A History of
Eastern Kentucky
University

A History of
Eastern Kentucky University

The School of Opportunity

by WILLIAM E. ELLIS
with a Foreword by THOMAS D. CLARK

THE UNIVERSITY PRESS OF KENTUCKY

Publication of this volume was made possible in part
by a grant from the National Endowment for the Humanities.

The University Press of Kentucky
Scholarly publisher for the Commonwealth,
serving Bellarmine University, Berea College,
Centre College of Kentucky, Eastern Kentucky University,
The Filson Historical Society, Georgetown College,
Kentucky Historical Society, Kentucky State University,
Morehead State University, Murray State University,
Northern Kentucky University, Transylvania University,
University of Kentucky, University of Louisville,
and Western Kentucky University.

Editorial and Sales Offices: The University Press of Kentucky
663 South Limestone Street, Lexington, Kentucky 40508-4008
www.kentuckypress.com

Photographs courtesy of Photograph Collection,
Eastern Kentucky University Archives, Richmond, Kentucky.

09 08 07 06 05   5 4 3 2 1

Library of Congress Cataloging-in-Publication Data
Ellis, William E. (William Elliott), 1940-
  A history of Eastern Kentucky University : the school of opportunity /
by William E. Ellis ; with a foreword by Thomas D. Clark.
    p. cm.
  Includes bibliographical references and index.
  ISBN 0-8131-2346-1 (hardcover : alk. paper)
  1. Eastern Kentucky University—History. I. Title.
  LD1741.E463E55 2005
  378.769'53—dc22   2004026886

Manufactured in the United States of America.

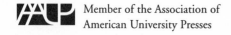

Member of the Association of
American University Presses

Contents

Illustrations follow pages 58 and 186.

Foreword

Thomas D. Clark

WRITING THE HISTORY of a century-old academic institution is akin to wandering footloose in a literary canebrake. By necessity an author must deal with founding years, bewhiskered presidents, hiring a skeleton faculty, gathering in students, placating an idiosyncratic public, and even overseeing construction. The historian must be concerned with all these elements. Too frequently the documentary record is skimpy or lost. The charge to the author is to be factual, inclusive, and coyly creative. The cardinal rule, however, is to be aware that he or she is writing about an extremely human institution.

In this instance, Professor Bill Ellis has brought skill and ingenuity to the task of writing Eastern Kentucky University's variegated history. He has revealed intimate knowledge of his subject drawn from years of being a faculty member, and from being diligent in the use of documentary and oral sources.

The tapestry of Eastern's history has been woven from a multitude of strands. Central University was founded in 1874 by the passions generated by the Civil War. That school exemplified all the frailties of southern Presbyterianism and Kentucky's swing toward the southern way of life after that terrible conflict.

Building on the ashes of Central University, the saga of Eastern has been layered, ring after ring, with each layer reflecting the penetrating stampings of succeeding presidents. To create a supply of teachers the General Assembly, beginning in 1906, created two normal schools and reformulated Kentucky A&M into the University of Kentucky.

As the scroll of Eastern's history has unfolded over the years, there is imprinted upon it the personal attributes of Ruric Nevel Roark, an argumentative and strong-willed normal school pioneer, who became Eastern's first president. Roark is deserving of remembrance as a doggedly determined founder.

Thomas Jackson Coates, 1916–28, shepherded the school through the years of World War I and the tough economic times of the early twenties. As his administration drew to a close, Eastern Kentucky State Normal School had advanced enough in its chrysalis stage to nearly becoming a teachers college.

Herman Lee Donovan, who succeeded Coates, was a classic example of the rural-agrarian Kentucky yeoman who was well endowed with self-confidence and determination. From his rural background experiences he brought to Eastern a strong sense of social and pedagogical order, including following in loco parentis to the letter and competing vigorously at the fiscal trough in Frankfort. His leadership helped the Richmond campus survive the tough Great Depression era.

With logic Ellis has organized his text in segmental conformity with presidential administrations. He has cast against this background a veritable collage of professorial, student, regent, political, and public personalities, even giving sentimental notice to campus dogs. There is something about athletics, academics, and the internal, sometimes petty, campus battles over the significant and the insignificant in this history of a place as well as a school.

There were always new unforeseen challenges. Within weeks of taking the helm, William Francis O'Donnell faced the horror of World War II. Then just as suddenly came the cessation of the conflict and the swarming to college campuses everywhere of GIs in a hurry to complete their educations and get on with disrupted lives. Though O'Donnell seemed incapable of making quick decisions, Eastern grew rapidly nonetheless, following rather than leading change in higher education in the commonwealth. Like most colleges, Eastern responded haltingly to the first stirrings of desegregation after the landmark *Brown v. Board of Education* decision in 1954.

Waiting in the wings at President O'Donnell's retirement in 1960 was a man of decisive action. Robert R. Martin was a complex personality with a sophisticated political background. Without the reservations of an O'Donnell, he exhibited an ambition to expand the parameters of the institution far beyond any past conceptions, especially into law enforcement and public health education. Though in virtual undisputed control of his demesne, Martin and the school adjusted to the trials and changes of the 1960s and 1970s. Martin worked diligently in elevating his beloved school to university status.

A well-schooled disciple of Martin, President J. C. Powell, between 1976 and 1984, fought to keep Eastern in an equitable position within the state's often contentious higher education system. Ellis portrays Powell as a low-key peacemaker, not just a caretaker, who tried to position Eastern for the technological and academic changes of the late twentieth century.

As one century closed and another opened, Eastern Kentucky University had transformed itself, spreading its academic net far beyond boundaries even remotely dreamed of in 1906. The whole structure of Kentucky public elementary and secondary education was revised in the Kentucky Education Reform Act of 1990. Six years later Governor Paul Patton pushed the General Assembly into reorganizing higher education, taking away the University of Kentucky's dominance of the state's junior colleges and creating the Council on Postsecondary Education.

The central issue, however, of all this reformism remained the same: the urge for better training of teachers and lifting the commonwealth out of the comparative statistical cellar of near-abject failure.

This book in many respects is a sound, microcosmic treatment of the history of public higher education in Kentucky. The author has escaped the infection of dullness, which permeates so much of academic history. There is a balance between the patriarchal presidential administrations and the human aspects of day-to-day classroom and campus affairs. This book has substantial credibility, with a text enshrouded in a comfortable blanket of benevolent understanding.

Preface

THE YEAR 2006 is the one hundredth anniversary of education at Eastern Kentucky University (EKU). Founded as a normal school, Eastern has evolved into a multipurpose regional university that is national in scope. Anniversaries are a time to take stock and reflect. I hope that those who read this book, in whole or in part, will find something important.

People might be replaceable, but institutions are not. H. G. Wells said: "Human history becomes more and more a race between education and catastrophe." Eastern, in its many forms and all things considered, has been a force for good and contributed mightily to the welfare of the region, state, and nation.

The book begins with a chapter on the history of Central University, a late-nineteenth-century "Southern" Presbyterian school that foreshadowed much of the good as well as ugly aspects of Kentucky, southern, and American cultures. I have chosen to organize this book chronologically by presidential administrations from 1906 to the near present.

I hope that faculty, staff, and alumni will find in these pages an accurate history of their time at Eastern. Some will read with a sense of nostalgia about a game in old Hanger Stadium, sellout crowds at Weaver Gymnasium, the long winning streaks and the tough losses to Western. The happy times and sad, the favorite professor and the one who was dreaded, all are part of the Eastern story.

In assessing the history of Eastern Kentucky University, one must look inward in the sense that all institutions have a life of their own based on time and place. Richmond and its vicinity had a great impact on the university and its earlier versions. But no place exists in a vacuum, and therefore the study must also look outward. State, regional, national, and international trends and forces have influenced the history of Eastern.

Eastern has been a "school of opportunity" throughout all its manifestations, from Central University in 1874 to Eastern Kentucky State Normal School in 1906 through its university status beginning in 1966 to the present. The historian of such a place must look at all kinds of records, public and private. Moreover, oral histories have been used extensively in this book to give the reader a sense of the personal side of the school.

Today's students might find it difficult to believe that during the Great Depression students fainted in the cafeteria from having denied themselves food for too long or that, during that same period, only a few people on campus, including faculty, had an automobile. Eastern has always prided itself on providing as good an education as possible for the least amount of money.

In the following pages the reader will find that Eastern has both reflected major trends in higher education and displayed its own personality. This will demonstrate the importance of such an institution as an example of a regional force in American education.

My perspective is that of a teacher, first and foremost. At Eastern we have always, owing to our origins and mandate, stressed teaching, service, and research in that order. At larger universities research and a "publish or perish" atmosphere would be prevalent. To write at Eastern has always required going the extra mile, and many faculty members have done so. My opportunity to write this history of Eastern came with retirement in 1999 and the generous support of Presidents Robert Kustra and Joanne Glasser. I am honored to be both a Foundation Professor and the University Historian after a twenty-nine-year career at Eastern.

The collection of the history of an institution like Eastern Kentucky University should never end. The Centennial Oral History Project is now in the process of collecting one hundred oral history interviews of faculty, staff, alumni, and supporters.

I am grateful for the support of Presidents Kustra and Glasser and their administrations. Several people, including two readers for the University Press of Kentucky, made valuable suggestions leading to publication. Other readers who saved the author from numerous mistakes include retired Eastern Archivist Charles Hay, current University Archivist Chuck Hill, Special Collections Librarian Deborah Whalen, Eastern alumnus and administrator Doug Whitlock, and Eastern's longtime Sports Information Director Karl Park. University Records Officer Jacqueline A. Couture facilitated the use of pictures in this book. Thanks also to university photographer Chris Radcliffe for the jacket photo. The Kentucky Oral History Commission, directed by Kim Lady Smith, has generously helped with interviewing and transcription grants.

Thomas D. Clark not only read the manuscript but also provided a generous foreword. Many others, including dozens who contributed oral histories, have aided this effort. To alumni, former students, and friends of Eastern, I hope that you enjoy reading the account of a truly unique institution in American higher education. But more than that, you are reading about a place that has been, if only temporarily, the home of many thousands of students, faculty, and staff since 1874. This book is dedicated to all those individuals who have found Eastern to be a school of opportunity.

Although several people have read drafts of this work in its various stages and made suggestions, the end result is totally mine. I have been mindful that objectivity is difficult when writing about one's own time. However, I also remember the sage advice Tom Clark gave me some years ago: "Do your research, and then sit down and write."

CHAPTER 1

Center of a Storm

Kentucky Presbyterians, Central University, and American Higher Education

CENTRAL UNIVERSITY, founded in 1874, formed at the nexus of several important nineteenth-century themes in American history: political, regional, national, religious, and educational.

If the Civil War officially ended in April 1865, it had just begun for many Kentuckians. Though Kentucky never officially seceded from the Union, it has been frequently said that the state joined the South after the war. While more than two-thirds of Kentucky combatants fought for the Union, after the war, former Confederates, from governors to members of the General Assembly to local county officials, dominated leadership in the commonwealth. Moreover, Kentucky's economy became more directly attached to the South with the rapid growth of the Louisville and Nashville Railroad and its southern trade.[1]

American higher education rebounded after the Civil War with the founding of more colleges and universities than ever before. Increasing numbers of high school graduates, including females, swelled the pool of available students entering the public and private school systems of America.[2]

Before the war, American Protestant churches battled over the slavery issue, with Baptists and Methodists splitting into distinct groups, while Presbyterians, southern and northern, continued their tenuous connection. After war began at Fort Sumter in 1861, the Presbyterian General Assembly convened in Philadelphia to chart its course. Dominated by pro-Union northern delegates, the group voted to support the Union and the United States Constitution. Angry southern dissenters bolted and formed the Presbyterian Church in the Confederate States of America. True to its border state position, politically and religiously, the Kentucky Synod of the church began to splinter during the war. Firm northern Presbyterian Dr. Robert J. Breckinridge, whose own sons divided over secession, branded any pro-southerner as a traitor. Relations did not improve for the remainder of the war, with the majority of Kentucky Presbyterians supporting the Confederacy.[3]

When the Civil War ended in 1865, Kentucky Presbyterians found themselves at a critical crossroads. Southern sentiment among Louisville Presbyterians forced the issue, and before long two competing synods vied for the soul of their church in Kentucky. Breckinridge led the northern faction, and Stuart Robinson and Bennett Young guided the southerners. By this time, the southern wing had adopted a new name, the Presbyterian Church in the United States, popularly known as "Southern Presbyterian."[4]

The issues separating northern and southern Presbyterians in Kentucky soon became the center of courtroom battles. At stake was governance of various church properties and of Centre College and a seminary in Danville. When the northern faction won control of Walnut Street Presbyterian Church in Louisville through litigation, the southern party was already at work forming its own institution of higher education. Consequently, when a later case gave the northern synod sole proprietary claim over Centre, the pro-southerners, styling themselves the Alumni Association of Central University, had already organized. Many members were alumni of Centre, and all supporters determined to found a new college with a southern ethos. Only indirectly connected with the southern synod in Kentucky, the college was controlled primarily by those who endowed it and by the Alumni Association. With the passage of enabling legislation by the Kentucky General Assembly in 1873, Central University took its first halting steps toward independence.[5]

The charter for Central University provided that the Alumni Association, not strictly confined to Presbyterians, would elect a Board of Curators, responsible for the educational control of the university, and a Board of Trustees, accountable for its business affairs. The boards would later be merged in 1884, and the southern synod of Kentucky would assume more control. The curators had the responsibility of electing a chancellor and president of the school. From the beginning, the Alumni Association had a heavy Confederate identity, which included Civil War veterans such as W. C. P. Breckinridge, Bennett H. Young, W. N. Haldeman, Governor James B. McCreary, and Stuart Robinson. W. C. P. Breckinridge and his father, devout northern Presbyterian Robert J., demonstrated the divided mind and heart of Kentuckians at the conclusion of the Civil War and during the divisive period of Reconstruction.[6]

Although an endowment drive easily oversubscribed a goal of $150,000, the panic of 1873 struck Kentucky hard, causing the actual cash to come in slowly. There were other problems as well. One leader noted that "much time was lost, and much angry dissension was stirred up by competitive struggles for the location." Initially, the Alumni Association chose Anchorage in Oldham County, but later changed to Richmond after Singleton P. Walters and several other Madison Countians made the largest block of money pledges.[7]

After more indecisiveness over leadership, Rev. Robert L. Breck, pastor of Richmond First Presbyterian Church, accepted the post of chancellor of Central University. A second-generation Kentuckian and graduate of Centre College, Breck had strong southern credentials. He believed that Central would appeal to the "southern-ness among a people homogeneous," in reference to the overwhelming majority of southern Presbyterians in the state. The Board of Curators also elected the Reverend J. W. Pratt as president, the presiding officer over the faculty of the institution in Richmond. With little money in hand, Central University opened its College of Philosophy, Letters, and Science and a preparatory school in that city in September 1874, along with the Hospital College of Medicine in Louisville.[8]

Central entered a field of burgeoning academic competition with little more than promissory notes, pledges, and a strong will to succeed. Advocates for a public institution in Lexington rekindled their efforts, as did the drive of Southern Baptists to revive Georgetown College from the scars of the Civil War. Berea College, a few miles south of Richmond, but worlds apart from Central, had been founded by Cassius M. Clay and John G. Fee in the pre–Civil War maelstrom over slavery. While Central would become an all-white institution, representing all that was sacred to the "Lost Cause" of the Confederacy, Berea attempted racial integration.[9]

The charter of Central University allowed for up to six preparatory schools, and, in addition to the one in Richmond, others were added in later years: S. P. Lees Collegiate Institute in Jackson in 1891, Hardin Collegiate Institute in Elizabethtown in 1892, and Middlesboro University School in 1896. A law school at Central never found much favor, lasting only a few years on two separate occasions and graduating only fifteen. A proposed school of theology, to hotly contest the errors of northern Presbyterianism, finally formed in

Louisville under separate authority. The most successful of the arms of Central University operated in Louisville as schools of medicine and dentistry. Both received strong support from the Louisville community, graduating more than thirteen hundred physicians and dentists through 1901. Eventually merged with the University of Louisville, these schools served a vital role in improving life in late nineteenth-century Kentucky.[10]

Just prior to opening in 1874, Central University in Richmond advertised tuition at sixty dollars a year, free for candidates for the ministry, and forty dollars for the preparatory department. Room and board with Richmond families could be found for an additional five dollars a week. Breck informed prospective students that if they did not have sufficient funds, they could pay "in the future."[11]

After an initial purchase of forty acres of land, construction began on what would eventually be called the Main Building, at a cost of $30,000. In that structure on September 22, 1874, Chancellor Breck declared, "We fling to the breeze our banner bearing the words we have put on the tablet in front of this edifice, *Lex, Rex-Crux, Lux.* We have no sectarian or partisan ends to accomplish here. These are our only distinctive principles: The Law is our King, the Cross is our Light." Madison Female Seminary property nearby became the plant for the preparatory school. In addition to Breck and Pratt, who both taught classes, eight other professors were appointed. Enrollment during the first year fluctuated, and the year ended with only thirty-six "collegiate" and eighty-six preparatory students in attendance in Richmond.[12]

The faculty assembled by Breck and Pratt compared favorably with those at other schools. Pratt had previously served for twenty years as a professor of English at the University of Alabama. He, like Breck, was an ordained minister and served as pastor of the Richmond First Presbyterian Church while at Central. Thomas William Tobin, a native of England, probably lent a luster unmatched by any of the earliest faculty members. He spent only six years at Central, but he charmed the area with his speaking, writing, and research in physics, chemistry, and geology. The inventor of a type of pendulum, Tobin also installed a primitive telephone system, connecting Central with a Richmond store, the only such service outside of Louisville at the time. After several students' stomachs "rose in rebellion" during the dissection of a cow in one of Tobin's classes, "It was said that the beefsteak consumed by that class during the remainder of the year was at a minimum." Some professors served longer tenures, including James V. Logan and L. G. Barbour, who were on the faculty from 1874 to 1901. The tenures of other full-time professors varied, and more than fifty men taught part-time as adjunct professors through the years.[13]

Financial constraints limited compensation for the administration and staff of Central. The chancellor never received more than $2,000 plus a house, the president around $1,300, and the faculty salaries, even during the best days of the nineties, only ranged between $800 and $1,200. In 1882 salaries were reduced "because of the utter impossibility of the Institution to pay more in its present financial condition." Again, in the last years of Central's existence, the chancellor reduced salaries, including his own. With an income of only $11,800 and expenditures of $14,100, the chancellor cut salaries in 1898. Even more ominously, he had to dip into the endowment to pay everyday expenses.[14]

In addition to the Main Building, now known as the University Building, other structures graced the campus of Central. A residency built for the president (called Blanton House today), completed in 1886 at a cost of $6,500, stood along "Faculty Row," where four modest brick residencies housed professors. Plans for other buildings materialized slowly. The Miller Gymnasium, with two stories and a basement, "heated by furnace and lighted by gas," became the focus for physical training. Memorial Hall, built at a cost of $15,000 to $20,000 and paid for by southern Presbyterian women to commemorate their centennial in Kentucky, served as a men's dormitory beginning in 1883. Library facilities proved to be inadequate, with many old books of little practical value.[15]

Although admission to the university was based on rather capricious standards in the beginning, by 1890, admission of a graduate from a recognized high school became automatic. The first degrees awarded included the Bachelor of Arts and the Bachelor of Science. A Bachelor of Letters, added in 1891, along with a master's program for an extra year of study, completed the rigors of academic life in Richmond. An entering freshman in the B.A. program faced a typical nineteenth-century classical curriculum with half-year courses in such areas as algebra, Latin, Greek, and English testing his mettle. Geometry replaced algebra in the sophomore year. The junior and senior year courses added chemistry, geology, and physics, as well as more practical courses in bookkeeping. True to the school's Christian foundation, religion crept into Central's courses in logic and ethics. The B.S. degree enforced more study of the sciences while substituting the study of German for that of Greek.[16]

Chancellor Breck faced many problems, ones that eventually forced his resignation. Claiming never to have turned anyone away because of a lack of funds, he scolded Madison Countians for not sending enough of their sons to Central and its preparatory school. "I appeal to you now to aid in maintaining it," he implored, "by giving to us your sons for education." Moreover, he claimed that the county's reputation for crime discouraged enrollment from outside its boundaries. Difficulty in collecting pledges, some resulting in litigation, drained Breck's energy. The problems of Central multiplied when President Pratt resigned in 1880. Breck, in failing health and citing a continual problem with funds, soon followed.[17]

After more instability, new leadership stepped into the breach. The Board of Curators appointed Rev. J. V. Logan, a professor of logic, ethics, Christian evidences, and psychology, as president of the faculty and Rev. Lindsay Hughes Blanton as chancellor. Blanton, a former chaplain in the Confederate forces, served one of the strongest "southern" churches in Paris. Although the prospects of Central seemed to initially improve, Blanton fought against declining revenues and tried to resign in 1886, worn out by the constant battle against insolvency. However, "the Board after mature consideration unanimously refused to accept the resignation, and voted and urged Dr. Blanton to take a few weeks for rest and recuperation." Though the chancellor did as suggested, the fiscal problems of Central refused to go away. As the pressure mounted, even Blanton lost some of his ministerial dignity. "What an old ass," he exclaimed, critiquing the machinations of one of his fellow Presbyterian clergymen.[18]

Central University did not live in a vacuum, as competition among Kentucky colleges continued to escalate. Commonly called State College and later State University, the Agricultural and Mechanical College in nearby Lexington became a state institution in 1880 after being separated from Kentucky University (Transylvania). With tuition of only fifteen dollars, it easily offered a much cheaper education than other colleges in the state and would continue to grow as Central's enrollment fluctuated. In 1881 Blanton and other private college and university presidents at Georgetown, Kentucky Wesleyan, Bethel, and Centre published *A Protest from Some Private Institutions against State Aid to Their Rival in the Field of Education*. Knowing that public taxation for higher education placed them at a disadvantage, the private institutions asked, "Do the people of the State desire to drive these institutions from the field and replace them by a costly State institution supported by special taxation?" Blanton declared, "The mass of the people everywhere are against taxation for college education." In the long run the citizens of the Commonwealth of Kentucky did indeed support a public college, and the legislature bowed to their will.[19]

The students of Central University came from a not too diverse background, initially being young white males from middle-class families. However, in a cash-strapped economy, many students depended on scholarships for tuition paid for by personal benefactors. Most students came from Kentucky, with a few from the southern states and fewer still from north of the Ohio River. The names of prominent Kentucky Presbyterian families appeared often among the student rolls, as did those of well-to-do Madison Countians. For example, Launey Clay, the son of a liaison between Cassius M. Clay and his Russian ballerina-paramour, graduated from Central in 1888. The student culture of Central had much in common with that at similar schools. The professions of graduates ran the gamut from distillers to missionaries and included ministers, engineers, farmers, lawyers, judges, politicians, soldiers, and businessmen. At least one became famous, if for all the wrong reasons. Admiral Husband E. Kimmel, who left Central after receiving an appointment to the U.S. Naval Academy, never overcame charges of not properly preparing the navy for the Japanese attack at Pearl Harbor on December 7, 1941.[20]

Campus authorities tried to keep a tight rein on their charges. By the mideighties, the list of regulations for students had become quite lengthy. Besides just appearing on time and arranging for tuition and other fees, Central students were expected to behave like Victorian and Kentucky gentlemen. They were to be in their rooms by eight thirty each evening, studying and contemplating the next day's activities. Archie Woods, a member of the first class in 1874, complained to his father that he never had time for anything but study. He observed that two students soon quit because the faculty were so strict "you have to come right to the mark in everything." Chapel attendance for morning prayers was expected, as was an appearance at "public divine services at least once on each Sabbath." Card games, billiards (including visiting "billiard rooms"), and the use of tobacco or alcohol on campus were prohibited. No secret societies were allowed, and any campus organizations had to be approved by the administration. A system of demerits kept miscreants in check. When class attendance became a problem, Central's administration added new rules of enforcement in 1887. Moreover, some students apparently did not pay their bills downtown, and in 1883 the Kentucky General Assembly passed a special law forbidding local merchants from advancing credit to Central University students. Beginning that year, catalogs printed this rule conspicuously. Religion was uppermost in the minds of the administration, and as late as 1897 a student would be "privately admonished by the President" for three unexcused absences from chapel.[21]

"The aura of the Confederacy, of course, was everywhere," according to an earlier chronicler of the school's history. Besides the southernness of the faculty, the students themselves thought in terms of being southern. The only African Americans on campus were workers, and their race was the object of derision in campus publications and a source of humor at campus events. The Central baseball team had a black adult male mascot, a quite common occurrence in southern colleges at the time. Appointments to the Board of Curators went to old Confederate sympathizers like Colonel W. N. Haldeman of the *Courier-Journal* family ownership, who had to flee Louisville because of his pro-southern sentiments during the war, or to local political kingpins such as former governor James B. McCreary, who had been a lieutenant colonel in the Eleventh Kentucky Cavalry. When W. C. P. Breckinridge and other southern apologists spoke on campus or attended commencements, they were treated as heroes. Articles in the local newspaper and in university publications treated the Civil War not only as a great and recent episode in southern culture but as nearly surpassing all other hallowed events. Central also exuded the "New South" mentality, a mind-set in which an attempt was made to retain the racial strictures of the old South while adapting to the new economic and industrial realities of the era. Significantly, state representative Carl Day, a Central graduate, exemplified that environment when he gave his name to the 1904 law that segregated Berea College and other Kentucky private and public institutions.[22]

The admission of women added a new dimension to Central University, the first halting steps to break the bounds of Victorianism. In 1887 the first women, Elizabeth Barbour, the daughter of a professor L. G. Barbour, and Bessie McDowell, graduated with diplomas, not degrees, meaning that they had been in attendance for a one-year course of study. Later in 1893, the Board of Curators gave the chancellor the power to admit any "young lady" who resided in Richmond or Madison County and who passed the entrance examination. Miss Barbour graduated the next year, as did Miss S. Russell Letcher, magna cum laude, described in the *Atlantis,* the student publication, with proper Victorian verbiage by an obvious male writer as follows: "Her dignified and graceful figure, dark hair and brown eyes, fair complexion and irresistible beauty command universal admiration." Two years later, two more women graduated. Increasingly, women became a more common sight on campus and in Central's organizations. Near the turn of the century, Kit Chenault graduated magna cum laude with a Bachelor of Letters degree. Paradoxically, a graduation picture shows her and the men all wearing hats and holding canes as symbols of their accomplishments and being southern "gentlemen." Women not only entered the halls of Central as students; one served on the faculty for a short time. Elizabeth Fauquier Bowden held the chair of elocution and oratory in 1897–98. On a limited but important basis and following trends in higher education, Central University belatedly offered women an opportunity for a college education.[23]

The addition of military science, tactics, and training added further depth to the Central experience. In 1892, a program began with Lieutenant W. H. Sage of the regular army assigned by the War Department. All freshmen and sophomores took the course, and student officers came from the junior and senior classes. Two companies of infantry and a battery of artillery were formed, becoming the Central University Battalion. The program added several Central University graduates to the U.S. Army officer corps, some of whom served in the Spanish-American War. "Strict, firm to his post," is how one "commandant" was described, "yet the college boys have no warmer friend in the University." True to its southernness, the Central University Cadet Corps marched in the 1900 parade for the Confederate Reunion in Louisville wearing gray uniforms purchased by "old stalwart Bennett Young," a most unreconstructed rebel who led the audacious raid on Saint Albans, Vermont, in 1864.[24]

Student organizations, illustrating the complexities of campus life, ranged from the serious to the frivolous. Along with the Philalethean and Epiphyllidian literary societies, fraternities, the Young Men's Christian Association (YMCA), the Epicurean Club, and the Mandolin, Banjo, and Guitar Club, weighty organizations all, were groups with such interesting, whimsical names as the Suicide Club, the Dynamite Club, the Ancient Order of Bloody Toughs, and the KHB Eating Club. Some groups were undoubtedly formed to combat the alleged snootiness of the literary societies and fraternities; others were up to date with current events, such as the "Cuba Libre" Club of 1898, the year of the Spanish-American War. That same year the Central University Engaged Girls' Club claimed a membership of seven, with five more "prospective members" available.[25]

The literary societies lent an air of intellectualism to Central. Oratorical competition, both on campus and intercollegiate, proved to be as exciting and important as sports among the student body. The Philaletheans, originally called Walters Literary Society and meaning "lovers of ease" in Greek, and the Epiphyllidians, "gleaners" in Greek, battled for membership among a limited student body and for honors as well. They debated topics of the day and held periodic oratorical contests that rivaled athletic games in intensity. For example, in 1898 the affirmative side won a debate on the topic "Resolved: That the flying machine would be beneficial to mankind." Dressing similarly and wearing contrasting red or white sashes, the participants cut quite a figure during campus debates. Competition became so intense and controversial that it necessitated the formation of an intersociety board in 1892. The societies published a monthly journal, the *Atlantis,* for several years, a cooperative venture that included alternating editors in chief annually between the two. The *Atlantis* proved to be a good source of literary news and published speeches. True to form, it stayed the course of southernness at Central. An oration on "The Old South," delivered by student J. L. Jacob in 1890, looked to the past while praising the South for its "renunciation of past errors." "Southern Heroism" was the topic of another student's published oration.[26]

Fraternities became the focus of social life at Central. At first operating undercover, sub rosa, because of initial faculty opposition, they prospered after receiving administrative sanction in early 1883. Several fraternities eventually formed, including Sigma Alpha Epsilon, Alpha Tau Omega, Sigma Nu, Delta Kappa Epsilon, and Phi Delta Theta. Their numbers ebbed on occasion; often the fraternities needed the membership and leadership of faculty and graduates to keep them alive. One of the leaders of Sigma Nu, Clarence E. Woods, kept up his interest after leaving the school and becoming a newspaperman. Upon his return to Richmond, he remained a loyal Sigma Nu and edited the fraternity's national journal for many years.[27]

Besides social and fraternal organizations, classes to attend, and examinations to take, writing opportunities also abounded for Central students. Official publications included the *Atlantis* (the literary journal), the *Cream and Crimson* (an annual), and the *Central News* (a newspaper). The *University Hot Times,* an independent publication that described itself as "a paper published semi-occasionally by the junior and freshmen classes," kept the campus astir. The latter once humorously chided life in Memorial Hall: "Truly it is a Memorial Hall—a hall of memories and nurseries [referring to bedbugs] not soon to be forgotten. Peace to thee, O, Memorial Hall. May the hilarious echoes of thy tumultuous halls never cease to resound, and may thy incomparable table fare improve somewhat." Then, as now, students could always find fault with college living conditions and campus food.[28]

As a sign of the times, Central students took an interest in sports. Athletic competition began with what we call intramurals today, but intercollegiate sports quickly became an important part of life on the Central campus. With football and baseball becoming sports of national interest, both were the centerpieces of Central sports. Rivalries soon developed with State College, Georgetown, Wesleyan, and especially Centre. Central also played much larger southern universities. Faculty became very concerned about what they considered an overemphasis on sports.[29]

Late-nineteenth-century football was a violent sport. Players wore only light padding and no helmets, though some protected their noses with rubber pads. With two forty-five minute periods, no forward pass, three downs to make five yards, and goals 330 feet apart, the game resembled rugby, its progenitor, more than modern football. Five points were earned for a touchdown, and two for a "kick for goal." The game was a brutal contest of pushing and shoving, and the "flying wedge" became a standard tactic until outlawed because of its dangers to life and limb. With "modernization," football became an increasingly national sport as Ivy League teams such as Yale and Harvard popularized the game. In 1880 Centre College and Kentucky University (Transylvania) played the first organized game in Kentucky, a scoreless tie. Some towns and schools outlawed the game for a short time, as Maysville did in 1877, declaring the game "of a character calculated to disturb the quiet of the people." Moreover, there was great conflict over players' eligibility, sometimes with "ringers" who played for several teams, and playing conditions. And, as important, college officials began to realize that winning meant as much to alumni as it did to students.[30]

Beginning in the fall of 1891 Central fielded a team after receiving a blood-inscribed sheepskin from Centre College challenging the university to a game. Coached by three local men who had some game experience, most of the Central eleven played in the first football game they had ever seen. One Central player described it as "a rough-and-tumble battle with plenty of slugging, kicking, and gouging." They played the whole game without substitutions—Central had only eleven players—and, as he recalled, wore baseball uniforms. When asked if he was hurt during the contest, he replied, "Oh, hell, yes."

Centre won by one point but would fall to Central by the same score the next year. Though a small school, Central turned out a representative team for the next decade, with only a few substitutes available and coaches also teaching full-time. The teams won more than they lost most years, and in 1893 Central won the mythical state championship by defeating Centre, Kentucky University (Transylvania), Georgetown College, and State College. An *Atlantis* editorial claimed that it had only been possible because of a lack of fraternity rivalry being channeled into college spirit. One such win over the Danville rival received a hyperbolic nineteenth-century appraisal: "The applause which greeted the approach of the gladiators dies away, the battle is fought and won, the shades of night fall over the field, it is deserted. . . . Central University is victorious, Centre College humbled in defeat."[31]

As part of the Southern Inter-Collegiate Athletic Association, made up of teams such as Louisiana State University, Vanderbilt, and the University of Texas, Central was not allowed to play Centre one year because of Centre's use of illegal players. A no-holds-barred game with State College ended with one of its players being thrown out of the contest, and, when the Lexington team walked off the field, the referee awarded the game to Central. In 1897 the team appeared well treated at Vanderbilt, but not so by the "ruffians" at Sewanee, where "the profanity and rowdyism displayed by the members of the team was extremely disgusting." The next year Central defeated Centre, 30–0, with the description of the game sent back to Danville via telephone. In 1899 a defeat by Centre brought the charge that a recent graduate had come back to play for the Danville team. Black eyes and similar injuries were worn as badges of courage by the Central eleven. One Central player, Keats Speed, who had transferred from the University of Virginia and went on to become managing editor of the *New York Sun,* is shown in the 1898 team picture, seated so that his injured left eye could be easily seen.[32]

There being no basketball played at the time, baseball proved to be just as competitive an intercollegiate sport as football and a spring favorite among Central's students. As usual, the greatest prize was defeating Centre College in what was already being called the "national game." When play was not up to high standards in 1897, the editor of the *Central News* complained about players returning late from a dance just in time to catch a train to a game. "This is entirely wrong and deserves severe condemnation," he exclaimed. After apparent criticism of editorial policy from the baseball team, the editor defended his action, saying, "We felt it to be our duty to publicly call attention to the condition of the team and to condemn the conduct of several of the members of it." Two years later, the next editor of the *Central News,* J. Edward Doughtie, exulted in bold headlines, "UNPARALLELED" about the joys of not only defeating Centre in baseball, 5–4, but also winning the state intercollegiate debating championship by defeating Centre. Moreover, in eight athletic, oratory, and debate contests with Centre for the year, the cream and crimson of Central had carried the day in seven. It should be noted that a Louisville Colonels pitcher coached the team for a brief spell, adding his expert advice for the Central nine.[33]

With the Philalethean and Epiphyllidian literary societies as the backbone of Central's debating and oratory, such activity flourished. The faculty much preferred these activities over sports. Just as much as the gridiron and diamond gave the chance for Central's young men to participate in intercollegiate athletics, the campus and intercollegiate debating and oratorical contests offered intellectual stimulation. The results of such contests often led to ill will among Kentucky colleges, just as much as squabbles about rules and even the number of and composition of judges for events. The *Atlantis,* published by the two societies, and the *Central News* were rife with articles about such debates and orations. The editor of the latter once cried sour grapes when venerable President James K. Patterson of State College complained about the judging of an oratorical contest that Central won.[34]

Central University was not without its own internal struggles, ones that are inevitable when the strong wills of student, faculty, and administration fail to mesh. Issues ranged over a wide spectrum. According to one historian, "College life was born in revolt." The antagonisms at Central were rampant: faculty versus students, fraternities versus nonfraternities, sports versus literary societies, chancellor versus faculty, town versus gown, and so on. Many students believed that almost any advantage, perhaps even cheating, was perfectly legitimate, if not entirely moral and ethical, in order to win out over, if not exactly defeat, the intent of the faculty to control their lives.[35]

Central's strong code of behavior clashed with the students' will and high spirits. Drunkenness and gambling led to immediate expulsion. One observer said, "I saw more drinking at Old Central University from 1884 to 1899 than in all the universities I have visited." Faculty feared secret societies, hence the reluctance to sanction fraternities except under direct administrative control. The struggle between faculty and students continued on several fronts. For example, when dozens of students boycotted class one Friday after Thanksgiving, they received multiple demerits. In a more serious incident, a student pulled a knife on Professor C. A. Leonard after refusing to extinguish a cigar. The situation escalated when Leonard "slapped" the student in the face. "He struck me with his knife on the thigh," the professor testified. After hours of hearings and deliberations, the faculty expelled the student. No one was exempt. For example, the Richmond faculty "voted that Dr. Blanton be requested to withdraw his son W. E. Blanton from college." The administration sometimes ran afoul of the editors of the *Atlantis,* who had to be restrained from excessively criticizing the faculty.[36]

A serious breach of rules at Central involved cheating, which became a hot topic in campus publications. When the son of a prominent Kentuckian was accused of cheating on an examination, the incident touched off a furor pointing to an undercurrent of conflict between Blanton and the faculty. The faculty took the charges at face value and voted to dismiss the student; in response, the father of the accused wrote a scathing letter to Blanton, who supported a milder punishment. "This whole matter has given me inexpressible pain," the chancellor explained. Only the intervention of the Board of Curators settled a potentially explosive situation. In a compromise, the student received a brief expulsion, then returned to Central and, after further education, became a well-respected physician. Another issue illustrated the breach between Blanton and the faculty. The latter argued that athletics were being overemphasized at Central, with some students being recruited and admitted only for their athletic prowess and not as "bona fide students."[37]

Central students also followed, and the faculty allowed, some time-honored campus traditions and a bit of foolishness, often to let off steam directed either at the faculty or against society in general. Campus high jinks included painting the president's carriage horse white and black to resemble a zebra or taking a calf to the roof of the Main Building on more than one occasion. The reasons for such behavior probably could be understood only by the young, bored, and often homesick students. One tradition, pitched battles by students over some object, appeared on many college campuses in the late nineteenth century. Contests over class flags led to more than bruised feelings. As reported by the *University Hot Times,* during the Grand Flag Rush of 1900, a war between students ended with a coalition of juniors and freshmen defeating seniors and sophomores. Fisticuffs probably took place, and some students were undoubtedly injured, but no public reports were made of them. Flags were torn down and burned. Charges and countercharges ensued for hours that evening, with thoughts about study far from the students' minds. Powerless to stop such events, the faculty usually waited out the tumult before resuming control.[38]

Like any college at any time, there were always numerous obstacles to overcome. Students and their parents felt the economic pinch as much as Central University. One parent, enclosing a check for seventy-five dollars, implored Chancellor Blanton to "please impress upon Jimmie that money matters are very stringent and he must not spend any more than is absolutely necessary." Moreover, the distraught father feared that his son's mind was not on studies. The impact on Richmond of Central's high-spirited student body was felt by one student left behind during the summer of 1896. "All of the boys have gone," he noted, referring to his Sigma Nu brothers, "and the town is as dead as you ever saw a place."[39]

At the bedrock of Central lay a devotion to a classical notion of education with southern and Presbyterian emphases. Even the advent of a new scientific idea did not cause much of a stir. Professor J. L. Howe taught evolution but did not believe that humans descended from a lower order. "The theory of the Evolution of life I understand to be the most satisfactory working hypothesis," Howe said, "which best explains the facts and phenomena as we find them." A committee of the Board of Curators studying a complaint about Howe found him to be "a fit and safe instructor." Through all the tumult and shouting, often quite literal, and the financial, educational, and social turmoil, hundreds of young men and dozens of young women received a creditable education at Central University, one that prepared them for the changing world of the early twentieth century.[40]

Commencements, which were events of great excitement at Central University, offer insight into what was most important to students and faculty alike. Beginning as a simple one-day event, by the mid-1880s the ceremonies had grown into a multiday celebration. In 1886 a Sunday morning baccalaureate sermon was followed by a YMCA event that evening. The literary societies performed in a series of events before graduation day on Wednesday. The winners of various contests received donated gold medals, such as the James B. McCreary Prize for the student who "stands the best special examination in Sophomore English." Honorary degrees, as well as those conferred on the students, rounded out the celebration. The graduation speaker became a highlight, with such luminaries as Delaware congressman Leven Irving delivering the commencement oration in 1898.[41]

While enrollment at the Louisville medical and dental schools and the preparatory units continually expanded, Central University in Richmond struggled to find its niche among the liberal arts colleges of its day. It became increasingly difficult to retain students. In 1888 only four graduates in the College of Philosophy, Letters, and Science were matched with four honorary Doctor of Divinity recipients. Even the addition of a master's program and admission of women in the mid-1890s failed to ignite a substantial enrollment increase. The 1899 graduation class, the largest in the history of Central in Richmond, included two women among the twenty-five honorees. Moreover, the prep schools in Richmond, Jackson, Middlesboro, and Elizabethtown never fed substantial student numbers into Central University.[42]

Toward the end of the century the handwriting on the wall appeared for Central University. If the impact of the panic of 1873 almost doomed the beginning of Central University, the aftermath of the one of 1893 placed more pressure on the school. Investments faltered. Bonds held on the Kentucky and Indiana Bridge Terminal Company had to be sold in 1895 for seventy cents on the dollar to stanch an even greater loss. Time and again expenses exceeded revenue, and salary cuts soon followed. Blanton received permission from the Board of Curators to borrow money to stave off disaster on more than one occasion in the late 1890s. Central even hired a financial agent to try to collect funds "as the only alternative to closing the doors of the University." Moreover, the chancellor claimed that the founding of a new Presbyterian seminary in Louisville in 1893 to compete with Danville Seminary siphoned funds that might otherwise have gone to Central.[43]

The wear and tear of competition with State College and other colleges and universities finally overcame Central's meager finances and its will to survive. Blanton explained that "we have been compelled to live from hand to mouth for twenty-one years" during his chancellorship. In what proved to be the last issue of *Cream and Crimson,* in 1901, he declared somewhat sarcastically: "If we combine with Centre, you will not have to change the names on your football suits. You might as well try to stop the Kentucky River as to stop this movement." Moreover, the majority of northern and southern Presbyterians, if not willing to end their decades-long dispute, called a truce. Talks about a merger with Centre College began by late 1898. Both schools needed each other to survive in the new century. If Central had a larger student body, Centre had more money.[44]

The Louisville newspapers and the *Christian Observer,* the Kentucky Presbyterian newspaper, supported consolidation while reporting the controversy that surrounded the merger negotiations. However, Madison County alumni and supporters of Central in the First Presbyterian Church protested the removal of their school to Danville, declaring that secret meetings had been held and a sacred trust had been broken. While the *Courier-Journal* of old Confederate Henry Watterson lauded merger as "another step in wiping out sectional feeling," fellow Louisvillian Bennett Young led the forces against consolidation. Even the approval of the proposal by both Kentucky Presbyterian synods, north and south, did not allay the suspicions of some. Madison Countians claimed that neither synod had the right to vote on the issue; that power rested only in the Central Alumni Association. When a Madison judge called the merger plan "abject surrender," another resident asked, "Shall 26,000 Southern Presbyterians surrender to 5,000 Northern Presbyterians?" From outside the state, a professor at Union Theological Seminary in Virginia charged, "If our Kentucky brethren associate with these U.S.A. [northern church] men, how long will they remain sound." But as a sign of the changing times, the *Central News* reported that in the last baseball game between the two Kentucky Presbyterian colleges, won by Central 15–9, the cream and crimson fans and team had been well treated in Danville.[45]

With the blessing of the two synods, assent by the Central Alumni Association remained the only stumbling block to consolidation. McCreary, true to his political form, acted as a peacemaker by chairing a meeting in Richmond. Blanton wrote at least one alumnus to be sure to attend the meeting "in order to prevent obstructionist tactics on the part of a persistent minority." "UNION, Delayed by Filibustering Tactics of Opposition," rang the headlines of the *Central News,* as Bennett Young and Madison Countians rallied the anticonsolidationists. The latter used delaying tactics during a nightlong alumni meeting. W. R. Shackelford spoke for four hours on a point of order, hoping that "reinforcements" would arrive at dawn and carry a winning vote. When word reached the meeting that the wife of Chancellor Blanton had died, the meeting broke up without a vote. Two weeks later the alumni voted 59–41 to consolidate. Some of the opponents swore they would go to court to block the move.[46]

However, cooler heads prevailed, and the "Agreement for Consolidation of Centre College and Central University, Under Name of Central University of Kentucky" finally became acceptable to the majority of Kentucky Presbyterians. While the Central University of Kentucky (it was changed back to Centre College in 1918) would have equal numbers of northern and southern Presbyterian members on the new Board of Trustees, by a "gentleman's agreement," the northerners would select the new president. Finally even crusty Bennett Young signed the agreement. Moreover, as another sign of Presbyterian peacemaking, the old seminary in Danville merged with the newer one in Louisville.[47]

As part of the consolidation, the Central campus passed into the hands of what would become the Walters Collegiate Institute. The preparatory schools and the medical and dental colleges remained as part of the new college. The president of the old Centre, Rev. William Charles Roberts, became president of the new Central University of Kentucky. Blanton assumed the vice presidency of the merged college, and Logan served as professor of psychology. While the undergraduate program in Danville retained the name of Centre College, Central University became the name of the umbrella now extending from Louisville to Danville and to the preparatory schools. Although the old Central University passed into history in 1901, for many years to come, its alumni would have an impact on their state, region, and nation. The closing lines of "The Old U-ni-ver-si-tee," the school song written in 1892, perhaps best summed up the sentiment of most graduates: "And we never, never, never shall forget. No! We never shall forget."[48]

Just as the founding of Central University in 1873 illustrated several salient themes in American history, the lives of two of its most prominent alumni, French Tipton, its first graduate, and Clarence E. Woods, who organized the first fraternity on campus, exemplified the southern ethos of the region in 1900, just one year before the consolidation of the two Presbyterian schools. The conflict between the two men, who became bitter enemies, involved politics, newspaper competition, and, ultimately, honor. The candidacy for president of William Jennings Bryan split the country and Madison County in 1896, with Tipton editing the Republican *Pantagraph* and Woods overseeing the Democratic *Kentucky Register*. While Tipton fully supported the gold standard platform of his candidate William McKinley, Woods did the same for the free silver ideals of Bryan. Bryan narrowly lost Madison County and Kentucky in 1896. Three years later the stakes were even higher in a hotly contested gubernatorial race featuring Republican William Taylor and Democrat William Goebel. Tipton and Woods continued their personal war in the local newspapers.[49]

In a political farce that rivaled the 2000 presidential furor, the 1899 race for governor nearly ended in civil war in Kentucky. It did end in the death of Goebel at the hands of one or more assassins. Although several men went to jail for the killing, the only such murder of a governor in the history of the United States, even today we do not know for sure who killed William Goebel. Tipton and Woods not only sparred over this issue but became participants in a debate over whether the Richmond Light and Water Company should be public or private. The thin veneer of civility in Richmond that had pervaded the conflict between the two men shattered on September 1, 1900. Witnesses later claimed that while Woods was talking to some friends on Main Street, Tipton came up from the side and struck his adversary in the face. Momentarily stunned, Woods fell to his knees. Rising to his feet, he pulled out a pistol and fired one shot into Tipton's abdomen. The bullet ripped through vital organs before exiting his back. Slumping to the pavement, Tipton cried for mercy. Although Tipton lingered in great agony for two days, physicians could do nothing to save him. Only hours before his death, Tipton exonerated his assailant by corroborating Wood's story and that of witnesses. Clarence Woods did not stand trial for the killing of French Tipton. The southernness of the Richmond, Kentucky, and Central University environments held firm and true. In effect, "southern honor" had been vindicated, a corruption of the biblical adage "An eye for an eye, a tooth for a tooth."[50]

Tipton and Woods represented the best Kentucky and Central University had to offer. They were both progressives. To the best of their abilities, they searched for what could best serve the interests of their town, university, state, and nation. However, the fact that their struggle against each other ended in such terrible violence illustrated that Kentuckians had much to learn about peaceful public discourse. Central University left a mixed legacy as its former students and graduates faced the new century.

CHAPTER 2

"The Best Is Hardly Good Enough"

Founding a Normal School, 1906–1916

AS THE TWENTIETH century opened, public school education in Kentucky limped along at the bottom of the states. Walters Collegiate Institute occupied the old Central University site and turned out semi-elite graduates, young men who would take their places in Kentucky society with a better than average education. Only in Louisville and a few other urban areas in the commonwealth did children receive a reasonably good education. The best that most children could expect was a grade school education, perhaps graduating from the eighth grade. There were no county high schools in the state. In a rigidly segregated society, the public schools followed the color line at the turn of the century. Ironically, while there were no state normal schools for whites, the State Normal School for Colored Persons in Frankfort made a halting attempt to educate the state's African American teachers.[1]

Teachers in the white public schools of Kentucky relied on locally taught courses and normal school education in the commonwealth's colleges. Normal schools themselves were little more than public high schools. Elementary teachers received the least training, sometimes none at all in the poorer rural districts, where they only had to pass a test given by the local school board in order to enter the classroom. Unfortunately, following a hierarchy that would persist into the late twentieth century, elementary school teachers also did not receive as much training, salary, or prestige as secondary teachers. Private normal schools at Glasgow, Bowling Green, and a few other towns provided some of the training. The Agricultural and Mechanical College in Lexington trained the most high school teachers and probably did the best job in the state of preparing young men and women for the rigors of teaching. Dr. Ruric Nevel Roark headed the Normal Department of State College under the di-

21

rection of "benevolent dictator" President James K. Patterson. Men of strong personalities and ideas, they clashed over how much emphasis should be placed on normal education at the Lexington school.[2]

In the late nineteenth century, most colleges and universities did not emphasize training teachers, and land-grant colleges, like State College, did not fill the need. Initially, major universities did not want to emphasize public school education, and any training was based on a typical American laissez-faire educational philosophy of competition and need. As public normal schools in Wisconsin and Illinois and other of the more progressive states improved the educational systems in their states, Kentucky education languished. Moreover, many normal schools had begun to evolve into teachers colleges. At the turn of the twentieth century, when Teachers College of Columbia University had become the premier trainer of teachers in America, only two states, Kentucky and Arkansas, did not have publicly financed normal schools.[3]

A movement to improve the training of teachers in Kentucky had been under way long before the demise of Central University in 1901. Central began a normal course in the 1890s but contributed few teachers to the public schools of Kentucky. After the turn of the century and many years of unfulfilled dreams, momentum for educational reform peaked. The leadership of superintendent of public instruction James H. Fuqua and the Kentucky Educational Association culminated in the formation of the Kentucky Educational Commission. The commission advocated what had become obvious to many leaders in the state: little progress in education would occur until training for teachers improved. There was no wheel to reinvent because the normal school movement had already ignited educational reform in many states. Many of the state's newspapers and public school supporters entered the battle. The *Southern School Journal,* the official publication of the Kentucky State Board of Education, encouraged "every friend of education" to urge their representatives in Frankfort to pass the normal school bill.[4]

That struggle would involve many forces in the meeting of the 1906 Kentucky General Assembly. Public meetings spread the word of a new day dawning in Kentucky education. The Educational Improvement Commission circulated petitions urging enactment of a law "to provide for the establishment and maintenance of an efficient system of State Normal Schools." Even though many legislators visualized that the time had arrived to act, Governor J. C. W. Beckham, a graduate of Central University, doubted that the money could be found for such a venture. Representative Richard W. Miller of Madison County introduced a bill on January 9, 1906, proposing three normal districts, each with a school. The contest was on to name sites for the schools before passage of the bill. Henry Hardin Cherry, president of the proprietary Southern Normal School in Bowling Green, and boosters in Richmond offered their cities and existing educational plants for the effort. Political intrigues in Frankfort abounded. Thrown into the mixture was an irreconcilable conflict between Patterson and Roark, who disagreed on the place of normal education at the state's largest college. Described as "elderly, aloof, and somewhat cantankerous" by one historian, Patterson also suffered from a distinct generation rift with the much younger Roark. After several years of bitterness at the Lexington institution, Roark resigned his post in mid-1905 and enthusiastically threw his support into the normal school movement.[5]

Boosters in Richmond, including Mayor Clarence E. Woods and lawyer Jere A. Sullivan, promised to turn over to the state the $150,000 old Central plant, now occupied by the Walters school. State senator Curtis Field Burnam, from an old Richmond family, pushed the bill as well. The *Richmond Climax* touted "The Advantages Offered by Richmond for the State Normal." With the tacit consent of the trustees of Walters Collegiate Institute, the Richmond Commercial Club offered that site for a normal school.[6]

Most of the opposition to the normal school bill came from State College and the private colleges of the state. When the bills ran into trouble, with Bowling Green's proposal getting a more favorable reception than Richmond's, Jere Sullivan set to work. First, he helped draft a substitute bill specifying only two sites. Second, knowing the antipathy between Richmond politico and former governor James B. McCreary and Governor Beckham, Sullivan arranged for an ally to persuade the governor to commit to the two-site bill. While Beckham agreed to the latter, he threw a monkey wrench into the machinery by proposing that a committee, appointed by him, choose the two locations. With faith in the merits of their proposal, the Richmond supporters agreed, and the amended bills went to both senate and house committees.[7]

After more minor intrigues, both houses unanimously passed the normal school law. Understanding the importance of the moment, the legislature announced that "an emergency is therefore declared to exist and this act shall take effect from and after its passage and approval of the Governor." The law specified a school in the western and eastern districts, a board of regents for each, and, most important, appropriations of money. When Louisville did not pursue a normal school site, Bowling Green and Richmond became the only and obvious choices. The location commission met with Bowling Green and Richmond representatives and visited both sites. In Richmond, its members were entertained at the Glyndon Hotel. Sullivan and Woods worked particularly hard. Meanwhile, the Kentucky Synod of the Presbyterian Church of America supported the Walters trustees in deeding most of the old Central University property to the state.[8]

In a flurry of activity, Beckham appointed boards of regents for the new schools. One member had to come from the local area, and one had to be of the opposition party. With Superintendent Fuqua as ex officio member, J. W. Cammack of Owenton, P. W. Grinstead of Lexington, Fred A. Vaughn of Paintsville, and Jere Sullivan of Richmond composed the first Eastern board. The Eastern Kentucky State Normal School, designated District 1, elected Ruric Nevel Roark as president, the regents granting him "liberal powers of authority." District 2 in Bowling Green chose, as a foregone conclusion, Henry Hardin Cherry. Both new presidents hustled to open their schools for the fall term of 1906. Thomas H. Pickels, a Central University graduate, summed up the feelings of many Madison Countians in a *Kentucky Register* editorial: "We'll get ours all right and Danville can have Central University, and welcome. For we've got a much bigger thing."[9]

Opponents refused to give up, challenging the constitutionality of the normal school law. They sought an injunction to prohibit appropriation of $5,000 for equipment and repairs for each new normal school. Meanwhile, the Eastern and Western regents ignored the lawsuit and spent the funds, assuming that the statute would be upheld. Regent Jere Sullivan helped represent Eastern in the courts. In April 1907, the Kentucky Court of Appeals ruled in favor of the normals, upholding a lower court opinion.[10]

The antipathy between Roark and Patterson did not lessen in intensity. If the older educator chaffed at the thought of some power being taken from his school, the younger relished the idea of having an opportunity to strike out on his own. After passage of the normal school law, Patterson referred to "his old nemesis Roark" in very uncomplimentary terms. "Instead of a loss," the crusty president told a correspondent, "we have gotten rid of an incubus" who retarded the growth of the State College normal department. Roark saw his school as being in direct competition with Patterson's in 1907. To Cherry he warned: "I am still very distrustful of our friends at Lexington. . . . By so much as they get, by that much we lose." A short while later Roark had not changed his mind. "I am certain that President Patterson and all under his control will seize and use any advantage they may get, no matter how slight, to block the State Normal schools, now or at any other time."[11]

Immediately after his appointment as president of Eastern Kentucky State Normal School, Roark began organizing for an immediate opening of the institution. With local banker Robert E. Turley appointed as treasurer, plans developed for setting about repairing the old Central buildings. It was soon seen that neither normal school could open in the fall because of a lack of funds and another pending lawsuit. Nevertheless, Eastern opened its Model Elementary School in September 1906 and convened its first normal school classes in mid-January 1907, a few days after the opening of Western.[12]

Owing to the emergency in the state's educational system and the lack of high schools, graduates of the eighth grade were readily admitted to Eastern. With the state divided into two parts, Eastern was designated as "normal school district No. 1" and encompassed sixty-nine counties in 1915 with a line, not including Jefferson County, running nearly straight south to Clinton County. County superintendents could appoint one normal student to receive free tuition for every five hundred "white children" in the district. Students with free tuition were to attend the school in their districts and afterward teach there for at least three years. For others, tuition was set at $10 per term, or $40 for the five terms of the school year. Women housed in Memorial Hall paid up to $2.75 per week for room and board. Men had to room in town but could take their meals at Memorial.[13]

The curriculum was kept simple because there was only one purpose for Eastern Kentucky State Normal School: take students without a high school education and mold them into teachers as effectively, efficiently, and quickly as possible. Those with the least qualifications took a review, or remedial, course, which prepared them to pass the county examination needed for teaching in the typical one-room schools in the state. After some early experimentation, Eastern settled into a simplified system. The elementary certificate required one year of study, and the intermediate certificate was a two-year program. The advanced certificate evolved over the next eight years to prepare teachers for teaching the youth of Kentucky, particularly in the rural districts. After three years of satisfactory teaching, the advanced certificate became a "state life certificate." Students were taught subjects they themselves would teach in their classrooms. The number of English, history, mathematics, reading, penmanship, and other courses taken depended on the level of certification. The course work became progressively more difficult, with

Latin, German, French, geometry, and chemistry added to the curriculum for those preparing for high school teaching. Instructors and administrators worked hard. Dr. Virginia Spencer, with a doctorate from the University of Zurich, taught German during her two years on campus, 1907–9, in addition to being dean of women. Special courses were offered for those preparing to become school administrators and those already in the field. A student could enter at any time, taking up where he or she had finished the previous term.[14]

There was more work to be done for the reform-minded. In a Kentucky version of the progressive fervor sweeping America, educational reformers launched another campaign. A movement led by state superintendent John Grant Crabbe and the Kentucky Federation of Women's Clubs culminated in state senator Jere Sullivan's sponsoring of a far-reaching law, Government and Regulation of the Commons Schools of the State, enacted on March 24, 1908. The "Sullivan Law" marked an end to the old inefficient school laws of the state. Henceforth, each county, now the basic unit of education, had to provide for a high school, paid for with a new local tax levy. Crabbe then led what became known as "whirlwind campaigns" to drum up support for the reforms. Dozens of speakers fanned out across the state, and most of the commonwealth's newspapers joined in the effort. The hue and cry of the state's teachers, coupled with like-minded reformers, radically altered the old patterns of thought. When a legislative committee visited Eastern, the students had a song, with a message, especially prepared for it. "We think our school beats all the rest, Kentucky, Kentucky. We try to make our work the best, Kentucky, Kentucky. We could do better yet, if we could only get A good big sum of money from Our Kentucky, Kentucky." Part of the same legislative package changed State College to State University. An apparent truce between Patterson, Cherry, and Roark brought a promise of continuing cooperation. Moreover, State University received an appropriation of $200,000, and the normals received $150,000 each for buildings and equipment. When the state attorney general challenged the new appropriations, he faced a united front from the three state schools.[15]

With the school on more solid financial footing than when it was founded in 1906, the future looked bright for the Roark administration in his second and third years. After only five women graduated in 1907, men became part of larger graduating classes of 1908 and 1909. With a faculty of only eight, including the president, in 1907 there were more students to teach and house at Eastern Normal than there was room. More women than men attended, creating a need for a new women's dormitory. Additional buildings were needed, and quickly. The library, housed in the old College Prep building, contained only three hundred books; the first librarian, Ada Barter, received a forty-dollar monthly salary. By 1908, the library had grown to more than fifteen hundred volumes. Interestingly, when it came time to destroy old books, Eastern Normal received permission to do so from the old Walters Collegiate Institute board, "provided that none of the books treating on the subject, 'Original Sin,' shall be destroyed." Conditions improved so substantially that the Eastern Board of Regents considered the question of sanctioning athletics.[16]

Roark's plans for a greater Eastern Kentucky State Normal School included construction of a new women's dormitory, a power plant, and an addition to old Memorial Hall. There was also a crying need for more classrooms and administrative space. The hand-to-mouth financial existence of Eastern continued during Roark's tenure. In April 1909, he told Cherry: "We are heavily overdrawn and are feeling the pinch of poverty." When Governor Augustus O. Willson, a Republican, slowed the rate of funds flowing to the normals, both Roark and Cherry suspected the ominous hand of Patterson in it all.[17]

Roark had no greater ally than Jere A. Sullivan, who did more than any early supporter to assure Eastern's success. After working hard for the passage of the normal school law, Sullivan served for twenty-four years as a member of the Board of Regents. Also a member of the executive committee of the board, he, the president, and the treasurer met monthly and dealt with many of the school's day-to-day problems. Moreover, the executive committee and the full board of regents usually met in Sullivan's home in downtown Richmond. The Sullivan Law of 1908 testified to his energy and belief in improving all education in the state. In contact with politicians and school officials across Kentucky, he exemplified the best of progressivism in the state. A Catholic and a lifelong Democrat, he promoted religious tolerance and encouraged his party to run members of his faith for public office.[18]

The first years of Eastern demonstrated the Roark imprint, planning for the future and working within the political realities of the state. While trying to squeeze in as many students as possible, he also encouraged the intellect. On March 21, 1907, teams debated the suffrage issue. "Each side carefully drilled its body of 'claquers,'" the *Eastern Kentucky Review* reported, "and the yells were given with force and gusto." The affirmative lost, but a few days later suffragist Laura Clay, daughter of the redoubtable Cassius M. Clay, spoke on campus. After only a few months of operation, Eastern adopted a strong motto: "The Best Is Hardly Good Enough."[19]

The energy and ambition that propelled Roark into an extremely active presidency led to health problems. In mid-February 1909 the Board of Regents opened bids for a women's dormitory, a model school, a power plant, and an addition to Memorial Hall. They also granted Ruric Nevel Roark a leave of absence and named Mary Creegan Roark, his wife and the dean of women, acting president. Only two months later, Roark, one month shy of his fiftieth birthday, died in a Cincinnati hospital, probably from brain cancer. Originally his condition had been described as a "general nervous breakdown." The regents voted that his wife serve out the remainder of the year at her husband's salary. Roark was memorialized across the state in the press and at other schools as a farsighted education leader; the *Eastern Kentucky Review* declared that he had "been called from the presidency of the Eastern Kentucky State Normal School to sit at the feet of the Great Teacher." The Board of Regents voted to name the new Model School building in his honor. One student who knew him well said, "Dr. Roark possessed a wonderful mind but I really wonder if he could have adapted himself to the changing times." Mary Roark bravely went about the tasks of mother and administrator, but with a broken heart. "I trust that God will mercifully grant that you and Mrs. Cherry may be spared to each other until old age," she wrote to the Western president, "and that it will not be yourself to know what it means for the light of your life to go out."[20]

Mary Roark served as acting president of Eastern until April 9, 1910. She took her role seriously, knowing that it was only temporary. She presided over the sanctioning of athletics as well as the laying of the cornerstone for the building named for her husband. When a faculty member disobeyed her instructions not to use the chapel, she charged him with "insubordination," and the Board of Regents voted for censure. When he did not publicly apologize, he was fired. As she left the post of acting president, students and faculty rewarded her diligence with a special commemoration. After speeches by faculty, staff, and Sullivan, and the presentation of a painting and silver loving cup, the students gave her special cheers. The men sang, "You know, I know, speak up loud, We know, they know, all the crowd, Thank her, thank her, this is meant, For our woman President." Then the women proudly replied, "There's a lady we know; for a year she has led us, And full was the table of learning she spread us, From mountain and bluegrass she called us and fed us, And we're proud of the work she has done." Mary Roark, reappointed as dean of women, served until the 1914–15 school year.[21]

With Mary Roark as acting president, the regents searched for a permanent administrator. John Grant Crabbe, elected superintendent of public instruction as a Republican in 1908, became the leading candidate because of his growing national fame and experience as ex officio member of the Eastern regents. A graduate of Wesleyan University in Ohio, he served as superintendent of Ashland City Schools for eighteen years. Deeply religious, he also played the organ and wrote sacred music. These years of service, plus more study, culminated in a doctorate of pedagogy from Miami University. After Mary Roark served for nearly a year, Crabbe became Eastern's president on April 9, 1910. At a time when many normal schools across the country were becoming four-year teachers colleges, Crabbe's efforts to raise Eastern to that level would be tested by a stingy legislature and competition with State University and Western, where wily President Cherry proved to be a crafty rival. During his first chapel appearance Crabbe declared, "I am to be more than president of this school. I am to be your co-worker in the greatest cause in the world—the upbuilding of schools."[22]

The new president determined to build Eastern into a first-class normal school, and he was impatient to get there. A disciplined man, he could not abide laziness or wasted time. Not wanting to embarrass talkative visitors, Crabbe had a worker devise an ingenious device to speed up their departure. After a few minutes Crabbe's secretary pushed a button under his desk. In the president's office a tiny bell rang, and the word "NEXT" appeared in a red lighted window in a box. "So when you have business with the Dr.," explained the maker, "you had better hurry up." As classes changed, Crabbe would stand on the steps in Roark Hall, repeating rhythmically, "All right, students, file and to the right, single file and to the right" as he clapped his hands. And they marched "single file from one building to another." When Crabbe managed a week-long Farmers Chautauqua, he rented a "big car" to shuttle the speakers. The driver recalled he had "eat enough dust to kill any one" on the terrible roads of Madison County keeping the busy Crabbe on schedule.[23]

Crabbe determined to open more and diverse opportunities for Eastern's students. He understood the difficulty of developing school spirit because the majority of students attended after the closing of the six-month rural schools in January. For example, during his first year as president, only 131 students attended Eastern normal in the fall of 1910. In January 1911, 559 students crowded into the inadequate facilities in Richmond. Even more students, 762, entered during the later term in March, followed by 921 for summer school. Enrollment of the model school also continued to increase.[24]

The new president planned on stimulating both the intellect and the sporting nature of Kentucky students. The school fielded a football team for the first time in 1909. This proved particularly difficult, since most of the players had never seen a game, and only three had played before. They found the recently invented forward pass completely incomprehensible. Nevertheless, they played hard, losing more than they won against high school teams. Crabbe also divided the student body into literary societies with imposing names such as Periclesian, Eutopian, Excelsior, Carpediem, and Cynthian. Women, a majority of the student body, participated fully, with one serving as president of the Eutopians. Faculty members led the groups. The societies held events, such as a special program prepared by the Carpediem on one occasion. There were other activities as well. William Jennings Bryan spoke at an Eastern chapel assembly under the auspices of the YMCA in May 1911. The entire student body lined the driveway into campus, welcoming the three-time presidential candidate. Introduced by Senator McCreary, the "Great Commoner" rose to speak to "deafening" applause. The audience apparently never flinched during his two-hour speech about religious work and politics. Crabbe also planned an annual lecture series and cultural events, such as visiting orchestras.[25]

Following a national trend, sports, originally limited to the high school level, became a more significant part of life at Eastern. Women participated first, playing basketball as early as 1907. In 1911, the women won a local tournament. The *E.K.S.N. Student* urged excellence in all of Eastern's endeavors, including getting the basketball season off to a good start. "A school is known in a good measure by the athletics it affords," the editor exclaimed. When the basketball team lost to Kentucky Wesleyan, but played a much better second half, a reporter rather bellicosely declared that "every man went back in the game determined to stay with his man or hurt some one in the attempt." Although athletics were important, after the 1911 football team won only one game, the sports editor consoled his audience, "In the first place, to have any kind of football team is better than not making the attempt at all." After a close baseball game at Stanford, the sports editor blamed the loss on the umpire giving numerous close calls to his son, the local pitcher. "Several of the base decisions were so rank that even Prof. Grinstead was protesting." When the Eastern catcher and Coach C. H. Wilson tried to "adjust the matter, the umpire said he was right and could lick anyone who disputed him." Believing that discretion was the better part of valor and "being slightly outnumbered, our boys left." Students and coaches alike understood the reason for so many defeats: "Our student body changes too often."[26]

In 1912, first-year teacher Charles A. Keith, a Rhodes scholar as well as a former professional baseball player, coached both football and basketball. Winning three football games that fall, while tying one and losing four, he presented an unusual chapel program one day. "To instruct the uninitiated in the mysteries of the game," Keith "explained from a diagram on the blackboard the various points of procedure in a foot ball game." In a disputed game the next year, Kentucky Wesleyan walked off the field and forfeited, 1–0. The next football coach, Ben H. Barnard, who also doubled as the manual training teacher, led the Eastern eleven, with no nickname as yet, from 1913 to 1916. His charges lost 7–6 to Stanford High School in 1914 but defeated Western, 34–6. An Eastern cheer of the time promised to "Stand 'em on their heads / Stand 'em on their feet / Eastern! Eastern! Can't be beat." Well, at least some of the time.[27]

Roark and Crabbe assembled an interesting faculty. Ernest Clifton McDougle, who served in several roles, eventually earned a Ph.D. at Clark University and became dean of the school. Longtime art instructor Maude Gibson, who painted various scenes of the campus, received far less salary than her male counterparts. George Drury Smith, who came to Eastern in 1908, enjoyed leading students on field trips, earning the nickname "Bug" because of his knowledge of biology. After a student-recruiting trip far into the mountains, he told a humorous story about crossing the South Fork of the Kentucky River in a horse and buggy: "All went lovely for a few feet, then all of a sudden our horse disappeared except for his ears. The next moment, before we had time to think, our buggy followed the horse. It would have done you good to see the Educational Collaborator of the State of Kentucky and the Head of the Science Department of the Eastern Kentucky State Normal splashing water and scratching gravel."[28]

A member of the original faculty, Wren Jones Grinstead combined a love of literature and languages with sports, and remained long enough to earn a Ph.D. before moving on to the University of Pennsylvania. The most unusual of the early faculty members had to have been Helena Piotrowska, always referred to as "Madame." Forced to leave her native Poland because of political activities, she returned during World War I to aid the fight for liberty there. A teacher of French and German, she lent an air of old-world charm to a school struggling to enter a realm of academia beyond the level of a high school. However, sensing that there was more mundane work to be done, she also organized sewing clubs in Richmond. Years after she left Richmond and Eastern, people recalled the formidable Madame riding her small horse, sidesaddle, wearing "her voluminous upper and nether Polish garments."[29]

With only a few professors having graduate degrees in this period, Crabbe and the Board of Regents searched for ways to upgrade the education of the faculty. The regents granted Piotrowska and Grinstead leave at half pay to study for higher degrees. Moreover, to encourage faculty study, the regents adopted prerequisites "to retaining a position," added to teaching contracts. At a minimum, faculty were to be involved in "some professional study," prepare "at least one professional paper," attend a professional meeting, read "studiously and regularly at least one professional journal," and be prepared for a classroom visit by the president himself. If these rules were not followed, "the contract automatically terminates." If President Crabbe and the Board of Regents could be helpful to faculty in giving leaves with half pay, they could also be quite harsh in some administrative decisions. For example, the regents not only refused to approve Crabbe's recommendation of an extension of Mary Roark's leave of absence with pay but also unceremoniously told her they "did not need your services during the coming year." By this time Marie L. Roberts had become dean of women, beginning a long period of service.[30]

"We must teach teachers to teach," declared the *Eastern Kentucky Review* in 1915. From the beginning of its existence, Eastern used several publications to share its message with the state. The *Review* began immediately in 1906. A quarterly, it publicized official information about the school, course work, and the issues confronting Eastern and education in the state. The *E.K.S.N. Student* allowed students to develop their journalistic skills, beginning in 1908 and ending in 1915, to be briefly succeeded by the *Talisman*. The *Eastern Progress* began publication in 1922, superseding the *Talisman*. The *Milestone* also began publication in 1922 and continued until 1999 except for a brief hiatus during World War II.[31]

The *Review*, the *Student*, and the *Talisman* all exemplified the progressive zeal of the early twentieth century, particularly of the southern variety. One of the founders of the *Student* declared, "It didn't amount to but little but it gave us a chance to develop a little in writing and in managing of a small business." The early years at Eastern coincided with the progressive presidencies of Teddy Roosevelt and Woodrow Wilson, and to a lesser degree that of William Howard Taft, administrations that highlighted public service and reform. While progressives never totally agreed on a single agenda, temperance, woman suffrage, prohibition, and literacy were all subjects that fit the mood of the time. Fiction in the *Student* often had an uplifting, Christian message. "The Awakening of the American Conscience," by Lelia Gore Buchanan, editor in chief of the *Student* in 1911, stressed the need for helping the poor, a classic example of an offshoot of progressivism, the Social Gospel. Lelia E. Patridge, a teacher at the Model School and director of the rural school, even wrote "Song of the Leaders of Kentucky," sung to the music of "We're Tenting Tonight on the Old Camp Ground." "We are thinking of our dear old State," she wrote. "Of its future, not its past. For the children's cry hath snapped the spell." The liquor trade was seen by many Eastern students as the bane of society. G. Mansfield Moore urged the citizens of Richmond in 1911 to "march to the ballot boxes of this town and under the avalanche of freemen's ballots bury beyond resurrection the Richmond saloon." That same year President Crabbe and several faculty members attended the Great Kentucky Convention, which had sections meeting on improving education, agriculture, and roads and reforming the tax system. Showing a typical female perspective on the suffrage movement, student Ella M. Trammel's prizewinning speech argued, "Who is against it? The liquor dealer, the keeper of the gambling den, the white slave dealer. . . . The liquor dealers hate the words woman suffrage, as the Devil hates Holy Water."[32]

But if the foregoing were examples of the uplifting message of Eastern's early publications, the southernness that had tainted old Central University continued to weaken the social message of its successor in Richmond. Touting the area as "the best place in the *South* to spend six weeks in one of the most beautiful cities of the *Southland,*" Eastern and Richmond exuded and rejoiced in its southern ambience. Fittingly, the Board of Regents authorized an expenditure of sixty dollars, a substantial sum for the time, for a set of books entitled the *Library of Southern Literature.* In addition, the United Daughters of the Confederacy gave a scholarship to the school. William J. Moore, who entered the normal school in 1913, recalled that "an old Negro man used to patrol the dormitory halls every morning . . . , rousing us boys by announcing, 'Risin' time, six-thirty!' in a sing-song chant." Eastern's racial strictures would have differed little from those at a school in the Deep South. Like the state of Kentucky, Eastern remained rigidly segregated. The only African Americans on campus were laborers, always referred to as "colored" or "Trusties," as pictured in the 1910 *Bluemont,* issued by the life certificate class. When a black cook died, Maude Gibson praised her with typical white southern paternalism: "'Sallie Ann' was a faithful, hard-working negress [*sic*] of the 'old-time' type." These were the days when a student could be admonished for referring to "one of the colored servants as a colored lady," recalled a 1910 graduate. Blacks in Richmond at the turn of the twentieth century were expected to live and react in a society little changed from the immediate post–Civil War era, the years of old Central University.[33]

In a more positive way, Eastern's early years demonstrated one of the most important trends of the time: the "democratization of higher education." Normal schools, more than state universities or old elite colleges and universities, contributed to the most rapid changes in American educational history. Particularly in a poor state like Kentucky, normal school education offered the quickest, most cost-efficient method of training teachers. With so few high schools in eastern Kentucky, the task of attacking the "virus of illiteracy" became the primary goal of the normal school movement. "The work has begun and the cry is 'Forward,'" exclaimed the first issue of the *Eastern Kentucky Review.*[34]

"If the Normal Schools are true to the spirit of the State's demand," President Crabbe explained to a meeting of the Kentucky Educational Association in 1912, "they will train teachers in this educational trinity—Hand, Heart, and Head." These teachers would then "train pupils in this same trinity." That effort tested Crabbe's abilities to the utmost. Though described as a "very authoritarian person" by one observer, Crabbe set a tone for the campus by wearing a tuxedo to chapel services and taking part in musical presentations, often playing an instrument himself. He encouraged pageants and commemorations to build student-faculty esprit de corps. His biggest problems included finding the money necessary to fund a growing school and coordinating the normal school movement in Kentucky with President Cherry at Western.[35]

Without overall state direction in a central agency, State University, Eastern, and Western cooperated only when necessary. They competed for appropriations from the Kentucky General Assembly and for students in the state. While State University probably drew a more qualified student body, it still had to compete for those students who wanted teaching degrees. Though Patterson retired in 1910, he kept close watch over State University's new president, Henry Stites Barker. Cherry proved to be an adept educator-politician and even considered running for governor on a couple of occasions. He was as determined to expand his school and influence as were the presidents of Eastern. Having a longer tenure, from 1906 until his death in 1937, Cherry enjoyed advantages in Frankfort. When Western received a $50,000 appropriation in 1912 and Eastern only $40,000, leadership at the Richmond school could not help but see unfairness.[36]

Crabbe and Cherry not only fought the normal school battle in Kentucky but also often disagreed over such substantive issues as state appropriations and curriculum. The competition was not always friendly. With the state divided between the two normals, they bickered when students crossed over the line for their education. When Western apparently lowered its residency requirement for obtaining an elementary certificate, Crabbe protested, "I am of the opinion that this materially lowers our standards and we certainly should raise rather than lower any of our standards." After a few Eastern students who "could scarcely carry very ordinary certificate work" transferred to Western, Crabbe railed at the thought of their getting "high class certificates" at Bowling Green. Apparently, Cherry backed down on this one. Finally Crabbe and Cherry agreed on an "ironclad rule," requiring both schools to coordinate any plans of transferring students. In 1916 they realigned their districts so that the state's population would conform to the 1910 census.[37]

Eastern Kentucky State Normal School was always living on the edge financially. On several occasions Crabbe had to borrow money to pay the faculty. The state warrants, which the normals used to obtain appropriated money from Frankfort, often arrived late. To get $500 worth of gravel spread on the campus in 1910, the contractor had to agree to wait until the legislature met. When members of the life certificate class of 1910 published the *Bluemont* on their own initiative, Crabbe and the board of regents refused to pay for the cost overrun. In 1913 the shortfall became so critical that certificates, IOUs, in effect, bearing 8 percent interest, were given to the faculty in lieu of salary. They could then exchange these, at a discounted rate, at a local bank. Even in such dire straits, Eastern had to defend itself against a 1913 state inspector's report that implied lax fiscal management at the school. The regents put up a strong defense of their school's expenditures. Eastern defended spending $444.65 for medical assistance to fight the threat of a smallpox outbreak at the school as a "good investment" because disbanding would mean losing valuable class time.[38]

As it struggled for financial security and its place in the education of teachers in Kentucky, Eastern Kentucky State Normal School grew in its first decade. Enrollment increased each year in a usual pattern. Younger, beginning students attended the two fall terms, while their older colleagues taught. After Christmas and the closing of the rural schools, older students joined their younger colleagues, and enrollment more than doubled for the third, fourth, and summer terms. The number of advanced certificates increased each year. Course work in everything from agriculture to pedagogy, manual training to German, offered a wide range of opportunities for study at Eastern Normal. From the beginning, a few students took only academic courses and did not prepare to become teachers. Crabbe, even more so than the Roarks, stressed preparing the normal student not only for the academic side of teaching but also for the rigors of disciplining pupils and classroom methodology. Believing that teachers needed "some 'stage-presence,'" Crabbe encouraged students to develop their public speaking skills in the literary societies. He wanted a well-rounded, as well as academically skilled, graduate.[39]

Who were the students of the pre–World War I era? Some of the earliest students interviewed for the Eastern Kentucky University Alumni Oral History Project revealed what it was like to attend the Eastern Kentucky State Normal School. After passing the eighth-grade examination, Virginia H. Waters entered Eastern in 1914. She worked in the cafeteria to help pay for room and board and had to study hard to keep up with her classmates. Being at Eastern during a transition in the dean of women, she recalled Mrs. Roark as being "more social," while Miss Roberts "was a little bit on the stern side." After graduation in 1916 at the age of nineteen—at that time teachers in Kentucky had to be at least eighteen—she began teaching. After a forty-five-year career, mostly in Jefferson County, she praised the foundation that Eastern provided. Students from eastern Kentucky, many of whom had "never seen the outside world, blossomed," she declared. The *Talisman* of 1916 identified Waters as "one of Eastern's best-read girls. She has a commendable sense of genuineness to her nature."[40]

"One of the sprightliest, one of the brightest, and one of the worthiest members of the Senior Class" were the accolades given Ethel Merritt Lisle, a classmate of Waters, in the *Talisman.* Having graduated from high school, Lisle represented a somewhat older type of student. The women of Sullivan

Hall, where she lived, were not always angels. When the young men on campus decided to sing to the women in Sullivan Hall after a basketball victory over hated rival Western, Lisle and a few other girls "decided we'd get up and put on our kimonos and raincoats and serenade the boys." Mrs. Roark and her chaperones "swooped down." "What have I ever done to you all to do that?" asked Dean Roark. Apparently the Eastern men took up for the women, persuading the dean and President Crabbe not to keep them "campused" for long, taking their social privileges away. Lisle remembered Crabbe as "a wonderful man" and a person of good humor. Teaching for the first time could be a shock. Although Lisle "loved" teaching, she disliked the drudgery. "You had to be janitor and everything. You got there at eight o'clock and you were off at four. But sometimes you had to carry the water and make the fires, and clean the windows and clean the floors." And all for the grand salary of forty-two dollars a month.[41]

Other students had similar positive experiences at Eastern during the Crabbe years. After finishing the spring term at Eastern, Raymond Layne had to borrow money to get him through his first few weeks teaching in a Harlan County coal camp. Digging the pits for outhouses was part of his duties, as well as teaching the three R's and handling discipline. Not knowing that a mischievous boy had matches in his back pocket, the young teacher administered a rapid lick of the hand. "The matches ignited and burned a hole in his pants and blistered his hip," Layne recalled many years later. "The word soon got around that 'Mr. Layne sot a boy on fire at school.'" Another student, Fannie Noe Hendren, remembered, "Oh, we had such good times." She attended during the transition in the dean of women's office. The girls discovered they could always get around Mrs. Roark by taking her daughter, Kathleen, along with them. Once they held an all-night party in the still uncompleted annex to Sullivan and got away with it with only a warning, escaping the dreaded threat of being campused. However, the Roberts regime changed all that. "Miss Roberts was an old maid and didn't understand young girls like Mrs. Roark did," explained Hendren.[42]

Most students were overawed by the physical setting of Eastern. "The Campus Beautiful," as it was being called as early as 1917, aptly described the effort, if not always the buildings and landscaping of Eastern. Olmstead Brothers of Brookline, Massachusetts, planned the landscaping. The Weber firm of Fort Wright, Kentucky, handled most of the architectural duties, developing a classical revival style for the campus until after World War II. Building on the physical legacy of Central University, a $150,000 state appropriation of 1908 constructed the Roark Building, Sullivan Hall, and a power plant. Memorial Hall again became a men's dormitory, accommodating 130 students. An annex added to Sullivan in 1912 increased its capacity to 150. A new multipurpose building named for longtime regent J. W. Cammack came into use in 1918. Purchases of more land, primarily farmland, expanded the campus. All the older structures required extensive refurbishing. Modern heating, plumbing, and lighting were added to the older buildings as money became available. In 1912 the Thompson Burnam home again became part of the nucleus of the old Central University property, eventually renamed the Blanton House. More building plans were in the offing later in the decade and at the beginning of World War I. Plans for a new library had to be shelved temporarily when Andrew Carnegie refused a grant application.[43]

In mid-1916 John Grant Crabbe decided to leave Eastern for the presidency of Colorado State Teachers College, nearly doubling his salary. His legacy after six years of service included expanding the campus facilities and curriculum and developing budgeting procedures. The number of faculty increased, and they became more qualified for their posts, with several returning to universities for more graduate work. Active in state, regional, and national education organizations, Crabbe set a good example for his faculty, serving as president of the National Education Association in 1913.[44]

After the early years of the Roarks' leadership, Crabbe's style was more systematic, though still personal. "I want to help you to make a man of yourself," he said at a "special mass meeting of the men" in 1914. Part of his program of uplift was to introduce Eastern students to the arts, literature, and the world beyond. His former students would remember him as a deeply moral man, who often led religious services during chapel time. Daily chapel attendance added to Crabbe's regular influence over the students. His talks to students were homilies about success in all walks of life. Though something of a martinet, he listened to others and developed an administrative structure for Eastern. His energetic, hands-on leadership came from a firm conviction that Kentucky had far to go in improving educational opportunity for its young people. He received one further honor before leaving Richmond. Music teacher John G. Koch wrote "Eastern Rally," dedicated to Crabbe. "Raise the name of Eastern, publish her virtues rare. Boom the fame of Eastern. E.K.S.N. fair!"[45]

CHAPTER 3

From Normal School
to Teachers College, 1916–1928

THE RESIGNATION OF President Crabbe quickly drew thirty applicants for the job as president of Eastern. Within days, however, the Board of Regents settled on Thomas Jackson Coates, a native of Pikeville. Apparently Coates did not seek the presidency and had to be persuaded to take the post on a one-year trial basis. Educated at Southern Normal in Bowling Green and at State College in Lexington, he served as superintendent of Richmond schools before becoming supervisor of rural schools for the state of Kentucky in 1911. A lifelong friend of Cherry, he told the Western president, "I am going to lean on you hard" for support. They would soon fall into the same pattern of rivalry that typified relationships between Western and Eastern.[1]

With a wealth of experience in education, having taught in a rural school, and with even a stint as editor of a small-town newspaper, Coates agreed to a contract of $3,600 in salary and free use of the president's home. There would be many challenges over the horizon, but one of the first was mundane but pungent. One of Coates's first accomplishments was to hook Eastern onto the city sewer system. As the minutes of the Board of Regents reported, "Practically all last year, sewage, almost in its natural state, arose from this filter bed [septic field] and flowed down the valley on the back of the campus and into the little creek, which flows through the farm joining the Campus, and finally through a portion of the City." Richmond's Water Street must have smelled much better after this needed change. A conflict between town and gown had been averted.[2]

Not long after assuming the presidency of Eastern, Coates, along with the faculty and students of Eastern, faced the challenge of World War I. "The world is afire," Coates wrote. "The German must and will be beaten. The world of democracy expects every Kentuckian to do his duty." With the dormitories full and some students living on the outskirts of town, prices inflated, and all costs skyrocketed. Buying up canned goods before prices went up even higher and canning college farm produce did not help much. Coal became a prime commodity, and its price became a burden to the Eastern budget. Then enrollment decreased because of the military draft and men volunteering for duty. To keep up enrollment, the Eastern Board of Regents agreed that "men and women eighteen years old and over be accepted provided they have the appointment of their County Superintendent whether they sign the agreement to teach or not." Although probably unseen at the time, this was the beginning of the end of the old normal school strictures and the evolution toward a senior teachers college.[3]

Coates made a special trip to Washington to get a Student Army Training Corps (SATC) unit assigned to Eastern. With a contract for one hundred soldiers, the army agreed to pay one dollar a day for room and board and seventeen cents a day for their tuition. An army lieutenant was assigned to the school. Like all American institutions, Eastern threw itself into the war effort. The *Eastern Kentucky Review* instructed those in the field with "Some Things Every Rural Teacher Can Do." From buying a Liberty Bond to seeking out "treasonable statements" to becoming "more efficient," everyone could help defeat Germany. Several teachers made patriotic speeches, including one by Professor Keith at Western. "He covered himself with glory," Cherry reported to Coates. "I enjoyed his splendid thoughts, words and achievements with the same degree of enthusiasm as if he had been a member of my own faculty."[4]

Even Professor Grinstead, an original member of the faculty and a classicist, went off to an SATC camp with four students and another teacher for a few weeks. "Worth while?" he asked. "Of course it was worth while. Apart from service to the country, every man came back with a straighter bearing, tenser muscles, a better digestion, a healthier color, a closer contact with life as it is, and a more wholesome respect for scientific fact and hygienic habits." Actually, only twenty men enrolled in the Eastern SATC program because of the terrible influenza epidemic and the impending end of the war.[5]

The cost of the war for the country and Eastern was high. A son of the Roarks died of pneumonia at an army camp in Wisconsin. Several former students and graduates died the same way or in combat. Hobart Galbraith, a former student and budding poet, wrote about his experiences. In "Weep Not," he proclaimed, "If I die on the battle front / Sing no sad songs for me /

For the flowers will soon grow above my head / And my mind from these horrors will be free." He did not reach the battle zones of France, dying during the influenza outbreak at Camp Zachary Taylor in Jefferson County. Lee Shearer, class of 1916, president of the YMCA, and editor in chief of the *E.K.S.N. Student,* died in the Battle of Château-Thierry.[6]

Even after the armistice concluded the "war to end all wars" on November 11, 1918, problems continued. A pandemic influenza outbreak of worldwide proportions threatened all institutions. For a while, the state health department ordered schools, movie houses, and churches to close down. One Eastern alumna lost five of her elementary students to the malady. More than fourteen thousand Kentuckians died during this outbreak of the "Spanish Lady," the nickname given to this form of influenza. More than one-tenth of that number died at Camp Taylor. Eastern's enrollment declined, but the school remained open. The State Board of Health sent physicians to vaccinate all students against pneumonia, and it took until the fall of 1919 to build enrollment back to prewar levels.[7]

New and old challenges faced Eastern in the immediate postwar era. With the old Walters Building condemned in a "dangerous condition," a new library became imperative if Eastern was to grow. Other needs such as a new dormitory were put on hold. Construction did not proceed without difficulties. Even with permission from Frankfort and the money promised by the legislature, Attorney General M. M. Logan ruled that Eastern should not contract for a building that could not be paid for out of "one year's appropriation." Finding a builder created problems. When a local man did not get the contract, he committed suicide. Then the Richmond contractor who did win the contract defaulted soon after construction began on the multipurpose Cammack Building. The bonding company saw to the completion of the building to be used for the Training School and library at a cost of about $68,000. President Frank L. McVey of the University of Kentucky spoke at a conference highlighting the new building on a topic on everyone's mind because of the just ended world war: "Americanism of All Citizens Through a Better Civic and Patriotic Instruction." One local critic later claimed that the building had not been well constructed.[8]

Construction in the generally prosperous 1920s greatly expanded the Eastern campus. When millionairess Mary Lily Flagler Bingham died in 1917, state coffers benefited, with Eastern gaining $35,000 from taxes imposed on the settlement of her estate. The money was used wisely, spread out over several projects, including the purchase of farmland and construction of a temporary gym and the new library. Burnam Hall, a badly needed women's dormitory named in honor of Judge A. R. Burnam, a state senator from Madison County, came into service in 1921 at a cost of $129,000, with an addition in 1926. The basement was used for many years as a cafeteria. A new wing to Memorial Hall gave more space for men. The Crabbe Library, named for Eastern's second president, was completed in 1923 at a cost of $67,000. A new administration building, constructed in 1926 for more than $200,000 and soon named for President Coates, served as an administration center and for classes. Three years later an auditorium, seating eighteen hundred, was added to Coates and named for longtime regent and state senator Hiram Brock. A disbursement of more than $465,000 in early 1928, which included new buildings, was the largest in the history of Eastern up to that time.[9]

Life on the campus was not without some danger. A series of mysterious fires in August 1920 threatened the safety of the Eastern campus, necessitating the hiring of a night watchman for the first time. A fire in the barn at the rear of President Coates's home not only destroyed his Ford touring car but also killed "about 100 chickens roosting in the loft." Later that same evening, a fire broke out in the old gymnasium, destroying it and threatening the nearby University Building. A fire in the basement of another structure was put out quickly. Although no culprit could be brought to justice, rumors circulated around Richmond for years that the firebug was the scion of a prominent family.[10]

Although the Coates years were a time of growth, the president, known for his cost-saving measures, often appeared reluctant to ask the legislature for money. The high inflation of the war years placed a strain on Eastern's finances. To keep workers, the school had to raise their wages. As stated by Western's historian, relations between the normal schools were "a mixture of hostility, suspicion, and cooperation." I have found nothing to the contrary. The dog-eat-dog competition for money in the early twenties apparently worked to the disadvantage of Eastern. When the University of Kentucky and Western asked for increased appropriations prior to the meeting of the 1920 General Assembly, Coates kept strangely silent. Perhaps this was because of criticism of Eastern by the state examiner in 1918. While generally favorable, the examiner censured the purchase of the president's home and subsequent improvements, suggesting that the house be used for a library. The report also criticized the school for supplying free electricity to school treasurer R. E. Turley, whose home joined the campus. Moreover, the examiner scored Turley's handling of the majority of the school's insurance.[11]

When Coates got a raise in 1918, the faculty did not. He received $4,600 "on account of the high cost of living," but had to pay $600 for staying in the President's House. Dean E. C. McDougle had the next highest salary at $2,750, and Keith and a few others received as much as $2,200. At the lowest end of the scale was an assistant librarian, who was paid only $700 for the year. In a confidential report to the regents, Coates could be quite critical of the faculty. In 1921, he declared Keith to be "a strong man but a big boy" and "untactful at times." Maude Gibson he found to be "a good teacher with the usual characteristics of an old maid; rather homely; not an attractive dresser." The faculty was expected to keep to the proprieties of the day. Because of the Training School, there were usually a few more women than men on the faculty. While F. Scott Fitzgerald might publish the short story "Bernice Bobs Her Hair" in 1920, it was not until the middle of the decade that faculty women could adopt such a hairstyle.[12]

In 1921 major changes began brewing in the normal schools. With Cherry and Western leading the way, the move toward the normals becoming state teachers colleges began in earnest. Judge J. W. Cammack provided much of the leadership on the Eastern side as both boards of regents met for strategic sessions. While Cherry asked for $335,000, Coates said Eastern needed "only $225,000 for the immediate future, although it could use to advantage a greater sum." It was decided that both schools "shou'l present their cases separately" for money, while combining forces to "draft a bill for the purpose of asking permission of this legislature to become State Teachers' Colleges in the future." The General Assembly reacted favorably but also insisted that the two schools could not provide enough elementary teachers for the state. Adding two new normal schools touched off the same political struggles as in 1906, when Richmond and Bowling Green won out. This time forces in Morehead and Murray carried the day during the 1922 legislative session, and these schools opened in the fall of 1923. Now that there were six schools at the public trough, including the African American school in Frankfort, the competition for state funds would be even more intense.[13]

The Richmond school evolved into Eastern Kentucky State Normal School and Teachers College by adding a third and fourth year of curriculum that became increasingly uniform because of national, regional, and state standards. Students as young as sixteen were entering Eastern; some were as old as sixty-four. By 1919, Eastern already had a two-year program for those who had graduated from a four-year high school, making it, in effect, a junior college. The elementary and intermediate certificate courses had been at a high school level, with the advanced certificate "of college grade," making Eastern "both a Normal High School and a Normal College." The days of the old-fashioned normal school curriculum were numbered. The Sullivan Law increased the numbers of high schools and high school graduates in Kentucky. In 1908, at the time of passage of the law, there were only 106 high schools in the state and no county high schools at all; by 1920 there were more than 400. Moreover, Eastern was already developing outreach programs. It offered many courses by correspondence and staffed a study center in Frankfort, taking classes directly to teachers.[14]

More changes took place at Eastern in the early 1920s. When the school became a four-year college in the fall of 1923, its calendar changed to two eighteen-week semesters and a summer school with two six-week terms, with courses earning semester hours for the first time. "Cheaper Than Staying at Home," ran an advertisement for the $225 per-year cost. The ad assured, "This will cover Tuition, Board, Room Rent and All Necessary Expenses." The act of 1922 required that Eastern increase its faculty and equipment "for the purpose of enabling it to go on a full four-year college basis." One of the most important steps forward was the hiring of Herman L. Donovan as dean of the faculty in 1921. The first student to register at Western Normal in 1906, Donovan finished an undergraduate degree at the University of Kentucky and an M.A. at Columbia University and had done work on his doctorate at George Peabody Teachers College before coming to Eastern. Like many of his students, he began teaching at the age of eighteen in a rural school. He provided valuable service in the transition to a four-year teachers college before leaving for more graduate work at Peabody, with some time also spent at the University of Chicago. After joining the faculty at Peabody, his place as dean was taken by Homer E. Cooper.[15]

No matter what the program, Eastern and Western and now Morehead and Murray often had to cooperate, whether they wanted to or not. Meetings between representatives of the schools in the twenties covered curriculum, number of hours required for graduation, and extension and correspondence courses. Without a state oversight body, they all tried to get the upper hand in the maelstrom that was Kentucky politics. Henry Hardin Cherry of Western, the ultimate political practitioner as educator, usually held the upper hand as he actively sought political alliances in Frankfort. However, Eastern kept up its enrollment with fewer resources. In 1925, Superintendent of Public Instruction McHenry Rhoads reported that Western had an approximate enrollment of 1,000; Eastern, 1,200; Murray, 700; and Morehead, 500.[16]

An insight into Eastern academic life is found in a 1926 document of faculty rules. In the twenties, the administration suggested the bell curve for grading. The school was very protective of students, particularly the young ladies. Any woman who wanted to participate in "any competitive contests" had to have the written consent of her parents. While the rules prohibited "all forms of dancing permitting undue familiarity [i.e., touching]," folk dances and rhythmic games were permitted. Dean of Women Marie Roberts, "Miss Strict" as some called her, ran a tight ship, having the power to decide what "social games" were permissible. She and trusted student monitors carried a ruler and enforced the "six-inch rule." Any couples who violated that invisible barrier were forced to sit down. "We also believe that sentimentalism is a menace to wholesome manhood and womanhood," the faculty declared, "and that the presence of love-making couples who can neither accept nor set limitations to their being together, 'in season and out of season,' is detrimental to the tone of the school." Men could visit women "legally" only for forty-five minutes after supper each evening, for a slightly longer period after Sunday dinner, and from seven thirty to ten o'clock on Saturday night, when promenading couples walked around the campus under the watchful eye of Dean Roberts. Sometimes the men would serenade the women. Chaperones were required when women went off campus. The men were given more independence, but not much. Study time for males in Memorial Hall from seven thirty to ten o'clock each evening was rigidly monitored. Not only liquor but also the use of tobacco was prohibited on campus. Any teacher, regardless of subject matter, who determined a student to be "seriously deficient in English" had the right to give the student an incomplete and require him or her to retake second-year English. Discipline was harsh, with one young man being denied a teaching certificate because he was judged to be "not of a good moral character." For "loafing on the campus and not attending classes," Coates sent one young lady home. "I am sorry your daughter has acted in this way," the president wrote the father, "but we cannot help it." And students did not always pay their bills. In 1928 business agent G. M. Brock complained about "the number of worthless checks given by students."[17]

When young ladies attended the downtown theaters, they walked hand in hand, so heavily chaperoned that the procession must have looked like an army platoon entering enemy territory. If the movie at the Alhambra Theater or the Opera House became a bit racy, a chaperone rang a bell and then whisked the ladies from the iniquitous scene. There is even the story of married students being forced to take a chaperone with them on downtown excursions. Students could sometimes run afoul of the rules. "Barge parties" on the Kentucky River were a highlight of student life in the 1920s until the Eastern administration got wind of dancing of the forbidden modern variety. Breaking the rules meant days or perhaps weeks of being campused. In a gentle teasing of Dean Roberts, Sullivan Hall women revealed in the *Eastern Kentucky Review* that they often indulged in a bit of subterfuge. After having "sumptuously partaken of a meal of beans and light-bread" in the cafeteria, they surreptitiously enjoyed peanut butter and sometimes even cooked "winnies" under the cover of darkness. When they heard the dean approaching they quickly got rid of the evidence and appeared to be sound asleep. The ladies of Sullivan also gave advice to prospective students about how to survive a fire drill: "Grab your blanket off the bed and wrap it completely around you so that it will reach your ankles" and then "run" for the steps. Sometimes students could not adjust to being away from home. The school refunded the fees of one young lady in 1920 who, upon arriving on campus, "immediately became greatly homesick," refusing to eat or to leave her room. But most students adjusted and thrived in the Eastern environment. Events such as a "pound party," to which members of the Periclesian Literary Society brought a pound of peanut butter, cheese, crackers, candy, and so forth, gave enjoyment and helped build school spirit.[18]

Before publication of the *Milestone*, the *Student's Review*, a senior issue of the *Eastern Kentucky Review*, gave students the opportunity to tell of their days at the school. The pictures of the thirty-one women and three men in the 1921 version demonstrated the normal school predominance of women in the school, most of whom were going to be elementary school teachers. "Myrtle Lee [Baker] is one of the rare kind who makes all 'A's' and is lovable still," read one caption. "To know her is to love her." Some of the men and women were obviously older students, ones who had already taught for several years in the public, probably rural, schools before finishing the three-year program of requirements. The caption under Delaney Roberts illustrated the alternate teaching and schooling regimen of most Eastern students in the old normal days: He "really is going to graduate this year. You needn't look incredulous. . . . He has been one of the shining lights of the school for many terms." Ovie and Elsie Watts of Harrodsburg, "The Twins," graduated together, both being members of the Periclesian Society. Poems, prophecies, and other humor filled the pages of the senior issue. To Professor Keith, already becoming a noted institutional character, one senior left a "darning set," perhaps in response to the teacher's occasional use of profanity in the classroom. Another left a stuffed mouse to Professor "Bug" Smith because so many live ones had been caught in her room in Sullivan, that she feared he would never find enough for his biology classes again.[19]

Interviewees in the Eastern Alumni Oral History Project revealed much about college life in the twenties. Playing cat and mouse with Miss Roberts occupied some of the girls' time. Studying and playing by candlelight after lights were turned out must have created a booming business for the stores of Richmond. Pranksters abounded. On one occasion someone put jam on some of the toilet seats, infuriating Roberts and the girls of Sullivan. Although described by one alumnus as "rough as a cob," and often emitting a bit of profanity during class, Charles Keith was beloved by most students. Of course, it did not hurt his popularity that he could still hit a baseball with authority. With only two student cars on campus in the twenties, students had a close camaraderie. Trips off campus were controlled by in loco parentis and were difficult at times for most students. A ten-cent chocolate soda or five-cent cherry coke at a downtown drugstore was about the only off-campus entertainment one alumna could afford.[20]

There was always time for humor on the Eastern campus, from the raucous stories of Professor Keith to the unintended little embarrassments of everyday life. When the father of a new normal student insisted that she take a family prescription for a "tickle" in the throat with her to Eastern, she complied. After riding in a student "jalopy" from the railroad station, the eager male students threw the suitcases out. "And my suitcase flew open," she explained with a laugh, "and my little bottle of whiskey for my tickle in my throat flew out." The first printing of the inaugural *Eastern Progress* in February 1922 contained an egregious error in an advertisement for a men's store. Editor Lucille Strother Hogge recalled the circumstances many years later. With the student body waiting in the chapel, she tried to find out why no one appeared with the hundreds of copies. "I went to the office and I could hear them laughing in there," she said. "And they wouldn't open the door. So the next day they had the papers." The downtown printer had misspelled the word "shirt," leaving out the *r*. With the offending word corrected, the first issue of the long-running student newspaper made its way into history.[21]

Although students might now major in other fields, everything at Eastern revolved around teacher education. Almost all students had contact with the Training School Department. The Model School consisted of twelve grades except for a brief time. Just as important was a rural school of eight grades. For many years, first Lelia E. Patridge and then Miriam Noland in the rural school trained hundreds of students who went out into the hinterlands of Kentucky. Eastern contracted with the Madison County school district for elementary students. After using various spots on campus and in the county schools such as Watts, Kavanaugh, and Green's Chapel, in 1929 Eastern built a rural school on the college farm at a cost of $10,000. Replicating all conditions to be found in the rural districts, it came complete with a potbellied stove and privies. True to its role in Kentucky education, Eastern never lost sight of its responsibility for rural education. In such schools, one teacher taught all eight grades. There might be two-teacher schools or even larger, but the idea was the same: one teacher had responsibility for sometimes forty students or more, ranging in age from six to the teenage years. Katie Carpenter, who later became an Eastern instructor, began her first year of teaching at the age of eighteen in a one-room school with sixty-two students; her salary was thirty-five dollars per month. Teaching in such a school required skills in management and sheer grit that seem daunting today.[22]

Most of the teachers at the Model School were women and were more poorly paid than the men. The school first occupied the building of the old Walters Collegiate Institute, with Eastern leasing the property. Simultaneously, high school work went on at both the Eastern Kentucky State Normal School and the Model School. Three high schools operated in Richmond for a time, with Madison Female Institute folding in 1919. The Richmond city board of education took over the property, and over time its Caldwell High School became known as Madison High School. Ironically, just when Eastern was about to become a four-year school and was in need of a demonstration high school, the city gave it up in 1922. There undoubtedly was some local political finagling involved, and superintendent of public instruction George Colvin sided with the city superintendent and local school board. In the mid-1920s, the staff of the Model School expanded to nine, one for each grade. Under the leadership of R. A. Edwards, a junior high school was organized for grades seven through nine during this time. When Eastern tried to place student teachers in the city schools, some Richmond citizens "thwarted" the plan, and it was not until 1934 that the college's students were allowed to student-teach in the city schools. After years of sacrifice, Eastern finally paid off the note for the remainder of the old Walters property in 1920.[23]

Eastern began to leave the old horse-and-buggy days quite literally during the Coates administration by tearing down the "hitching sheds" in late 1919. Purchase of a 1919 Wayne School Car, Model 0068, with a fourteen-foot body at a cost of $1,323, gave the school the opportunity to move students about. At the same time President Coates asked for this "auto bus," he reported to the Board of Regents that "the old gray horse" that had so faithfully served the school was so broken down that it had to be retired to the college farm. Before long, a "radio receiving set," as well as "one of the new type Victrolas for furnishing music for games and entertainments on the campus," a modern refrigeration plant for the cafeteria, a 1925 Ford Coupe for a recruiter, and a motion picture projector for campus movies on Monday and Saturday evenings, added to modernity at Eastern Kentucky State Normal School and Teachers College, as it became known after an act of the General Assembly in 1922. As another sign of the times, the business culture of the twenties, Eastern began a publicity department in 1926. And Coates found holding a regional high school basketball tournament on campus "the best piece of advertising the School had ever sponsored." Although forming soon after the beginning of the normal school, the Alumni Association did not become a viable group until the 1920s.[24]

Eastern also modernized its finances in some ways. Beginning in 1918, revenues to Eastern and the other state schools came on a "millage basis," at first necessitating a slowdown of funneling money from Frankfort. In fact, Coates had to borrow money on several occasions. An attorney general's opinion approved Eastern's right to borrow money for a short time "within the limits of the annual appropriations to the institution." And they needed it. Coates recognized that "the change of Eastern from a Junior to a Senior College is going to entail quite an expense for teachers and equipment." Money was an ever-present problem. For example, under the old state warrant system, Eastern could get only ninety-six cents on the dollar from willing buyers. Coates not only asked for less money than Cherry from the 1922 General Assembly but also got outmaneuvered in 1924 in sharing a new inheritance tax. Half of the revenue would go into the state's general fund, one-quarter to the University of Kentucky, three-sixteenths to Western, and one-sixteenth to

Eastern. The 1928 legislature, however, appropriated $250,000 for new buildings on the Richmond campus, the same as for Western. Coates continued the budget processes initiated under the Crabbe administration. As Eastern moved beyond its normal school days, student tuition and fees added to its coffers. At $225 a year for "Tuition, Board, Room Rent and All Necessary Expenses," how could anyone resist? On the rare occasions when there was a temporary surplus, Eastern quickly invested the money in war bonds or in local banks. There were also expenditures owing to unforeseen problems. For example, because of the inflationary crisis of World War I, Eastern paid students living with "landladies" in town a "room equalization" to compensate for cheaper campus housing. In one month alone the school paid out $2,000. As inflation eased, the board stopped making the payments.[25]

All through the twenties, Eastern sold and bought land, including what became known as the New Stateland Farm and the adjoining Gibson place. For a short time, the house on the Gibson Farm, known as Ellendale, was used as a men's dormitory. A. B. Carter, the farm director, often appeared at regent's meetings to advise how to improve the Eastern farm, including adding "thoroughbred" stock. Other properties were added, completing the general outlines of the campus today. Into the late 1920s, the Board of Regents, and more specifically the executive committee, consisting of the secretary of the committee, the treasurer, Regent Sullivan, and President Coates, took an active role in running the school. Either R. E. Turley or Paul Burnam could propose motions, and both had serious input in the affairs of Eastern. A reading of the Board of Regents minutes gives the impression that the regents, consisting of four appointees, were very proactive. The fact that most of their meetings were held in "the rooms of J. A. Sullivan" testified to the hands-on approach of the "local" regent who became a patriarch of Eastern. Often one regent took on a specific problem. For example, in 1926 Charles F. Weaver was delegated the responsibility to study and sign a contract for the improvement of boilers at the campus power plant. All expenditures were important, and none were too small for the regents to consider at length. When it came time to choose the type of beds for a dormitory, regular beds won out in a close vote over Murphy "disappearing" beds for an addition to Memorial Hall. The regents also studied the design of a new dairy barn as much as other expenditures and did not always agree with President Coates or faculty recommendations.[26]

If Eastern did not lead in national trends in American higher education, it certainly followed them. This was quite obvious in health, physical education, and athletics. As training for health and physical education teachers became more formalized, Eastern developed programs to fill the need for public school teachers. The teaching of health began in 1919, and the first full-time health teacher was employed in 1925. Physical education, or physical culture, as it was known in the early days, began in 1910 in a course called School Games and Plays. After the 1920 General Assembly passed a law requiring physical training, Eastern responded with more courses and plans for an enlarged gymnasium. Manual training and physical education were taught by the same teacher for several years. Then physical education and athletics were combined. After the introduction of football in 1909, athletics became more formalized. History professor Charles A. Keith coached all sports during his first year on campus. Ben H. Barnard was in charge of athletics from 1913 through 1916. George Hembree took over in the fall of 1920. While a normal school, Eastern played mostly high school teams, slowly adding more college teams. The 1915 football team played five games against three teams, losing to Kentucky Wesleyan, winning and tying games against Millersburg Military Institute, and tying Western at Bowling Green but winning at home, 6–0. When Eastern lost to Centre College in 1916, a local paper noted with pride that the score was only 0–26. A win over Western, 13–12, was more than enough to heal the wounds of that defeat.[27]

Athletic facilities at Eastern in the twenties were modest to say the least. After the mysterious fire that destroyed the old gymnasium inherited from old Central University and Walters Collegiate Institute days, Coates looked for funds to build a temporary gym. An improvised gym in the basement of the Training School was used, and both men's and women's basketball teams used the local public high school facilities. Using some of the money from the Bingham estate and other revenues, Eastern built a temporary wooden structure for about $8,500, humorously called the "Barn" by students. The regents advanced money in 1926 to improve the old multipurpose field, seeing "that 1000 Knock Down Bleacher Seats be installed." These were spartan facilities, to be sure, but they were all Eastern could afford at the time.[28]

As in previous years, most of the men going out for the football squad had never played, many of them never having seen the game played before stepping onto the practice field in September. In 1921, when only two men had ever played in a college game and three others had played football in high school, the season was "not a grand success." In 1927 and 1928, the Board of Regents voted to pay Henry Triplett thirty-two dollars for two teeth "knocked out in one of the games" and to pay other medical bills for injured athletes. Athletics had become important enough to begin an insurance program for the players, and by this time Eastern had added a campus physician to the staff. The rivalry with Western continued to be heated in the twenties, with Coates and Cherry even being forced to act as peacemakers after an altercation at a football game in Bowling Green. Coates told his counterpart at Western that the results of a 1922 football game showed that the Hilltoppers had the better team, Eastern losing 47–6. He regretted a "little misunderstanding" after the game. The next year rumors circulated that Eastern and Western might stop playing each other because of growing tensions. Although Cherry told Coates that a "feud . . . does not and must not exist," in reality, the rivalry remained at a fever pitch. If there was to be nearly constant bickering over students jumping from one district to another, athletic contests could not help but be rather bitter.[29]

Eastern's teams of the twenties won more than they lost, the 1924–25 women's basketball team, which won the state title, and the 1927 football team being exceptionally good. After the team returned from a victory over Union College, the *Eastern Progress* reported that students marched en masse downtown after breakfast, carrying "their hilarity on till chapel and appeared at chapel and 'took it' [over]." Beckham Combs attended eight years of high school and college on the Eastern campus in the twenties, playing football all those years. Basketball proved to be an increasingly popular sport for both women and men. In 1919, Coach Charles F. Miller's men's squad played Sue Bennett, Union, Cumberland College, Transylvania, the University of Louisville, and Centre. His duties as teacher of manual arts must have stretched his abilities to the limit. Track and field also became important on the Eastern campus, where defeating Western was the making of a successful spring season.[30]

One of the greatest athletes in the history of Eastern, and Kentucky for that matter, appeared on the Richmond campus about the time of World War I. Owsley Countian Earle Combs, playing basketball and his first love, baseball, soon caught the eye of a Louisville Colonels baseball scout. The "Gray Fox" played for two years in Louisville before joining the New York Yankees. Playing center field and hitting leadoff in the vaunted "murderers' row" lineup that included Babe Ruth, Combs had a lifetime batting average of .325. He helped the Yankees win the World Series in 1927, 1928, and 1932. Combs once told an old Eastern friend that playing center field forced him to field a good part of paunchy Babe Ruth's right field position. His playing career cut short by injuries sustained from smashing into an outfield wall, Combs coached for several years before returning to Madison County and farming. The first Kentuckian elected to the Baseball Hall of Fame, Combs served on the Eastern Board of Regents from 1956 to 1975.[31]

There were also plenty of opportunities for the development of the intellect as well as the muscles of Eastern students. From its beginnings as a normal school, Eastern always had students who were interested in the arts. Literary societies created during the Crabbe years prospered into the early twenties and, with additions, were known as the "Seven Sisters." For several unknown reasons, perhaps dwindling numbers among them, they were abolished and replaced by the Horace Mann Society for college students and the Ruric Nevel Roark Society for normal school students in 1923. Class and regional organizations became increasingly popular. The editor of the *Eastern Progress* disliked this change, claiming that literary standards had been lowered and that regional groups would create divisiveness. In March 1921, Rucie Miller organized the Little Theater Club. After Miller left Eastern in 1924, Pearl Buchanan led the group for many years, eventually having a theater named in her honor. From 1912 through 1932, the Redpath Chautauqua came to Richmond each summer. Many Eastern students took the opportunity to see dramas and musicals like *The Mikado* and to hear orchestras that would never appear back in their home counties. Moreover, they could hear great orators like William Jennings Bryan and hear of faraway places they could only dream and read about. Many probably saw their first motion picture at the conclusion of an evening at the Chautauqua.[32]

Music and art were also emphasized at Eastern. From its earliest days, Eastern Normal taught drawing, vocal music, forensics, and penmanship each term. By 1908, the normal school employed a vocal music teacher. As Kentucky school law began to require more music and art, so did Eastern courses. First vocal and then instrumental music was added. Instructor John K. Koch wrote "Eastern Hymn" and "Eastern Rally" for the normal school. Longtime music teacher Brown E. Telford came to the school in 1917. In 1926 Jane Campbell joined the faculty to lead the new Eastern orchestra. Possibly in response to the fact that Western already had an orchestra, Coates asked the Board of Regents for $850 to purchase instruments. While the combined women's and men's glee clubs performed *The Messiah* as early as 1919, the performance did not yet appear on a regular basis. Maude Gibson was the only instructor in the art department until the mid-1920s, when other art teachers began to join the staff. Although not as much money was spent on art as music, Coates set aside $200 in 1920 for a two-week exhibition of thirty-three original oil paintings from the New York Metropolitan Museum of Art.[33]

From the earliest normal school days, the Eastern library held a place of prominence. Although small and always inadequate, slowly the volumes accumulated in the old brick building known as Walters Collegiate Institute, which was condemned in 1917. The faculty library committee constantly sought more funds for books. A $1,000 book fund in 1918 was big news to book lovers on campus, as was hiring an assistant librarian a year later. In the fall of 1918, the library moved into part of the Training School, or Cammack, Building. Five years later, the John Grant Crabbe Library opened. With sixteen rooms, it was expected to be adequate for many years. Librarians Mary Estelle Reid and Carrie M. Waters in mid-1923 refused to sign their new contracts because they had not been given adequate raises. A few weeks later the Board of Regents relented, knowing that their services would be invaluable with the move into the new Crabbe Library. Construction of the library coincided with senior college status and the legislative mandate to improve facilities.[34]

There was also something for the spirit in the 1920s. With required convocation attendance, often of religious nature, it was difficult not to be influenced by the civil religiosity of the Eastern atmosphere, which combined religion and progressivism. Field representative I. H. Boothe said it best in 1919: "Eastern has a mission. Its faculty is the missionary station. Its students are the missionaries. Eastern Kentucky, in particular, is the mission field." The Young Women's Christian Association (YWCA) and YMCA were always active on campus, offering serious messages to Eastern's students. There was fun as well. On one occasion the YMCA held a "backwards party," during which everyone dressed, walked, and played backward. "Rarely has a scene of more merriment been witnessed than that which presented itself when the guests and friends began to assemble," ran a report. Many students also attended the churches downtown. Although a few Jews and Catholics attended Eastern, Protestants predominated. For every Rose Dobrowsky, identified as "one of the fairest of the daughters of Judah" in the graduating class of 1916, there were dozens more Protestant students. In 1923, Coates ignored an anti-Catholic diatribe sent to him. Moreover, Jere A. Sullivan always demonstrated to the Richmond and Eastern communities the best attributes of a Catholic layman. Coates also regularly invited Patrick Henry Callahan, a prominent Louisville Catholic layman and prohibitionist, to speak on campus.[35]

A man very much unlike Crabbe, Coates was under unrelenting pressure to build a strong teachers college out of the old normal school. One graduate of the school recalled occasionally driving the president downtown to a movie house in the late 1920s, not to see the afternoon showing but to find a place of relaxation and sleep away from the stress of the job. Then, in early 1928, President Coates entered the hospital. After an emergency appendectomy, he died on his sixty-fifth birthday, March 17, 1928. In an emergency session two days later, the Board of Regents appointed Dean Homer E. Cooper as acting president and announced it would "welcome suggestions and advice as to the selection of a President for the Eastern Kentucky State Normal School and Teachers College."[36]

The condolences to Coates's family and praise of Eastern's third president came from numerous sources, including President McVey of the University of Kentucky. At a memorial service, R. A. Edwards of the Training School delivered a long tribute praising Coates as "an indefatigable worker." William L. Keene of the English department read a specially composed poem, "White Silence," in reference to the snowfall on campus: "The night he died white silence shrouded deep / The little world he loved." "The Passing of a Great Man and Administrator," an editorial in the *Eastern Progress,* described a man who was always seeking ways of "saving money." "He allowed his task to kill him as Roark also did," Jere Sullivan told Dean Cooper.[37]

A critical review of Coates's nearly twelve years at Eastern reveals mostly positive change. The school went from a normal school in 1916, offering little more than a good high school education, to a four-year teachers college by 1928. Coming late to the state normal school effort, Kentucky lagged behind the curve of development in other states. But, better late than never, and Coates and others who contributed to this effort should be given credit for their accomplishments. The size of Coates's faculty more than doubled, from thirty-three to seventy, and the quality improved as well. Eastern's campus took on the look of a real college with more than a quarter of a million dollars of construction. From a budget of only $75,000 in 1916, current expenses grew to nearly $280,000 annually and $160,000 for capital outlay by 1928. If Coates was frugal, Eastern did lead the way in the state by adding a commercial department in 1926. When Eastern chose a "hand-power" freight elevator over an electric one in 1927, it symbolized not just penny-pinching but much-needed economy. Coates was not always up to the political battles inherent in the Kentucky educational milieu. Until his death, he continued to spar with his nemesis at Western, Henry Hardin Cherry. After 1922, Coates also had to challenge the new administrators at Murray and Morehead in the competitive field that had become teacher education in Kentucky. No more fitting tribute to Coates could be found than Eastern's admission to the American Association of Teachers Colleges with a Class A rating, announced at a Board of Regents meeting just after his death.[38]

During that same meeting the regents discussed a retirement program for the faculty, another sign of the maturing of Eastern. The faculty at Eastern changed during the Coates years. Whereas in 1906 few had college degrees, a degree became the norm. The majority received their bachelor's degrees at the University of Kentucky, George Peabody College, or Eastern. As Eastern's faculty obtained graduate degrees, the number of men began to predominate over women. Beginning in the Crabbe years, Eastern granted leaves of absence after seven years of service at half pay for faculty returning for more education. The teacher, of course, had to agree to return to Eastern. This sabbatical policy became standard in the midtwenties. In 1925 Eastern began listing faculty by academic rank, soon requiring that an instructor have a bachelor's degree, except for music, art, and handiwork. By 1927 a salary schedule was in place. However, that same year Coates noted that the school was losing faculty because of low pay, declaring it was "absolutely necessary that we watch our salaries." For example, Herman L. Donovan had decided not to return to Eastern and took a higher-paying teaching position at Peabody. The Eastern president also cited the need for more doctorates, especially for the heads of departments.[39]

Because of either the restlessness of World War I or the instability of the Jazz Age, student discipline became something of a problem in the twenties. Dean of Men Charles Keith—he became dean in 1921—may have overawed his charges in Memorial Hall with his physical stature and tales of his baseball career, while the changing times caused Dean Marie Roberts more problems with holding her women in check with old Victorian standards. Even a few student pregnancies occurred in the twenties, although Dean Cooper believed that these originated before the women entered Eastern. But if it was the Roaring Twenties, explained one alumna, "we didn't roar so much, we didn't have the opportunity." However, the times were changing. A tradition called "show rush" began the twenties. Students gathered en masse on campus after a football victory, then walked downtown to the movies. If Eastern students were clamoring for change, some listened. In 1928, Professor Anna Schnieb, who had a Ph.D. from the University of Vienna, sponsored the "Open Forum Committee." A forerunner of student government, the committee helped develop a badly needed student loan fund. By far the greatest change came to Eastern with college status, as enrollment and graduation numbers increased. Second-semester enrollment continued to have higher numbers because teachers in the field returned for work toward their bachelor's degree. In 1926, students were allowed for the first time to major in subject matter fields rather than in education alone. Though more and more students attended consecutive semesters toward the 128 hours of classes required for a bachelor's degree, Eastern continued to educate the student who could only afford to attend one semester or summer term each year. And, if a student did not work hard, he or she would receive a letter from Dean Cooper advising the unsuccessful "to withdraw because it appeared that continuing here would be an unproductive use of time and money."[40]

Many students still followed the old pattern of the normal school, some teaching for several years before arriving in Richmond. One alumna began attending Eastern in the early twenties but did not graduate until 1937. "Lawsy me," one woman said. "I would teach awhile and then go to summer school." Others, like Emma Case, found a haven as a young widow. Living with her two daughters in an apartment belonging to "Bug" Smith, she flourished in the Eastern atmosphere. She soon joined the faculty, teaching in the elementary program, before becoming dean of women in 1932. Most students were fairly poor, needing to teach or work in order to attend Eastern. Beckham Combs fired stoves, swept and mopped floors, and drove President Coates and others around town. "To me Eastern was a great place," exclaimed Susan Fields in an interview. "I was from a small town, I loved everything about it, it was a big time for me."[41]

One thing did not change. The racial mores of the day restricted Eastern's social and economic influences. Eastern exuded a southernness little different from that found at schools much farther south. Although the relations of white faculty, students, and staff with black workers might have been cordial, the school retained the old paternalism of the nineteenth-century South and did not change from the Roark and Crabbe years. The school's first geography teacher, Mary B. Dean, was recalled by many as very much an unreconstructed rebel. "She was a fine, proud, Southern lady," recalled longtime Training School director R. A. Edwards, "always ready to stage a good fight in defense of her religious or political convictions."[42]

Eastern students faced many crises during the Coates years. The end of World War I placed tremendous economic pressure on many of them. The twenties in particular were turbulent times. Neither could Eastern students and faculty escape the intellectual, cultural, and educational flux of the period. For example, they must have discussed the advent of antievolutionism, when, for example, the Kentucky General Assembly debated the first restrictive laws in 1922. In 1925, a jury in Dayton, Tennessee, judged Kentucky native John Thomas Scopes guilty of teaching evolution and breaking the first antievolution law in America. In the future, there would be even greater challenges to the comfortable world that was Eastern Kentucky State Teachers College.[43]

As Eastern faced the era of a new president, it was quite a different school than it had been in 1916. The years of World War I and the 1920s had generally been prosperous, and if Eastern did not always receive its full share of state funds, it came very close. Moreover, Eastern had moved from a normal school to a four-year teachers college, maturing as an institution. The coming years would present changing financial, social, and political challenges.

Ruric Nevel Roark, 1906–1909.

Mary Roark, interim president 1909–1910.

John Grant Crabbe, 1910–1916.

Thomas Jackson Coates, 1916–1928.

Herman Lee Donovan, 1928–1941.

William Francis O'Donnell,
1941–1960.

Robert R. Martin, 1960-1976.

J. C. Powell, 1976–1984.

H. Hanly Funderburk, 1985–1998.

Robert W. Kustra, 1998–2001.

Joanne Kramer Glasser, 2001–Present.

CHAPTER 4

The Donovan Years

*Prosperity, Depression,
and the Shadows of War, 1928–1941*

DURING THE COATES YEARS, Eastern grew from a normal school into a state teachers college. From its founding in 1906, the school—its students, faculty, and administration—faced numerous challenges. Eastern was never isolated from the world. The coming decades would place even greater stress on a college, region, and state with limited resources.

When Coates died on March 17, 1928, the Eastern Board of Regents soon moved to name his replacement. With Dean Homer E. Cooper serving as acting president, business went on as usual. However, there must have been undue pressure on the regents from some quarters. In its minutes, the board flatly declared that while it appreciated "suggestions and advice as to the selection of a President," it would not "employ any person to that position who personally makes application for same or causes his friends to urge the Regents to employ him."[1]

Before the board met in Louisville on March 26, the regents had already decided on the man they wanted. Hiram Brock made a motion to nominate Herman L. Donovan, who appeared briefly before them. They elected him unanimously.[2]

Forty-one years old at the time, Donovan already had a long career in public education, from elementary school teacher to dean of Eastern from 1921 to 1923. After taking a leave of absence from Eastern to finish his Ph.D. at George Peabody College for Teachers, he joined the faculty there. Regarding his return to Eastern, he told the *Courier-Journal,* "I intend to give my time, energy and ability to the programme of the school. . . . My life will be vested in that position. I feel that I know best the education problems of this state and I am going to give my best." The *Courier* praised the appointment in an editorial "A Kentuckian Reclaimed." "No one rejoices more on account of your coming back to Kentucky than I do," confided one of the state's premier school superintendents, Lee Kirkpatrick of Paris.[3]

All the previous presidents of Eastern brought to the post certain skills and ambitions. Roark was indefatigable, overworking himself into an early grave while laying a strong foundation for the normal school. Crabbe tried to elevate Eastern scholastically and its students intellectually to a higher plane than just a normal school. Coates, known for his strict economizing, was dull but dogged in his quest to improve the school. Donovan brought new skills, including an uncanny political savvy, to the position. This ability would be needed during the tough economic times ahead, because politics always simmered near the surface of Kentucky education. A protégé of H. H. Cherry at Western, Donovan would soon find that administrative necessity often brought him into conflict with his old mentor.

In the twenties, Eastern, like most normal schools in the country, moved steadily toward teachers college status. Educational historian Jurgen Herbst has argued that normal schools, in contrast to land-grant universities and elite eastern colleges, represented the true democratization of education in America. Eastern and its cohorts across America offered opportunity to the masses, those with few resources. These teachers, in turn, would inspire a new generation of students.[4]

Donovan's ambitions to lead a school such as Eastern even took precedence over monetary reward. Earning $8,000 at Peabody, Donovan took a big pay cut; his first contract at Eastern was for $5,250, which was offset somewhat with free use of Blanton House and paid utilities. With hindsight, Donovan stated in his memoirs, "I knew I could administer a college; I was full of confidence, enthusiasm, and dedication. My health was excellent and my energy was unbounding. I was ready to accept a challenge." Very soon, Donovan would find it impossible to finish writing projects. "I didn't know being a college president so completely robbed one of his time," he told a friend.[5]

Even before assuming the presidency on June 1, 1928, Donovan began attending regents meetings and working his way into office. At the time, Eastern consisted of a physical plant valued at $1.5 million on a campus of about two hundred acres. That fall, 465 students enrolled in sixteen academic departments. The library had only about twenty-five thousand volumes. Although the school was somewhat larger than when he left in 1923, it was much the same, struggling to end its days as a normal school and finding its way as a fledgling teachers college.[6]

An alumni banquet preceded Donovan's inauguration on October 25, 1928, a sign of the new president's plan to seek more support from that growing source. Representatives of twenty-two colleges and universities attended the ceremonies. W. C. Bell, state superintendent of public instruction; Bruce R. Payne, president of Peabody; and Frank L. McVey, president of the University of Kentucky, spoke before the administration of the oath of office by the chief justice of the Kentucky Court of Appeals. Donovan spelled out his philosophy of education in his address, "The Duality of the Teachers College." In contrast to the old normal school days, now the student should not only learn how to teach but master subject matter as well. With religious fervor he declared that "we again publicly avow that this college shall be consecrated to the high and holy task of preparing teachers for the children of this commonwealth." Praising the rise of the relatively new teachers college, he championed the role these institutions would fulfill in the future. "This institution is pledged to quality rather than quantity production," he maintained.[7]

The new president threw himself into the challenges of administering a teachers college. Because of competition with other state schools and the vagaries of an often-stingy legislature, he would need all the cunning of a Kentucky politician to keep Eastern alive in the tumultuous days ahead. If the college was to grow, it needed a broader student base, and renewed efforts would be needed in recruiting. If the faculty were to be more efficient, they needed to be better educated, and that would require increased expenditures. Donovan wanted a smooth working operation, and he set about the task immediately.

Described as "characteristically authoritative" by Eastern contemporaries W. J. Moore and W. C. Jones, Donovan balanced his prerogatives as president with some faculty and student input. He depended even more heavily on the Eastern community, giving administrators and faculty leeway to make some decisions on their own. Although a firm believer in the policy of in loco parentis, he urged students to form a student government, eventually placing a student on most committees. Apparently he always had good relations with the Board of Regents; at least there is no sign of tension in the minutes.[8]

The Board of Regents, with the exception of some minor political intrigues, remained remarkably stable during the Donovan years. J. W. Cammack anchored the board until his death in 1939, even while serving as attorney general of the commonwealth. With his expertise he remained the college's most important regent and unofficial legal counsel. But the board was not safe from the turmoil that often roiled the political waters in Kentucky. In 1930 Republican governor Flem Sampson replaced longtime regents Jere Sullivan and Hiram Brock with H. D. Fitzpatrick Sr. and John Noland of Richmond. Crusty old Sullivan, the survivor of many a political tussle, did not take kindly to his "ouster" by a Republican and fussed about it across the state. Keen Johnson, publisher of the local Richmond paper, became more politically active in the thirties; he served on the board while lieutenant governor, after being appointed by Governor A. B. Chandler. After the deaths of Sullivan and Cammack, Johnson became Donovan's closest ally and confidant.[9]

Soon after returning to Eastern, Donovan clashed with Dean Homer E. Cooper, who had replaced him in 1924. There is some evidence that Cooper may have wanted the presidency. Although Donovan appeared to approve of Cooper's "high standards" during their first year of working together, that relationship began to turn sour. First Donovan found Cooper negligent in not visiting each classroom at least once a semester. In addition, teachers Pearl Buchanan and Emma Case reported run-ins with the dean that rankled the new president.[10]

After serving as president for two years, Donovan roundly criticized Cooper for being a sloppy administrator and failing in "human relations." "Students come to me saying that you are 'rude' to them when they must see you," Donovan charged. The president urged the dean to mend his ways quickly. When that did not occur, notes in the Donovan Papers indicate, he thought about several remedies. Taking advantage of a revenue shortfall in March 1931, Donovan and the Board of Regents decided not to rehire Cooper and suspended the deanship. Donovan later told a fellow college president that he and Cooper did not see "eye to eye" on many issues. "Since it became quite impossible for us to harmonize our views, it became necessary for one or the other of us to leave the institution," Donovan explained. "In view of the fact that I was president, I had the advantage and, consequently, made a change in the office of dean."[11]

There were several changes in the administration during Donovan's tenure. William C. Jones wore several hats. Serving as director of research and head of the education department, at the dismissal of Cooper he became de facto dean until being officially appointed dean of the college in 1934. After teaching elementary education for several years, Emma Case began her long deanship of women in 1932, "with some trepidation." The easing out of Dean Marie L. Roberts took all the persuasive powers of Donovan, who understood that she had lost contact with more modern students. Case believed in allowing students to set their own rules, within limits, what she called "allowance of great personal freedom in as much recognition of small details as is possible." William J. Moore also began his career at Eastern in the thirties, eventually becoming dean. The hiring of Dr. J. D. Farris as school physician also added a faculty member who taught health courses, as well as someone who helped beautify the campus with his landscaping skills.[12]

Although Eastern had never had an official tenure policy for faculty, Donovan tried to regularize it more in the thirties. "After a professor serves for a period of two years," Donovan explained, "we regard his appointment as a mere formality." However, to the end of his administration, Eastern could not begin a retirement system. While he claimed that "members of the faculty are free to speak and write on any question on which they desire to be heard," there was little doubt who was in charge of Eastern. Seeking better organization and efficiency, Eastern combined eighteen departments into eight divisions in 1932. These included applied arts and sciences, fine arts, biological and physical sciences, education, health and physical education, languages, mathematics, and social sciences.[13]

One of Donovan's greatest ambitions was to upgrade the faculty, and he was quick to weed out teachers whom he thought were substandard. Though he did not involve himself in a "house cleaning," a few people were let go, and others were held to a higher standard. For example, after getting rid of a recalcitrant music instructor, Donovan declared that the miscreant's letters to Regent Sullivan "stamp him as an ass." The hiring of replacement James E. Van Peursem paved the way for a much-needed upgrading of the Eastern band and instrumental program.[14]

Donovan held the faculty's feet to the fire. Even though Anna A. Schnieb helped found the Open Forum, she ran afoul of many students, who placed a notice on campus bulletin boards proclaiming "Schniebology 314" to be a bum course. Citing her lack of concern for students—59 percent failed in one class—they suggested that she be transferred to another "Eastern Institution," to the asylum in Lexington, or failing that, "to the Bush League." After an investigation, Donovan agreed with the students, particularly criticizing Schnieb's teaching of freshmen. "I have concluded that this is a problem of human relationships," he stated. "It is your problem rather than ours. You are going to have to solve it, or it will become necessary for you to find another position before long." Apparently she improved enough to remain on Eastern's faculty for several more years.[15]

Longtime tobacco-chewing, profanity-spouting Professor Charles A. "Bull" Keith remained his lovable, gruff self, giving grades at the opposite end of the spectrum from Schnieb. A study of grade distributions in 1928–29 showed that he gave no Fs and only fifteen Ds among a student load of 903 that year. He claimed to have simply thrown student papers down the stairs, the more weighty ones falling to the bottom and receiving an A. He used student graders, even allowing them to grade their own papers. If students complained about a grade, he shut them off quickly. However, he was known as a great storyteller and an entertaining public speaker. During the depths of the Great Depression, many students signed petitions to get him to give a lecture on the topic "What May Be the Sociological Results of Our Present Economic Conditions?" Somewhere in between Schnieb and Keith came chemistry Professor Meredith J. Cox, who apologized to Donovan for making the "blacklist" of teachers alleged by students to grade too hard.[16]

Donovan inherited a faculty that appeared to him short on both education and professional preparation. He pushed instructors to finish their Ph.D.'s or at least obtain a master's degree. To D. T. Ferrell, he granted a leave of absence on the premise that "we must have in the department of Education several teachers holding the degree of Doctor of Philosophy." During the Donovan years, 1928–41, the number of Ph.D.'s increased from three to twenty-three. Amazingly, from 1927 to 1931 the percentage of instructors with no degree or only a bachelor's decreased from 61 percent to 25 percent. Most instructors taught a fifteen-hour course load, though science labs accounted for higher loads. By the late thirties, Eastern had developed a limited use of student evaluation of instruction, a "Rating Scale of Teaching." Although I do not know the extent of its usage, this measurement instrument falls in line with Donovan's philosophy of systematizing the teaching process. Eastern also entered a new age with implementation of a salary scale based on education and merit. Donovan encouraged faculty to continue their education, to read, conduct research, and publish when possible.[17]

Recognition of Eastern's strides in improving its role as an educator of teachers came with memberships in the Southern Association of Secondary Schools and Colleges and the American Association of Teachers Colleges (AATC) in the twenties. While entry into the AATC was not too difficult,

Eastern had to increase its number of doctorates on staff before being admitted to the Southern Association in 1928. Students celebrated that recognition with a bonfire and speeches by Donovan and other faculty members. In the Southern Association, Donovan led a mini-rebellion of a "liberal group" in 1933 and 1934 against what he saw as "self-perpetuating" leadership in the group. Writing numerous college presidents and other educators in the South, he successfully garnered the votes to appoint "new blood" to committees and other positions of leadership. As evidence of Donovan's growing stature as an educator, he was elected president of both these groups during his tenure at Eastern: the AATC in 1934–35 and the Southern Association in 1938–39. A capstone reward came in 1932 with Eastern's selection as one of the top twenty-five teachers colleges in the country.[18]

Many changes came to Eastern academic life in the thirties. In 1930, the old normal school was dropped. When the state department of education took over certification of teachers, it still required only one semester of college work to obtain minimum certification to teach in Kentucky. Model High School opened again in 1930, after an eight-year hiatus, serving Richmond as well as taking a few remaining students who had no high school education available in their counties. Eastern also began offering courses of study leading to degrees other than for teachers, especially in commerce. These programs became well established by 1932. Students interested in entering the professions of medicine and dentistry were encouraged to study at Eastern for their first three years of education. Eastern also increased its offerings off campus and through other extension work.[19]

In contrast to Coates, Donovan had definite ideas not only about how the school should be run but about the world in general. Donovan firmly supported the United States joining the Permanent Court of International Justice. Before the development of the Civilian Conservation Corps in 1933, he suggested a similar idea to Senator Alben Barkley. He closely adhered to the Democratic Party in local, Kentucky, and national politics. A southerner of the enlightened progressive variety, Donovan urged greater educational opportunity in the region. "Educating the Teacher for the Progressive Public School" became the topic of one of his speeches. In 1933 he gave an address before the National Education Association entitled "Teacher Training for the New Age." In many ways he represented the dry progressivism so evident among a number of Democratic leaders in the state. "So far as I am concerned," he told Clarence E. Woods, "I am a militant advocate of prohibition. I am not a crusader in many causes but this is one in which I am willing to fight." However, Donovan found himself spread too thin and declined to take a primary leadership role for the prohibition cause as the repeal of the Eighteenth Amendment appeared imminent in early 1933. Early in his presidency he adhered closely to the views of progressive senator Alben Barkley.[20]

Donovan was not afraid to attack the localism of Kentucky education. On one issue, elimination of the subdistrict trustee system in Kentucky schools, he took a strong and active position. In many rural schools a teacher was forced to pay a "kickback" to the local trustee for obtaining the job. The Eastern president saw this as a corrupting influence, particularly in the mountains. Using anecdotal information, gathered from a survey of the commonwealth's school districts, he armed himself for a crusade. He approached the major papers and political and educational leaders in the state unrelentingly in the early thirties to get rid of the system. Arguing that rural teachers made such low pay anyway, he asked, "What will be the effect if they are forced by a nefarious system to hand over to a subdistrict trustee from $25.00 to $150.00 of their meager salaries?" The effort paid off when the *Courier-Journal* and several local newspapers editorialized against the subdistrict system. Finally, a new school code outlawed the subdistrict trustee system in 1932, allowing a county board of education and the superintendent to select teachers.[21]

Students, the object of all of Donovan's and the faculty's efforts, offered challenges. Eastern fought an uphill battle to maintain its enrollment. Western had the largest enrollment of the state's normal schools early in Donovan's tenure. Initially Donovan appeared uneasy about recruiting students. Although many students followed the old tradition of getting a year of training, teaching, and then returning to Eastern for a spring term and the summer school, more and more attended full-time. These students did not often mix well with each other. The older students kept their noses to the grindstone. The more carefree younger students, some of whom now did not intend to go into teaching, offered quite a contrast. They joined clubs, played sports, and took a more active role in all campus activities than their older counterparts.[22]

Following the norms of the times, Donovan advocated in loco parentis. At the beginning of his term, the Eastern catalog flatly stated: "Students are to be ladies and gentlemen under all circumstances. This is the chief requirement. Parents may send their boys and girls here with the assurance that their safety, their general culture and their education will be carefully guarded."

Donovan took it upon himself to impose his will on students. Moreover, through chapel, or convocation, services he sought to inform and uplift their lives. Finally, he had strong beliefs about the education they should receive.[23]

Most students went along with in loco parentis, with the old basic premise of controlling the male students by having even more control over the females. Although Emma Case worked toward the Women's Residence Hall Organization allowing more freedom, Dean of Men Charles A. Keith did so more slowly. From complaining about Mrs. Keith confiscating some higher wattage lightbulbs to her predilection for walking in on the men in the Memorial Hall showers, Eastern students were not silent. All kinds of issues in student affairs surfaced in the 1930s. Some were important and others not. For example, an old administrative policy forced students to turn out the lights as early as nine thirty, but a campaign by the *Eastern Progress* resulted in a twenty-four-hour light policy in 1935. By the midthirties, women could go out two nights other than the weekend.[24]

Like his predecessors, Donovan firmly believed in punishing those students guilty of infractions. While more than one coed might have explained her late return to the dorm from downtown Richmond with the excuse she "couldn't walk up the hill any faster because my date has asthma," the consequences were usually the same. Indeed, Donovan intervened personally in many such cases. "It is impossible for any college to educate a boy," he told one mother, "unless he has the urge to take an education." The president suggested that this young man return to farming, "since that is the thing he seems to be interested in." Not attending classes or chapel, failing grades, drinking, stealing, gambling, and fighting did not exhaust the list of infractions for which a student could expect a trip home. Students could be summarily dismissed for a very serious infraction or have their suspension "undated," meaning they could remain in school. However, a future problem could lead to immediate dismissal.[25]

As soon as he came to campus, Donovan took the offensive against unruly student behavior, including those "frequenting questionable places." A number of students, "whose morals were of a low order," he maintained, were soon expelled for sharing nighttime revelries off campus. Two girls who stayed out all night with two men in "a one-seated Studebaker car" were given their walking papers. Donovan charged Dean Case with finding any coeds who drank alcohol off campus. "I am dreadfully shocked to learn that any young woman who would attend our institution would think of drinking," he said.

When the president observed men picking up Eastern coeds on Lancaster Avenue, "I even blocked several cars and made the girls get out and accompany me to the office of the Dean of Women." When one young couple was convicted of staying in an apartment overnight, Donovan told them, "We never want you to return here again." Moreover, "I think the best thing for you to do is go down to the clerk's office and get married now." "No one should be permitted to sit in dark or shadowed spots on the campus after it gets dark," Donovan ordered a student night watchman whom he found to be lax in enforcing Eastern's moral code. Those rules extended to "petting parties," a practice Donovan challenged the faculty to stop. "Let us teach gentility of manners," he admonished them. Emma Case held teas at which the young men were expected to be dressed in coats and ties. Although Donovan believed that conversion to a dining room situation rather than a cafeteria would best suit Eastern, he ran into "considerable dissatisfaction among students" and gave up on the idea in the late thirties. He told the regents "that this was no time to attempt any new policy that would cause us to lose in attendance." But he did expect a "well-ordered" cafeteria, even though one student wrote a letter to the *Courier-Journal* complaining about the low quality and high prices of food. However, all things considered it must have worked; by the midthirties Donovan reported a great improvement in student behavior.[26]

"The auditorium is my classroom," Donovan once told an old Peabody colleague. Moreover, he desired close contact with students, even acting as an academic adviser to freshman and having a few men at a time living in Blanton House. He took an interest in the health and diets of students, including what they were eating in the cafeteria. All of this was part of his hope to keep his finger on the pulse of Eastern.[27]

In effect, chapel, or convocation, at Eastern became Donovan's "bully pulpit." Borrowing from his mentor Cherry, he instituted mandatory chapel attendance at Eastern, now made possible by the nearly eighteen-hundred-seat Brock Auditorium, which held the entire student body. Although Donovan had a slight impediment, a hesitation in his speech, he never missed a chance to speak to the Eastern students and faculty and in other venues. "In the assembly, students become acquainted with me," he maintained. Three days a week for one hour he expected students and faculty to attend. Roll was taken, and if a student missed too often, he or she received a dreaded summons to the president's office. Speakers ranged from faculty members to those of the larger community. Sometimes there was a reading of scripture and a prayer, but the "chapel" was intended to be both inspirational and informational. Plays, debates, music, and speeches were presented by students. Foreign visitors included Chinese, Finnish, and Polish spokesmen, as well as Kentucky politicians, bankers, lawyers, writers, and businessmen. Donovan even invited a French Communist and an Italian Fascist on separate occasions, the latter nearly touching off a near riot with an inflammatory speech.[28]

Donovan was not afraid to bring in Catholic and Jewish spokesmen. Just before the outbreak of World War II in Europe, Rabbi Fred I. Rybins gave a speech entitled "Tolerance Today." Rabbi Joseph Rauch of Louisville delivered an address entitled "We the People" on another occasion. Other speakers came to Eastern for extended periods. In the summer of 1939, for example, famous historian Harry Elmer Barnes, who had taught Kerney Adams, spent a week on campus leading the "Conference on Contemporary Affairs." While Eastern was not afraid to expose its students to the ideas of a changing and often volatile world, it, of course, adhered closely to its southern moorings on the subject of race. The only African Americans on campus were hired help. In the late 1930s Donovan served on the Governor's Advisory Committee on the Equalization of Higher Educational Opportunities for Negroes, chaired by President McVey. He believed in a typically southern racist noblesse oblige toward blacks. "I am in favor of the Negroes having educational opportunities equal to those of the whites," he told McVey. But, like most southerners and not a few northerners, "I think that there should always be in our region separate schools for the two races." He could not see that "separate but equal" was "inherently unequal." Moreover, with limited state funding, black children could never receive equal educational opportunity.[29]

Students of the thirties did not always take kindly to Donovan's governance. In an age of apparent student complacency and obeisance, students were not averse to complaining about chapel, food, and housing. Ruth Catlett wrote an editorial in the *Eastern Progress* explaining "that there are some noticeable signs of boredom in some parts of our chapel. An opened book or a bowed head are not intended to be signs of rudeness." Many students opposed mandatory chapel, proposing that juniors and seniors should be exempt. Donovan relented somewhat. After experimenting with allowing seniors to voluntarily attend chapel, Eastern cut chapel back to Monday and Friday, with the Wednesday hour set aside for class and other student meetings.[30]

The Open Forum Committee, spearheaded by Professor Schnieb, offered some hope for more student involvement and even a student government. However, the idea never seemed to catch on, particularly among the older students who were only there for short spells. Although Donovan appeared to be interested in a student government, his support was lukewarm at best. In the late thirties, the *Eastern Progress,* under the editorship of Edward Eicher, proposed a "Progress Platform" that included a "modified system of student government." A measure sponsored by the *Progress* and the Open Forum failed in 1938 when 335 voted for and 371 against a mild form of student government. W. J. Moore later revealed that students failed to pass the student government because they thought control was "slanted toward faculty and administration." However, students were placed on most of the college committees and helped govern the residence halls. The biggest positive student turnout of the era came with a 743–29 vote approving a five-dollar fee for the *Milestone.*[31]

One tangible outcome of the Open Forum was the development of a meager student loan fund in the late twenties. For example, in early 1928 the fund had less than $175.00 in the account and needed refreshing by the Board of Regents. At one time all the girls in Sullivan Hall donated one dollar to the fund. Most faculty members also invested small amounts. Many students received limited loans in the thirties, including a tall, skinny male by the name of Robert R. Martin. A loan of thirty dollars in 1934 helped this struggling student through the year. Although most loans were small, being under fifty dollars, they were helpful, and most alumni paid back their debts.[32]

Donovan sometimes had a short fuse with students. In an assembly, "A Family Chat," as he called it, the president lectured students on "proper use of property," including avoiding wearing "paths across campus." Moreover, he asked, "What do you talk about in your bull sessions?" When students persisted in "path making," he had temporary fences erected. He could be just as abrupt with faculty. "A faculty member who is not learning and growing intellectually," he asserted in another "Family Chat," "is ready to retire." In the same chapel program where he announced that chapel would be cut to two days a week, he also lectured that "eating is an art among civilized people." Today, fussiness about such topics would be laughed at, but in the climate of in loco parentis of the 1930s it all made good sense to a serious-minded president like Herman L. Donovan.[33]

Eastern students followed most of the college trends of the era. Although freshmen hazing began in the fall of 1924, in 1930, with a more stable fall enrollment, upperclassmen refined this rite of passage. The rules changed nearly every year. By the late thirties, the "Mystic Six," an ominous-sounding name for the senior controllers, had a well-developed plan for "Hell Week." Among other things, freshmen were to wear the letter *F* drawn with lipstick on the forehead, wear red bandannas, and be prepared to sing for seniors at any moment. On Friday of that terrible week they had to ride a stick horse on campus and carry a shoeshine kit. "Kangaroo Kort will be held as often as necessary," the Mystic Six announced. Eventually, as in most things of this sort, some students went too far, and Donovan called it off after skirmishes between freshmen and upperclassmen "resulted in injuries to several students." The Mystic Six, after one basketball victory, vowed to rebel if the team was not allowed to join a "grand rush" to the "picture show." On a more positive note, Pi Omega Pi, a national commercial teachers honorary fraternity, came to campus in early 1935. Until then fraternities had been forbidden by faculty edict. A few months later Kappa Delta Pi, the national honorary for students of education, installed its first members.[34]

If Donovan had a "pet" student in the early thirties, it was Robert R. Martin, who become president of Eastern in 1960. In many ways Donovan acted as mentor for the young man, who served as president of the class of 1934, freely giving advice as Martin began his career in education. One of Martin's contemporaries maintained that he led a clique that controlled campus elections and politics. Tall and gaunt at the time, "sort of hungry looking," he became the big man on campus. Martin, never lacking in self-confidence, led the Eastern student contingent in the march on the state capital in early 1934, advocating the passage of a sales tax.[35]

Donovan also considered physical education to be of utmost importance in the life of the student body and the preparation of teachers. In the fall of 1928, Thomas E. McDonough and Gertrude Hood joined George Hembree, who had come to Eastern in 1920. With McDonough as head of the division, Eastern took the lead in training physical education teachers in the state. Charles T. "Turkey" Hughes took over the head coaching job in both basketball and football in 1929 and would hold both posts until 1935. However, the staff, student, and president all lamented the poor physical education and athletic facilities at Eastern.[36]

Donovan needed all the political clout he could muster in approaching the legislature for funds. The old wooden temporary gym, appropriately called the "barn" by students, was a disgrace to the campus. Testifying before a state senate appropriations committee, the Eastern president passed around the worst possible pictures to illustrate the school's plight, complaining that the building was not even as good as one of the senator's cow barns. "I kept repeating that the dairy cattle were better housed than the young men and women," Donovan said. The senator later told Donovan that when he passed around the pictures to the committee, he knew he was "licked." Of course, it was always good to point out that other schools, particularly Western, had better facilities. Calling in all of Eastern's political support, the General Assembly approved what would become the Weaver Health Building, named for longtime regent Charles F. Weaver of Ashland. The Greek Revival structure, based on a similar facility at Washington and Lee University, came with the usual construction delays and problems. Apparently there were also some problems with laborers at a previous work site. Donovan had a clause placed in the contract stating that workmen who made indecent remarks to coeds would be summarily fired. Formal ceremonies in October 1931 dedicated the new $204,000 building, which contained a large basketball arena and other facilities. As part of the festivities, athlete T. C. McDaniels, posing as a Greek god, was wheeled in on a platform. A pale light highlighted his gilded body, clad only in a pair of briefs. "I think it took him several weeks to get all that paint off," recalled alumnus James C. Burnett. The facility housed the basketball Maroons for more than three decades. During one stretch the team won thirty-eight straight home games and lost only fifty-one games from 1931 to 1963. Wonder of wonders, the new indoor pool, which had inherent leaks, drew swimmers from far and wide.[37]

When Donovan came to Eastern in 1928, he had no intention of the school's fielding anything but representative athletic teams, placing no emphasis on winning. Athletes received no scholarships, working on campus to help pay their expenses. Eastern's basketball teams had some success. Maroons Zelda Hale, Herman Hale, and Ben Adams played on the famous Carr Creek team that lost to Ashland High School in the 1928 state tournament in four overtimes. After joining the Southern Intercollegiate Athletic Association (SIAA) in 1928, Eastern played in its tournament from 1929 through 1933 with the help of the "Carr Creek boys," as they were called. The 1931–32 team was runner-up in the Kentucky Intercollegiate Athletic Conference tournament and at the conclusion of the 1935–36 season lost to Western in the finals. However, Donovan complained that such small crowds attended sporting events, particularly football, that it was difficult to fund a program.

Furthermore, being so close to Lexington and the University of Kentucky hurt the Maroons. The latter nickname was still not entrenched when Donovan arrived at Eastern in the summer of 1928. As another sign of his forcefulness he nixed a plan of students, including *Eastern Progress* editor Edgar T. Higgins, to change the name of athletic teams to "Leopards."[38]

Football struggled in the late twenties and early thirties against seemingly impossible odds. Coach Hughes faced a difficult task. The president reported to the Board of Regents in the fall of 1929 that prospects for the football team were "not very bright." With most players "not of the football type," Eastern had to get SIAA permission to play a few freshmen on the varsity team that year. It was not unusual for Eastern athletes, many of whom came from small eastern Kentucky high schools, to play in the first football game they saw. J. Ed McConnell, from a small Franklin County high school, recalled being told to go into a scrimmage and play tackle. "I said, well, show me where it is," he said. "We need more husky fellows who are interested in playing the game," Donovan told a recent graduate. Even more embarrassing was having to drop Western from the schedule in 1932. "OUR TEAM TOO LIGHT TO ENGAGE MAJOR TEAM WITHOUT DANGER OF INJURIES," Donovan explained in a telegram to President Cherry. Eastern's lack of success on the gridiron was not for lack of effort. Players of the time found head coach Hughes "wasn't mean enough," but line coach Tom Samuels and freshmen coach Al Portwood were taskmasters. Halfback Jimmy Burnett recalled that Portwood amazed him because "he could get up in the air and he'd kick you twice while he was still in the air."[39]

Donovan's term of office had hardly begun before the Great Depression struck. The stock market crash of 1929 did not immediately impact Eastern, although Donovan, like many middle-class people, lost money in some securities. The fall of 1930 brought the first sign of the hard times ahead. Eastern, with its largest enrollment, 715, and biggest freshman class in its history, nearly ran out of water as drought hit the region. Richmond could supply water for only twelve hours a day for several weeks. A young woman interviewing for a position in the library recalled muddy water coming from the water faucet of the Glyndon Hotel during this time. However, even in early 1931, Donovan did not seem overly worried, with a surplus of nearly $30,000 on hand. He even got a raise to $6,000 a year after a favorable decision by the attorney general, who said that college presidents were exempt from the old constitutional salary limit of $5,000. By spring, the crunch had begun to be felt, coinciding with the firing of Dean Cooper. Notwithstanding, Donovan could report to the regents that a half million dollars had been spent on capital improvements like the Weaver building in the previous three years. More ominously, business agent Marshall Brock, whom Donovan found to be "one of the most efficient men I ever knew," reported more "dishonored checks" than usual. And more and more students showed up at the president's door asking for part-time work. Some were able to eat regularly only by signing notes for meal tickets. One knew it was a tough time when even the daughter of a banker had to plead for a loan. Even Wren Jones Grinstead, one of the original teachers at Eastern Normal, lost his job at the University of Pennsylvania and attempted, unsuccessfully, to return to Eastern.[40]

During the hot summer of 1932, as the presidential race between Franklin Roosevelt and incumbent Herbert Hoover also heated up, Eastern's fortunes turned downward, reflecting the growing national crisis. Although Eastern enrollments declined by only three hundred, income shrank drastically in the next three years. From 1930–31, with a high of $478,615 in state appropriations, income fell to only $195,000, or a decline of nearly 60 percent by 1933–34. Donovan set to work on a plan to save the school. To make up for the shortfall, the regents voted to raise student fees to $10 per semester and out-of-state tuition to $27. With an estimated cost of $250 to $300 for nine months of schooling, Eastern began to be beyond the reach of many of the commonwealth's aspiring students. Draconian economy measures included letting seven faculty members go, a 15 percent reduction in all teaching salaries, and a 10 percent reduction for other workers. Fifteen percent of the instructors either left or were not rehired. Teachers taught heavier loads. The curriculum also came under intense scrutiny, with several courses being eliminated. Other slashes included discontinuing library science and industrial arts for one year, suspending the band director, and cutting out all purchases of books. A few teachers, like language instructor Mabel Pollitt, even volunteered to resign or take some time off so that they would not be on the payroll. With declining state revenues, all faculty were told that they could be terminated with thirty days' notice if the crisis deepened.[41]

From calling off the twenty-fifth anniversary celebration of the school to replacing lightbulbs with ones of lower wattage and reducing fire insurance, the efficiency of Eastern was cut to the bone. "At the present time, we are unable to pay our regular staff," Donovan told an unemployed teacher asking for a job. "Our budget is so 'shot to pieces' that it is impossible for us to operate in a normal manner." To the wife of a Whitesburg principal who had not been paid in two months, the president advised her to tell her husband not to resign. "A man must hold whatever he has and be contented for the present," he said. How severe was the crisis? "The state-maintained institutions will almost be out of business unless some relief is given during the school year 1933–34," Donovan told the president of Centre College. "We have no money with which to repair a leak in a roof, a broken window, or any other damage to our buildings." However, the Eastern president placed great faith in "our program of retrenchment."[42]

Like most American colleges and universities, Eastern survived the crisis of the Great Depression surprisingly well, although not without difficulty. Increasing costs made it ever more difficult to attend American colleges. A study by Dean Jones indicated that many Eastern students could not afford to pay tuition. Some potential students never made it to Eastern, and others would be scarred for the rest of their lives. Although college enrollments decreased nationwide, they did not fall as much as one might suspect. Some students were able to attend by using savings and finding small loans. With $70 in savings, one student entered Eastern and, like many students, was kept afloat by small jobs. One day he worked seven hours for $1.40 erecting bleachers. Some girls chose the cheaper rooms in Sullivan at $1.35 a week over the more expensive rooms in Burnam at $2.25 a week. Student Millie Prater and others recalled the top floor of Sullivan being called the "Attic." Students denied themselves in other ways. They shared books and ate sparingly. The Business Office sold coupon books worth $5.00 for cafeteria board. Alumni of the era recall witnessing female students passing out while waiting in the cafeteria line at Burnam Hall. Having fasted for several days, they were overcome at the smell of food. Working in the cafeteria was considered the best job on campus, particularly cleaning up in the evening. At that time the opportunity presented itself for a little innocent pilfering of food, especially ice cream.[43]

Even before the Great Depression hit Kentucky, Eastern was under attack. Donovan told his old mentor Cherry in 1930 of the impending conflict with the University of Kentucky. "If the University takes over a Junior College in Paintsville, why would it not take over a Junior College in Russellville, Hopkinsville, or Campbellsville," Donovan explained, "or any other place in the State where there is a struggling church school about to pass out?" Here was an issue that would dog relations in Kentucky higher education into the twenty-first century. The state colleges against the University of Kentucky and warring among themselves for students and state appropriations had an early origin. Moreover, even the private colleges, sensing weakness, according to Donovan, attacked the state schools at this crucial time in Kentucky higher education.[44]

When the budget crunch hit Frankfort in 1932, Donovan complained far and wide about Western getting a bigger appropriation than his school and about Eastern being dragged down by the weaker schools at Morehead and Murray. The General Assembly panicked when state revenues dropped precipitously in 1930–31. "The recent Legislature practically destroyed every good school law on the statute books," Donovan said of the 1932 General Assembly. "Nothing seemed to be able to check this wild spirit of destruction." Tension ran high in Frankfort as fiscal disaster loomed. When "a mob of some one hundred stormed" the mansion of Governor Ruby Laffoon, everyone in the state felt a sense of impending doom. Disunity in higher education made everyone wary of the future. Donovan felt besieged by the University of Kentucky. When Donovan asked for a united front from his fellow presidents in the state, he did not get much support. Even the creation of the Council on Public Higher Education (CPHE) in 1934 did little to allay suspicions between schools or lessen tension in the state.[45]

To offset widely circulating rumors of Eastern's demise, Donovan sent a blanket letter to students assuring them that the school would remain open for the second semester in early 1932. Two years later, he had doubts that Eastern could remain afloat unless the General Assembly passed the sales tax. It seemed that attacks came from all directions at once. State inspector Nat B. Sewell on Governor Rudy Laffoon's staff appeared to take particular glee in attacking Eastern in the early thirties. Donovan countered with a well-reasoned explanation of his expenditures. "There has been no attempt to pad this budget," Donovan averred. Later he charged Sewell's report as replete with "neat and cleaver phrases," but signifying only "some literary ability" and nothing more.[46]

Donovan was not one to take lightly attacks such as Sewell's or any others. He enlisted Vance Armentrout at the *Courier-Journal* to defend Eastern in particular and public education in general in the thirties. Calling in political help from Eastern's constituency, the president encouraged alumni to come to the defense of their school. "See your Representative and Senator and tell them what Eastern has meant to you," he pleaded. To a Peabody friend he exclaimed: "You have no idea of the attacks being made on the Teachers Colleges of Kentucky. The very existence of these institutions is at stake."[47]

The Eastern president also wrote pieces for the press and made speeches defending higher education against tax cutters looking for an easy opponent in those troubled times. "Are There Too Many Teachers in Kentucky?" he asked in a broadcast over WHAS radio in Louisville. "The answer is emphatically 'No,'" he answered. Instead, more and better-trained teachers should fill the state's schools. To the charge "Are Teachers Colleges a Menace?" he responded in an education journal. Of course not, he said. Only they could have raised the educational level of the American population in the last decades. While the typical public school teacher in 1923 had only high school training, ten years later the majority of teachers had at least two years of college work.[48]

Thrown into this mixture of conflict and intrigue was the Griffenhagen Report of 1933, a state-mandated study of education that touched off a flurry of activity in the state. Donovan and his allies, particularly Keen Johnson, the editor of the *Richmond Daily Register,* railed against the report. Claiming that "their so-called 'educational expert'" visited Eastern's campus for only two days during vacation time, Donovan found numerous errors and omissions in the report of Griffenhagen and associates. He included nearly five pages of objections in a letter to the group. From "a malicious falsehood" to "a joke" to "a gross misrepresentation," Donovan found most of the report far from an accurate view of his school. Absurd comments included a criticism about using "too much salt" in the cafeteria and a suggestion to cut out the music program. To the president of Murray, Donovan confided, "I do not think you need to worry about the Griffenhagen Report. Nobody seems to be taking it seriously." Nevertheless, out of the report came some resolutions of problems facing higher education and urging more cooperation. More ominously for Eastern, Western got tentative approval to begin graduate work.[49]

Just when prospects at Eastern appeared the bleakest, the New Deal stepped in to bolster the economy through its myriad relief, recovery, and reform programs. If President Franklin D. Roosevelt's New Deal did not end the Great Depression, it certainly ameliorated conditions. Over the next few years, Eastern not only revived with the infusion of federal money but actually thrived. Eastern competed with all the other state schools for Kentucky's allotment. Donovan was not afraid to go to Senators Alben Barkley and Virgil Chapman and other politicians to get his word across in Washington. First came aid through the Federal Emergency Relief Administration for student work. Civil Works Administration funds in late 1933 helped complete work on three tennis courts, the athletic fields, and a sewer project. Later the National Youth Administration kept many a student in the classroom. Then funds through the Public Works Administration (PWA) and Works Progress Administration (WPA) aided the building program.[50]

From distributing songbooks to working in the library to handing out towels in the gym, Eastern students found work, and dozens stayed in school because of the infusion of federal work-study funds. Some students returned to school in early 1934 only because of a very small increase in federal funding. Twenty students were promised $.30 an hour, which could add up to from $15 to $20 per month, depending on how many hours they worked. The funds were never great enough, with usually no more than about two hundred students receiving federal aid at any one time, as with a grant of more than $20,000 in 1936. Donovan had to constantly fight to get Eastern's share of the state's allocation. "It is absolutely necessary that we protect the children of a democracy in such trying times as these," Donovan told Aubrey Williams, the federal director of the National Youth Administration. In April 1934, Donovan estimated that 40 percent of men and 28 percent of women worked on campus to pay their way through school.[51]

After completion of Hiram Brock Auditorium and the Rural School in 1929 and Weaver Health Building in 1930, Eastern's construction plans languished because of the Great Depression. Those buildings created a lot of pride on the campus. Local wag Josh Cosby never lived down voicing his first impression of Brock: "Man, it sure would hold a heap of hay." While Donovan pointed with pride to the fact he had been able to add "talking picture equipment" and a public-address system to Brock Auditorium in 1934, only New Deal programs and some improvement in the economy salvaged construction plans. The first new project was a badly needed football stadium. A new field with a five-thousand-seat concrete stadium, with locker rooms and dormitory space for athletes, highlighted the initial plans. To supplement a $20,000 PWA grant and $18,000 from Eastern's funds, faculty, alumni, and friends of the school bought hundreds of barrels of cement for construction. With an estimated cost of $45,000, a $2.50 donation for a barrel of cement gave many people a share in this facility. A sizable donation from the family of H. B. Hanger Sr. gave the new facility its name.[52]

With a grant from Washington, Eastern hired O. V. Arnett of Berea, the lowest bidder, to begin construction in 1935. Difficulty in finding and keeping skilled workers at the site led to some poor workmanship throughout the construction. Confusion over the type of concrete to be used added further delays. Continued sparring, Arnett versus Donovan and the PWA inspectors, became almost comical. In one indictment, Donovan had a fifty-item complaint against Arnett that included a dangerous unvented gas heater and a useless septic tank filled with mud. Finally, an exasperated Donovan exclaimed, "As President of this institution I would not want Mr. Arnett to erect another building for us." Nevertheless, on October 17, 1936, Eastern played Louisville at Hanger Stadium on homecoming day. Governor A. B. Chandler, Lieutenant Governor Keen Johnson, and "other notables" dedicated the building at halftime. A 9–6 victory began an auspicious opening for Hanger Stadium, where for more than three decades the Maroons would have a winning record. But that was not the end of the story. So many problems remained within the stadium that the bonding company held Arnett's feet to the fire. It would take nearly another year to repair the faults and for Eastern to officially accept the building.[53]

Eastern alumni, no matter how far they roam, can never forget the Ravine. Part of the original landscaping designed by Olmstead Brothers, the Ravine replaced an old pond and offered a natural hillside setting for outdoor plays and meetings. With a WPA grant, more grading and construction completed an amphitheater with a stage and terraced seating for twenty-five hundred in 1935. In 1936 the first Foster Music Camp held outdoor summer concerts there. Many a campus romance begun in the Ravine resulted in marriage. Longtime Eastern administrator Donald Feltner proposed to his wife there in 1956, for example, and there must be many more such stories. Improvements in the circle drive were paid for in part with WPA money, hiring both student and outside labor. A new concrete roadway and an improved sewage system added much to the appearance and safety of the campus.[54]

If the Weaver Building and Hanger Stadium improved the physical nature of Eastern's students, an enlarged Crabbe Library was just as important for their intellectual development. Donovan, who placed a high priority on enlarging the library, searched for funds from the time he came to Eastern in 1928. With a 30 percent grant, and the remaining 70 percent a loan from the PWA to be paid for in bonds for the first time in Eastern's history, an addition to Crabbe began in 1934. Like all such work, there was constant wrangling with the library contractor to complete the job and fix numerous problems. Eventually the work had to be completed by the bonding company, a nearly

$94,000 project all told. To pay for the finishing touches, the regents shifted $3,000 from other sources. Finally, at Alumni Day on May 26, 1936, Eastern dedicated the addition to Crabbe Library.[55]

Like all facets of Eastern work, the library suffered greatly from the Depression era budget cuts. From $6,000 spent on books in 1928, expenditure for books declined to zero in 1931 and only rose to $2,500 in 1933. Donovan scrimped and saved from other projects to purchase the John Wilson Townsend Library in 1930, a seventeen-hundred-volume collection of Kentucky books. In 1938, the Carnegie Corporation granted Eastern $6,000 for books for each of three years. Apparently some things never change at Eastern's library. Often it was too hot, both summer and winter, for students to properly study in the library. However, students enjoyed working there for head librarian Mary Floyd.[56]

New Deal programs also played a role in the next stage of construction on the Eastern campus, all designed by architects C. C. and S. E. Weber. But first, the president had to do some old-fashioned Kentucky politicking. About old Memorial Hall, the men's dormitory, Donovan told the state health commissioner, "I believe it is the worst public building to be found in the Commonwealth today." It did not hurt to have U.S. Senate majority leader Alben Barkley on your side. Describing Memorial Hall as being in a "dilapidated condition and unfit for occupancy," Donovan told the senator, "the building will have to be wrecked whether we can get a new dormitory or not." Later, when other state schools got ahead of Eastern in a round of PWA grant acceptances, Donovan complained bitterly to Barkley: "It appears strange that our modest request cannot be granted. Our school is the only one to be left out." So the Eastern president redoubled his efforts. All the struggles of Donovan, the regents, alumni, and their allies worked. In the late thirties, Eastern received both state and federal money for just over $700,000 in capital improvements for construction of men's dormitories, an arts building, and an addition to Burnam.[57]

At a cost of nearly $177,000, Miller, Beckham, and McCreary Halls were named for political leaders who helped promote the founding of Eastern in 1906. Student Jim Squires experiences in old Memorial Hall testified to the need for new men's dormitories. "The key grated in the lock, the door swung open and there was the room. The plaster was beginning to crack; the beds were taking on the sway back appearance; there was one small, rough study table and no sign of a dresser where clothes might be kept; and nowhere did

I see a study lamp or any place where one might be plugged in." In a Masonic ceremony, longtime Eastern professor and acting Kentucky grand master Charles A. Keith led the formal laying of the cornerstone for the men's dorms. "With the completion of the new buildings under construction at Eastern the building program would be finished for several years," Donovan revealed in a speech at this ceremony. The multipurpose Fitzpatrick Building initially housed art, home economics, and industrial arts. Named for Regent H. D. Fitzpatrick, it came into service in 1939 at a cost of $111,000.[58]

The crowning touch of Donovan-era construction came with completion of the long-anticipated student union. In addition to state capital improvement funds and a PWA grant, Eastern sold bonds for financing part of the $354,000 facility. As usual, the contractor dragged his feet, blaming subcontractors for numerous construction delays. Built with a colonial Williamsburg exterior and art deco–style interior, the student union would be named for the Governor Keen Johnson, a key Donovan ally. Donovan wanted a building that would awe as well as inspire Eastern's students. He was not disappointed. Attached to one side of the building was the Pearl Buchanan Theatre.[59]

At a Founders Day ceremony on March 21, 1940, in Hiram Brock Auditorium, the governor accepted Fitzpatrick, the men's dorms, and the Keen Johnson Student Union Building for the state. In what would be considered a conflict of interest today, the governor remained an Eastern regent throughout his tenure in Frankfort. Student Clyde Lewis, who later became a longtime administrator at Eastern, took part in the ceremonies. With tall black marble columns and modernistic lighting in the second-floor dining room and magnificent Walnut Hall on the first floor, the new union dazzled students, faculty, and local citizens alike. The first wedding held in Walnut Hall took place on February 1, 1941, with Jane Case, the daughter of Dean Emma Case, marrying Gene Wright. Sixty years later they renewed their vows there, testifying to the longevity not only of their marriage but of the building as well.[60]

When Donovan came to Eastern, he appeared to be content with little emphasis on sports. Although the basketball teams of head coach Turkey Hughes were successful, his football teams struggled because of a lack of numbers, good players, and scholarships. "He didn't have any material to work with, including me," recalled one of his players, who praised Hughes as "one of the nicest persons I've ever met." As a sign of his growing intensity about sports, Donovan complained about Western recruiting student-athletes in Eastern "territory." Momentous changes were in the offing. Freshman coach

Al Portwood was fired after running into a conflict with Donovan and McDonough over his coaching methods. In early 1935, Hughes, clearly under pressure, resigned as head coach of both basketball and football. Although Donovan hailed Hughes's efforts at a banquet, the president had clearly changed his mind about the merits of winning and losing. First, Eastern began offering a limited number of room and board athletic scholarships. Next, Donovan brought in Rome Rankin, a highly touted Ohio high school coach. "I required of the new coach certain promises relative to his success," the president told a friend. "In brief, I told him that the position was his for one year and after that his contract would be renewed, only if there was marked evidence of improvement. If he cannot meet these conditions, a new coach will be employed." In a personal letter to Rankin, the president was equally blunt: "Within two years I expect you to be winning a good percentage of your games." With the coming of head coach Rankin in early 1935, the school began to experience a golden age in sports. "This is one game you've got to eat, sleep, live, and dream," the new coach told the press. For the first time, Eastern held spring practice. At this point, the new stadium was being planned. By early August, athletic director McDonough assured Donovan, "I checked with Mr. Rankin the efforts which have been put forth in bringing a football team to Eastern. No stone has been left unturned and I feel rather optimistic over the prospects for this fall."[61]

The new coach moved into the dormitory in Hanger Stadium and kept a close watch on his players. Bachelor Rankin would appear well dressed at each game with a red carnation in his lapel. He demanded that his players fit into the campus culture, including attending Dean Case's teas. "You all are going to dress up and we're going to the tea," tackle Fred Darling recalled Rankin ordering. "He believed that that was part of the training." But Rankin's first priority was building a strong football program. Richard I. "Puss" Greenwell, the captain of Rankin's first team in 1935, recalled this drive to bring a winner to Eastern. Rankin recruited at quite a distance. When three young players came in from Salt Lake City, Rankin gave Greenwell the task of keeping them from going home that first summer. "Rankin told me, if those kids get away from here, I'm gonna get rid of you," Greenwell recalled with a smile during an oral history interview. "I had to take care of them all summer long and they finally enrolled." Art Lund, one of that threesome, became a triple-threat back. Known as "Eastern's passing crooner," the six-foot, four-inch blond later went on to a long career in the entertainment business as a singer and actor, starring in the 1956 Broadway musical *The Most Happy Fella*. Rankin promised only work for players. If a young man did not make the team, he did not get a job, known as an "athletic workship." For example, Virgil McWhorter cleaned the gym, and Fred Darling had responsibility for the towel room.[62]

Donovan certainly had had a change of heart about football. In particular, he wanted to beat Western, a prospect that appeared impossible in the thirties. After rescheduling in 1934, Eastern did not win against the Hilltoppers in football until 1942. Although the new coach delivered on most of his promises, Donovan grumbled about the Morehead loss in 1936, a game now being called the "Hawg Rifle Classic." "We dropped the football game with Morehead," he lamented to regent Cammack. "I have never seen such playing." Keeping a close watch over athletics, even before the beginning of the 1938 season, he told McDonough, "I am afraid Rankin has neglected to get good material. I think he has too many boarders and not enough athletes." The *Eastern Progress* even got in the act, complaining about the lack of student support in 1938.[63]

The highlight of Rankin's football coaching at Eastern came in 1940 with the Maroons' first undefeated season. Not playing Western for the first time in six years, Eastern outscored its eight opponents 273 to 27 that autumn. Abandoning the old single wing, the Harlan County backfield of Spider "The Benham Flash" Thurman, Travis "Tater" Combs, Joe Bill Siphers, and Bob Mowat ran a wide-open offense using the Notre Dame box, or short punt formation. End Charles "Chuck" Schuster made Little All-America, second team, and Thurman made honorable mention. Ahead of his time, Schuster even fashioned a face mask using his industrial arts training. At the end of the year Rankin's six-year pigskin record was enviable, winning thirty-six football games while losing only twelve. Rankin was just as successful in basketball; his 1939–40 basketball team won fifteen games and lost only one. When Western returned to the football schedule in 1941, the Hilltoppers handed the Maroons their only blemish, 20–27, which was all the more galling because Eastern led at halftime, 20–0. More important, that loss cost Eastern the possibility of playing in the Sun Bowl, according to Fred Darling. Eastern also turned out excellent baseball, track, and golf teams in the late Donovan era. George Hembree won five straight state college baseball championships, and several players went on to professional careers. All-around athlete Roy Pille was honored with a trip to the 1936 Berlin Olympics, a sign of Eastern's standing among trainers of physical education programs in America. Competition with Western never ceased. After a "gentleman's agreement" had been made that the dividing line between the two schools should be at Bardstown, Donovan bitterly charged Western president Paul L. Garrett with breaking his school's vow.[64]

Football players were not above a bit of innocent brownnosing. After spending forty cents on a vase from a Chinese restaurant on a road trip, several players presented it to Dr. Schnieb to add to her collection of objets d'art. "She went ape," according to one account, and "the rest of the students hated us with a passion." "She really didn't care much for the athletes before then, but from then on, whenever we were going to play, she'd have the rest of the students clap for us before the game," recalled another player. Ironically, both alumni who told this story went on to long careers as, you guessed it, college professors. Students were also not above other chicanery if it seemed necessary. Knowing that mathematics professor Fred A. "Speedy" Engle would be upset if he found out a student was a Baptist and did not attend his Sunday school class, Jimmy Burnett made sure that he did. Even though he was not a Baptist, Fred Darling signed up for Engle's Sunday school class and also helped in the professor's garden. But it was all in good fun, and each student appreciated the extra help that Engle provided so that they could pass his difficult algebra class.[65]

With all the economic problems mentioned here, what was it like to be a student at Eastern during the Great Depression? Viebie Lee Catron Cantrell, one of fourteen children, struggled successfully to get that all-important teaching certificate. As a "child of the depression," Fred Darling recalled tough times at home and at school. But, he added, "It didn't take a lot of money to survive back in those days." At any one time only a few students had automobiles on campus. Though an old Model T of one male operated like a taxi ferrying students around, most walked nearly everywhere. "We had a lot of dances," recalled one coed. "I never got bored." At the "Vice-Versa" dance, a coed selected a male from a stag line and escorted him to the dance floor. "Girls never expected a boy to pay, because we knew they couldn't," said one female interviewee, so many dates were of the dutch-treat variety. Kenneth W. and Shirley K. Perry walked downtown to the movies for entertainment off campus. For twenty-five cents, "We'd split a sandwich and each had a coke at the drugstore." Fred and Edna Darling took long walks downtown and out

Barnes Mill Road. He proposed to her on the steps of Weaver Health Building. Campus romances led to many successful marriages. The Ravine and other campus haunts away from the prying eyes of college watchdogs served Eastern students well.[66]

There was also much to do on campus besides going to classes or attending sporting events, or dating, for that matter. Firm believers that "idle hands are the devil's workshop," Donovan, the administration, and faculty offered many activities for students. There were plays, oratorical contests, and debates, even one against a touring team from Harvard University. Besides chapel, there was frequent entertainment on campus, even of the avant-garde variety. Ted Shawn and His Men Dancers, often scantily clad, presented modern renditions of their art at Brock on several occasions. Eastern students thrived in contests of all sorts, with two ranking high in an essay competition sponsored by the American Chemical Society in 1931. In 1939 Louise Holman, as Miss Eastern, represented Kentucky in the Miss America contest. She took first in the bathing beauty contest and second in the evening dress competition, was voted Miss Congeniality, and finished sixth overall. One evening nearly fifteen hundred people crowded into Brock, a real showplace of the times, to see one of the most important documentaries of the thirties: *The Plow That Broke the Plains. The River,* another documentary, would soon be shown there.[67]

Students also could hear interesting discussions at the World Affairs Club, first organized by Professor L. G. Kennamer, and attend its annual banquet. The Hanging of the Greens became an annual Christmas event beginning in 1930, as did the presentation of Handel's *Messiah.* Departmental clubs and those based on students' region of origin had large memberships and attendance. Moreover, the administration encouraged students to attend church, and a few "chapel" programs each year were given over to religion. Although there was undoubtedly some prejudice on campus, Catholics and Jews attended Eastern apparently with little difficulty. However, a Florida school superintendent told Donovan that athlete Carl Kemp's Catholic faith "would prevent his being acceptable" for a teaching and coach position. When a hypervigilant Harlan County Baptist attacked Eastern as "subversive of true religion," Donovan fought back. Listing nineteen faculty who were Baptists, he defended Eastern's role as a leader of spirituality. "The founding fathers of our Nation very wisely, I believe, separated church and state," he replied. The churches of the community reached out to students, as did the Baptist Student Union, the Catholic Club, the YMCA, and the YWCA on campus. A student did not have to look far for extracurricular activities of a religious nature.[68]

In many ways, Eastern modernized in the thirties. Although formed in 1909, the Alumni Association became much more active under Sam Beckley in the thirties. He also served as the school's first real publicist. "I am convinced that a college, just as a business, must be publicized," Donovan told Beckley, urging him to work harder. A short while later Beckley could report that he had visited seventy-eight high schools, attended nineteen county teachers meetings, and organized six extension classes. At the annual meeting of the Kentucky Education Association, Eastern held a breakfast for alumni. Donovan kept in close touch with school superintendents, particularly those with Eastern connections and leaders such as Lee Kirkpatrick at Paris, who proved to be a particularly close confidant of the president. Each year Eastern held a meeting with superintendents in its region, and every summer a guest superintendent taught at Eastern. Eastern redoubled its efforts to teach extension courses. The Eastern Club of Harlan County praised the teaching efforts of Professor L. G. Kennamer on one occasion. To find jobs for alumni, Eastern began publicizing its recent graduates through greater efforts of the Placement Bureau headed by M. E. Maddox. For example, 1939 graduate Arthur Logan Wickersham is listed in letters to superintendents as "Prepared to teach Mathematics, Chemistry, and History."[69]

Competition for students increased as the number who could afford to go to college shrank. Student recruitment became more systematized. Donovan never promised more than he could produce. Rarely was a prospective freshman offered campus labor. Rather, the president urged a student to enter; if his or her studies proved successful, a student job might be available for the sophomore year. The president also warned students that they needed savings or loans and help from parents in order to attend Eastern. It was a tough time when even the daughter of a banker asked for campus work and was told she would have to wait until her sophomore year to receive a job. But one prospective student got the promise of campus work because "he is the type of student we desire to help at Eastern." In contrast, Donovan told one young woman with ten siblings to forget about college and try to get into a National Youth Administration camp. Many students attended only because they were allowed to pay on an installment plan throughout the year.[70]

To get the word out about Eastern, the school also demonstrated another example of its modernity, communication by radio. Donovan placed commerce professor R. R. Richards in charge of a weekly series of broadcasts over Louisville's WHAS in 1935. "The depression, unlike war, does not exact life of youth," Donovan said on a WHAS speech, "but it does take a terrible toll." The programs covered a wide range, everything from drama to music to true educational lectures. Eastern also took part in *The Teachers College of the Air* broadcasts over WSM in Nashville, sponsored by Peabody College.[71]

As economic conditions improved, Eastern finally celebrated its founding, originally put off in 1931, five years later with publication of *Three Decades of Progress: Eastern Kentucky State Teachers College, 1906–1936*, edited by history professor Jonathan Truman Dorris. Dorris and other faculty members contributed fifteen chapters on the history of higher education on the campus, going all the way back to the days of Central University. The book cost $571.18 to publish fifteen hundred copies, which sold for $1.00 for the clothbound version and $.25 for the paperbound version. *Three Decades* continues to be an excellent source of information about Eastern's early years.[72]

Competition among Kentucky schools of higher education continued unabated in the thirties. A strong supporter of Governor Chandler and Keen Johnson, Donovan worked their offices and the legislature for the benefit of Eastern. If Western was Eastern's primary competition for student, athletes, and appropriations, the University of Kentucky, just twenty-five miles away, always seemed to Donovan to be crippling his school's efforts. Schools like his, he maintained, "are the poor man's colleges." Donovan told the president of Murray, "I do not think that we should always have to go to the University [of Kentucky] to secure their consent to achieve what may be desirable for the teachers' colleges."[73]

By the midthirties, the drive to offer a master's degree increased, with the University of Kentucky (UK) College of Education opposing it and Western jumping the gun on the issue. The CPHE, made up of individuals appointed by the governor and the presidents, began offering some direction. For his part, Donovan believed that the state colleges were not ready to offer such degrees. However, he also felt that as long as Eastern graduates went to UK for graduate work to become principals, superintendents, "or teachers in better high schools," the "University secures their last loyalty." And, he argued, that meant that these Eastern alumni would give more support to UK. The lack of a graduate program, Donovan felt, led to lower summer school enrollment in the midthirties. After Eastern offered graduate courses in 1935–36,

Governor Chandler brokered a compromise under which UK would not teach undergraduate education courses and the state colleges would not teach graduate courses. Although the CPHE did some planning, it took the iron hand of Governor Chandler to persuade all state colleges to accept a much-needed fifty-dollar student fee in 1936. Donovan even sparred with his old friend Cherry at Western over the graduate degree issue, and although he got along well with President Frank L. McVey at UK, the Eastern president was sure that other university officials were out to get Eastern. When Keen Johnson became governor, Donovan worked hard to get a master's program reinstated. After a concerted effort, he got approval from the CPHE for an M.A. in late 1940. The Eastern president also labored to get "Teachers" dropped from the school's name.[74]

Eastern never fully escaped the trials of the 1930s. Eastern's students and faculty not only heard more and more about the world's political problems but also attended lectures and discussed events in such groups as the World Affairs Club. Like most Americans, Eastern's family moved slowly toward the realization that they could again become embroiled in a war. Donovan was probably a bit more hawkish than the rest of the faculty. Eastern became one of the first campuses to apply for a Reserve Officers Training Corps (ROTC) unit. By early 1936, the Department of the Army approved a field artillery unit for the Richmond campus. Initially, Eastern was to get three officers assigned and $85,000 worth of equipment. When students did not sign up in large enough numbers, Donovan had to fight to keep the program and used some congressional help in doing so. As war tensions increased in the world, voluntary enrollment in ROTC increased in the unit's two batteries. A pistol team and the annual Military Ball added to Eastern's growing list of extracurricular activities. Eastern graduated its first eleven cadets, who received commissions as second lieutenants in the reserves, on May 31, 1940, including longtime Richmond accountant William E. Adams. In 1940, enrollment grew to more than 250 men divided into three batteries. Early the next year, Donovan urged the regents to approve plans for an armory for ROTC the same month that Professor George Hembree, an officer in the Kentucky National Guard, went on active army duty.[75]

Eastern showed a divided mind about the growing tensions in the world. While the ROTC drilled, the *Eastern Progress* urged the forming of a peace club. The editor of the student newspaper declared that "war would bring a dictatorship to the United States" and warned of "false propaganda" from both sides in Europe. While there still appeared time to worry about college dances and airing complaints about chapel, war crept ever nearer. In early 1941, six Eastern men were accepted for Army Air Corps training. War still was not foremost in people's minds. It was major campus news when Rex, the campus mascot dog, had to be retired to the Eastern farm. The *Eastern Progress* declared that although "Rex was sort of a nuisance," he "was such a lovable old pooch."[76]

Herman L. Donovan found out early in his presidency that it would be a nearly all-consuming job. He no longer had time to work on his elementary school readers, although the older editions continued to sell well. Elected a trustee of his beloved Peabody College in 1932, he had only limited time for that responsibility. His health remained good except for one siege of illness in early 1935. He prospered, being able to purchase a Madison County farm during his days at Eastern. In the summer of 1936, after depression conditions eased somewhat, he took an extended tour of Europe. As with all successful college presidents, rumors circulated that Donovan might take another job. In 1938, he received one such offer but decided to stay at Eastern even though his salary did not increase over that of $6,000 per year.[77]

If Eastern survived the Great Depression, even seeing its enrollment grow in the late thirties, it was not without problems. Donovan knew that the school could no longer simply appeal to Kentuckians as only a teachers college. It had to have a broader appeal. Although Eastern had a loyal faculty, Donovan lost teachers to better-paying positions in other states. Ominously, he found that Eastern ranked twelfth from the bottom in salaries among schools in the American Association of Teachers Colleges. Moreover, the Southern Association complained about Eastern's high teacher-student ratio. It was a constant battle to hire more teachers and raise salaries within the confines of a poor state budget. Although the topic was often discussed, Eastern could not follow the lead of UK and Western and initiate a retirement program during the Donovan era. On the positive side, Eastern's enrollment increased steadily after 1934, rising to well over one thousand students each semester by 1939–40. Also showing Eastern's maturity, male enrollment increased to 45 percent of the student body.[78]

With the retirement of President Frank L. McVey at the University of Kentucky in 1940, speculation about his replacement circulated. When Dean and Acting President Thomas P. Cooper declined accepting the university's Board of Trustees offer of the presidency, the leading candidate became Herman

Lee Donovan. In the end, Governor Johnson's support of Donovan proved essential. The hand of the governor, also a member of the UK Board of Trustees, was everywhere. At the same meeting of the Board of Regents that announced the resignation of Donovan, the governor moved for the approval of longtime Richmond school superintendent William Francis O'Donnell as Eastern's chief executive. The regents approved unanimously and saved money to boot, with O'Donnell making $1,000 less than Donovan. In a *Courier-Journal* interview, O'Donnell "expressed his intention of continuing the program which Dr. Donovan has begun at Eastern."[79]

"And politics—The Damnedness in Kentucky," the last line of Jim Mulligan's quintessential paean to Kentucky life, might well explain the series of events mentioned here. Speculation and rumor about the deals cut illustrate some of the political currents in Kentucky at the time and the relationships between Donovan, O'Donnell, and Johnson. Longtime Eastern administrator and alumni director Mary F. Richards said that in order to reward O'Donnell for his political assistance, Johnson had to move Donovan up to the Kentucky presidency. Martha K. Barksdale, another alumna and longtime secretary, said substantially the same thing in an oral history interview. A well-done dissertation about the commingling of education and politics in Kentucky found substantially the same conclusion: "Governor Keen Johnson, under pressure from the KEA, elevated H. L. Donovan to the presidency of the University of Kentucky so that he could appoint the superintendent of schools in his hometown of Richmond to the presidency at Eastern."[80]

A graduate of Transylvania with a master's degree from Columbia University, and described by the Richmond paper as "an Irishman by blood, a Texan by birth and for 33 years a Kentuckian by choice," O'Donnell would face challenges just as daunting as those so skillfully negotiated by Donovan.[81]

CHAPTER 5

Trials of War and Peace

The O'Donnell Years, 1941–1960

THE ADMINISTRATION OF a new president started uneventfully enough in mid-1941 with life on the little campus in Richmond flowing much as it had for years. Most students came to Eastern to prepare for teaching, while a minority sought a degree for other careers. The sons and daughters of farmers, shopkeepers, and factory workers, Eastern students were career-oriented and self-directed. They wanted to escape the privations of the Great Depression that were still on everyone's mind.

Whereas Donovan tended to be something of an autocrat, William Francis O'Donnell, "O'D" to his friends, was much more low-key, perhaps even intimidated by his new position. Neither an intellectual like Crabbe nor a plodder like Coates, O'Donnell brought talents to the post that would become more and more evident in the years ahead.

Enrollment for fall 1941 declined to just below one thousand students. Women outnumbered men because of increasing war pressures as more and more males entered military service or war work. However, with a graduate program in education approved by the Council on Public Higher Education, summer enrollments increased.[1]

After the undefeated season of 1940, the football Maroons looked forward to the 1941 season as war heated up in Europe and Asia. With the Darling brothers at tackle, Chuck Schuster at end, and Bert Smith at halfback, the team ran through most of its early opponents. "In answer to the howl of the fans," the *Eastern Progress* announced, "Western was rescheduled and both teams are out for blood."[2]

Eastern retained the old Hawg Rifle by defeating Morehead 32–13. Alas, hopes for another undefeated season ended at Bowling Green, as the

Hilltoppers, after trailing by 20 at halftime, defeated the Maroons by seven points, 27–20. The basketball team prospered as well with a 10–4 season led by Rome Rankin, who continued to see double duty as head coach of both basketball and football.[3]

Eastern students and faculty became increasingly uneasy in the fall of 1941. More and more graduates of the ROTC program and other students entered the military. Bill Bright, a recent alumnus, wrote back from an air base: "Here I am, 'way down here in Texas, trying to learn to fly Uncle Sam's way, but I wish I was back in the Student Union, having a real time before and after the games, seeing all my old pals who have come back for the tilts." Two weeks later senior Claude Rawlins predicted in the *Progress* that if the United States entered the war, "We will be ruthless because others are ruthless."[4]

Like most Americans, people at Eastern heard about Pearl Harbor on Sunday afternoon, December 7, 1941, while listening to the radio. Senior Ken Perry was lying in bed recovering from a broken leg suffered in the Morehead game when he heard the broadcast. "My first reaction was, they can't be that stupid," he recalled. "I think everybody's reaction was the same." Being an ROTC cadet, "we all thought we'd end up in Europe." Students and faculty convened the next day in Brock Auditorium to hear President Franklin D. Roosevelt before Congress excoriate the Japanese for that "day which will live in infamy." Like the Great Depression, Americans were again caught up in events over which they appeared to have no control whatsoever. Paul Brandes, in the first issue of the *Progress* after the brazen attack, encapsulated the thoughts of many in his front-page editorial, "Let the Darkness Be Light." "But we beg to call to your attention that this war must be won," he said, "and that its results must be so administered as to effect justice and goodwill, not hatred and the desire for revenge."[5]

Even under these trying conditions, life continued much the same at Eastern. Clubs and religious organizations met and prospered. O'Donnell continued chapel two times a week, but the content remained much the same as under Donovan. However, a freshman reported that security at his home in Rahway, New Jersey, included searchlights and air wardens and that such measures might soon reach Richmond. Meanwhile, in basketball, the Maroons suffered "the usual defeat at the hands of the Western Hilltoppers in Bowling Green," the *Progress* lamented.[6]

But things were soon to change as the war news deepened in intensity. Eastern, like other state schools, adopted the quarter system, beginning in the summer of 1942, to provide shorter courses for men who would be entering the armed forces. Several faculty members followed their colleague George Hembree into service or war-related work. The longtime head of the physical education department, Thomas E. McDonough, resigned to take a similar post at Emory University. Families began raising Victory gardens on Eastern's grounds. Construction of the army ordnance facility south of Richmond drew off enough campus maintenance workers that O'Donnell felt compelled to raise salaries to keep his own staff.[7]

Enrollment plummeted in the fall of 1942 to 692, a drop of nearly 300 students. Under the new quarter system, fees remained comfortably low: $22.50 for in-state and $35.00 for out-of-state students. Some students and the *Progress* still clamored for more input into college policy with student government. "WE WOULD LIKE TO SEE SOME REAL RESULTS," screamed one editorial in early 1942. However, the war seemed to override everything. The 1942 *Milestone* led off with a tribute to the ROTC program. The next year the staff of the annual dedicated the issue to the theme "1943, America's Year for Victory" and included pictures of Eastern men on active duty.[8]

After the 1943 basketball season, sports were suspended as most of the athletes entered the service. With the cancellation of basketball, Eastern lost the services of Arnie "Shorty" Risen, a promising six-foot, nine-inch freshman who would go on to fame at Ohio State University and the National Basketball Association.[9]

Like many other colleges and universities, the Richmond school began exploring the "Possibility of Cooperation with the War Department." Dean W. C. Jones suggested a naval cadet program. In early 1943, army officials met with the regents to discuss bringing a training unit of the Women's Army Auxiliary Corps to campus. Meanwhile, all ROTC students were called up as male enrollment plummeted. Some of Eastern's female students entered the armed forces, while many more took jobs related to the war effort.[10]

It did not take long for the full brunt of war to hit the campus. Eastern's sons went missing in action and were killed in battle. Lieutenant Donald Hugh Dorris, the son of Dr. Jonathan Truman Dorris, was lost at sea in the Battle of the Solomons on the cruiser USS *Vincennes*. Not long afterward, Captain Thomas Farris, the son of campus physician Dr. J. D. Farris, died while tending the wounded in Normandy. One of the greatest athletes in Eastern's history, Bert Smith, who earned four letters in football and also starred in track, basketball, and baseball, died in the Pacific. Athlete James

Gott and Mack Childers, a team trainer, also died in combat. O'Donnell, with two sons in the military, kept up a steady correspondence with Eastern's men in service.[11]

Still, some semblance of the old college life remained in Richmond. Eastern's literary magazine, *Belles Lettres,* sponsored by the Canterbury Club, published short works by Eastern students. Concerts and movies gave some respite from the often terrible war news. Speakers kept the campus informed of the larger world. Geographer L. G. Kennamer directed the World Affairs Club and led discussions of the war on and off campus. Before the war was a year old, Harvard geologist Kirtley Mather told his audience that it would be decided by the Axis powers' lack of oil. Another "expert" warned, "Victory is in the bag but we may lose the peace." Eastern knew the world was in this war for freedom. While a *Progress* editorial could hype a scrap drive, "With Scrap—Slap a Jap," another piece by the same editors warned that all was not right in Richmond. "Although Richmond appears peaceful, there is war on. Not like in Europe. But in Richmond there is something startling. Ignorance, prejudice, poverty, and disease are in Richmond in alarming proportions. And these are both the causes and effects of war. In Richmond people live in homes which provide inadequate shelter from the cold and which are unsanitary." Without mentioning African Americans, the editors sensed the coming social, economic, and political struggles of the postwar period. A few months later in the *Progress,* a reviewer of a book about blacks concluded, "Can we continue that program [segregation] and still have any real growth of liberalism?"[12]

The dwindling campus rebounded in 1943 with the introduction of military programs. Negotiations between Eastern and the War Department saved the college, like many in the country, from near financial oblivion during the war. One thousand people turned out to welcome the first contingent of three hundred members of the Women's Army Auxiliary Corps as they arrived in early March 1943 at the railroad station. Officially known as Army Administration School, 3589 Service Unit, WAC Branch No. 6, the unit trained secretarial workers in six- to eight-week courses. In all, ten classes, with more than sixteen hundred women, graduated from the school through February 9, 1944.[13]

"We found that a WAAC is a lady and a soldier in the best sense," wrote a reporter who visited Eastern. From six o'clock reveille to evening "mess" at five thirty in the Student Union cafeteria, the women had a busy day. Eastern faculty filled in some positions, but most of the staff came from army personnel. The few hundred regular Eastern students and female soldiers seemed to meld into a happy unit.[14]

The Richmond campus bustled even more when an Army Specialized Training Program (ASTP) unit came to town to teach a basic course in engineering. ASTP overlapped the WAC unit by several months, beginning in September 1943. Most of the men had some college experience; about 450 finished the course on the Richmond campus. O'Donnell borrowed several science faculty members from the University of Kentucky to round out the civilian staff, while Rome Rankin and Charles T. "Turkey" Hughes gave the men army-style physical training. With women army personnel in Sullivan and Burnam Halls and the men just across campus in Beckham, McCreary, Miller, and Memorial Halls, the campus took on a busyness that had been missing for several months.[15]

With the arrival of the engineers, O'Donnell admitted that "fraternizing" with the locals was a bit of a problem. "I am told that when study hall is dismissed at 10:00 in the evening the town girls descend upon the campus like paratroopers," he explained, tongue in cheek. "We are taking steps, however, to put a stop to that. Military guards are being placed around the campus and the State Patrol is lending its service."[16]

Notwithstanding, the town, regular students, WACs, and ASTPs seemed to get along rather well. With at least one wedding of army personnel in Walnut Hall reported in the newspapers, there must have been a lot of such romances on campus. Nightly movies in Brock Auditorium, dances, and swimming in Weaver pool offered enough opportunities for cupid to sling his arrows. One dance even invited personnel from the navy program at Berea College and the Darnall Hospital outside Danville. For a few months, the campus newspaper became the *Eastern Progress and Engineer.*[17]

Necessities of war struck the campus. First the War Department decided to consolidate all WAC programs in a single location. Then, more ominously, because of "imperative military necessity" to get more men into combat duty, Secretary of War Henry Stimson ordered termination of the ASTP program at Eastern. When the two military schools left the campus by early March 1944, there was a big hole in the college and town. "So we say goodbye as the ASTP unit leaves," Imogene Blair declared in the last issue of the combined *Progress and Engineer.* Wartime romances were bittersweet. "From every window you could see a boy waving or smiling or looking," a female observer said, "as the train began to move faster so did each girl and heart."[18]

Life at Eastern, an alternative to the *Milestone* published by Harvey LaFuze's Eastern Photo Club in May 1944, gives a sense of the impact of the army programs on the Richmond campus. Most of the photos contained soldiers, but there was even room for one depicting an old Eastern student gripe, "Schniebology." Although Eastern appeared to be overwhelmed by such programs, it was not ungrateful. Without the military programs and the thousands of dollars, about $10,000 a month, they brought in, Eastern's campus might have fallen into such disrepair that it would have been unable to face the great growth of the postwar period.[19]

For much of the remainder of World War II, Eastern operated on reduced finances and services. After the end of the army programs, Eastern's enrollment dropped to a low of 270 for the fall quarter 1944. With intercollegiate athletics at a standstill, the University of Kentucky borrowed the services of Rome Rankin for a short time. Eastern continued to offer off-campus programs in regional centers. Owing to the rationing of tires and gasoline, it was easier to take the faculty out to centers in Lee, Harlan, Knott, Perry, and Bell counties and other locations than for students to come to the campus.[20]

After Congress passed the Serviceman's Readjustment Act of 1944, commonly called the GI Bill of Rights, O'Donnell predicted that enrollment would soon increase. After spending a short while as commissioner of revenue in Frankfort, W. J. Moore returned to Richmond to became dean of the college when W. C. Jones moved on to become graduate dean at Peabody. Longtime school physician and director of health Dr. J. D. Farris left for Emory in 1943. The coeds on campus continued to pack "Buddy Bags" to be sent by the Red Cross to servicemen overseas.[21]

Throughout the war, Eastern kept in close touch with former students. After alumni secretary Sam Beckley went into the service, Mary Francis McKinney took over. The campus paper included several pages of alumni news, and McKinney also sent out a mimeographed "Alumni News Letter," which included former students as well. On one occasion, the *Progress* received a serious reprimand from the Office of Censorship when it published a wartime no-no, the unit and ship identification of an Eastern student.[22]

Even as the war raged on, the Eastern administration began planning for the postwar era. Several dozen former students replied to a questionnaire mailed out by Eastern. Most had only positive things to say about the school and a feeling of nostalgia about things as they were, and they intended to return to Eastern if possible. However, some were not afraid to speak their minds. Some wanted student government, a study of world affairs, and a current events course. While most respondents praised the staff, at least one thought it was time for teachers "who were unable to impart knowledge" to leave, particularly Anna Schnieb. One woman, overseas, scrawled on her form: "Sorry but I can't see myself returning to college now or even after the war. After being here almost a year and a half all I want to do is someday return to the states and then make plans. Post war plans are so futile it seems."[23]

Beatrice G. Dougherty, class of 1945, observed Eastern during the war, pouring out her feelings in prose and poetry. With poignancy, pathos, and humor, she told of life on campus. "During one summer when 'civilian' campus enrollment was small we coeds appeared as only a few tiny specks of brightly colored dresses amid a sea of olive green uniforms." Once she was left spinning by army women and men marching in different directions. A keen observer, she witnessed one of the stressful results of war. When a plane flew low over Richmond, a soldier in uniform sitting in a downtown drugstore dived under the table. Returning to his seat, "he looked real sheepish and embarrassed like he thought somebody would laugh. Not a soul in that room laughed. And this guy just sat there and relaxed. That was the greatest respect we could have paid a soldier."[24]

In the fall of 1944, things began to change on the Eastern campus with the improving fortunes of the war effort. The Normandy landing in June and the island-hopping campaign in the Pacific gave everyone hope that the war would soon be over. "G.I. Joe Back to School at Eastern," read a *Progress* headline. Rankin came back from the University of Kentucky to coach a resumed basketball program that included Fred Lewis, a native of Brooklyn and a marine veteran, and James Lewis Argentine. The team won twenty of twenty-five games and went on to win third place in the National Intercollegiate Basketball Tournament in Kansas City.[25]

As the war ground on into the spring and early summer of 1945, Eastern began to recover even as the war news often included tragedy as well as miracles. Word came that Major George Hembree died in an accident at an airfield in Texas, the only faculty member to die in uniform. In the last year of the war, Eastern's death toll increased. All told, of the more than one thousand Eastern men and women who served in World War II, eight graduates and forty-five former students died in the service. However, Stanley Todd and three other Eastern men survived prison camp life. Eastern held several commemorative services during and after the war. Professor W. L. Keene wrote a touching tribute on one such occasion, "Our Unreturning," which concluded: "They will be still a memory brave and young / When children's children hear their story told." Eastern also named a badly needed structure, Memorial Science Building, in 1952, with an inscription on a bronze plaque at the underpass connecting with Roark: "Dedicated to the sons of Eastern who lost their lives in World War II."[26]

The frugal administration of O'Donnell during the war years helped Eastern prepare for physical growth of the campus. Longtime teacher and administrator Turkey Hughes called O'Donnell "more or less fairly tight." With "$225,000 in cash," the regents and O'Donnell paid off some debt and refinanced the men's dorms and Student Union at lower interest rates. Although O'Donnell often complained to the regents about inadequate faculty salaries, he did not aggressively pursue state appropriations to raise them. In the immediate postwar period Eastern continually lost faculty to higher-paying jobs. In his defense, it must be added that O'Donnell never, in his nineteen years at Eastern, asked for a raise for himself. However, when it looked like Rankin might go back to UK as an assistant to Coach Adolph Rupp, O'Donnell recommended a healthy increase because "we will need a man of his type to direct the energies and training of returning veterans."[27]

With the end of the war, student enrollment burgeoned beyond what anyone anticipated. The GI Bill brought a flood of men and a few women to the campus. Freshmen enrollment for fall 1946 set a new record, with 555 male and 14 female veterans in attendance. Men outnumbered women that fall, 699 to 385, a pattern that would continue well into the 1950s. Student culture also changed, at least temporarily, because many of these individuals wanted an education quickly and efficiently presented to them. The urgency of one veteran fit them all: "I've lost three years now so you can well see why I want to start back as soon as possible."[28]

Veterans did not take kindly to frivolous regimentation after several years in the armed forces. Hell Week, an Eastern tradition for freshmen, came under attack in the fall of 1946 when many veterans adamantly refused to take part. One hundred twenty freshmen veterans signed a petition, personally given to the president, that if exempted they would not take part as upperclassmen. "We have decided that we took enough (hell) in the service and this is no time to start it again," read the petition. The ubiquitous "Kilroy" also signed the document. They took some flak from civilian freshmen for not participating, as one recalled, and the furor sparked some campus debate.

However, the campus soon settled down, though Hell Week would continue for a few more years, with "Rat Court" for men and "Cat Court" for women. Life was not always serious, as the *Progress* reported one week. "Mysterious Singers Serenade Maidens," ran a headline about a spur-of-the-moment chorus showered with candy bars, popcorn balls, and even sandwiches by an appreciative audience.[29]

By the fall of 1945, everyone recognized that married veterans would need new housing. Married couples moved temporarily into McCreary Hall, the first floor of Memorial Hall, and all of Sullivan annex. O'Donnell worked hard to get surplus buildings and housing from government facilities, pressuring Kentucky senators and congressmen for their aid. The newly formed Veterans Club urged O'Donnell to speed up acquiring housing. By early 1946 surplus prefabricated housing began arriving and thus began officially Veterans Row, more commonly called "Vet's Village" or "Mattoxville" for Eastern's registrar, Melvin E. Mattox. Eastern had to pay for moving and erecting the buildings. Paying only twenty-five dollars a month in rent, Carl and Mary Ward recalled the rather spartan life in the wooden barracks. "Four families and a big black coal stove in the living room. The school furnished all the utilities and a coal pile out at the end of the building." By the early fifties, the village had become so entrenched in the Eastern community that the Veterans Club elected a mayor and eight councilmen "to control speeding and check prowlers." With "peepers" an apparent problem, one veteran took on the role of "special deputy."[30]

For veterans, students just out of high school, and returning teachers working on their degrees, who had only emergency certificates, Eastern offered an interesting mixture. "I talked to my minister and he said he thought that Eastern was one of the places where you could get the best education," said Anita Allen, "so I chose Eastern." Many students continued to work on campus or at other jobs to finance their education. "I dished out food" at the cafeteria, said one. "It was essential that I do something." The master's program also drew an increasing number to the campus.[31]

In the first years after the war, Eastern's athletic teams flourished. The Maroons resumed football in the fall of 1945 with one of the few all-civilian teams in the state, winning its first postwar game against Indiana State Teachers College and finishing with a 4–3–1 record. Owing to the "starvation diet" that former halfback Casey J. Nowakowski had endured as a POW, it was announced that he would not be able to participate. Two-time all-American

Fred Lewis, who went on to play professional basketball, and Goebel Ritter led the 1945–46 Maroons on the basketball court as Eastern won the Kentucky Intercollegiate Athletic Conference (KIAC) that year. Lewis's wife, Eileen, served as a cheerleader, and the couple was elected king and queen of the Sweetheart's Ball. The 1946 football team beat Western, 6–0, to win the KIAC crown, with returning servicemen like Norman Deeb and Bill Shannon leading the way. For the first time in many years, Eastern also fielded a women's basketball team, though not at the intercollegiate level, in 1947.[32]

Though Rankin always wore his trademark red carnation and dark suit to games, he continued to be a taskmaster. "He could be meaner than hell," recalled tackle Deeb. One time while yelling at a player, "who was always goofing up," Rankin's "false teeth fell out on the ground. And he was so mad, he kicked his teeth! Everybody wanted to die laughing, but they didn't dare." However, beneath that tough veneer was a lovable father figure. Everyone was shocked when Rankin decided to leave Eastern. Upon completing his doctorate at UK, he went to the University of Maine for the remainder of his career.[33]

Paul McBrayer took over the basketball duties even before Rankin left, relieving him for graduate study after the 1946 football season. The "Big Irishman," an all-American for Rupp and an assistant coach for the Baron, McBrayer led the Maroons to winning seasons in the late forties and early fifties. The 1949–50 team ranked as high as eleventh nationally at one time, winning the newly formed Ohio Valley Conference (OVC). Athletic director Turkey Hughes was one of the leaders in organizing the OVC in 1948, a conference that included Eastern, Western, Murray, Morehead, Louisville, and Evansville. Marshall and Tennessee Tech soon joined. With Chuck Mrazovich and Jim Baechtold leading the way, Eastern won the 1950 OVC championship over Western before eight thousand fans in Louisville. Not long afterward, the Board of Regents raised McBrayer's salary after O'Donnell reported that "his reputation as a coach and as a gentleman is a real asset to the college." Home games were nearly always at capacity in Weaver Gymnasium, where the Maroons were virtually unbeatable. A much-needed addition to the gymnasium increased seating from fifteen hundred to thirty-seven hundred, as well as increasing locker room and recreational space. The 1952–53 Maroons won the OVC crown but lost to Notre Dame in the first round of the National Collegiate Athletic Association (NCAA) tournament.[34]

The football team was nearly as successful as McBrayer's Maroons. Long-time assistant coach Tom Samuels became head football coach after Rankin resigned. Alumnus Fred Darling returned to the college as line coach, soon to be joined by Glenn Presnell as backfield coach. Presnell, whose fifty-four-yard field goal held the National Football League record for many years, introduced the T formation into the Maroon offense. The 1947 Maroons defeated Western, 27–7, at home, while losing a heartbreaker away the next year, 13–14. Adding lights to the football field increased attendance. For a few years, the Madison County horse show also used the facility during the local fair.[35]

Eastern continued its evolution when, along with Western, Morehead, and Murray, it received permission from the General Assembly to drop teachers from its title, becoming Eastern Kentucky State College in 1948. The advent of the Council on Public Higher Education (CPHE) in the midthirties did not end the conflict. Rivalry with Western continued unabated; only the characters changed. O'Donnell became incensed when Western basketball coach Ed Diddle recruited cheerleaders from London. "It is also quite disturbing to learn that Western has a field worker in the territory usually served by this college," the Eastern president wrote President Paul Garrett. When a letter came to the Bowling Green school announcing that "Kentucky needs Eastern State Teachers," Garrett hit the roof. "I want to assure you that we do not need Eastern State teachers here in Bowling Green where this letter was delivered," he snapped.[36]

After a vote by the CPHE, Eastern and the other state schools returned to the semester system in the fall of 1948 with fee increases and the old standard of three hours credit for most work. Another Griffenhagen report urged higher salaries, and O'Donnell reported to the regents several times that he was losing faculty to higher-paying institutions. Professor of physics Arnim D. Hummel, for whom the planetarium would later be named, moved to Ball State College for this reason. A few others received increases if they appeared to be preparing to go elsewhere. The Southern Association of Colleges and Secondary Schools (SACS) also nagged Eastern about its low salaries. However, salaries were raised only slightly in the late forties, while the cost of living soared. With the cost of food increasing, the college raised a large garden, as did many of the faculty.[37]

For several years the large number of veterans at Eastern carried the budget. The college received $260 in tuition for each veteran, while for others the state appropriated $67.50. With such small state appropriations, only that extra money made it possible for Eastern to grow substantially. Although Eastern finally received full title to 108 veterans' dwelling units, two laundry build-ings, and six other buildings for ninety-six single people, the upkeep was expensive. When veterans' enrollment declined in 1949, O'Donnell timidly approached the General Assembly for only enough money to cover operating expenses for the school "to hold its own." Even the *Progress* chafed at the thought that Murray and Western, while serving smaller student bodies, got higher state appropriations for operating expenses. Separately, the president was at work chasing "capital" state money to build needed dorms and other structures. Doubling the size of Weaver Gymnasium, increasing dormitory space, and erecting a new science building became the greatest priorities. Only limited campus housing kept Eastern from enrolling two thousand students in the late forties, with more than fourteen hundred in school on the Rich-mond campus each semester.[38]

State politics was never far below the surface in Kentucky education dur-ing O'Donnell's tenure at Eastern. The *Courier-Journal* often pointed out that political interference at Kentucky colleges was endemic. The 1943 elec-tion of a Republican governor, Simeon Willis, appeared to threaten O'Donnell's reelection a year later. With the board evenly split between two Republicans and two Democrats as required by state statute, Republican state superinten-dent of public instruction John Fred Williams held the swing vote. Omi-nously, political intrigue seriously disrupted Morehead with the ousting of President William H. Vaughn. More predictions were made that O'Donnell, an avowed Democrat, would be ousted in 1946. Then Governor Willis and Superintendent Williams fell out over education funding. A short while later the Board of Regents unanimously reelected O'Donnell in May 1947. The American Association of Teachers Colleges (AATC) in a 1947 report claimed Governor Keen Johnson seemed "to have dominated" the meeting that elected O'Donnell in 1941. Why should one who appointed members also be al-lowed to sit on the board, it asked? When Johnson's term on the Board of Regents expired while he was governor, he temporarily left the state in order to be reappointed by Lieutenant Governor E. C. Dawson. The AATC and SACS disaccredited Morehead and threatened to do the same with the other Kentucky colleges and UK unless the process of appointing regents was depoliticized. With the election of Democrat Earle C. Clements as governor in November 1947, the furor abated somewhat, at least for the short run. Local politics could also be a headache for O'Donnell, as when the regents debated whether to deposit funds in Democrat Spears Turley's State Bank or

Republican Paul Burnam's Madison-Southern National Bank. Eventually they compromised, promising to split these duties between the two local banks.[39]

The continuing challenges for O'Donnell and Eastern during the 1950s were much the same as for the war years and the immediate postwar period. Increasing enrollment brought demands for more housing, teachers, and classrooms. The State Property and Buildings Commission hired Dr. Charles Spain of Peabody to make a study of the building needs of Eastern. He echoed O'Donnell's pleas for new construction. Coupled with increasing costs of higher education, the Eastern community would be hard-pressed to find both the money and the will for change. With Western and Murray receiving larger appropriations than Eastern, the political sagacity of O'Donnell, the regents, and Eastern supporters would be tested.[40]

During the 1950s, the cold war continued to have a great impact on the lives of Americans. The beginning of the Korean War in June 1950 added new trials to an already dangerous world, with enrollment dropping slightly for a short while. The ROTC program at Eastern, after a brief hiatus at the end of World War II, began again in 1946. The program prospered, with thirty-five men receiving their commissions at graduation in June 1948, and regularly turned out an average of forty commissions in the 1950s. The unit changed from field artillery to branch-general training. Marksmanship matches with Western's ROTC were just as hotly contested as the football and basketball games. O'Donnell backed the program without exception. When questioned by the regents about building a rifle range for the cadets, he showed his lighter side, as recorded in the minutes of the meeting: "The President said that it may seem to the Board entirely unnecessary to spend money to teach the Hatfields and McCoys how to shoot, but the ROTC program requires this type of instruction." Six-week summer camps, the annual Military Ball, parades, and other traditions became firmly entrenched by the end of the decade. The Pershing Rifles continued as an honorary society for ROTC.[41]

Students in the fifties, while not as serious-minded as those of the war and immediate postwar eras, nevertheless were still very goal-oriented. They found it hard to change from old, well-worn Eastern traditions. While the *Progress* often encouraged students to "unpack and stay" on weekends, Eastern remained pretty much a "suitcase college." Editor Edith Ann Taylor pleaded, to no avail, with students to stay on campus and attend the 1953 homecoming football game and not go home to "Lostville, Deadburg, Deceased, or some other out-of-the-way village where you spend a big week-end doing nothing." There was lots of time for fun on the Richmond campus, perhaps too much. "Grillology is a major subject," the 1959 issue of *Milestone* jested, and the *Progress* often noted that it took up the time of a lot of students. One student joked that his entire time was spent "loafing and contemplating newer and better ways of loafing." In the late fifties, a frivolous nationwide college phenomenon also struck the Eastern campus: the "panty raid." After a KYMA Club pep rally ended with a snake dance from Hanger Stadium through the grill to downtown and back, a "mass of boys stormed" the girls' dorms, according to an *Eastern Progress* report. "At least two boys were seen displaying silk trophies." Some girls countered by rushing into Keith Hall. At first males were summarily dismissed after such incidents, but the administration later softened its action. Moreover, boy-girl relations remained much the same with the Ravine still favored as the best place for "applied Home-Ec."[42]

The times were changing in the fifties. Television sets were purchased for the dorms and Student Union in 1954. More and more students now had automobiles, and parking became a problem. Students were not as silent as they had once been. As has been common for students in all periods, they complained about food in the cafeteria. On at least one occasion O'Donnell promised to lower prices and improve quality after a "very caustic editorial" in the campus newspaper. And there was often criticism of bookstore prices. Pizza finally made its way to Richmond, with a large combination selling for two dollars at Luigi's downtown. More important, students got something for which they had campaigned for years: student government. "After 26 years—a constitution," the *Progress* exulted in April 1954 after students approved it by a nearly 72 percent vote. First-time student government president Ronald Coffman claimed, "We have what we asked for, a group trying with very limited power to aid the students in voicing their opinions." After a year's trial, the Student Association became permanent in the fall of 1955.[43]

In the postwar period, Eastern students had numerous extracurricular opportunities. Religion played an important role in the lives of many. An annual Religious Emphasis Week began in 1946, bringing speakers and ministers to the campus. The YMCA and YWCA were active, as were groups for Baptists, Catholics, Methodists, Presbyterians, and others. The Baptist Student Union was the first to purchase land for the construction of a building just off campus. Although O'Donnell and the faculty were "definitely opposed" to social fraternities and sororities, there were several societies. National honorary societies included Pi Omega Pi, the commerce honorary,

Kappa Delta Pi for education students, Alpha Psi Omega for drama students, Kappa Pi for art students, and Sigma Tau Delta for English majors. Dean Emma Case also spearheaded the formation of honorary societies for men and women. Clubs for specific majors and for regions and counties also enjoyed large memberships in the fifties.[44]

Plays and concerts abounded, too. The Little Theatre production of *Stalag 17,* directed by ex-POW Gerald Honaker, took on special poignancy in 1957. With the exception of one year during World War II, the Foster Music Camp continued its service each summer to high school musicians. Not only did the music, art, and drama departments contribute, but numerous groups and individuals were brought in from the outside. The Jewish Chautauqua Society provided regular speakers, for example. When student enrollment finally outstripped the capacity of Brock Auditorium, O'Donnell softened the old mandatory chapel attendance rule for all students. Then convocation lost the intent of Herman L. Donovan as a weekly classroom directly under the control of the president. Moreover, seniors disliked having to attend and finally won their battle. However, underclassmen were exposed to fine entertainment and speakers every week.[45]

Enrollment grew by leaps and bounds in the fifties, much as at other colleges and universities. Owing to the GI Bill, male students continued to outnumber women, though by a smaller percentage through 1960. O'Donnell, the regents, students, and faculty complained about overcrowding. Throughout the decade, Eastern enrollment was limited only by dorm space. Often three and sometimes four men were crowded into one room. The question was how to get the money for capital improvements. With a ten-year doubling to nearly twenty-eight hundred students by 1957, and nearly five hundred at off-campus centers, the Southern Association of Colleges and Secondary Schools continually pressured Eastern for improvements. Eastern responded by adopting a specific tenure policy with a five-year "probationary period" in 1948. Not spending enough on students and the library or having a lower faculty-student ratio drew the attention of SACS in the fifties. Only after Eastern increased its expenditure above the minimum of $350 per student did the group remove an asterisk beside Eastern Kentucky State College in its listing.[46]

The cost of attending Eastern did not increase much in the fifties. The incidental fee increased from $35 to $45 per semester, while room rent varied from $36 to $72 per semester by decade's end. Out-of-state students paid slightly higher incidental fees. Including board, room, fees, and books, a student could attend Eastern for about $300 per semester. Nevertheless, many students of modest circumstances needed all the help they could get. Usually about two hundred students worked on campus at various jobs. To one student, a small increase in work hours kept her in school. Emma Case and others on campus helped out with personal loans and small gifts when students' money ran short. The regents set aside fifty $50 scholarships to be used at O'Donnell's discretion to help worthy "superior" students. "I would like to attend Eastern in the fall," said one prospective student, "but I haven't enough money." O'Donnell soon replied that a $50 scholarship was granted. To *Sputnik* and the apparent Russian challenge to education in the late fifties, Congress responded with the National Defense Student Loan program. Eastern paid its one-ninth matching sum, and its students became eligible for these loans in 1959. Each year a few graduate students, like Janet Hibbard, who went on to teach at Eastern for many years, were given fellowships for teaching, counseling, or aiding in the dormitories.[47]

Most Eastern students succeeded, getting their degrees and becoming teachers and joining other professions. Some, like Fran Herndon, who received a Fulbright grant to study in France in 1958, did especially well. As in the old days, some students, teaching full-time, took years to graduate. Golda M. Cooper, who shared a room with her daughter one summer, finally finished her degree in 1956 after several decades of taking summer classes and correspondence courses. However, there were always the miscreants who did not take advantage of their opportunities for one reason or another. O'Donnell was not averse to telling students to try their luck elsewhere. "Your record in class was one of the poorest we have ever had," he told one student. About one young woman who appeared incorrigible and had to be dismissed, O'Donnell explained to Dean Case, "No matter how hard we have tried to help someone, I must say that it always makes me very miserable when our efforts fail." Most trends in the country were reflected on the Richmond campus. Wearing "I Like Ike" buttons, a majority of students voted for President Dwight D. Eisenhower in a straw poll just before election day in 1956.[48]

Eastern students and faculty kept their sense of humor throughout the era. At a time when students were concerned about the Russian satellite *Sputnik,* launched in October 1957, "The Sputniks," described as "the team from outer space," won a men's intramural basketball tournament in April 1958. Mozart, the successor of campus dog Rex and named for his apparent interest in music and marching with the band, often entered the news section of the

Progress. His disappearance during a Christmas break trip to Louisville became big news, even being reported in the *Courier-Journal.* After spending a night in a Louisville police station, he gladly returned to the quiet of the Eastern campus. Students noted that he was so tired that he cut all classes except for English. When many students and even the president complained about too many dogs on campus, the *Progress* reported it should not be blamed on "Mo." O'Donnell complained to the sheriff: "I like dogs. We all do, but barking dogs at two o'clock in the morning, and stray, unattractive looking dogs roaming through the house at all times during the day cannot be endured by the best of dog lovers. Help us if you can!" Alas, poor Mozart, like Rex, at last died in 1964 and was buried in the Ravine.[49]

If there is any justified criticism of Eastern's fifth president, it is that he was uneasy about asking for money from the legislature. A fiscal conservative, O'Donnell believed his first responsibility was to save money. The refinancing of bonds in 1945 instead of using a $225,000 surplus for the building of a new dorm, for example, pointed to his mind-set. He understood the importance of the money coming in for veterans' education and anticipated the inevitable shortfall when their numbers decreased, with no increase in state appropriations. In the 1950s, O'Donnell became more aggressive. "Operating a college is like carrying on a war in that we have to keep fighting all the time to hold our own position," he told the faculty in November 1950. It galled him as much as anyone that Western and Murray, despite having smaller student populations, got higher appropriations than Eastern. The regents urged more effort in building for the next meeting of the legislature. A decline of state revenue in 1953 brought renewed crisis to the college's budget. By the next biennium O'Donnell, "delighted with the appropriation," pointed with pride that now only Western received more state money. Local member of the state House of Representatives, Josh Cosby, deserved some of the credit.[50]

With the election of Eastern alumnus Robert R. Martin as state superintendent of public instruction in 1955, the college got more of a hearing in Frankfort. Also, Martin pushed Eastern to plan for the growth anticipated for the 1960s. O'Donnell appeared emboldened. Record enrollments each semester also helped the arguments presented to lawmakers. Eastern's appropriation now exceeded $1 million annually. Finally, in late 1957, Eastern's share of the state budget increased slightly over that of Western after the presidents of the five state colleges, working through the CPHE and the Department of Finance, arrived at a formula agreement. In early 1958, Eastern had the largest appropriation and student enrollment of any state college. Just as important, Attorney General Jo Ferguson said that revenue from existing dorms "could be pledged to finance the construction of new ones." A building boom was about to begin.[51]

Buildings did appear on the Eastern campus after much struggle in the early and middle years of O'Donnell's administration, and the record is admirable. Even the development of Vet's Village, costing more than $125,000, was no small accomplishment. The Weaver addition at $260,000 was important, as was the new Memorial Science Building, at nearly $700,000, for badly needed classrooms. Renovation of Sullivan and the building of Keith Hall in 1954, at a cost of $556,000, added much-needed dorm space, making it possible to return the former to a full-time women's dormitory. Still, the *Progress* complained everything was too "crammed" together.[52]

One of the most pressing needs was for a new music building. Again, the bonding process made it possible to construct buildings with the payoff delayed until far into the future. The State Property and Buildings Commission added some regularity to the process of planning for a $375,000 music building. At first, the regents voted to name the new music building for O'Donnell but later voted to honor the composer of "My Old Kentucky Home." By 1955, Eastern was planning to replace Vet's Village with better family housing. One of the most pressing needs was renovation of Burnam, particularly its "spider-work of electric cords strung across the rooms from the ceiling outlets to study tables and radios." Planning for another men's dorm led to a $600,000 bond issue, to be paid off in 1997. Superintendent Martin made the motion that the new dorm be named for O'Donnell in honor of his years of service to Eastern. The regents unanimously passed the resolution. Bonding through the federal Housing and Home Finance Agency proved invaluable for growth. However, buildings could not be built fast enough in the fifties. As a sign of the changing and improving times, the old Rural Demonstration School was discontinued in 1958, and two years later the last vestige of old Memorial Hall was demolished. Students were sometimes not in awe of the new construction. "The Students of Keith Hall" petitioned about a common complaint to President O'Donnell in winter 1958. "This just isn't fair to have to pay this much per year for a room and then have to freeze to death," they implored. "Please do something about this for us before someone in Keith has to go to the hospital with pneumonia." The opposite was true for the women living in the basement of Burnam. Mary Cole recalled that they had to keep the heat turned off even during the coldest weather "or we would have burned up."[53]

Eastern athletic teams entered another golden age of Maroon sports in the 1950s. After the "Big Irishman," Paul McBrayer, coached the basketball team into the OVC championship by defeating Western 62–50 in 1950, he had continued success. He was "pretty-hard nosed," recalled Carl Cole, an all-American guard in 1961, "a very strict coach with the voice to go with it." Though never again reaching a ranking of eleventh nationally, McBrayer's teams were always competitive. More important, his players gave him the utmost loyalty and praise for his coaching and character.[54]

Jim Baechtold, whom McBrayer called "the best all-around player I have seen in my 22 years of coaching," Shirley Kearns, and Bob Mulcahy were outstanding players of the early fifties. Baechtold and his future wife, Shirley Spires, were elected junior prom king and queen. Baechtold went on to a professional basketball career with the New York Knickerbockers. He came back to Eastern as an assistant coach to McBrayer after five years in the National Basketball Association.[55]

Jack Adams played great basketball in the midfifties, leading the Maroons back to the OVC crown in 1955 along with Guy Strong and Jim Mitchell. When Adams graduated in 1956, McBrayer called him "the greatest player that I have seen in my twenty-five years of coaching." Adams set nine all-time scoring records, having led the state in scoring his senior year with an average of twenty-four points per game, and had his number retired.[56]

O'Donnell's attitude toward sports, as toward most other things, was conservative. When regent John S. Juett brought up the subject of "enlarging and improving the sports program" in early 1951, the president quashed any such thought. He argued instead that, while athletics did not pay for itself, it did bring in students, and the program did not need more emphasis. Eastern's chapter of the American Association of University Professors (AAUP) even wanted a de-emphasis on sports in order to save money to put into faculty salaries. With so many financial needs, O'Donnell worked to keep all costs under control. In the midfifties, athletic scholarships came under scrutiny. Again, the president defended a prudent approach, maintaining that by using an inter-accounting system no money was actually disbursed. Moreover, he explained to the regents that athletes also helped pay their way through school. Most students liked the level of play at Eastern, although *Progress* editor Bert C. Bach in 1958 sometimes complained about the "Overemphasis Problem."

By the late fifties, football and basketball "scholarships" usually covered room and board and fees. Spring sports were given less emphasis, and student-athletes received only partial scholarships. Football players were expected to keep up maintenance on their dwelling under the football stadium, as were the basketball players in Stateland Hall. With separate training tables for football and basketball players, they ate abundantly.[57]

Beginning in the late 1920s, women's sports struggled thereafter for years. Most activities were of the intramural variety in the Donovan and early O'Donnell years. Gertrude Hood, who came to Eastern in 1928, introduced field hockey soon after arriving on campus. Then she moved the physical education intramural programs toward outside competition, with "field days" and "play days" in basketball, field hockey, and softball. The Women's Athletic Association (WAA) of 1946 became the Women's Recreation Association in 1950. Hood's philosophy was "whoever wanted to go got to go" when the Maroonettes competed against other schools. "Eastern Girls Plaster UK Gals 32–31," the *Progress* announced proudly in early 1947 as the Richmond school won its first basketball game of the postwar period. Betsy Tandy, president of the WAA, led the team in scoring. Throughout the fifties women's sports gained momentum, with field hockey joining basketball as an increasingly competitive sport. However, enjoyment over competition was emphasized for women's sports in this era.[58]

After being at Eastern for twenty-one years, Tom Samuels resigned his head football coaching post in 1953 to enter the pharmacy business in Orlando, Florida. Glenn Presnell, who had served as an assistant under Samuels for seven years, took over the challenge of improving on the Maroons' enviable 8–2 1953 season, led by a left-handed quarterback from Corbin, Roy Kidd. The next year Eastern rolled to an undefeated season in the OVC, beating Western, 21–0, in Bowling Green before a record homecoming crowd. Only a tie against Toledo spoiled an otherwise perfect season. Led by all-conference seniors Don Daly, Frank Nassida, Jim Hanlon, Bob Muller, Jerry Johns, and Fred Winscher, the Maroons had hopes for a postseason game.[59]

Though the Maroons barely missed out on a bowl bid in 1941, the 1954 team played in the Tangerine Bowl in Orlando. Eastern received the princely sum of $7,500 for the effort. In a hard-fought defensive game against Omaha University before a crowd of thirteen thousand, Eastern lost, 7–6. Eastern football teams for the remainder of the fifties, while competitive, did not fare as well, though they continued to dominate the other Kentucky state colleges.[60]

The rivalry between Eastern and Western continued unabated in the fifties in athletics, for state appropriations, and for students. In the midfifties, O'Donnell, always looking for a way to save money, agreed with President Garrett at Western to limit the total number of athletic scholarships to fifty. However, contests between the two schools heated to a near frenzy, especially when Western's coach Ed Diddle whipped out his trademark red towel. In a rough-and-tumble basketball encounter at Bowling Green in February 1960, an incident marred a mostly healthy competition. There were several accounts given, perhaps depending on whether you were a Western or Eastern fan, player, or representative. Toward the end of the first half, as a Hilltopper drove for the basket, Eastern's Ralph Richardson was whistled for a foul. After the two colliding players fell to the floor, Diddle charged Richardson and had to be restrained by others. McBrayer asked Richardson if Diddle had touched him. When the Eastern youngster replied yes, McBrayer, ever the gentleman, decided that the circumstances were too troubling and took his players off the floor, forfeiting the game. Hyper Hilltopper fans assaulted the Eastern players with taunts as they walked to the locker room. They also pelted the bus with snowballs as it headed toward Richmond. With tempers inflamed on both sides, Richardson even filed an affidavit swearing that he was not guilty of any wrongdoing. However, a few days later President O'Donnell and Western's President Kelly Thompson were seen walking "arm-in-arm" to committee meetings in Lexington and Frankfort. When asked about the incident by a reporter, O'Donnell replied that the "sooner forgotten the better." There was not much chance of that, however, as sports fans unfortunately have long memories.[61]

In the fifties the Eastern faculty grew substantially in size as the student body doubled, but the school was always understaffed, never quite keeping up with the pace of change. SACS usually complained about this in its reports. When Eastern had a faculty of 85, the association said it needed at least 118. The trend of an increasing percentage of faculty with doctorates during the Donovan years actually reversed under his successor. At the insistence of SACS, Eastern adopted a formal sabbatical policy, with one semester at full pay after seven years of service.[62]

The faculty kept pressure on O'Donnell to raise salaries. O'Donnell continually told the regents of the struggle to compete with other schools. President William L. Keene of Eastern's AAUP pushed for raises. Everyone realized that each year Eastern lost some faculty to higher salaries elsewhere. When the state ran short of money in 1953, there were increases for no one. The next year, with an improved state economy, salary increases ranged from $300 to $400. More hefty raises came in the late fifties as more money became available. O'Donnell even contemplated merit increases. The faculty applauded a 10 percent increase in 1958. Salaries for staff remained abysmally low. For example, longtime secretary Martha K. Barksdale made only $2,600 in the midfifties. She took some solace in believing that the "office of eight," the secretaries, had a strong influence. "We eight, little old biddies in the office," she said, "ran the school in a sense, because we knew everything that was happening."[63]

Meanwhile, the enrollment set new records each semester in the late fifties, nearing three thousand by the fall of 1959. And O'Donnell could report salaries that were higher than those at other state colleges. One of the greatest problems was retirement for teachers, who, because of low salaries over the years, had built up small funds in the state teachers' retirement plan. For many years, Eastern provided part-time employment for nearly everyone retiring to supplement their income. For example, George Gumbert, an agriculture teacher until he had his voice box removed because of cancer, oversaw the tiny visual aids program for several years. It was not until 1956 that Eastern faculty were covered by Social Security.[64]

One of the biggest changes in the O'Donnell years came in the growth of the library, reaching more than one hundred thousand volumes by 1960. Of course, constant pressure from SACS had pushed that effort. Alumnus Dick Allen replaced Mary Floyd as chief librarian in 1957. Professor Jonathan Truman Dorris worked tirelessly in editing and organizing the publication of a new history of Eastern: *Five Decades of Progress: Eastern Kentucky State College, 1906–1957.* Numerous faculty members participated. Unlike *Three Decades of Progress,* which was delayed by the Great Depression, this one came off rather easily. After one thousand copies were printed at a total cost of $5,079.83, the book sold for $5.00 a copy. O'Donnell saw that copies were sent to many politicians, including Governor "Happy" Chandler. Dorris also kept working away at his small museum, increasing its holdings on a shoestring budget.[65]

After returning from his brief service in Frankfort, W. J. Moore continued as dean of the college. In the postwar years, the curriculum began to expand as the school faced new challenges. Every department added new courses and revised old ones. History 29, A Survey of the Global War, which was described as the "social, economic, and political background of World War II; problems brought about by world conflict; the importance of world peace," illustrated the efforts of Eastern to keep up with the changing times.[66]

There were attempts to raise the intellectual level of Eastern's students during the O'Donnell years. Kennamer's World Affairs Club became affiliated with the Foreign Policy Association and discussed the important issues of the day. Eastern brought important speakers like Alexander Kerensky, the old anti-Soviet Russian, to the campus. Kerney Adams and W. L. Keene led a Great Books Symposium from time to time. By the midfifties Adams had developed a history course, Ideological Foundations of Western Civilization, to stimulate thinking and develop a "questioning attitude." In such a course "one of the most important things a teacher must learn is not to talk too much," Adams said. Fellow historian Clyde Lewis was also developing his social science approach to the study of civilization as part of a general education rubric, which was part of a growing national trend. Although *Progress* editor Bert C. Bach and other student leaders scolded their classmates for not reading enough serious books, it should be recalled that this was the age of rock and roll and Elvis Presley. Even black-based rhythm and blues influenced the all-white Eastern student subculture. Students also listened to the records of the Hilltoppers, a transitional group of student troubadours from Bowling Green.[67]

True to its southern moorings, Eastern did not react quickly or positively to the desegregation movement of the 1950s. As a matter of fact, it took a long time for Eastern to end the procedure of listing African American employees as "colored" in the minutes of the Board of Regents. When the Kentucky General Assembly repealed the Day Law in 1950, O'Donnell told the regents that Negroes had applied and that both Eastern and Western had advised them "to go to the University [of Kentucky] or to Berea or the State College in Frankfort." About the only contact the faculty and students had with African Americans was with those who worked on the campus. Black janitors like Harvey Wilson and Oscar White, who led a noon hearts card game in Coates basement with some faculty in attendance, were respected by all on campus. Hazel Warford, janitor in the Weaver Building from 1931 to 1961, dispensed advice to young athletes and boxing lessons in addition to fulfilling his cleaning duties. In 1977, the Alumni Association placed a plaque in Weaver honoring Warford's years of service.[68]

With the desegregation case of *Brown v. Board of Education* in 1954, Eastern could no longer ignore what was happening in America. However, there was still no rush to welcome blacks to the campus, and the first minority student did not enter until two years later. Andrew Miller, a local teacher, became the first black student at Eastern in a summer graduate course and received a master's degree in 1958. Anne Peyton Spann, in the class of 1961, became the first black to attend all four years at Eastern and graduate. For a while she was the only African American student on campus. Although there appeared to be no problems in integrating the Richmond campus, it was not unusual for Eastern students to wave a Confederate flag at ball games as other teams began to bring along black players by the midfifties.[69]

The *Eastern Progress* changed from the blatant racism of an earlier time to a much more liberal stance. An editorial in late 1958 by Beverly Dansby and Tommy Logsdon commented on the racial divide, arguing that prejudice was a learned behavior and that teachers educated at Eastern should accept integration and teach it to their students in the coming years. "Our government does not ask too much of us to at least give this issue on integration a chance," the *Progress* said a year later.[70]

If Eastern haltingly entered a new age with the integration of the classroom, it still demonstrated a harmful insularity. In the fall of 1956, only one hundred out-of-state students attended out of a total of twenty-five hundred. Though several foreign students had successfully attended Eastern just after the war, O'Donnell refused to accept foreign students in the early fifties because of the housing shortage.[71]

In his last months in office, O'Donnell took some criticism for deferring maintenance. One alumnus recalled a piece of cardboard covering two broken windows for nearly two years in Cammack and complaints about leaky roofs. Moreover, State Superintendent Martin had other qualms about O'Donnell's leadership. Unless there was more strategic planning and capital construction, Martin said, "there are thousands of young people who will be denied a college education." The dynamics of the regents also changed as two more members were added during Happy Chandler's second administration. The regents, Martin, and O'Donnell all expressed themselves without reservation in a June 1959 meeting. At issue was how to fund badly needed faculty raises. While O'Donnell defended keeping a $100,000 reserve at all times, regent Earle Combs pushed to have half of that amount used to raise salaries. After a heated discussion, O'Donnell urged the regents to approve his recommendation. "If you find that you will have some money that ought to be distributed later on at Christmas time," he added rather sarcastically, "you can make their hearts glad by giving the faculty an extra amount at that time." In the end the regents accepted the president's recommendations but added $200 to each faculty member's salary.[72]

With O'Donnell nearing the age of seventy and mandatory retirement, there was much speculation about his successor at the end of the 1959–60 school year. O'Donnell's nineteen years of service to Eastern came during very trying times. With his leadership the school weathered the war years and pushed off into the postwar years of rapid growth. Some critics complained about his conservative nature and his indecisiveness. Others, including Martin, did not believe he looked far enough into the future. A fiscal conservative by nature and habit, O'Donnell did not challenge the other state schools for adequate funds until late in his presidency. Nevertheless, he led Eastern through some tough times and prepared the school for more enlightened and aggressive leadership in the coming years.[73]

Eastern's student body changed during O'Donnell's years, but not as radically as it would in later years. In loco parentis still operated; rigid curfews and restrictions for the girls kept the boys at bay most of the time. Dean Case kept a benign eye out for her charges. There were small intrigues. For example, if a coed wanted to wear shorts or slacks on campus during the school week, she wore a long raincoat over them. Springtime trips to Boonesborough Beach gave a little freedom from the prying eyes of a watchful administration. The faculty was also changing. Dorris and Keith and many of the old guard retired, their places being taken by younger professors. So, too, would the legends change over time. Meredith Cox, a longtime chemistry professor, had the reputation for being a taskmaster and threatening to jump out the window when students did not perform up to his demanding standards. However, he, like the rest of the Eastern faculty, were dedicated to guiding students who were not always well prepared for the rigors of a college education.[74]

CHAPTER 6

Robert R. Martin

"A Vision of Greatness," 1960–1976

AS PRESIDENT O'DONNELL neared the mandatory retirement age of seventy, the political nature of Kentucky education emerged. There is little doubt that Robert R. Martin, class of 1934, had in mind returning to Eastern as president. He plotted his course well, working his way through public school teaching into administration at the state department of education in Frankfort. All the while he kept a strong dedication to the Democratic Party.[1]

Before military service in World War II, Martin earned a master's degree at the University of Kentucky. With a postwar doctorate in education at Teachers College, Columbia University, specializing in school finance, he positioned himself for administrative work. After serving in the state department of education for several years in ever more responsible positions, he ran for state superintendent of public instruction in 1955, allied with gubernatorial candidate Bert T. Combs. The latter lost a bitter primary to former governor and U.S. senator A. B. "Happy" Chandler, while Martin won wide majorities in the primary and general elections. With his new position of state superintendent, Martin served, ex officio, on the boards of all the state colleges.[2]

As state superintendent in an initially hostile Chandler administration, Martin played a key role in the implementation and funding of the Minimum Foundation Program and the growing school consolidation movement. These were the early years of school desegregation, and Martin and Chandler worked together to bring about peaceful integration in an otherwise "southern"-oriented state. Chandler recalled in an interview, "He was a great big fellow, some of them called him 'fatso.'" The hurly-burly of Kentucky politics was always simmering just below the surface for old political foes like Martin and Chandler. Martin, a protégé of former governor and U.S. senator Earle

Clements, kept his political options open, perhaps even dreaming of running for lieutenant governor or governor someday. However, most of his contemporaries in the Democratic Party understood that politics always took second place to his desire to improve education in Kentucky.[3]

The naming of a new president of Eastern came down to timing and a majority of votes by the regents, six of whom were appointed by the governor. Chandler, limited to a four-year term, had appointed four regents, who could elect his choice as president of Eastern if O'Donnell resigned before Chandler's term expired in December 1959. In early 1958, Chandler named Robert B. Hensley and H. D. Fitzpatrick Jr. to the board, joining Thomas B. McGregor and Earle Combs, whom he had appointed in 1957 when state college boards were increased to six. Keeping with state mandate, the board had to be equally divided between the two political parties. Moreover, if a Chandler ally won the governorship for the next four years in the election of 1959, then the appointment of a pro-Chandler candidate was nearly assured. Rumors were rife about the impending replacement for O'Donnell. John E. Robinson, an Eastern alumnus and opponent of Martin in the 1955 primary, allied himself with Chandler and posed a threat as a possible candidate. Clyde Reeves, head of the state fair board, appeared to have the support of the *Courier-Journal,* the important Bingham paper in Louisville with a statewide influence. When Chandler tried an end run by urging the Eastern regents to name a replacement before the Eastern president retired, Attorney General Jo M. Ferguson, a Combs-Martin ally, shot down that idea quickly in a summary opinion.[4]

Strong-willed individuals, Martin and Chandler had locked horns over switching the surplus property division out of Martin's control to that of the governor. Moreover, when perennial state officeholder Wendell Butler did not receive a key post in the department of education, he blamed Martin, further straining their relations. It was payback time in a way, because during Butler's term from 1951–55, he "relegated" Martin "to a rather minor position in the department," according to Martin's longtime ally, James L. Sublett. Political seer Ed Prichard revealed in an interview that Martin had "a rough tongue" and often made light of Butler's abilities. When Butler ran for the state superintendent post in 1959 in his quadrennial game of political musical chairs, Martin kept silent. However, four years later, when Butler claimed the commissioner of agriculture post, Martin sarcastically opined, "He'll do less harm to a pig than he can a child."[5]

When time rolled around for the 1959 gubernatorial race, Combs ran again. After consulting with Clements, he chose Martin as his campaign manager. There was some grousing among "school people" in the state, but the greatest complaints came from Chandler and the *Courier-Journal*, both calling for Martin to resign from his state post. However, Ned Breathitt, who succeeded Combs as governor, saw this as positive because it forced education before the electorate. In a tight three-man race, Martin helped broker a deal whereby Louisvillian Wilson Wyatt dropped out and became a candidate for lieutenant governor, leaving Combs with only Harry Lee Waterfield to contend with in the Democratic primary. "He was on top of everything that occurred during the campaign," said Combs. An alliance with Chandler worked against Waterfield, who lost the primary by twenty-five thousand votes. Combs swept into office with a wide majority against Republican John M. Robsion Jr. in the November general election.[6]

Combs gave Martin an immediate "political plum," appointing him commissioner of finance in December 1959. "I was looking for the most capable man I could find," Combs explained, "and I thought Bob was that man." Martin set about budget planning for the new administration, with education getting special treatment. Meanwhile, rumors made the usual rounds about the presidency of Eastern. However, winning the presidency was no easy task. Although there is no record of such a conversation, Combs, and probably Clements, conferred with Martin about the best approach to ensure the Democrat's candidacy. Meanwhile, a faculty committee headed by Ralph W. Whalin, chairman of the industrial arts department, prepared a profile of the qualifications it thought the new president should possess. Giving it to the governor and the regents, Whalin believed it had a positive influence and pointed the way toward Martin as the prime candidate.[7]

With Chandler safely out of the way, the April 13, 1960, meeting of the regents became crucial to the future of Eastern Kentucky State College. There was old-fashioned Kentucky politicking afoot. When some suggested that L. Felix Joyner might be a candidate, Combs appointed him state personal commissioner. Adding to the intrigue, Superintendent Butler and three pro-Chandler regents met downtown for a "strategy conference" prior to the regents' meeting on campus. When they returned to Coates Administration Building, the meeting proceeded with two new members appointed by Combs, F. L. Dupree and Russell I. Todd, who had replaced former governor Flem Sampson and Dr. Ernest Begley.[8]

After some preliminary business, including accepting a budget for 1960–61, O'Donnell formally announced his intention to retire on June 30. Butler called for nominations for a new president. McGregor, who had not been part of the premeeting group, promptly nominated Martin, "a man dedicated to education and the best interests of this College." Fitzpatrick named Peabody College's Jack Allen, a relative of his, and an alumnus and former professor at Eastern. Finally, Butler nominated Clark Farley, another Eastern graduate and superintendent of Glasgow schools. To be elected, a candidate would need a majority, or four votes of the seven-man board.[9]

Butler suggested that the regents vote by secret ballot, and they all agreed. On the first ballot Martin received three votes, Allen two, and Farley one, with a single abstention. Butler burned the ballots and called for a new vote. On the second ballot Martin had four votes with three passes. After announcing that Robert R. Martin had been elected the sixth president of Eastern, the state superintendent burned the ballots. Then the regents voted, unanimously, to employ Martin for three years, the remainder of O'Donnell's term, at the same salary, $15,000. Butler telephoned Martin in Frankfort with the news. "I am honored to be chosen president of my *alma mater*," Martin replied.[10]

"I fully expected to be appointed," Martin said self-confidently in an interview just after his retirement in 1976. Though some members had an old commitment to Chandler, particularly Earle Combs, even Chandler ally Wendell Butler finally settled into the Martin camp, probably on the second ballot. And, whereas the other candidates had "soft" support, that of Martin was imbued with the power of a sitting governor. "I wanted the Board of Regents to appoint him," Governor Combs recalled, "and I let that be known." "Intelligent people know what the score is without having their arms twisted," the former governor insisted. Butler recalled: "Bob happened to be at the right place at the right time with the right qualifications." "I gave him the vote that elected him president," Butler insisted, realizing that if Governor Combs wanted Martin, then he had to vote for Martin or suffer the political consequences in the coming years. Therefore, on the crucial second ballot, McGregor, Todd, Dupree, and Butler voted for Martin.[11]

Foreshadowing the future, the *Lexington Herald* immediately hailed Martin's appointment, while the *Courier-Journal* chose to ignore it editorially. Robert R. Martin was not publisher Barry Bingham's choice for the presidency. Bingham could never forgive the former state superintendent's mixing of education and politics as campaign manager for Combs in 1959. Simply put, their "educational philosophies clashed," Sublett observed. Whereas, the *Courier-Journal* leadership wanted a pristine educational system in Kentucky, Martin understood that politics and education could not be separated.[12]

After his election, the forty-nine-year-old Martin continued to serve dynamically as finance commissioner while waiting for his July 1, 1960, takeover at Eastern. Already he was at work on financing for dormitories, declaring Eastern's "buildings in a bad state of repair." Martin later reminisced, "I gave my attention to building and did this without upheaval and letting" Dean Moore and older faculty and staff retire on their own. However, he did begin to put together a team to help him. He persuaded J. C. Powell and John Vickers from the Department of Education to join him in Richmond as executive assistants.[13]

As the time approached for Martin's coming to Richmond, he began to reveal himself more to the public. When asked about his weight by a reporter, Martin drolly replied, "Just say more than 250 pounds and let it go at that." "I always claimed he could eat anything," said his old friend Sublett half jokingly, having once witnessing him devour a pot of cold bean soup. If he had prodigious size, six foot two inches and well over three hundred pounds, he also had a quick mind and devotion to work. He could outwork most people, had a capacity for quick planning, and did what he could to get Eastern's case before the public. Al Smith, a longtime observer of Kentucky, credited Martin, as well as his archrival Morehead president Adron Doran, as hardly ever turning down a chance to boost the cause of higher education. For example, Martin delivered eleven eighth-grade and high school commencement speeches from late May through early June 1963. For parents Martin "always had the same sermon," Smith said. "Send me your children, we will find the money." One thing was certain about Martin, according to Kentucky's historian laureate, Thomas D. Clark: "He was the most astute of astute politicians."[14]

To Eastern he brought a style of leadership in contrast to that of the easygoing O'Donnell. In a hurry to move Eastern to where he thought was its destiny, Martin, as one of his longtime friends noted, demanded so much from people he would sometimes ignore them if he found them wanting. "He was intimidating," noted University of Kentucky president Otis Singletary. "He sort of took over a room with his presence," said another observer. Martin expected everything and everyone to be in its place, often calling late at night or early in the morning with an idea for staff or a political crony. He liked humor, sometimes even making fun of his prodigious weight, but found it more fun to play a practical joke on someone else. However, when speaking at an August commencement at Morehead, he said he would obey President Doran's admonition for a short speech because "fat men are not inclined to talk too long in August in Kentucky." Impatient, when he wanted to end a phone conversation, "he would just hang up." Only a few people like old high school friend and army retiree Shirley M. Castle, longtime director of Eastern's personnel services, could tell Martin "what he didn't want to hear" without fear of repercussion. "He'd get red-faced about it," Castle revealed in an interview, but soon relented. Martin sometimes irritated people, like long-time employee Larry Martin, for not lavishing praise for their efforts, as if they should expect none. He was as human as he was huge. The new Eastern Kentucky State College president liked food and plenty of it, as well as a tipple or two. All things considered, Robert Richard Martin was a complex man, with a complicated personality that far exceeded the exterior view that most people saw. With no major avocation, except for attending an occasional horse race, he gave about all he had to college administration.[15]

Several themes would dominate the Martin years on the Richmond campus. Eastern, like most other colleges and universities at the time, had a rapid growth spurt. Student enrollment outstripped efforts to build enough dormitories and classrooms. Despite the best efforts of Martin, Eastern could not escape student and faculty unrest during the Vietnam War era. In loco parentis came under fire as students asked for liberalized dorm hours for women and more student self-government. The ROTC program would become a lightning rod for those students and outsiders who wanted to radically change the college. Moreover, the restiveness of faculty would dog the latter years of Martin's tenure.

A wily administrator, Martin caught the leading edge of vocational change. In the early sixties he pushed the beginning of nursing and allied health programs as well as law enforcement education. University status for the Eastern campus in 1966 brought not only new programs but also turmoil. Turf battles intensified between Central University College and the new College of Arts and Sciences and their respective deans who, on philosophical as well as practical grounds, warred over general education requirements.

Eastern somewhat timidly faced the racial divide of the 1960s, slowly integrating in a town with many of the characteristics of one in the Deep South. While the Richmond public schools desegregated peacefully, a local swimming pool closed over the integration issue. Ironically, as African Americans began to join Eastern's athletic teams in growing numbers, the nickname was changed from Maroons to Colonels, complete with a stereotypical antebellum Civil War colonel mascot. Martin wanted an easily identifiable mascot and got his way.

In the middle of all these rapid changes and conflicts would be the strong presidency and presence of Martin. He viewed all this through his own prism, one based on ideas that were as old-fashioned as those of the Donovan years, as well as a vision that was far ahead of that of many of his contemporaries in higher education. The engine that drove Martin made him as competitive as any battlefield or athletic contestant. He loved winning, whether it was taking the "old hawg rifle" from Doran's Morehead football team or getting a bigger piece of the education appropriation pie in Frankfort. Foremost was Martin's burning ambition to make Eastern into the best school he could. And he was in a hurry.

Into what longtime aide J. C. Powell described as a "sleepy, slightly run-down easy-going campus" came Martin, "who hit the ground running" on July 1, 1960. With no planning or budget in place, Martin immediately set Powell to work on the deplorable dormitory problems (there were too few, and the existing ones were not in good condition). The new president's financial expertise in education immediately impacted Eastern. At Martin's first meeting of the Board of Regents, they agreed to renovation projects and a resolution entitled "Creating a Consolidated Building Project." Taking advantage of a new state law that allowed a school to collect fees in order to let bonds on new construction, a bill that Martin helped write, the regents approved construction of a laboratory school and dormitories. The new president also urged construction of a new gymnasium, one that would dwarf Weaver. By early September, the regents authorized sale of $2 million in bonds.[16]

The 1960 fall semester began with the old Eastern traditions; freshman hazing, Saturday football games, as well as the usual student misbehavior along with a record enrollment. The president warned students during an assembly that "ample sidewalks" made trekking across the football field unnecessary. Five students were expelled after a snake dance downtown got out of control, with Martin even declaring a campus curfew. However, students were also interested in the presidential election between Richard Nixon and John Kennedy. The *Eastern Progress* editorialized against the bigotry of anti-Catholicism.[17]

On November 16, Eastern held a formal inauguration of the new president in Brock Auditorium. Several state dignitaries, including Governor Combs, were in attendance. Building on a speech he had made at the fiftieth Founders Day in 1956, Martin outlined his philosophy of education in a refined speech, "A Vision of Greatness," taking a cue from philosopher Alfred North Whitehead. After paying homage to Eastern's heritage, Martin testified to the wonders that education held for the world by allowing a level playing field for the disadvantaged, nonelite, usually first-generation college student. He included a list of sixteen challenges as part of his vision for Eastern. Already attuned to the need for vocational education, the new president maintained that a college graduate "is expected to be a trained individual who can make his mark in our culture and civilization."[18]

"The American dream begins in the classroom," Martin averred. Moreover, he recognized the challenge of communism and the need for intellectual stimulation with "a faculty noted for its scholarship." Students, of course, were the center of his vision, his "imperatives" for the future. A stickler for formality and ceremony Martin had a mace and presidential seal, developed by faculty artist Dean Gatwood, in place for the inauguration.[19]

The year 1960 was a crucial one in America. With the nation ever under the threats of the cold war, the presidential election of that year was hotly contested. Although the 1950s had been years of growth in higher education, now high schools were turning out graduates in record numbers. Would there be room for those who wanted to attend college? Moreover, what new directions in vocational education would appear in coming years?

Martin's first year at the helm proved his dynamism. He pushed construction of new dorms and a new field house. Fearing loss of the ROTC program because of declining graduation rates, he proposed and the regents approved a two-year compulsory program. Although the Maroons lost their last three games of the football season and surrendered the "Old Hawg Rifle" to Morehead, a roundball victory over Western at home was indeed sweet. With Carl Cole scoring thirty-four points, students chanted, "We want a holiday," making old Weaver gym reverberate. "President Martin cancelled Friday afternoon's classes," the *Progress* reported, "and was wildly cheered by the three thousand plus milling students." But there was also more afoot. The editors of the school paper asked why their school did not have social fraternities while Western and Murray did. Other students found the name "Maroons" wanting and cited the need for "a fighting name and mascot that would help considerably to stir up spirit and enthusiasm." In November 1961, the *Progress* and the Student Council announced a campaign to find a "permanent name."[20]

In the midst of a whirlwind of change at Eastern, Martin proved his knack for publicity, as well as for pulling off a political coup. Looking for a way to publicize the school, Martin called on his old friend Clements to contact Vice President Lyndon B. Johnson about receiving an honorary degree at Eastern Kentucky State College's 1961 spring graduation. After graduation was changed to suit Johnson's schedule, the day almost did not happen when the assassination of Dominican Republic dictator Trujillo, coupled with President Kennedy's absence from Washington, almost scuttled the vice president's trip.[21]

"It was a frustrating experience," Martin later recalled. First, after arriving by helicopter at 9:00 A.M., Johnson kept warning Martin he might have to leave at any moment. Second, an activist professor, who hoped to embarrass the Washington administration over its civil rights record, was arrested beforehand, unknown to Martin, and lodged in the Madison County jail. Otherwise, the day went off without a hitch.[22]

With Governor Combs and other dignitaries on hand and much press coverage, the event drew attention to a vibrant institution and Martin's leadership. The graduation ceremonies, Johnson's speech, and the conferring of an honorary Doctor of Laws degree, Eastern's first such effort, went well. The vice president spoke about foreign affairs with a cold war tenor: "We seek friends, not enemies," he said. Afterward, Johnson helped break ground for the new Alumni Coliseum, had what turned out to be a leisurely lunch, and then made an obligatory trip across the street to Elmwood, the Watts estate. Miss Emma Watts, who requested this visit through her Texas connections, knew that Martin had designs on her property and wanted nothing to do with him. "We kept a respectful distance," Martin recalled (tongue in cheek) years later. Meanwhile, the mistress of Elmwood and the vice president shared glasses of bourbon and then a short walk through her garden before he rushed back to Washington. For years people have laughed at the following story about Martin and Miss Watts. When he asked her if Elmwood was for sale, she replied indignantly, "Is your campus for sale?" Although EKU did acquire 4.5 acres of her estate to be used for a parking lot, any attempt either to purchase Elmwood or break her will has failed.[23]

At the August commencement a few weeks later, Eastern conferred an honorary degree on Philippine general Carlos P. Romulo, continuing Martin's strategy of publicity. Famous people and useful political figures often highlighted graduation, it being obligatory to give each sitting governor an honorary degree. In 1964 Norman Vincent Peale and Congressman Carl D. Perkins received honorary degrees. March 21, Founders Day, also received special emphasis under Martin. After Eastern was granted university status in 1966, Governor Edward T. Breathitt received his honorary degree on Founders Day of that spring. To highlight the placing of a copy of Enid Yandell's statue of Daniel Boone in front of the Keen Johnson Building, Martin invited Fess Parker, television's portrayer of the vaunted frontiersman, to receive an honorary degree in 1968. And new awards were initiated when five Democratic Party leaders received Regents Awards for service to Eastern in 1964.[24]

Eastern appeared to grow so rapidly in the early sixties that *Courier-Journal* columnist Joe Creason once said that Martin should put up a sign reading, "Eastern Kentucky State College, Under Construction." At the nitty-gritty task of financing and building Martin had no peer in what now seems like a "golden age" of campus growth. The Richmond school grew from an estimated $7 million to a physical plant of $120 million under Martin's direction. In the 1960s alone, enrollment grew from three thousand to nearly ten thousand. Eastern, like most schools of the time, was confronted with the overwhelming problems of housing this burgeoning population. One way to get government funds for dormitories was to squeeze three students into a room designed for two, thereby proving the need for bonding funds to federal authorities. Martin excelled at tweaking the system for all it was worth. For example, why not use Model School tuition pledged toward constructing other classroom buildings? Or, by putting classrooms under a stadium, the new Hanger Stadium would qualify for "a sizable government grant," according to bond expert Cornelius Grafton. Martin also worked to consolidate bond funds and took every opportunity to reduce debt when interest rates fell. When the Housing and Home Finance Agency did not act quickly enough, Martin called on political friends like Congressmen Carl D. Perkins to see that it "expedited" the necessary paperwork. Martin also cooperated with Perkins to see that increased student assistance made its way through Congress. In the 1960s, many a graduation, Founders Day, or homecoming featured a groundbreaking or dedication ceremony on the Eastern campus. A local banker perhaps summed it up best: "He arrived one day and ever since there's been a cloud of dust all over the city of Richmond that seems to never settle."[25]

In the sixties it became customary to name the new buildings for regents as a reward for their service, with exceptions like one for Governor Combs, to whom Martin owed his post. Other structures were named for Eastern's presidents, including the new Model School complex for Donovan and a men's dorm for Martin soon after he arrived. Martin also understood the importance of infrastructure on an enlarged college campus, including expanded married housing, a new water tower, and other service buildings. Most of the buildings were completed on time. However, when one of the massive 308-foot-long laminated wood arches in the ceiling of Alumni Coliseum fell during construction, injuring several workers, completion was delayed for months.[26]

Students of the early sixties came in increasing numbers to the Richmond campus. Martin excelled at working on financing needed construction. Continuing a post–World War II trend, males outnumbered females on campus. Initially there was a need for more dorms for men than women. Black enrollment continued to lag behind that of other state schools. The majority of students still majored in education. However, some, like James H. Barrett, who excelled in chemistry, went on to graduate schools such as Ohio State University and into careers other than teaching. Like many students, he also met his wife on campus, Sue Campbell Barrett. One student of this era went into show business after befriending Hollywood star Rock Hudson. Harvey Lee Yeary, aka Lee Majors, became the star of television's *Six Million Dollar Man*. Other students like Dan Webster came from a small Kentucky high school to what he considered an enormous college campus. He took the ROTC curriculum seriously, getting his commission as well as an accounting degree. Roger Green also took the ROTC course but had to work on the maintenance crew to make his way through Eastern. Like many such graduates of the period, they spent tours of duty in Vietnam.[27]

With the building of a model fallout shelter in the Coates basement, the Eastern campus knew full well the extent of the threat of nuclear war at the height of the cold war. In the early sixties everyone on campus suffered along with the nation through the Cuban missile crisis and the assassination of President Kennedy on November 22, 1963. About the latter, Managing Editor Doug Whitlock of the *Progress* lamented, "A man is dead. The nation lives, but hangs its head in grief and shame." To show its sorrow Eastern held special memorial services, and thirteen hundred ROTC cadets marched downtown. However, life went on as only it could in the increasingly tumultuous sixties. A week after the assassination, a capacity crowd of sixty-five hundred cheered Eastern's victory over Louisville at the first game in Alumni Coliseum.[28]

Students could still find time for eating at Bales restaurant, where customers wrote down their own orders, or at Johnny Allman's on the Kentucky River. Nearly every issue of the *Progress* in the early sixties had an ad for Spec's, a local watering hole, as well as ads for several brands of cigarettes until 1963. There were dances and movies on campus, but if students wanted a bit of off-campus adventure they could see *And God Created Woman,* starring Bridget Bardot. If a mock wedding exercise in one professor's social science class was not informative enough, students could view *No Greater Sin* at a local drive-in theater, complete with scenes of an "actual childbirth." Campus life was changing, with increasing discussion of allowing social fraternities and sororities on campus. "Fraternities and Sororities: Should We?" asked a *Progress* editorial. More and more students went south to places like Daytona Beach or Fort Lauderdale for spring break in the early sixties. Some things do change. After many years as the beloved campus mascot, Mozart died in the summer of 1964, but not until he had been immortalized in a painting by a student artist. Music professor Donald Henrickson recalled one time that the lovable pooch slowly climbed a stage and lay down while one of Henrickson's students was giving a recital. When he tried to shoo Mozart from the stage, the audience rebelled, and the concert went on, complete with dog and singer doing what they did best. How could anyone forget such a four-legged campus character?[29]

Martin did not make many administrative changes other than naming Powell his chief adviser and executive dean in the early years. He preferred to allow older faculty and staff to retire. Most were given a final semester's leave with pay as a reward for their long service. Emma Y. Case retired in 1962 after thirty years as dean of women. Dean Moore stayed on into the midsixties as dean of the college. Martin encouraged retired military officers to come back as administrators. When personnel director Shirley Castle influenced one of his fellow retired colonels to come to Eastern as an administrator, it proved to be a mistake. Martin and Castle's friend were "both obstinate," and "neither one would ever admit to being wrong." The latter finally resigned. In contrast, Larry Martin got along well with the president because he could administer food services well and, just as important, turn a profit.[30]

"Teachers were kings in their classrooms," Powell recalled, when he came in the fall of 1960. In Martin's first year the *Progress* editors asked for more involvement by faculty as advisers and mentors in the lives of students. As the school began to grow rapidly in the midsixties, the nature of the faculty changed. With its emphasis on teaching and service rather than research, Eastern remained a haven for instructors without terminal degrees. However, Martin preferred to hire candidates with doctorates, and he usually met with them, which was more of a formality than they thought. Branley Branson's experience was similar to that of almost every teacher when they met Martin for the first time. "I went in there and my knees were knocking," said Branson, a biologist. "He's sitting there and he's gruff and he'd talk awhile and the next thing I knew I was hired." Although they often had differences, Branson admitted, "I liked the old rascal." "He loved to intimidate," alumnus and long-time administrator Larry W. Bailey recalled. Martin "could switch from an absolute fire-breathing dragon to the most gentle person that you've ever known," Bailey explained. "I mean instantly."[31]

Some faculty could not abide Martin's leadership style and left when they got an opportunity. For example, Robert L. Oppelt, who never felt like the president was willing to commit enough resources to the music program, resigned. Martin could be hard-nosed and would dismiss instructors, particularly if they lacked tenure. There could be tragicomic situations. One terminated professor not only went on a downtown shopping spree in which he charged items to the president but also took a shotgun to his Combs Hall office. His officemate, Leon Rottersman, talked the distraught man into leaving. Captured by the state police, the ex-prof agreed not to return to Richmond and later received psychiatric treatment.[32]

Faculty often went beyond just teaching, as did other supporters of students. When James Masterson dropped out of Eastern's industrial arts program, Jess Lewis, his former high school teacher, and department head Ralph Whalin gave him both moral and tuition support to help him complete his college education. Masterson returned the favor by teaching for twenty-eight years in that department. Eastern continued to provide students who had less than stellar high school careers an opportunity to succeed. Sometimes an energetic teacher like Gene Forderhase and his wife, Nancy, could encourage a student like Larry Bailey to stay the course and graduate.[33]

Though Eastern had been open to black students since action by the regents on March 21, 1956, it struggled to gain more than a handful of African Americans well into the sixties. The southernness of Richmond, although the city school system was one of the first in the state to desegregate, was partly responsible for the slow pace. The *Eastern Progress* and a few campus leaders appeared to push for more effort as violence erupted on southern campuses. When riots broke out at the University of Mississippi in 1962, Ben Cartinhour in the *Progress* pleaded, "The decisions of the courts of this land must be obeyed if America is to grow, prosper and remain the symbol of life [and] liberty." During his first year at Eastern, Martin replied to a *Courier-Journal* inquiry that of 3,452 students in 1960–61, he knew of only a dozen black students.[34]

However, a year later Martin could report more progress to WHAS radio and television in Louisville. He insisted that there be no discrimination in residence halls. Further opportunities for blacks at Eastern came in the way they did at most colleges and universities: through sports. Jack Jackson came to campus in the fall of 1961 on an athletic/work-study grant on Coach Don Daly's track team and was joined by three other African Americans from Dayton, Ohio. Martin apparently told the football and basketball coaches that it was time to integrate their teams. It was not long until Jim Parks in the *Progress* declared that "Blacks strengthen athletic teams," asking for integration of other Maroon teams. African American Aaron Marsh immediately made an impact on the Maroons' gridiron in 1964, and Garfield Smith took the basketball court in 1965.[35]

When the Eastern track team went to Nashville in May 1963, apparently Vanderbilt did not know that the Richmond school would be bringing a black athlete. However, "it was enlightening" for all concerned, Jackson found. "They wished me luck without any discrimination. Perhaps, the old traditions of the South will change," he concluded. It was not always so easy for black players. James E. Keller, later to become a Kentucky Supreme Court justice, recalled a time when his only black teammate, George Lee, the first black football player at Eastern, was refused entry into a movie house on a road trip in 1961. "I was never prouder than when the forty of us left that theater," he recalled in an August 2000 graduation speech.[36]

Like many Eastern students, blacks had to work hard to attend college and often overcame seemingly impossible odds. Charley E. Gillispie, who grew up on a Madison County farm, came to Eastern after military service. He wanted to go to a predominantly white college and brought with him a desire to succeed. Using veterans' benefits, he also worked for A&P grocery stores to pay his way through school. "You've got to have an integrated society in order for everything to be equal," he said in a 1987 interview, while working for one of the largest accounting firms in Chicago. And, like Aaron Thompson, another African American who came to Eastern after working for several years, Gillispie believed he had a duty to mentor young blacks. Moreover, Thompson knew what it was like to grow up in a large, poor eastern Kentucky coal camp family; in his own family he had nine siblings.[37]

Many of Eastern's white students shared these same challenges. Linda Preston Scott DeRosier, class of 1968, told of her hardscrabble but rewarding Appalachian life in *Creeker,* an award-winning autobiography. Eastern Kentuckian John W. Smith, who has more than two hundred semester hours at Eastern, started college at Asbury. "But I was in love with a girl going to Eastern," he explained, and so he transferred for his sophomore year. Scholarships helped, but he recalled working for two years, from four to midnight, at a Kroger store and catching only four hours sleep before arising and studying before class. "Eastern has really done a lot for people in my part of the state," Smith maintained in an oral history interview. "I felt that I got a very good education." Like many Eastern graduates, he moved from teacher to principal to superintendent over the course of his career. Another student of the era recalled that though dorm director Jack Adams ran a tight ship, there was always plenty of temptation downtown. However, the ROTC program instilled a bit of discipline in the wayward males, and there were enough difficult teachers and courses to keep most students in line.[38]

If the student body was only slowly becoming integrated, it took even longer for the faculty. In mid-1966 Martin informed the regents that he was trying to find "a qualified person or persons of the Negro Race." Several prospects did not sign contracts. Jim Way, with a master's degree from Eastern, got a call from John Rowlett, who offered him a job in the industrial arts department. In Way's interview the formidable Martin said bluntly, "If you want the job you can have it." Way came in the fall of 1967. Jim and his wife, Anna, who also worked at Eastern, were educated in a rigidly segregated Kentucky. They were among a vanguard of black teachers who helped integrate the state's public schools. "We've been kind of pioneers," according to Jim, who before he came to Eastern was the first black teacher in an all-white school in Cynthiana. Moreover, for a time the Way children were the only black students at Model. When asked about coming to Richmond, Anna said, "I think the Lord sent us here." Kara Stone, a Richmond native, soon joined the social science department as its only African American.[39]

Sports continued as an important part of life at Eastern. In 1964, longtime teachers and coaches Turkey Hughes and Gertrude Hood were honored by having athletic fields named for them. New sports like swimming, the "Electrifying Eels," had great success under Coach Don Combs, the son of

Earle Combs. The turnover of older faculty and staff in the early sixties extended to the coaching staff. Although baseball coach Hughes continued to have much success, winning his eighth OVC crown in 1966, the football program fell on hard times under Presnell, and stress finally wore down basketball coach McBrayer. After 219 victories over a sixteen-year span, including two OVC championships and two NCAA appearances, McBrayer abruptly retired, telling the president that his health was "declining." McBrayer had a great impact on his players, being much beloved despite his gruffness and his reputation as a taskmaster. Roland Wierwille summed up the opinions of many former players: Coach McBrayer "took me from nothing and made me something." Martin soon named former all-American and assistant coach Jim Baechtold to the post.[40]

The Eastern president attended most athletic events and kept his usual close watch over everything. At a 1963 basketball game Martin quieted Eastern students when they began to yell "Give 'em hell," a longtime tradition. Martin was not above scolding the students of other colleges. When Morehead students used unsavory signs at Eastern contests, the Eastern president noted to Doran, "I must comment that, apparently, your students are overly intrigued with indoor plumbing." The Eastern president ran a tight ship financially. When Hughes asked to use autos during a long spring break road trip instead of a "tiresome trip on a school bus," Martin replied with his usual folksiness: "I believe your boys are squealing before you are hurt." Large crowds turned out for contests, particularly against in-state rivals Morehead, Murray, and Western. Alumni Coliseum was usually near capacity, and old Hanger Field often overflowed. In 1963, as a reward for his support, local character Wes Eades was given membership in the E Club and free admission to sports events. For years people marveled at how he could get to away games, often meeting the team bus upon its arrival. However, when he went to the Tangerine Bowl in Florida, he admitted, "I was gone for seven days, and it almost broke me."[41]

Although Presnell's 1962 team had a 6–3 record, his 1963 team fell on hard times at 2–8, and he retired after ten seasons as head coach. He replaced Turkey Hughes as athletic director and served in that capacity for another eight years. Martin appointed Roy Kidd, a former Eastern all-American and current assistant coach, as head football coach. Kidd began an unprecedented career by demanding more of his players than had Presnell. Quarterback Larry Marmie recalled that Kidd moved players out of the "bowels of the old football stadium," where partying sometimes took place, and into a dorm. For miscreant players there was the "dawn patrol," running at daylight for a team infraction, even for all-American end Buddy Pfaadt. Kidd's teams suffered through some tough times, but they improved over the years. He pushed to get more black players. In 1967, quarterback Jim Guice and black receivers Aaron Marsh and John Tazel led the team to a winning OVC season and a bowl bid. With ABC televising the game, Eastern defeated Ball State, 27–13, in the Grantland Rice Bowl on December 9. Middle guard Teddy Taylor, who ran back a fumble for a touchdown, and a stingy defense controlled a much larger Ball State offensive line.[42]

Baechtold had some success early in his career as head basketball coach. After winning the 1964–65 OVC title with a 13–1 record, with Lee Lemos starring, the Maroons lost in the first round of the NCAA to DePaul. In 1966 Eddie Bodkin set an all-time Eastern scoring record. By this time the name "Maroons" had been completely supplanted by "Colonels." Eastern basketball integrated under Baechtold, with Garfield Smith, Bobby Washington, and Toke Coleman leading the way. After only five years as head coach, Baechtold resigned in May 1967, citing the "pressure" of the game. "I made a decision a year ago that I could not continue to coach for another 20 years," the thirty-nine-year-old said, "because of the way a coach has to live." Martin soon appointed alumnus Guy Strong as head coach.[43]

In the early sixties Kentucky higher education was rife with competitiveness of both a political and a practical nature. Although the Council on Public Higher Education (the word "Public" would be dropped from the title in 1977) had gained more control over the state system, from its inception in 1934 strong presidents like Martin at Eastern, Doran at Morehead, and Kelly Thompson at Western scrapped among themselves. Cooperating only when the largest competitor, the University of Kentucky, threatened to grab too big a share of the state's coffers, they dominated in the early sixties. When faced with a threat of a "superboard" proposed by the Commission on the Study of Higher Education in Kentucky in 1961, the state colleges bristled at such domination. They worked their friends and constituencies to thwart such a plan. And there was always concern about what would become of Kentucky State College, at one time the only school for African Americans, now that integration had been mandated.[44]

Meanwhile, UK, none too quietly, expanded its small community college system. President John W. Oswald of UK, coming from the California system of higher education, wanted to expand and rationalize Kentucky into a similar pattern. He ran headlong into the adamant opposition of Martin and Doran. Longtime Kentucky educator Lyman Ginger found Oswald and Martin "poles apart in understanding Kentucky," and "both were aggressive." Kentucky's newspapers were not silent. Barry Bingham Sr.'s *Courier-Journal* and E. J. Paxton's *Paducah Sun-Democrat* usually took the side of a larger, expansive University of Kentucky. In the early sixties the biggest bone of contention became UK's expanding community college system. Several conferences did not settle the issue, with Martin and Doran doggedly denying Oswald and his successor, Otis Singletary, domination of the state. Even mild-mannered President Ralph Woods at Murray urged the need for a united front to get proposed graduate programs accepted by the council.[45]

For all the political contention and education infighting, there were other major changes taking place at Eastern in the midsixties, particularly in academics. True to his "Vision of Greatness" inaugural address, Martin looked for ways for Eastern to catch the crest of vocational changes for schools of its type: older, predominantly teachers colleges. Moreover, Eastern was quickly moving toward university status, a battle that would also take all the political cunning of an old master like Martin. "We developed programs that young people wanted and needed," Martin said.[46]

After hearing about the shortage of nurses, Martin gave John Rowlett the task of finding a way for Eastern to get into the field. Although Rowlett had "many doors slammed in his face" while working with state officials, he persevered. One difficulty was finding hospitals for clinical training of students. Being shut out of Lexington hospitals by UK and having three private hospitals in Richmond, Rowlett worked out deals with Frankfort, Paris, and Winchester health facilities. The program began with an associate degree class of twenty-five students in the fall of 1965. Charlotte Denny came in 1967 to oversee the burgeoning nursing program move toward a baccalaureate degree. More than once the UK medical school tried to either stop or control the Eastern program. And there was always the problem of negotiating the minefield that the Council on Public Higher Education posed. The program grew and, after being housed in several locations, moved into a freestanding allied health and nursing building named for Rowlett.[47]

"Capable of very rapid planning," according to Rowlett, Martin also charged him with getting a law enforcement program under way after learning that UK did not appear to be interested. Rowlett met with state police officials like Ted Bassett and others to work out the details. With few college-level law enforcement programs available in the region, except for Michigan State University and Florida State University, the field seemed wide open. Robert W. Posey, with state police experience, taught the first class, beginning in January 1966. Again, Martin's foresight and ability to latch on to a trend meant a new vocationally oriented program for Eastern. Within months, Eastern received its first federal grant from the U.S. Department of Justice. Initiation of the Traffic Safety Institute in the fall of 1966 continued a trend of expansion in the new area. Eastern also became one of the first schools to receive federal aid to prepare college teachers of law enforcement.[48]

By the midsixties, Eastern had grown not only in student and faculty numbers but in expanded programs as well. With talk of university status in the wind, Eastern reorganized into schools in 1965 as enrollment that fall neared seven thousand. Separation into arts and sciences, business, education, technology, and Central University, a centralized advising and general education program, represented a radical change from the old single-college system. This new atmosphere was supercharged with rivalry and conflict. Fred Ogden, dean of arts and sciences, and Clyde Lewis, dean of Central University College, clashed from the beginning over the administration of general education, the two-year program for freshmen and sophomores, and the courses from their curricula that would fit the new requirements.[49]

All this realignment would go for naught if the CPHE and the Kentucky legislature did not approve the state colleges rising to university status. After CPHE approval, Martin said it was only recognizing that Eastern had already become "a large multi-purpose university." When the 1966 General Assembly met, the issue hit the front burner. Martin, Morehead's Doran, and Western's Kelly Thompson pulled out all the stops in getting their allies to work on state legislators. Governor Ned Breathitt, a UK graduate, supported the effort, but the university's bloc across the state did not. Oswald opposed House Bill 238, arguing that it would dissipate state resources and diminish the university's programs. As part of the bill, approved by the CPHE, state colleges would also be allowed to develop master's programs in disciplines other than education, a monopoly that UK had enjoyed for many years. University of Kentucky graduate dean A. D. Kirwan complained that these programs would be inferior to his school's and that his programs were not at the level they needed to be. Martin peevishly replied, "I'm right distressed they've had so little success with their graduate program at UK that classes are not full."[50]

After sailing through the Kentucky House of Representatives 83–0, the measure, demonstrating a bit of UK resistance, passed the Senate 32–5. In a well-distributed picture of the occasion, Martin hovered over the right shoulder of Breathitt, while a glum Oswald stood on the periphery, as the governor signed the bill into law on February 26, 1966. Eastern's regents approved the measure in early March. The five schools at the renamed Eastern Kentucky University could now be called colleges. Martin named Thomas F. Stovall as the school's first vice president for academic affairs and dean of the faculties. Just as important, the new law also changed the nature of the CPHE into a lay council with nine voting members, appointed by the governor. University presidents remained on the council as advisers and nonvoting members. And from now, on budgets had to go directly through the council.[51]

The 1966 law making Eastern a university and changing the composition of the CPHE did nothing to end the competitive nature of Kentucky higher education. While the UK community college system continued to be a divisive issue, the fiscal woes of the University of Louisville (UL) and a campaign for a new university in northern Kentucky pushed the tensions to new heights. Martin was outspoken against bringing UL into the state system. Neither did he believe that a new state college or university in northern Kentucky would be cost-effective. When Republican governor Louie B. Nunn (1967–71) pushed for both during his term, all the state universities stood against him. EKU alumnus John P. DeMarcus, as an aide to Nunn and then assistant to the president of what became Northern Kentucky University in 1976, worked tirelessly to mold UK's old community college in Covington into a four-year school. Although he was now a competitor with Martin and his alma mater, DeMarcus found Martin to be "very helpful," if for no other reason than they were now both allies against UK. With the bleak economy of the late sixties, everyone, including Singletary at UK, knew that this was only dividing the education pie ever more thinly.[52]

Although Martin preferred to work with political allies like Governors Combs and Breathitt, he also adapted to later chief executives. After the 1967 election of Nunn, whom he had opposed, Martin told a friend how he approached the new governor soon after the inauguration. "Hell, I put my hat in my hand and walked in and said 'here I am.'" Nunn and Martin developed a strong working relationship, particularly as student unrest developed in the late sixties. In 1971, faced with a difficult situation, having supported Combs in his losing race in the primary against Wendell Ford, Martin likewise immediately began establishing a working relationship with the new governor.[53]

In the sixties Eastern demonstrated many signs of becoming not only a university but a mature one. Martin, ever looking for a way to advance Eastern's position and image, pushed for initiatives that would have been impossible during the O'Donnell years. Soon after coming to Eastern, he began a process of forming a foundation, separate from the school but supporting its functions, including administration of a loan fund. Martin's idea, which sounded grandiose to some, included building a faculty club and golf course, something that no other school had at the time. After years of negotiations, the entrepreneur W. Arnold Hanger gave Eastern his mansion, Arlington, and a few acres. The EKU Foundation agreed to pay nearly $500,000 for an additional 165 acres. Eastern paid for construction of the first nine holes, at a time when many capital programs were in progress on the campus. Further construction, including nine more golf holes, a swimming pool, and tennis courts, along with other improvements led to one of the finest facilities of its kind in the state.[54]

Martin knew the importance of ceremony and concrete. Just as important was something that can only be described as "monumentalism," an attempt to construct and incise in stone, marble, bronze, and concrete the marks of a great school. From the installation of Enid Yandell's Daniel Boone bronze in 1967 to the Felix de Weldon Centennial Statue (1974), symbolizing America's space exploration, to another de Weldon equestrian creation for the new law enforcement complex in the midseventies, Eastern's statuary befitted a growing and well-established institution. Each statue was dedicated with Martin's usual attention to detail and ceremonialism. Students soon began rubbing Boone's left toe for good luck on the way to an exam. To honor one hundred years of education on the campus, beginning with Central University, Eastern celebrated in 1974 with a wide range of activities, including numerous arts events, a pageant, and the development of a centennial medallion. The Centennial Statue, dubbed "The Streak" by students and not a few faculty because of its scanty covering and the current streaking craze, became the scene of student vandalism on a few occasions. Martin defended the statue, paid for with $75,000 from the Alumni Association, as a worthwhile project against its critics.[55]

Eastern could not help but be changed by new student and faculty attitudes in the sixties and seventies, ones that would oftentimes clash with the views of Robert R. Martin. Frivolity like "mooning" might hit the campus, but there were more important issues at stake for everyone in the Eastern community. Pressures for social fraternities and sororities built in the early sixties. When other state schools added them, Eastern students pushed hard. After a sixteen-month study by the faculty, which was approved by a two-thirds majority, the Board of Regents accepted fraternities and sororities just as Eastern was becoming a university in 1966. Faculty and study committee member Smith Park said becoming a university had a lot to do with Eastern's acceptance of these organizations. Editorials in the *Progress* as well as statements by regents and faculty recognized that Eastern was entering a new era. From now on there would be social organizations beyond anything imagined by its founders. Was this a sign of the maturing of Eastern as a university? Many questioned whether it would be good for the school, including regent Russell Todd, who said it "would create differences in social standing." By early 1967, seven fraternities had organized and embarked on Eastern's first Rush Week, with the Inter-Fraternity Council overseeing the organizations. Sororities developed at a somewhat slower pace. While a fraternity housing area was considered too expensive by the regents, fraternities were allowed to rent houses where only a few students could live. This became a source of fierce debate in Richmond in the 1970s, as frat houses on Main Street led to friction with the city government.[56]

For all the changes coming in the midsixties, many students remained grounded in the eleven religious organizations on campus. The Baptist Student Union, the Newman Center, Wesley Foundation, Inter-Varsity Christian Fellowship, and others offered Eastern students a spiritual foundation. The Baptists, Catholics, and Methodists built new centers on the edge of the campus. Moreover, Century Club of the Alumni Association paid for construction of the Chapel of Meditation, built on the site of the old football field. George Nordgulen, campus chaplain, oversaw the chapel. *The Messiah* and the Hanging of the Greens continued as important Christmastime campus events. Older campus honoraries like Collegiate Pentacle, Iota Lambda Sigma, Omicron Kappa Alpha, Scabbard and Blade, CWENS, and Phi Alpha Theta, among others, continued to serve a vital function. Organizations such as Circle K, Kappa Delta Tau, and the YWCA taught service to the community. While the old regional and county clubs had long since disappeared, Eastern students still had great attachment to home. On most weekends the campus demonstrated all the signs of the "suitcase" college of old.[57]

However, the greatest challenges to Eastern traditions came with student unrest of the sixties as the academic world came under great stress. As the Vietnam War intensified and American casualties mounted in Southeast Asia, the draft and the ROTC program became a focal point of unrest, as they did on most college campuses. Moreover, when the Supreme Court ruled in 1967 that students had the same due process rights as adults, paternalism of the Martin variety and in loco parentis came under attack. In particular, under-graduate women asked for more liberal hours, noting that the men had no such restrictions, and faculty, like students, asked for more self-government. Martin, who tended to dig in his heels on matters of authority, called the "sorry sixties" an unfortunate decade.[58]

Another campus institution survived the turmoil of the Martin years. Eastern's ROTC, which began in the midthirties, became an important ad-junct to the educational program while offering students an opportunity to earn a military commission. From the beginning of his presidency, Martin pressed to make it a premier part of the Eastern community. When it ap-peared that the program might falter, by not producing enough graduates to continue in the U.S. Army's good graces, he had the program made manda-tory. "It teaches our young men—freshmen and sophomores—a greater ap-preciation of citizenship, and its many, many obligations," Martin told an army general.[59]

Increasingly, the college community became aware of the war in Vietnam. By late 1965 the issues were firmly implanted. Senator John Sherman Cooper framed the nation's and Eastern's predicament aptly in a campus address. "The war in Vietnam is in many ways more difficult than any the United States has ever faced," he said. While he did not approve of withdrawal, neither did he want to extend the war. At a time when antiwar demonstrations were just beginning on other American college campuses, Eastern students held a blood drive for the military, and the *Progress* editorialized in support of American troops. By late 1965 the campus paper told of more than a dozen Eastern graduates serving in Vietnam. Several had already been injured, including Captain Henry W. Giles, the son of deceased art professor Frederick P. Giles. Announcement of the wounding of First Lieutenant John B. Hanlon, a 1964 ROTC alumnus, who received the Silver Star for leading his troops to safety while "partially paralyzed," brought the war closer to home. Streets on the campus would later be named in honor of Hanlon and also for Paul Edwin VanHoose, who lost his life in Vietnam. In 1970 the new safety and security building was dedicated in honor of William Jackson Brewer Jr., who was killed in Cambodia. Veterans like Tony Cox and Mike Embry began streaming back into schools such as Eastern as the war ended.[60]

Eastern was not immune from the turmoil swirling around American campuses. Martin met occasionally with students, answering their questions about current issues, in what were called "gripe sessions" by the *Progress*. With the election of Steve Wilborn as student body president in 1967, a candidate for the KEG, or "Keep Eastern Growing," party, things heated up. Just as Martin wanted to keep things as they had always been, Wilborn determined to change the campus, with the Student Government Association (SGA) having a say in campus policies. In many ways, Vice President Stovall, and particularly Powell, were buffers between the administration and students. Owing to the legislation creating the state universities, a student, the president of the student body if a Kentucky resident, and a faculty member, now joined the Board of Regents as nonvoting members. The first of these new members were Steve Wilborn and Ralph Whalin.[61]

When the regents approved a new Student Association and Student Council constitution, Wilborn asked for further changes. Martin and Wilborn also clashed when the latter asked the regents to pass a fee of one dollar per student to be at the disposal of the student government. Martin continued to offer dialogue but increasingly balked when any substantive change came before him. Everybody seemed to be choosing sides. Craig Ammerman, editor of the *Progress,* even had to defend his paper as not being a rubber stamp for the administration. Each week during the 1967–68 school year, the student paper featured editorials, stories, and letters about the big issues of student government, Vietnam and the ROTC program, and women's hours. "ROTC: Mandatory or Voluntary?" asked one such editorial. Added to the divisive mixture on campus was a movement, eventually successful, to ban the Confederate flag and the singing of "Dixie" at athletic events.[62]

With Wilborn reelected to another term as student president, the 1968–69 school year turned out to be just as contentious. In a faculty address, Martin pledged to "uphold rights" but also warned that "the University will not be run by threats and will not respond to ultimatums." Moreover, the president said, in his inimitable style, that Eastern would "not become a haven for hippies, yippies, beatniks, and others of the unwashed." The gauntlet was thrown down. With a report from the Powell committee studying student affairs pending, the campus was tense. Added to the campus turmoil, "an Eastern black militant" maintained that there would be more riots like that at Watts in Los Angeles, "maybe at Eastern." Meanwhile, Martin and Wilborn sparred over control of student funds at a regents' meeting.[63]

If it looked like America was imploding with the assassinations of Robert Kennedy and Martin Luther King Jr. and the tumultuous presidential election of 1968, it was also a critical, divisive time at Eastern. While Eastern continued to grow in students and with more capital construction projects under way in the 1968–69 school year than ever before, old issues finally came to a head. The campus debated the Powell report on student affairs. Mandatory ROTC continued to be a center of contention, particularly during parades. One time word leaked out that protesters were going to disrupt a review of ROTC troops by Martin. "We knew what their plan was," recalled longtime dean of students, and later vice president Tom Myers. Members of the Veterans Club sat beside several of the suspected demonstrators, keeping them from leaving their seats. After a long study, critics received at least one concession when the ROTC program was reduced to a one-year required program, like that at Ohio State University, then made optional. Through all this turmoil, Eastern's ROTC remained a large program, usually second only to Texas A&M. One ROTC alumnus, who retired as a colonel, found that a person had to be careful if he joined in what he thought was an impromptu panty raid but was in fact an antiwar demonstration. One evening he joined in a group of young men locked arm in arm but after a short while was told its mission. "I didn't think Col. Smith [the ROTC commander] would like that," he said with a laugh, so "I dropped out."[64]

In what was undoubtedly the most tempestuous event in Eastern's history, Wilborn distributed university-duplicated copies of "The Student as Nigger," written by a California professor, in mid-February 1969. "Its flamboyant style and frequent obscenities have provoked the concern of a number of educational officials," wrote *Courier-Journal* reporter Richard Wilson. Martin reacted quickly and ordered Wilborn to return all copies. The student president complied; only about five hundred out of three thousand had been distributed. Martin maintained the worst parts of the pamphlet were the "unspeakable obscenities." In a heated meeting on March 19, Martin and the regents confronted Wilborn, who said he had not intended to cause a "riot but wanted the faculty and others to start thinking." The regents then voted unanimously to censure Wilborn. Reactions came from far and wide. Eastern's chapter of the AAUP urged restraint on both sides while upholding the right of the student leader to voice his complaints. *Progress* editor Craig Ammerman also urged peace and dialogue while claiming that the Student Council was not properly leading students. The *Courier-Journal* and *Herald Leader,* as expected, editorialized against the regents' actions, as did the state AAUP, while the *Lexington Leader,* a Republican organ, voiced its approval. A *Progress* cartoon of the time perhaps caught Martin's dilemma best. "Excedrin Headache #2001," the caption said, capitalizing on a popular advertisement for a pain reliever, as issues swirled about a distraught president with an ice pack on his head. Wilborn was not kicked out of school, graduating in the class of 1969; both he and Martin allowed the impasse to lessen in intensity. Some years later Wilborn admitted that he and Martin clashed because of a "lack of political savvy" on his own part and the president's inability to see "student involvement and student responsibility" in a positive way. Ironically, by then they were serving together in the Kentucky state senate.[65]

Other issues of the time were just as divisive. Dean of Women Mary K. Engels met with students in the Ravine about liberalizing women's hours. The Powell Report and ROTC recommendations became finalized by action of the administration and the regents. Though freshmen girls still had tight restrictions, those for upper-class women were liberalized, though not as much as desired by critics. Attorney General John B. Breckinridge backed up the administration in cases involving student disciplinary action, including the right to censure Wilborn and to regulate women's hours. If Eastern appeared to be in the backwater of student upheaval in America, it should be pointed out that at the conclusion of the 1968–69 school year, Robert Warfield, an African American and vice president of the Student Government Association, became the student representative on the Board of Regents. And editor Ammerman, in "Inside Scoop on Robert Martin," commended him because "he is unafraid to stand for what he believes." "It's about time to give a little credit where it's long overdue," he concluded.[66]

The fall semester of 1969 did not bring peace to the Eastern community. Just as Eastern was celebrating its inaugural win at the new Hanger Field, 29–10 over Austin Peay, plans were under way for a Vietnam War moratorium. On October 15 an estimated eight hundred students and others attended a meeting in the Ravine, where the names of the dead were read. On Veterans Day, November 11, a large crowd met at the Madison County courthouse to honor the war dead, and on ROTC Day, Eastern's twenty-five-hundred-man brigade took part in another war memorial ceremony.[67]

The conclusion of the decade that Martin called "the sorry sixties" did not appreciably change campus life in the short run. While some students were restive for more change, the majority went about the tasks of getting a degree with as little disruption as possible. Sports and clubs took up much of a student's out-of-class time. Some gains had been made for black students, with nearly 150 now attending each semester. The shootings of students at Kent State University in the spring of 1970 touched off disturbances at nearby University of Kentucky, including the torching of the ROTC building. Watching the fire while sitting in Governor Nunn's automobile, UK trustee Happy Chandler allegedly remarked, "You don't have to worry about this happening at Eastern." Although no such violence took place at Eastern, Martin got the regents to grant him the power to declare "a state of emergency" in case similar developments hit the Richmond campus. "Gutless wonders" among American college and university presidents, Martin contended, allowed the disruptions. However, he also admitted to a Lexington Kiwanis Club meeting in August 1970 that some reform of student government had been long overdue. Signs of latent conservatism remained on the campus. When the faculty suggested that Harry Caudill, the author of *Night Comes to the Cumberlands* and other books about Appalachia, be given an honorary degree, the Board of Regents refused because of the controversial nature of his writings.[68]

Change came for the faculty in the Martin years. As already noted, a plethora of new degree programs added to the diversity of the campus as never before. Some older faculty shifted to other programs. Faculty without a terminal degree, normally a doctorate, could remain at Eastern as long as they received adequate ratings for teaching. Because Eastern was a non-research-oriented college and then university, teaching and service were always more highly prized than research and publication during the Martin years. At the suggestion of a SACS study, Eastern added the Faculty Senate in 1966–67, the first year of university status. With the president as head of the senate because he was chairman of the faculty and the growing number of vice presidents and deans as ex officio members, the administration easily controlled this body. In the sixties Eastern's administrative hierarchy became more complex, with Powell being appointed vice president for administration; Neal Donaldson, vice president for business affairs and treasurer; Tom Myers, vice president for student affairs; and Don Feltner, vice president for public affairs. John Rowlett replaced Thomas Stovall as Eastern's chief academic officer, vice president for academic affairs and research, in 1972. Like the more inclusive student government, the birth of the Faculty Senate was a halting step toward a more democratized university community. Significantly, the senate began to review most all the major issues and studies on campus.[69]

While a fifteen-hour load had been the norm for many years at Eastern, the faculty finally got it reduced to twelve. Medical insurance was added in 1965, a plan that encouraged young faculty with children to stay. Promotion and tenure measures became ever more codified, with the regents in 1970 confirming the standard five-year probationary period among American colleges and universities. In 1970 Eastern joined a modern trend, ending the first semester before Christmas break, while adopting an alternating Friday schedule, which was not standard on American campuses. Although few teachers published books, Eastern, along with other Kentucky colleges and universities and two historical societies, formed the University Press of Kentucky. Some faculty members, like Dale Patrick in industrial education and Lloyd Graybar in history, published works of national importance. Martin encouraged an influx of new ideas as long as these were not subversive to his "vision" for Eastern. He brought in Florence B. Stratemeyer, a Teachers College, Columbia University, retiree; Thomas D. Clark, Kentucky's premier historian; and Jesse Stuart, among others, for short-term teaching assignments. While moderate African American leader Whitney Young Jr. was welcomed to campus for a speech, Martin nixed appearances of radicals like H. "Rap" Brown. Neither did the president grant freedom for the SGA to bring in outside speakers without administration approval.[70]

There was method to Martin's sometimes harsh stance against what he viewed as radicalism. He was making points with parents and others of "his conservative constituency," according to the *Courier-Journal*'s Dick Wilson. "Hurray for you!" wrote one woman after one of his strong pronouncements against campus unrest.[71]

The beginning of the 1970s brought more change at Eastern, though at a slower pace than during the dynamic 1960s. Construction on campus began to slow as the new dormitories filled. The dedication of the Wallace, Powell, and Jane Campbell structures in 1970 and the Rowlett Building in 1976 represented the high-water mark of capital construction. With rising interest rates it became nearly impossible to build new dorms. Nevertheless, Eastern annually had the largest on-campus dormitory population in the state. There was always the race to keep ahead of the other state schools. Martin could not have been happy when, in 1973, Western's full-time equivalency (FTE) exceeded that of Eastern, 10,301 to 9,734. Showing his usual financial prowess, Martin never missed an opportunity to consolidate debt and lower interest rates. Occasional state budget shortfalls hampered Martin in completing his "vision." A small minority of students continued to push for change. In August 1970 the regents approved the new constitution of the Student Government Association, which included a Student Court. Student regent Bob Babbage, grandson of Governor Keen Johnson, a former regent, moved its adoption.[72]

The furor touched off by the Kent State killings did not end quickly. Presidents of the SGA as well as the editors of the *Eastern Progress* continued to wrestle with the issues of war and student participation in Eastern's governance. As a young faculty member, I once saw a male student tugging a toy car on a string across campus as a sarcastic protest against his continued dependency on his parents and the adults at Eastern. Abolition of women's residence hall hours remained a bone of contention. At one regents meeting in 1972, at the instigation of SGA president Charles I. Kelhoffer and student regent Guy Hatfield, a few dozen students staged a peaceful "sit-in, stand-in, or a something-in on the main floor of the Administration Building," reported the *Progress*. Editor in chief Mike Park of the campus paper humorously scolded some students for misspelling words on their placards. He doubted "whether a couple of them had been to grammar school."[73]

When UK law professor Robert Sedler became involved as a spokesman for the Kentucky American Civil Liberties Union (ACLU), filing a lawsuit on behalf of some EKU coeds who wanted curfews eliminated and a fired teacher reinstated, Martin struck back. He declared that perhaps the UK professor was neglecting his teaching duties. President Otis Singletary of UK defended his instructor as being within his rights. The *Courier-Journal* took its usual anti-Martin bent, decrying his "depressing influence" on his own faculty. Martin shot back that, while only Eastern had been singled out by Sedler and the ACLU for having regulations over women's hours, all state universities had something of the same type, especially for freshmen. He even considered calling in his old political cohort Bert Combs to defend Eastern and others in a class action suit. Regent Henry L. Stratton boldly told Martin, with some humor as well, "Anyone who is denounced on the editorial page of the *Courier-Journal* cannot be all bad." Another constituent also supported Martin against Sedler's "meddling." Under Dean Emma Case's stringent dress code in 1960, coeds wore raincoats over shorts and slacks because they feared being campused if they ventured on campus in such clothing and were not engaged in physical education activities. By the end of Martin's first decade as president, not only had clothing restrictions changed but hours had been liberalized into a "self-regulated" system. However, during open houses "in rooms where guests are living," the code explained, "the doors must be kept open." Appointed dean of women in 1973, Jeanette Crockett faced a world that was nothing like that of Emma Case when she became dean. It should be remembered that none of the lawsuits against Eastern withstood judicial tests, with one case going to the U.S. Supreme Court.[74]

If Martin appeared hypervigilant in the day-to-day administration of a growing and often tumultuous university, he also participated in numerous off-campus organizations and causes. Always interested in history, he helped get a replica of Fort Boonesborough constructed, served as president of the Kentucky Historical Society, and also was one of the founders of the Kentucky Oral History Commission. The organization of Kentucky Educational Television, according to O. Leonard Press, its first executive director, was due in large part to Martin's "invaluable" service as a founding board member. Press observed that the Eastern president had "one of the sharpest, fastest minds I have ever met." After long years of service the American Association of State Colleges and Universities elected him president in 1971. Martin traveled a good bit. Among other honors he received a Danforth Foundation Grant to travel abroad.[75]

Friend and foe alike wondered how Martin did so much, particularly for a man so glaringly overweight. "I love homemade candy," he told one gift giver, "but the Lord knows I should not eat it." It was not unusual for detractors, behind his back, to call the Eastern president "hog jaws" or similar epithets. An anonymous alumnus once warned him to lose "about 150 pounds at once. . . . [I] don't know how you have escaped a heart attack this long." Other health problems seemed to only slow him a bit.[76]

In the seventies SGA presidents often locked horns with the intransigent president. Student regent Steven W. Slade also challenged Martin at meetings. Other issues, such as representation on the Student Senate, often arose. As in the past, editors of the *Progress* often disagreed with student leadership on campus. Jack Frost of the student paper appeared more pro-Martin and took Greeks to task for not doing enough worthwhile projects. When the February 22, 1973, issue of the *Eastern Progress* did not appear, conspiracy theorists claimed that it was only another example of Martin's dictation. While the president claimed "missed deadlines, poor style and 'shoddy research'" for an editorial as the reasons, his detractors saw this as censorship, pure and simple. The Faculty Senate even called an emergency meeting. After Martin explained his views at a Student Senate meeting, editor Bob Babbage defended his paper and claimed that the *Progress* would "never become a milktoast, weak publication." Ron Wolfe, *Progress* adviser at the time, later recalled that Martin often disagreed with the paper's content, but "he did, however, grudgingly let them have a pretty free rein on opinions." As proof of his leniency, one only has to see hilarious *Progress* cartoons of a naked Martin streaking across campus or preparing to throw a bomb at the Student Senate. However, he was not averse to calling in an editor or telephoning *Courier* reporter Dick Wilson if he did not agree with their opinions.[77]

New issues confronted the university in the early seventies. Self-studies as part of SACS and National Council for Accreditation of Teacher Education (NCATE) reaccreditation added to the crisis of a maturing campus. Both organizations suggested some "reorganization." Creation of Special Programs, a new College of Allied Health and Nursing, and a study of graduate education were among changes made. General education continued to be a sore point between Central University and the College of Arts and Sciences, and a new study brought out many of the old issues. The implementation of Title IX, granting women equity in athletics, brought change by increasing grants-in-aid to women, while decreasing those to male athletes. Moreover, the budget, to which students contributed less than 20 percent of their total college expenses, continued to be a problem. A continuing energy crisis drove up campus expenses. After the Student Senate voted to have a Robert R. Martin Day, the regents moved to make it a celebration of the president's years at Eastern as well as reelecting Martin to a four-year term.[78]

Some things remain the same on a college campus, there never being enough money to fix everything. The innovative Begley Building required extensive repairs from the time the state accepted it. When history department chairman George Robinson told the administration of the woes of the old University Building, including an uncontrollable heating system, leaks, and dangerous windows, he failed to mention the annual influx of wasps on the upper floors and crickets in the basement that human residents, myself included, often observed. "These lines seem endless," said one student about fall enrollment, held in the oppressive heat of a non-air-conditioned auxiliary gym of Alumni Coliseum in late August. However, sometimes money could be found for a worthy cause. Surplus from bonds, for example, helped build an indoor tennis center named for Greg Adams, the son of Jack and Barbara Adams, who was paralyzed in a high school football accident. Martin praised the young man for "the courageous fight he has made for his life."[79]

If the Vietnam War, student government, and women's hours continued as issues of the early seventies, there was always time for a bit of frivolity. Three straight nights of streaking turned out more than a thousand students in mid-March 1974. Taking pictures of the unclad males led to the expulsion of some students, a policy the administration eventually softened to probation for others. A few weeks later, on April 3, 1974, a tornado killed eight people in the county and brought the university to a standstill when electricity failed for several days. Many students and faculty helped the community in a massive cleanup that lasted for days. While Eastern students often went home on weekends, by the Martin years Thursday nights at downtown bars was already a well-established tradition for some students.[80]

If there was sometimes counterproductive student unrest in the sixties and seventies, there were also signs of positive change at the Eastern campus for African Americans and women. When Oscar White retired in 1975, the elderly black custodian lamented that integration came too late for him. Whereas he had to drop out of school in the fourth grade, an increasing number of young African American Kentuckians took advantage of desegregation and educational opportunity. Delma Francis, who in 1974–75 became the first black editor of the *Progress* in its fifty-three-year history, went on to work for the *Minneapolis Star Tribune*. Eric Abercrumbie, B.A. 1970, M.A. 1971, went on to direct diversity programs at the University of Cincinnati and established the Black Man Think Tank. While a student he helped found the University Ensemble, an African American choir at Eastern. Another sign of positive change occurred when Angie Taylor became the first female student regent in 1975.[81]

President Robert R. Martin not only weathered the storms of student revolt in the sixties and seventies but also protected his turf with gusto. Never liking the intrusion of a private bookstore in Richmond, Martin fought Wallace G. Wilkinson's enterprise on Second Street at every turn. When the Kentucky Government Council, the *Courier-Journal,* and others pushed for a stronger CPHE with tighter controls over higher education, Martin stayed the course. Although he acquiesced in admission of the University of Louisville and a new college in northern Kentucky into the state system, he fought any attempt to create a "super board." When one such feeble effort came before the General Assembly in 1970, Martin, Doran, and Sparks viewed the defeat from the senate gallery in a famous *Courier-Journal* picture. Governor at the time, the acerbic Nunn recalled he telephoned Martin, saying that the three-some looked like "Winkin,' Blinkin,' and Nod," which really should be attributed to Lieutenant Governor Julian Carroll, who presided over the vote. Martin "just sort of grunted," Nunn said. Sometimes the Eastern president let Morehead's Doran be the point man in trying to wedge the community colleges from UK, a "divorce" both could agree on, if nothing else.[82]

Anxious to build a new law enforcement complex, Martin came into conflict with a renewed attack on Eastern's primacy in that field. The 1971 Crane report, under which UK and UL would predominate in law enforcement, emerged and met the full fury of Martin. In his classic style Martin retorted, "That dog won't hunt." Coming just as a new state requirement specified that all major projects be approved by the CPHE, timing was important. In a whirlwind effort Martin and Rowlett pushed for public support, including getting the *Lexington Herald-Leader* to come on board. With Ed Prichard on Eastern's side, the CPHE unanimously approved construction, and Governor Wendell Ford helped break ground on October 16, 1972. Even as severe a critic as Bob Schulman of WHAS-TV, a Bingham property, found that "Martin and Eastern truly deserved the go-ahead." As usual, the hard effort to get federal assistance paid off, as the bulk of construction money for the $7 million project came from federal grants. Dedicated on August 7, 1975, the complex would soon be called the Robert R. Martin Law Enforcement, Fire Science, and Traffic Safety Center. Another de Weldon statue, this time a mounted policeman, became further evidence of Martin's dedication to a monumental style.[83]

By becoming a leader in vocational and technical training, Eastern drew the notice of the nation. An article in the *Chronicle of Higher Education* in 1975 praised the effort, one in which more than 30 percent of Eastern students were engaged. With colleges of law enforcement and nursing and allied health continually growing, there was envy on the part of some of the older arts and sciences faculty. However, the support courses and general education curricula provided by arts and sciences for the new vocational degrees also added to its own growth and student loads for faculty.[84]

Athletics at Eastern in the late sixties and early seventies proved successful within the context of a limited program. Martin kept a close watch over it all. Never having the money or fan support for challenging the bigger schools, the Colonels nonetheless fielded representative teams in all sports. More important, expanding women's sports to include basketball, tennis, volleyball, gymnastics, hockey, and track and field began compliance with Title IX. The Becky Boone Relays, guided by Coach Dorothy Harkins, soon became one of the largest women's track and field events in the region. Grant Colehour and Ken Silvious were all-American cross-country stars in the late sixties. Wrestling, gymnastics, and baseball turned out successful teams year in and year out. Debbie Battle was the first female on the always successful swimming team, competing in diving for Coach Dan Lichty. "I am not a women's liberationist," she said. "I just love diving."[85]

After several successful basketball seasons, including one OVC championship, Guy Strong moved on to Oklahoma State University. His replacement, Bob Mulcahy, also an Eastern alumnus, stayed only three years before being replaced by assistant coach Ed Byhre. In many ways the basketball program fell on hard times, particularly with so many changes in coaches. Victories over archrival in-state OVC teams came at a premium.[86]

In contrast, football flourished. After victory in the Grantland Rice Bowl, head football coach Roy Kidd took full advantage of the new Hanger Field, which opened in 1969. Winning over Morehead usually brought an extra day off at Thanksgiving, compliments of Martin. Wally Chambers, who anchored the defensive line in the early seventies, became the first OVC player to be drafted in the first round of the National Football League draft. He went on to a great career with the Chicago Bears before being struck down early with arthritis. In 1974 the Colonels won the OVC for the first time since 1968, with all-American tailback Everett "Poo-Loo" Talbert setting a rushing record of 1,478 yards.[87]

Speculation about Martin's retirement during his sixteenth year as president coincided with faculty regent Morris Taylor and a minority of faculty aggressively pushing for more involvement in university governance. At the April 3, 1976, regents meeting, Martin, to the surprise of many, abruptly announced his retirement. He explained, "I do not believe that I have the vigor, or at the age of sixty-five the expectancy of time to give [Eastern] the direction it needs." Asking to retire as of September 30, he urged the regents to find a new president by that time. The "Organization of a Presidential Search Committee" of six politically appointed regents would be headed by board chairman Robert B. Begley. As Martin requested in his resignation, a committee of faculty and students would act in a purely advisory capacity.

Taylor and some others criticized the "rush" to appoint a new president by the end of September. Some foresaw the election of Vice President J. C. Powell as a done deal.[88]

During Martin's term of sixteen years as president, change at Eastern came by evolution rather than revolution. Martin's strong hand, coupled with the dominant innate conservatism of the faculty and student body, thwarted the radical change so evident on many American university campuses. As president of the Faculty Senate in 1975–76, I witnessed firsthand the conflict that marked Martin's last months at Eastern. Although the administration set the agenda for the senate, increasingly the faculty had its say, even if it was often voted down in meetings. In a vote to strip ex officio members, nine deans, and vice presidents of the voting privilege, the measure failed, 24–23, in early May 1976. Times were changing. An insider like Vice President for Student Affairs Tom Myers understood that the days of Martin's methods "are over" when interviewed in 1978. Time, wear, and a changing university atmosphere prompted Martin to admit to being "happy" to be on the outside soon after his retirement.[89]

University status beginning in 1966 was the highlight of the Martin years. If a person looks at the statistics of Martin's tenure, from 1960 to 1976, the change is indeed breathtaking. Enrollment increased from three thousand to thirteen thousand. Campus value increased from $7 million to about $120 million. Faculty increased from 126 to more than 500 members, with a lowering of the teacher-student ratio and a doubling of the number of faculty with doctorates. Majors increased tenfold, from only twenty-six in 1959, with law enforcement and allied health and nursing highlighting the change. In bricks, mortar, stone, and bronze, Martin left a lasting legacy at Eastern. "His weakest spot was in dealing with faculty. He was very autocratic. He wouldn't last twenty minutes now with modern faculty. He was fading even when he went out," concluded Kentucky historian laureate Tom Clark in 2002. In his farewell remarks to the regents on September 30, 1976, Martin admitted that faculty development had not been his strong suit. However, when the *Lexington Herald-Leader* called him an "education evangelist," in an editorial obituary in 1997, it could not have been more right. Dick Wilson's comparison of Martin and Doran was more telling than anyone could have limned. "If the two men were orchestrating a parade, Martin would be satisfied with planning it flawlessly," the *Courier-Journal* reporter said. "Doran would insist on being the grand marshal."[90]

Allan Ostar, executive director of the American Association of State Colleges and Universities, perhaps best summed up Martin's presidency, for all its flaws, just after the Kentuckian's retirement. "His philosophy is to provide education opportunity to all who can take advantage of it no matter how modest their means and to give them the best education at the lowest possible price." The successor of Robert Richard Martin followed a giant in Kentucky education and would face the problems and legacies of the past, as well as a whole new set of challenges in the years ahead.[91]

CHAPTER 7

J. C. Powell

The Maturing Years, 1976–1984

FROM 1976 TO 1984, Eastern Kentucky University matured as a regional university. In contrast to the Martin era, program growth slowed as student enrollment stabilized. Students continually asked for change but not with the insistence of the Martin years. In addition, they increasingly felt the consequences of tougher economic times.

Change came mostly from within, a tendency that demonstrated both good and bad aspects. Several trends from the Martin years continued. For example, faculty became increasingly involved in university governance. Periodic state budget shortfalls kept EKU, along with other state schools, from developing to its fullest potential. Moreover, by the end of this era, the "graying" of the faculty and administration would eventually lead to a turnover of personnel.

As President Robert R. Martin neared retirement, speculation about a successor centered on his longtime aide, Julius C. Powell. "Of course, there wasn't any doubt in my mind J.C. was going to get the job," said Richard Wilson, *Courier-Journal* higher education reporter. Though Emma Y. Case believed Powell would win out no matter what the process, she also suspected that Vice President John Rowlett aspired to the Eastern presidency. Martin told a prospective candidate, with typical humor, "My position in the race for my successor is strictly 'hands off'—I wish all my friends well who are competing and won't know whether to extend congratulations or condolences to the winner."[1]

Martin's retirement announcement and the rush to appoint a successor stirred up a campus furor. The *Eastern Progress* asked for faculty and student input and eventually called for the appointment of "someone outside of the

University." On May 5, 1976, the Faculty Senate passed a resolution urging the Board of Regents to include faculty regent Morris Taylor on its presidential search committee. The regents denied this request, with chairman Bob Begley stating that his intent had been only to place an equal number of Republican and Democrat members on the committee. However, the regents did allow for faculty and student advisory committees to "help in the screening process." Each worked on criteria needed for the new president. The final decision, though, would rest with the regents. Meanwhile, the *Lexington Leader* openly endorsed Powell.[2]

The student and faculty/staff advisory committees, using a scaling system, helped cull the list to sixteen names from more than two hundred applications. To Bob Bagby, who represented the College of Law Enforcement and Safety on the faculty/staff committee, it seemed to be a foregone conclusion that Powell would be one of the top choices. While the regents' presidential search committee ranked Powell as its top candidate, the student and faculty/staff groups did not. In both majority and minority reports, the faculty/staff committee claimed not to have received enough information and access to candidates on which to base a decision. However, on a tally sheet totaling points for each candidate, Powell ranked fourth in the faculty/staff column. The student advisory committee adamantly stated, "Dr. Powell does not possess demonstrated academic and leadership credentials in comparison to other candidates." The tally sheet in the Powell Papers used by the regents' committee, now housed in Eastern's Special Collections and Archives, shows that he received more points than any other candidate.[3]

When the Board of Regents met on August 14, Taylor and student regent Mark Girard cast the only votes against Powell. The board elected the seventh president of Eastern to a two-year term at a salary of $45,000 per year. The press reacted with no surprise, most fully expecting Powell to be named. But if "good old boy" Kentucky politics still operated in an educational sphere in the election of Powell, times had indeed changed compared with the completely closed-door election of Martin in 1960. Powell reacted pragmatically and with magnanimity. "I guess no one has ever been the unanimous choice of the faculty and student body," he said. "I don't look at it as a personal thing." Regent Beverly Yeiser flatly stated that Powell, from the beginning, had been the best candidate.[4]

Powell, except for the nagging baggage of being thought of as Martin's man, appeared well prepared for the job of president of EKU. "It's got to be a hellacious job," declared former Martin antagonist SGA president Steve Wilborn. Described as a "manager" by some, Powell admitted in an interview that he had been part of the Martin team for so long because their "different natures" complemented "one another." "I thought we made an awfully good team," he said. While Martin operated with a heavy hand at times, the well-spoken Powell always did so with a velvet glove. How would students, faculty, the administration, parents, alumni, and that all-important entity, the Kentucky General Assembly, react to such leadership?[5]

Powell would preside over an institution that had entered a maturing state, what he called "a plateau of growth." Enrollment fluctuated, as often regressing as increasing slightly. The Council on Higher Education (CHE) imposed more restrictions and demanded coordinated planning. From the perspective of Eastern and its sister regional universities, the council favored the University of Kentucky and the University of Louisville with its new funding formulas. The mission statement of Eastern stressed "teaching, public service, and research," in that order, within its "primary geographical area." However, there was some room for "flexibility and adaptability," with Eastern being given a key role in developing "especially programs of a technological nature." And the university would continue to produce more teachers than any other school in the state.[6]

At his last regents meeting, Robert R. Martin admitted, "I have not been a popular leader . . . , but rather, I have sought respect." With typical wit he said he would go through his last working day, and then "I expect to come over in the morning and bid Dr. Powell well and get back in the car and get out of town as fast as I can." The Eastern community could not let Martin go without a big send-off. On September 16, 1976, a tribute dinner for Martin included guests as politically antagonistic as former Republican governor Louie B. Nunn and Democrat Party guru Ed Prichard. They and others of a more compatible political cast gathered in a love feast that for once included no controversy. Representatives of students, faculty, staff, and alumni all praised Martin for his contributions to Eastern and higher education. However, if anyone expected Martin to retire completely, they were mistaken. When John Lackey retired from the Kentucky Senate, Martin got back into politics and won that seat in 1977. There, he championed education. He also helped found the Kentucky Oral History Commission during the nation's bicentennial. Even the *Eastern Progress* had good words to say about Martin, particularly the "many years of freedom of expression." "There have been a few visits to the office from time to time," the student editor admitted, "but always after the fact never before."[7]

Meanwhile, the 1976–77 academic year opened with the traditional faculty/staff assembly in Brock Auditorium. Vice President Rowlett opened with an academic pep talk, urging faculty and staff to improve the quality of their performances. Listening to Powell's recorded address many years later, a person cannot help but detect a bit of nervousness at the beginning. However, when he got into the realm of his expertise, including funding, the legislative process, and working with the CHE, he warmed to the task. The audience laughed when he told an old joke, saying, "Some of us who work with the General Assembly think it might be better if it met for two days each sixty years" rather than sixty days every two years. Significantly, Powell announced the creation of a planning council and his intention to work hard to raise faculty salaries.[8]

With all the pomp and circumstance that could be mustered, Eastern officially installed Powell as its seventh president during a special Founders Day celebration on March 19 and 20, 1977. The transition from the Martin to the Powell administration was nearly seamless. For example, no immediate major changes were made in the administrative personnel of the university. However, the much more low-key approach of the new president would contrast greatly with the full-steam-ahead, no-prisoners-taken demeanor of Martin. Everyone recognized that the boom years were over. The following period would be a time of consolidation, the maturing of a school only ten years a university.[9]

A college or university, no matter how large or small, is not without internal rivalries; fraternities versus nonfraternities, students against faculty, faculty against administration, and the list goes on. Even within departments there were usually factions, personality conflicts, and sometimes petty bickering. Eastern had its own "chattering classes," as the English say, who were never at ease with the slow change coming at the school. Moreover, the decade-old rivalry between arts and sciences and Central University College (CUC), their deans and faculties, continued into the early Powell administration. The Academic Planning Council, with Deans Fred Ogden and Clyde Lewis as recently minted associate vice presidents along with Vice President Rowlett, Graduate Dean Charles H. Gibson, and Joseph Schwendeman, dean of the Office of Undergraduate Studies, looked for a way out of this impasse.[10]

These efforts resulted in a series of changes starting with the division of arts and sciences into natural sciences, social and behavioral sciences, and humanities colleges. Moreover, CUC departments that taught survey classes would be transferred to these colleges. Military science and mass communications were transferred to the College of Applied Arts and Technology. In all, EKU now had nine colleges, with the creation of a new College of Health, Physical Education, Recreation, and Athletics. Schwendeman's office had already taken over the advising role for undecided students previously done by CUC. Dean Ogden, in his history of the College of Arts and Sciences, noted that from the beginning, he and Dean Lewis had never seen eye to eye on the administration of the general education program. While the 1979 reorganization apparently "resolved" this conflict, it never completely ended the rivalries. General education, owing to the great number of departments involved and courses taught, continued to be a much debated issue. How much was enough, particularly for the technologically based majors? One study in 1982 indicated that EKU did indeed do a good job, with students gaining in general education knowledge because of these lower-division courses.[11]

The Powell administration faced other challenges. In early 1977, Governor Julian Carroll announced a "money squeeze" in state government and suggested greater oversight by the CHE led by director Harry Snyder. At times the prickly relationship between Powell and Snyder, who had earlier served as an administrator at UK, came into the open, especially in conflicts over the mission of the regionals like EKU. During the governorship of John Y. Brown Jr. (1979–83), three state budget shortfalls and reductions in Eastern's budget in thirteen months severely challenged even Powell's financial expertise. "Perhaps more fundamental, though," the Eastern president told Snyder, "is the truly erosive effect of two consecutive years of substantial reduction in state support to this institution with no apparent prospect for relief." Moreover, Eastern had to continue paying on two principal construction bond funds.[12]

Brown, who brought some business acumen to the governorship based on his success in franchising Kentucky Fried Chicken, pushed the CHE to higher fiscal vigilance and even suggested a superboard. Brown claimed Kentucky needed a "flagship" university to compete with other states. To the regional universities like Eastern, the governor's mandating of funding formulas appeared to favor UK and UL. Powell fought hard but could only do so much against the Brown, Snyder, and CHE combine during the 1982 session of the General Assembly. The Eastern president argued to all who would listen that because of budget cuts, inflation, and higher energy costs, the university had already lost 30 to 40 percent in purchasing power by 1981. "It is an erosion of quality," he claimed. Of course, one way to meet costs was to raise tuition, which no one liked. Throughout the era, Model School survived attacks claiming that it was either elitist or too costly to maintain.[13]

Through these difficult times Powell continued to put faculty and staff salaries first while deferring maintenance. This retrenchment extended into the early years of the administration of Governor Martha Layne Collins. With the meeting of the 1984 legislature, there was a somewhat fairer formula in place for the distribution of state funds. However, then the General Assembly had to be persuaded to fully fund the CHE recommendation. Powell would be bedeviled by budget crises throughout his presidency. Even the smallest expenditures were important. If in the Martin years it was often difficult to get more than one electric typewriter in each department, now it became increasingly difficult to borrow one for a short time outside of a departmental office.[14]

Lack of funds impacted the campus, according to longtime director of buildings and grounds Chad Middleton, because long-range maintenance became difficult to plan. Severe winters, beginning in the late seventies, forced conservation. Facing a worsening energy crisis, EKU successfully saved on costs by turning the thermostats down in winter and up in summer. Only the ceaseless efforts of people like Raymond Gabbard, Middleton said, kept "the campus and grounds in good shape." The reality of the new era of energy usage also forced EKU to begin investing in small computers to monitor heating and cooling of campus buildings. Of course, everyone complained about the health risks of teaching and learning in the Wallace Classroom Building. Students and faculty fumed about either too much heat or too little cooling in classrooms and dorms. "We sure did work around here for a long time without air conditioners," an exasperated Powell responded.[15]

Powell was always much more low-key than his predecessor and did not favor the grand gesture that Martin relished. For example, in contrast to Martin's ritual of announcing a Wednesday holiday if EKU beat Morehead in the last football game before Thanksgiving, Powell set it as policy, whether we "win, lose, or draw." Moreover, Powell changed spring commencement from Alumni Coliseum to Hanger Stadium. Likewise, commencement no longer included laboriously calling out the name of each student and the president shaking hands with each recipient. Martin had especially enjoyed the latter.

To a critic of these moves, Powell rationalized, "A large majority of the audience and many of the graduates left during the proceedings," in the usually sweltering Alumni Coliseum in May. Faculty cheered now that only one-third were required to attend in order to make room for friends and family of the graduates.[16]

In contrast to the boom times of the Martin years, only one structure, the multipurpose Carl D. Perkins Building, was completed during Powell's term. The Arnim D. Hummel Planetarium, openly opposed by the *Courier-Journal* as an unnecessary frill for a regional university, was another matter. Billed as the "second largest campus planetarium," it did not open as planned in late 1978 because its director, Jack Fletcher, refused to accept defective equipment designed and installed by Spitz Space Systems. Finally, a lawsuit that dragged into the mideighties forced the company to fix the nearly $1 million device to the satisfaction of Fletcher, Eastern, and the Commonwealth of Kentucky.[17]

Owing to high interest rates, no new dormitories were built in the Powell years. A year after taking office Powell predicted that "tripling" in some dorms "would become a way of life." All the complaints by *Progress* editorialists and in SGA meetings came to naught. A Dieter Carlton cartoon featuring a forlorn Powell overlooking students crammed three deep into a sardine can added a bit of humor to the facts of life in tough financial times. Even though the state fire marshal's office complained, the *Progress* finally had to admit that "tripling was here to stay." With Keith Hall and Case Annex converted into faculty offices, in response to a Southern Association suggestion, EKU had spaces for only about sixty-five hundred students in rooms of two. Usually at least five hundred more students were crammed into the dormitories. However, the university did purchase the University Inn on the Eastern bypass to house police cadets in training at the College of Law Enforcement complex.[18]

The difficult financial times of the late seventies and early eighties forced hard decisions on the administration. Maintaining the library proved to be a challenge during this period, according to director of libraries Ernest E. Weyhrauch, with book purchases being cut. Weyhrauch, who earned an M.A. in history at Eastern, also filled in to teach when needed. The Jonathan Dorris Museum operated through 1982, until Powell closed it because of "reductions of state appropriations for two consecutive budget years, combined with increasing enrollment." While Powell hoped to revive the museum, boxed materials were moved to Perkins, and it has never reopened there. Much-discussed plans for a fraternity row also had to be shelved. The controversy over off-campus frat housing continued; one student regent called these accommodations "firetraps."[19]

Meanwhile, Larry Martin continued to tweak the food service facilities, turning out good meals and making an annual profit for Eastern. Students complained occasionally, but how could anyone resist the "dollar line" Martin opened in the Powell Cafeteria to utilize leftovers? The head of the visiting Governor's Scholars Program extolled Martin's virtues one summer: "You are my kind of person—no B.S., no hidden agendas, no phoniness."[20]

Eastern accepted new ways to serve the commonwealth. Charles Hay in the University Archives had already initiated oral history projects, most notably one for President Robert R. Martin, by the time the Oral History Center (OHC) opened in 1977. The OHC's director, William Berge, taught a course on oral history, as well as encouraging the collection of interviews on a wide variety of topics. On a much larger scale, the Office of Natural Areas under William Martin looked after preservation of Lily Cornett Woods, Maywoods, and Spencer-Morton Preserve. Martin called Lily Cornett Woods the state's prime example of an "unaltered mixed mesophitic forest," one that needed to be protected at all costs. WEKU-FM continued to give an alternative to the usual claptrap on commercial stations, particularly stressing public service, news, and classical music. Ron Smith, Loy Lee, and later Marie Mitchell gave Eastern a first-class operation.[21]

In other areas Eastern also made halting progress in the Powell years. The school followed trends and federal regulations but did not especially lead in opening opportunities for minorities. The effort to enroll more African American students and employ more black faculty and staff continued. When the federal government ordered Kentucky to implement a desegregation plan, Doug Whitlock, Powell's executive assistant, took on this difficult task. Like all public institutions, EKU developed an affirmative action plan and included a nondiscrimination statement in all its advertisements for positions. In the Powell years, black enrollment increased slightly. There were other signs of progress. The creation of an Office of Minority Affairs gave new impetus to this effort. Two black students, Clayburn M. Trowell and Charles M. Floyd, were elected to head the SGA in 1980. The next year Dr. Rodney Gross became the first black regent. However, women still struggled to climb the administrative ladder. Carol Teague became the first female to reach the director level as head of academic computing. In particular, female editors of the campus paper often noted this lack of progress, with no women as vice presidents or even regents. Joining Dean of Women Jeanette Crockett, Virginia Falkenberg was named acting dean of the Graduate School in late 1984.[22]

If many traditions continued, Eastern did display more cosmopolitanism than ever before. Teachers with foreign backgrounds added an international flavor to the campus, as did an increasing number of foreign students. Kenneth S. Hansson, a native of Sweden, became dean of the College of Applied Arts and Technology. Heino Luts, of Estonia, and Milos Sebor, of Czechoslovakia, escaped Communist oppression after World War II to find a home in America and at Eastern. Native Netherlander Wietse de Hoop became founding chairman of the Department of Special Education. Italian native Francesco Scorsone taught mathematics. Klaus Heberle, a native of Germany who became deeply involved in university governance, came to this country as a young boy just before World War II. Ursel D. Boyd came as a German war bride and added her vivacious charm to the campus. Samuel and Esther Leung, Amiya K. Mohanty, and others gave the campus an exposure to faculty of Asian extraction. Others, like Joan Boewe, studied abroad before coming to Richmond for an academic career. In 1980 Eastern joined the Kentucky Institute for European Studies, a group that sent faculty and students to study abroad. In addition, Eastern began celebrating Culture Week, with Eastern Europe the first subject of study, in 1984.[23]

The clientele of Eastern Kentucky University, the students, also faced old problems as well as new challenges during the Powell years. Did Eastern students change much during the Powell years? More important, did the university develop better ways to serve them?

"Some of the people were pretty unfriendly and I got all messed up with my cards," said one unhappy coed after a particularly stressful August registration day in an oppressively hot auxiliary gym in Alumni Coliseum. In the early eighties a new computer registration system began to end the seemingly endless lines. To encourage the entry of students with excellent academic potential, the EKU Foundation began funding scholarships in 1979 for twenty-five entering freshmen each year.[24]

Students could be just as serious or as silly as their Eastern antecedents. "Horny corner," the plaza between the Powell Building and the campus bookstore, often was the scene of hormonally charged exuberance during good weather. Greek societies on campus could just as easily work hard for a charitable cause as hold a juvenile contest like a "milk my baby" event in which

161

coeds sucked on bottles. Most of this campus folderol was good fun and, more important, a useful venting of youthful steam. Homecoming came and went with the usual queen election, including the reign of Elizabeth Cummins, my future daughter-in-law, in 1983.[25]

Many Eastern students longed to be at a more liberal university, but the sixties were over. Perhaps the lack of a war around which to center protest led to a calmer campus life. While Eastern would never return to in loco parentis, change came slowly for such issues as open houses. "We are approaching the situation as best we can," Powell told students soon after taking office. "I know and you know that we will not have open dorms." Student regent Mark Girard accused Vice President Tom Myers of using delaying tactics in approving more open house hours. One student regent opposed a slight change, saying it was "eight to ten years behind the times." However, the regents soon approved lengthening open houses to sixteen hours per week, and they doubled that a couple of years later. Guests had to be checked in and out, the door left ajar, and, an alumna revealed in an interview, "You had to have at least one foot on the floor."[26]

Even with annual changes in staff, the *Eastern Progress* continued to be an award-winning weekly campus newspaper. Weekly editorials, articles (some quite excellent), cartoons, and high-quality pictures filled out each issue. For a short while in the early eighties each issue featured a "Miss" or "Classmate of the Month," a mostly harmless titillation for male students. As a sign of the times, the coed ordinarily posed in a swimsuit. Each young lady's written profile usually included as "turnoffs" people who were "rude" or "snobs."[27]

Students succeeded as they always had at Eastern. Tom Rebilas, crediting voice teacher Don Henrickson, became the first EKU graduate to be selected for a Fulbright-Hays graduate study grant in Germany. Barry McCauley blossomed into a successful opera singer, starring with the New York City Opera as well as singing in Europe. Football player Steve Frommeyer, a good example of student-athlete, made all As except for two Bs by his senior year and won a NCAA graduate school grant. Craig Ammerman, who sometimes locked horns with President Martin as editor of the *Progress,* headed the New York Associated Press Bureau in the1970s.[28]

Most Eastern students worked and studied hard. Oklahomans Lowry and Joyce McKee took nine years all told to finish college, including his years in the navy. These accounting majors with two young children had little time for play. Many students labored long and hard to accumulate several degrees

162

at Eastern. Nancy Elliott Simpson may have set an all-time record, with 235 semester hours accumulated at Eastern, including a B.S., an M.A., elementary endorsement, Rank I, and principalship accreditation to her credit.[29]

Though Eastern had a reputation as a party school and for bleary-eyed Thursday nights downtown, religion played a key role in the lives of many students. While toga parties prospered at a downtown bar, so did religious services on campus. Student activities director Skip Daugherty explained that Rev. Jed Smock was within his First Amendment rights when he harangued jeering students at "horny corner." More important things were going on. University chaplain George Nordgulen believed religion to be on the upswing on campus. Father Ron Kettler of the Newman Center said, "I think it's a very religious campus." The Baptist Student Union, directed by Rick Trexler, moved into a new building on the edge of the campus and served hundreds of students each week.[30]

The experiences of most Eastern students mirrored those of past years. Lisa A. Irwin came to Richmond from a small town in Ohio, lived through some of the trials of dormitory tripling, and, like many students, had some difficulty settling into a major. She finally chose occupational therapy, a program in which Eastern led the state, after taking a class with Joy Anderson, and she joined Sigma Tau Alpha, a service sorority. Dorm life could be fun and full of good-natured pranks. Once a girl in Case Hall "snuck this guy up the back staircase," Irwin revealed in an interview. "We penny-jammed her door, which is cramming as many pennies as you can in the doorjamb. They couldn't open it from the inside and then you could hear them in there cussin' and stressin'," she said with a grin. For Irwin, college life was fun, interesting, and hard work academically. To pay for her college experience, she labored in a factory during summer "vacations" and sold blood plasma during the school year. "I thoroughly enjoyed college, the whole experience, all the friends," she explained. "It was a real cultural experience to meet all these people from different places."[31]

As a transfer student, Tim Tingle found many of the same challenges. Life in the dorm could be "loud, raucous, and despite the best intentions of the cleaning crew, kind of dirty at times. At one point there was a contest between the various floors in Commonwealth Hall to see who could find the biggest cockroach." Sometimes dorm mates could have obnoxious traits, like the guy who played the same song, Ted Nugent's "Cat Scratch Fever," over and over on his stereo. Now an archivist in the Kentucky Department for

Libraries and Archives, Tingle also has high praise for the education he received at EKU: "My background and training in history at Eastern has proven invaluable in preparing me to contribute to the preservation of Kentucky's historic public records."[32]

Powell-era graduates found success in various ways. Cynthia Bohn went on to work for IBM and later opened a successful vineyard and winery in Woodford County. Carl K. Greene is a good example of a "nontraditional" student, who came back to college later in life to get a degree in journalism. Black graduates Rev. Kevin Cosby, who became a Baptist leader in Louisville, and Douglas Jackson Jr., who developed a program for at-risk children, the Center for Academic Success in Sierra Mesa, Arizona, gave back to their communities. And the entire Eastern community cheered the courage of an alumna in her fight for life and in founding the Cynthia Shaw Crispen Endowed Chair in ALS Research at the UK Chandler Medical Center.[33]

Some things always remain at Eastern. Alcohol and Thursday nights downtown will always be with the university. The *Progress* editorialized occasionally about student apathy and "suitcasing" on weekends. Faculty groused about grade inflation, low salaries, and the erosion of standards. Even though students could now have refrigerators in their dorm rooms, they pushed the envelope a bit by cooking illegally on hot plates. They complained about the aforementioned roaches, parking, higher tuition, heat and cold, and the faculty on occasion.[34]

To bring about better communication between faculty, administration, and students, Eastern followed a trend of the seventies and created an ombudsman office. As much a counselor as a buffer between groups, Dixie Bale Mylum, who served in that post longer than anyone else, observed, "I dispense a lot of Kleenex." Although a relatively cheap program, with the professor-ombudsman getting only a reduction of one class, it was scrapped because of budget concerns in the mideighties.[35]

The Eastern ROTC program prospered from 1976 through 1984, often leading the nation in enrollment. Joint programs with Cumberland College and Union College added to the numbers. The Pershing Rifles and Valianettes continued to do well in contests with other units. Colonel Hollis L. Roberts, class of 1957, became the first alumnus to return to head Eastern's ROTC. The program also became more attuned to the changing times and offered more opportunities for women. Three married couples received commissions on the same day in 1981. Jackie Truesdell, the first female brigade commander in 1983, could proudly state, "I got it because I was first out of advance camp. It's equal opportunity." A United States Marine platoon leaders training program also operated on campus.[36]

One student enrollment trend became even more visible from 1976 through the early eighties. Female enrollment grew as male numbers declined slightly, now at a nearly 60-40 female-male ratio, with overall numbers declining slightly. Vice President Don Feltner cited several causes for the decline in enrollment, including a troubled economy, less student aid in the Reagan era, a lower number of eighteen-year-olds in the population, and tuition hikes. Tuition at Eastern, dictated by the CHE, went up 15 percent just in 1983, a not inconsequential sum to struggling students. They, of course, failed to realize that while tuition and fees paid for about 18 percent of their costs, state appropriations paid for as much as 60 percent.[37]

With questionable state support, President Powell viewed the alumni, one-third of whom graduated during his presidency, as an important source of revenue along with the EKU Foundation. The Margin for Excellence Fund campaign became one way for graduates to bolster the school's finances. Clarence Gifford and Leslie Anderson, classmates in the first graduating class of 1909, became leading pioneers in this effort. Alumni found numerous ways to help their alma mater. Karl Bays, a 1955 graduate and founder of American Hospital Supply, sponsored a scholarship. Thomas S. Logsdon, an aerospace engineer who graduated in 1959, never forgot the impact of Eastern on his life. He praised Smith Park, who helped him through tough times by giving him a job as an office assistant when he was a freshman. In addition, there were changes in the alumni office. Ron Wolfe, former *Eastern Progress* adviser, replaced Director J. W. "Spider" Thurman in 1982 as the association went through reorganization to become more self-sustaining.[38]

In many ways the Powell years were golden for Eastern athletic programs. There were increasing challenges, particularly economic ones. Title IX continued to pose problems as well as offer opportunities for women as it was pushed by the federal Office for Civil Rights. Martha Mullins became assistant athletic director, with the responsibility of improving opportunities for women. Although interpretation differed from time to time, in effect, for each male sport, Title IX required that there should be a comparable female sport, as well as equality of scholarships and other expenditures.[39]

The Powell years were indeed magical for Colonel football. After switching to a new classification for football only, I-AA, the Colonels became a powerhouse. With national championships in 1979 and 1982 and finishing as runner-up for the two years in between, Roy Kidd's teams seemed nearly invincible. ABC-TV sportscaster and former Arkansas coach Frank Broyles called Eastern's double-overtime playoff victory over the University of Nevada–Reno in 1979 "the most exciting football game I've ever seen." Eastern went on to defeat Lehigh, 30–7, in Orlando for the title.[40]

Some things could always be counted on. Victories over archrival Western Hilltoppers came hard no matter what the sport, and Wes Eades continued to show up at most away games. Paul Love, class of 1951, always returned to play his bassoon in the alumni homecoming band. Although a graduate of the dreaded Western Kentucky University, Greg Stotelmyer began broadcasting Eastern games in his exciting style in 1979. All-American defensive back George Floyd starred in a victory over the Hilltoppers in 1981. The next year Eastern won the 1982 I-AA national championship with a perfect 13–0 record. Steve Bird, a first-team all-American receiver, and quarterback Tuck Woolum led the offensive machine.[41]

The founding of the Colonel Club in 1978 helped with extra funding and highlighted sports activities. It would be transferred to the EKU Foundation five years later. EKU also experimented with something new. The first football game at night came to Hanger Stadium in 1982 when portable lights were brought in for a game with Murray State University.[42]

In contrast to Kidd's longevity as football coach, the head basketball job at Eastern was less secure. Coach Ed Byhre had one great season sandwiched between several not so successful ones. Improving in 1977–78 to a winning record, Byhre's Colonels won the OVC the next year when walk-on Dave Tierney sank two free throws to defeat Western in a packed Alumni Coliseum. Colonel's playmaker Bruce Jones on that team came up the hard way; when playing basketball as a child, he had to nail a lard can to a tree and use a ball that did not bounce. Teammate James "Turk" Tillman broke the single-season scoring record. However, two years later the *Milestone* lamented about the basketball team: "Every way they turned was the wrong way." Assistant coach Max Good took over in 1981.[43]

Women's basketball became more competitive in the Powell years. After overcoming a serious childhood injury, Peggy Gay led the women's basketball team in scoring in the late seventies. Eastern women began competing in the NCAA in 1982 under coach Dianne Murphy. For two years Lisa Goodin led the nation in free throw percentage.[44]

In nonrevenue sports Eastern always fielded representative, if not championship, teams. The men's tennis team of Coach Tom Higgins (a former FBI agent), led by Joe Shaheen, had an undefeated OVC record in 1976 but more often did not fare as well. Kenny Glover became an all-American high jumper and nearly an Olympic competitor. Swimming continued as a successful sport. Jim Ward began his long, successful career as baseball coach in 1979. While men's and women's gymnastics were a big part of the athletic program in the early 1980s, by 1983 the women's program fell victim to the economic woes. Wrestling was cut to address Title IX concerns.[45]

All aspects of life at Eastern during the Powell years came under the stresses of the economy. Even the *Milestone,* in 1982, highlighted the theme: "Economy vs. the University." The Eastern president emphasized that "the thrust of the 80's in higher education will be toward quality, not quantity." The programs that EKU offered to its students had to meet two basic tests: marketability (whether it was competitive with other institutions) and outcomes (whether the graduate could find a job).[46]

The old tension between the liberal arts and the newer technical training often surfaced at Eastern. The university had already established itself as a leader in law enforcement and allied health and nursing education. As a sign of the times, Eastern suspended Latin and other foreign language degrees while adding programs in public relations, real estate, and paralegal studies in the Powell years. Technology programs like horticulture and the development of cooperative education led students into the workplace. All programs had to receive accreditation. Nursing, for example, failed in its first accreditation bid but received it two years later from the National League of Nursing. Older programs in the arts and sciences, like English, history, and political science, continued to keep a "share" of the Eastern student clientele. There were always teachers to train for the public schools. Moreover, students came to the university for preprofessional training. Adviser John L. Meisenheimer oversaw a small number of premed and predental aspirants each year. As part of the Powell administration's long-range planning, groups like the Program Evaluation Committee periodically studied all facets of the university and made recommendations. Vice President John Rowlett reported to the regents in 1984 that since 1978, EKU had suspended thirty-one programs. He might have added that it was not without feeling the hot breath of the CHE on Eastern's neck.[47]

The faculty of Eastern also adjusted to these changing times, the years of maturity. Now, almost all those hired held a doctorate. Faculty who had come in the rapid growth years after World War II began retiring in greater numbers. Younger faculty with children particularly appreciated something as simple as being paid every two weeks rather than with ten monthly checks. All worried about that academic bugaboo known as grade inflation. "Are we getting too soft?" some asked. There was frequent discussion of this topic in committee meetings, the *Progress,* and Faculty Senate meetings. As part of Eastern's maturing, the regents approved supporting faculty publication with a subvention with presses other than the University Press of Kentucky. As a sign of the "graying" of the faculty, as well as a method of shifting resources to those departments that were growing, faculty meeting the Kentucky Teachers' Retirement System's minimum requirements could begin retiring under an early retirement option in the mideighties. Drawing full retirement pay, the retiree could teach half-time for half pay for a few years. As another sign of budget constraints, as well as more planning, the granting of sabbaticals now became more competitive through a tougher screening process. Executive assistant Whitlock announced that no longer should faculty consider sabbaticals to be "vacations."[48]

Faculty Senate reorganization and faculty evaluation by students became two hot-button issues during the Powell years. The senate evolved out of full faculty meetings that were still held into the early Martin years. As the number of faculty mushroomed in the midsixties and some chaffed at Martin's dictation, a rudimentary Faculty Senate organized. A major sticking point in the early seventies included the ratio of ex officio members, including all the vice presidents and deans, in comparison with full-time faculty members. Paul Blanchard and some younger faculty representatives worked to limit the number of ex officio administrators who could vote on Senate measures. Change came slowly. Although the senate elected a chairman each year, Powell as president had the right of presiding if he chose. He did not do this, but he did make personal informative reports at most of the monthly meetings. He often referred to the young Turks on campus as "the loyal opposition" in his remarks and was very open about the problems that Eastern faced. The Powell years ended with an administration bloc of ex officio members and others still holding the floor on key votes. However, like all other aspects of the Powell years, the Faculty Senate was on the move toward greater autonomy, which was another sign of the maturity of the university. Eastern faculty also joined the Congress of Senate Faculty Leaders, which sought to advise the CHE.[49]

Student evaluation of faculty became another controversial issue in the late 1970s. With the Student Senate supporting mandatory evaluation, *Progress* editor Nancy Hungarland said, "One gets the impression the Faculty Senate is looking for any excuse to block a mandatory evaluation system." A short while later the Faculty Senate approved a committee report supporting mandatory student evaluation for teachers, with a long list of regulations. President Powell supported the senate's recommendation, and the regents put their stamp on it. The central question remained: How would the data be used? Some faculty thought that such questionnaires should be used only for "improvement of instruction." While some departments already used them for promotion and tenure decisions, others did not. The Committee on Student Evaluation of Instruction in the Faculty Senate studied the issue and invited faculty input. The whole issue became even more complicated when educationists and those of a psychological bent supported using a standardized format such as the Individual Development and Educational Assessment (IDEA) "instrument." Others wanted to design their own forms, as some departments like history had been doing for several years. Even the greatest supporters of the IDEA device knew that it contained all kinds of variables, and faculty had to learn to use it "properly." For example, faculty were warned by "experts" not to mark an item for student evaluation that was not a strong suit. After some faculty rebellion, mandatory evaluation was suspended for a short time. However, it was finally reapproved in 1983 with the proviso that administrators would also be evaluated. The Faculty Senate finally adopted IDEA, with the amendment that it would be "a factor in determining merit pay raises." Eastern had firmly entered the brave new world of technocracy by the end of the Powell era.[50]

Richmond and the Eastern community have never been isolated from the violence of American culture. The addition of the position of investigator and crime prevention specialist in the Division of Safety and Security in 1977 was recognition that crime on campus was a serious problem that needed addressing. While the student court handled many problems, the Student Disciplinary Board, the only group appointed directly by the president, had responsibility for the most serious offenses.[51]

These were serious times indeed. Safety and security director Thomas Lindquist felt compelled to outline guidelines for avoiding rape. While the administration might be more concerned about fire safety, completing installation of smoke detectors in all dorms, and students throwing things out windows and turning in false alarms, students themselves seemed more aware of petty theft. No one was prepared for the shocking brutal murders of regent chairman Charles C. Combs and his wife at their home in 1983.[52]

After months of speculation about Powell's continuing tenure, the fifty-eight-year-old announced his retirement at the spring 1984 regents' meeting. "I do not have the energy and enthusiasm" for the continued stress of the years ahead, he said. This timing would give the regents eight months to find a new president. The regents' approval of a "bare-bones budget" that "will provide for meager continuation of programs and services" pointed to the probable cause for Powell's fatigue.[53]

The Powell years represented the shortest presidency since those of Ruric Nevel Roark and John Grant Crabbe. In 1982 the seventh president of Eastern summed up the thrust of his time in office. "This institution is now past its teenage years," he said. "I see my term of administration as a time of trying to flush out the things of quality, with improvements in the way we're doing the things we do rather than growth in them." His was a correct assessment.[54]

Even with all the budget woes, Powell's watch included highlights such as beginning computerization on campus, twelve new academic programs, and the reaccreditation of the remaining programs. He had proved to be more than a caretaker. The lack of new money, the expanded role of the CHE, and the state of the economy and stabilized enrollments marked the Powell years, according to Vice President William E. Sexton. Unfortunately, many buildings showed the wear and tear of having deferred maintenance for too long. The *Eastern Progress* praised Powell as a peacemaker after the tumult of the Martin years: "Powell maintained a calm atmosphere at the university and kept a working relationship between students, faculty, and administrators." An important part of the Powell legacy would include the importance of long-range planning, with the development of five-year planning cycles.[55]

Meanwhile, as the 1984 fall semester opened, some things seemed to drag on or never change. The planetarium suit remained unresolved, long lines persisted at registration despite a new computer system, and enrollment declined slightly. EKU ranked sixth among state schools in faculty salaries. In an autumn ritual, students and faculty complained about uncomfortable, overheated classrooms, dorms, and offices when invariably warm days returned after the buildings and grounds division fired up the steam plant. To student complaints about parking, Lindquist had once replied, "A parking sticker doesn't guarantee a space, only a 'hunting license.'" Students still rubbed Daniel Boone's left toe for good luck on the way to an exam, especially if they had not studied adequately. The benign ghost of the Blue Lady in Pearl Buchanan Theatre continued to intrigue the campus. And one could still pig out at Ma Kelly's on her famous fried chicken and meatloaf.[56]

With at least 150 hats in the ring, including those of Vice Presidents Myers, Schwendeman, and Rowlett, there was no shortage of aspirants for the Eastern presidency. If EKU continued to grow in the years ahead, it would have to be with an influx of nontraditional students. Students would have to continue to work at pizza and hamburger joints, borrow money, and seek grants to pay for an increasingly expensive education. And many students would now take five or more years, under the best of circumstances, to complete a bachelor's degree.[57]

CHAPTER 8

"To Make a Good University a Better One"

The Funderburk Years, 1985–1998

THE WEAR AND TEAR of the years on J. C. Powell led to his retirement. Even with the relative decline in state support, stagnant student enrollment, and the uncertain state and national economy, much progress had been made during his administration. Older and newer programs matured, women made some progress on campus, and the Faculty Senate now had more say in university governance. However, Powell could never escape the considerable shadow of Robert R. Martin and the impression that he had been handpicked by his predecessor.

With Powell's resignation some of the old demons of Kentucky education and politics arose. There were important questions to be asked and answered. Would the good old boy political system again cloud the selection of a new president? As Eastern faced the uncertain years ahead, would it be able to adjust to the increasing competition for students, faculty, and funds, while keeping up with national trends in higher education?

The regents made the selection process, thankfully, much more transparent than in 1976. This time the search committee would be made up of the chair and vice-chair, the faculty and student regents, and two other regents elected by the board. Faculty/staff and student advisory committees became a prominent part of the process. An alumni advisory committee would also aid the effort. More important, the selection process would not be as rushed as it had been in 1976, with a new president not due on board until January 1, 1985. However, not everyone was happy with the projected eight-month-long selection process. Department chairs asked, unsuccessfully, that the date be extended to July 1, fearing many candidates might not be available until midyear.[1]

Over the summer and into the fall, the regents and advisory committees labored long and hard. The names of internal candidates kept popping up in campus conversation. The candidate list was cut to ten and then to the top three by November. The finalists were H. Hanly Funderburk, a professor at the University of Alabama at Montgomery; John L. Green Jr., president of Washburn University in Kansas; and Joseph P. Giusti, chancellor of Indiana University–Purdue University at Fort Wayne.[2]

All three candidates appeared well qualified and made impressive visits in open campus forums. However, to say the least, Funderburk came with some baggage. A compromise presidential selection at Auburn University in March 1980, he never had a consensus of support on that campus. Beset with serious financial problems and a budget deficit, arts and sciences professors claimed he favored science, engineering, and agriculture over their needs. Even a prominent politico in the Alabama Farm Bureau became involved in the fracas on the side of the embattled president. After two veteran vice presidents resigned and the faculty passed an overwhelming no-confidence resolution, Funderburk finally stepped down just short of three troubled years on the job. His interest in the Eastern presidency grew after he did some research on the university. "My name got into the hopper," Funderburk maintained in an oral history interview, "and this thing just kind of developed."[3]

On November 26, 1984, the regents deliberated for more than three hours in a closed-door session, according to Chairman Henry Stratton, because they wanted to fully discuss each candidate. After going back into open session, they voted unanimously, 10–0, in favor of Funderburk, making him the eighth president of Eastern. The fifty-three-year-old Alabamian received a three-and-a-half-year contract at an initial salary of $76,500.[4]

Faculty regent Bonnie Gray expressed the hope that her colleagues would rally around the new president "and get behind him on the basis of his strength that he will bring to the office." In contrast, Faculty Senate chair Michael Bright said the faculty was perplexed by the choice: "People are apprehensive. It's going to be tough for Funderburk. He has to prove that he will be good." Tim Cowhig, the student regent, claimed that his constituency, while they had some reservations about the new president, would find him to be "fair, blunt, and they'll know where they stand with him." The *Eastern Progress* added, a bit ominously, "The University must long remember Funderburk's past." Political pundit Al Smith, host of KET's *Comment on Kentucky*, got a telephone call from regent Stratton just after Funderburk's appointment. "Al, you've got to support us," Stratton told him. "I know what they're going to say. He got fired at Auburn. But, he's the best man we could find and we really love him. He's going to be all right."[5]

"We see a lot of good things and we want to be a part of that," Funderburk reacted, "and we're excited about it." A botanist by training and a longtime college administrator, Funderburk would be tested by his new charge in Kentucky. First, he would have to allay fears of the faculty, staff, and students about a repeat of the imbroglio at Auburn. Second, he would have to build bridges to the political hierarchy in Kentucky. However, anyone who had lived and worked in the Fob James–George Wallace political maelstrom had a possible leg up in the less highly charged Kentucky sphere.[6]

"What I'd like to accomplish is to make a good university a better one," the new president said. Perhaps based on his Auburn experiences, Funderburk declared his intention to involve "faculty, students, staff, alumni, and the public in general" in the process of running EKU. He met with these groups soon after coming to campus, espousing his belief in "shared accountability" while impressing all with his strong suits in finance and planning. Moreover, he said the magic word for faculty, "salaries," claiming that this was his first priority. A snowfall during his third day on the job and a subsequent bad cold only briefly dampened this southerner's enthusiasm for the presidency of Eastern.[7]

For an incoming executive the financial outlook could not have been any better, with an 8 percent budget increase in place. Impressed with the "quality of the buildings" on campus and the planning for the future already under way, Funderburk knew there were serious maintenance problems to be addressed. He found a "stable" Board of Regents at Eastern without, as in Alabama, having to contend with direct membership of the governor. Remembering his problems and the turmoil at Auburn, Funderburk made no changes in administrative holdovers from the Powell era. He wanted stability.[8]

The official inauguration of Funderburk as president of Eastern Kentucky University, being merged with graduation on May 11, 1985, at Hanger Field, was indicative of his style and stress on frugality. After being given the oath of office by Chief Justice Robert F. Stephens, Funderburk declared, "I do not assume the presidency of this fine institution for us to be average." "True excellence" would be his watchwords, and quality faculty and staff would be the means of reaching this goal. Eastern did not have to be "bigger," but to carefully plan for the future. He challenged everyone to work hard. Then the new president told 1,962 graduates: "Presidents and faculty come and go. You will be alumni of this institution for the rest of your lives."[9]

The early Funderburk years were blessed with initial increases in state support and an upsurge in enrollment, which made it possible to have 10 percent salary pools in 1990–92. The opening of extended campus centers in Corbin, Manchester, and Danville between 1990 and 1995 added students. In Eastern's designated twenty-two-county service area, an influx of "nontraditional" students, those over twenty-one who did not come to college directly out of high school, helped the total enrollment grow steadily to 16,866 in 1992. However, then a decline began again at EKU, with enrollment bottoming out at 14,657 in 2000. There were several reasons, including a less than aggressive recruitment program by Eastern, the eventual end of the nontraditional boom, and the vagaries of the economy. In good times, many young people who do not come from traditional college-attending families tend to get full-time jobs. When the economy takes a nosedive, many instead go to college if they can get part-time jobs and financial assistance. Because of these demographic changes, the average age of an Eastern student went from 21.8 years in 1970 to 25 years in 1990.[10]

The Board of Regents during the Funderburk presidency evolved into a more proactive group, meeting often for committee work, for example. In addition to faculty and student members, a staff representative was added by state law in 1994, with Ron Mink elected by his peers. The president received extraordinary support from the board, even during the biggest controversy of his tenure in the late eighties and early nineties. That conflict arose over administrative pay raises, the president's included. A *Progress* cartoon in 1987 showed a bloated administrator with a skinny teacher asking, "Anything left for me?" The faculty salary pool was usually evenly divided between across-the-board increases and merit raises. Some faculty groused about having to competitively seek increases with their colleagues and about overpaid administrators. Also, younger faculty members argued that higher-paid senior faculty and administrators always received a larger share than those at a lower salary, if the increases were made on a percentage based on current salary. It took some effort by faculty to get budget documents showing percentage increases placed on reserve in the library for all to see. On the whole, faculty received much higher increases than in the Powell years, and Funderburk always placed this at the top of the agenda for expenditures.[11]

The faculty debated many issues during this era. Faculty input increased as Funderburk encouraged important items to begin at the departmental level and then proceed upward through channels to the Faculty Senate and, finally, to the Board of Regents. New or revised policies for sick leave, retirement, promotion and tenure, syllabi, merit pay, sabbaticals, and faculty and administration evaluations worked their way through the system. There was debate on most issues, a far cry from the Martin years, when faculty felt left out of the decision-making process. Now some faculty complained about too much committee time cutting into teaching and research activities.[12]

Eastern's relations with the governors and the General Assembly followed the normal ups and downs of Kentucky politics. Governor Wallace Wilkinson (1987–91), who was more critical of higher education than previous chief executives, initially locked horns with the state's universities. A February 16, 1988, student march and rally in Frankfort, with President Funderburk heading the Eastern contingent, failed to move the combative governor. When Eastern gave Wilkinson an obligatory honorary degree a few weeks later, *Progress* editor Mike Marsee claimed it appeared to be "something of a peace offering," though undeserved. But, if Wilkinson was not kind to higher education in 1988, two years later budget director James R. Clark could report that the governor's higher education budget "was clearly the best recommendation we have seen in the 1980's."[13]

About this time an announcement that two of Eastern's regents had made substantial contributions to the campaigns of Wilkinson and his wife surprised no one. Politics was still a big part of the university system in Kentucky. The next governor, Brereton C. Jones (1991–95), determined to reform the system. For the appointment of trustees or regents, he proposed a seven-person board that would screen candidates and give the governor the names of three people for each post. The legislature passed such a law, and all boards were purged with the ruling that at least half were to be new appointees. In the end four new members were appointed to the Eastern board. Sadly, the state's economy turned sour again, and budget crunches returned under Jones. This encouraged Funderburk to redouble his economy measures, particularly to save money for the educational "rainy day" that could bring severe budget cuts.[14]

Student evaluation of instruction continued as a hot-button issue among some faculty, myself included, particularly if it was used as an integral part of merit-pay decisions. Was IDEA the best "instrument" for plumbing students' opinion of their instructors, or should there be an alternative that could be chosen by individual departments? After several years of discussion and debate, the Faculty Senate adopted a resolution in 1987 allowing "the IDEA Evaluation Program and/or another evaluation questionnaire for student opinion of instruction chosen by the department." Like everything else at Eastern during Funderburk's presidency, bureaucratization of instruction grew apace.[15]

Quality teaching became one of the thrusts of the Funderburk years. The EKU Foundation found a way to encourage and reward good teaching by creating Foundation Professorships in 1987. At the end of tight competition, three honorees each year received special recognition, as well as a $4,000 stipend for two years. Later this sum would be added to the recipient's salary for as long as he or she remained at Eastern. Following its charter as "a corporation affiliated with the University for the promotion of the educational, civic, and charitable purposes of the University in any lawful manner," the foundation became more active as the chief repository for private gifts.[16]

The general education program at Eastern continued to be controversial even after the reorganization of the Powell years. At a colloquium early in the Funderburk tenure, where the debate became heated, suggestions ranged from no change at all to scrapping the system entirely and allowing students to take almost any class they wanted. As another sign of a maturing institution, the Eastern community could now debate improving both the quality of the student body and the university's offerings to them. However, no major changes were made in general education, though the regents' Academic Quality Committee and the university's General Education Committee studied the issues often. In the late eighties, the idea of adding a foreign language requirement in certain suggested majors fell by the wayside, as did other major innovations.[17]

Eastern could not escape what one expert called "the cacophony of teaching," in which subject matter often became the extension of a professor's political, social, or intellectual mind-set. Eastern had its own version of the chattering classes, sometimes "blathering" might have been more correct, as the professoriate often went off on tangents. The Eastern "left" mostly copied trends in larger universities, being more reactive than proactive. A few professors pushed ideological hobbyhorses. For example, one zealot required some of his English survey classes to indulge his dedication to animal rights, which the *Progress* gleefully lampooned in a cartoon showing the professor shoving a chicken down the throat of a student. For the most part, however, Eastern faculty, staff, and students appreciated an open forum in the typically conservative atmosphere at EKU. Such opposites as Phyllis Schlafly and Sarah Weddington could debate women's rights in the University Centerboard series, although many students and even some faculty were no-shows. How could anyone have stayed away from a debate between Abbie Hoffman and G. Gordon Liddy? Many did. Most of the time no more than 10 percent of students turned out to vote in student government elections.[18]

With tenure, unfortunately, "academia is a place where lazy people can hide," observed one longtime professor. Most teachers worked hard, though, often going that extra mile to inspire and encourage their students in the classroom and with counseling. For example, Elizabeth Fraas, in addition to her teaching duties, completed a fifteen-year stint as *Eastern Progress* adviser, pushing the venerated campus paper into winning the prestigious national Pacemaker Award for college newspapers, as well as being designated the Best All-Around Weekly Campus Newspaper for two straight years and the Best All-Around Non-Daily Campus Newspaper in 1997. Merita Thompson, professor of health education and faculty regent, won an Acorn Award given by the Kentucky Advocates for Higher Education as one of the state's top professors in 1995. "The bottom line is genuine concern for the student and a passion for wanting them to learn," she said.[19]

Although teaching and service have always come first at EKU, some faculty published extensively in the Funderburk years. Jerry Faughn in physics and Karl Kuhn in astronomy published textbooks used by high schools and colleges. English professors Hal Blythe and Charles Sweet continued a long collaboration as mystery and scholarly writers. For many years they often met at a McDonald's restaurant, where their nom de plume "Hal Charles" worked out nefarious plots and stratagems that oftentimes turned into television programs and publications. Geographer David N. Zurick published books in his realm of expertise, tourism in the Himalayas and the cultures of that region. These are only a few examples of the many faculty who made their imprint outside the confines of the classroom.[20]

Moreover, Eastern's faculty served the wider world in numerous ways. Governor Martha Layne Collins appointed Ronald Marionneaux as state geographer for one year in 1987. The state government used several faculty members to great advantage during the administrations of Governors Brereton Jones and Paul Patton. William H. Martin spent six years as commissioner of the Department for Natural Resources, while Elizabeth R. Wachtel served for five years as commissioner of the Department of Mental Health and Mental

Retardation. Other Eastern faculty lent their expertise as consultants to both private and public organizations.[21]

Funderburk kept the faculty happy with higher salaries, and he filled most administrative posts with faculty and staff already on board. This saved money, as did the practice of reorganizing and combining some posts. When John Rowlett retired after forty-two years of total service at Eastern, Russell F. Enzie, who had served as associate vice president since 1986, was elevated to vice president for academic affairs and research. At the same time, Eastern labored to comply with federal and state hiring goals for minorities by initiating an administrative internship program. Women received more consideration for advancement than ever before, with Ethel Smith becoming Eastern's first female registrar in 1986. After Virginia P. Falkenberg and Marijo LeVan served as acting associates in academic affairs and research, Rita R. Davis became associate vice president in 1995. Falkenberg became dean of graduate studies and research. In addition, Donna Masters became director of grants and contracts, and Marsha Myers, director of libraries in 1992.[22]

Although some innovative programs were begun in the Funderburk years, EKU lagged behind its sister regionals, the University of Kentucky, and the University of Louisville in establishing such programs. While it had been discussed for more than twenty years, EKU was the last university in the state to introduce an honors program—a twenty-eight–credit-hour program developed by philosophy professor Bonnie Gray—in 1987. A National Endowment for the Humanities grant for a faculty workshop early on and development of scholarship funds aided this effort. Another program that was late to develop was women's studies. Many colleges had had such programs for decades, but it was not until 1996 that Eastern developed a minor in this field.[23]

Programs in law enforcement as well as allied health and nursing continued to lead the state and, in some areas, the nation in graduating students. The College of Business and the College of Education played important roles in the university. Although there was always some tension between the old "arts and sciences" rubric and the newer vocationally minded colleges, they coexisted increasingly well in the Funderburk years, when many of the former conceded that they, too, were primarily in the business of training graduates for the world of work. The College of Law Enforcement became a leading candidate for designation as a "Program of Distinction" as part of a matching program developed for regional university development. Truett A. Ricks, who proved to be very innovative, replaced founding dean Robert W. Posey in 1983. In 1997 Gary W. Cordner became dean. The name was changed to the College of Justice and Safety in 2000 to reflect the changed roles of the institution. Pressure from the CHE and other accrediting agencies, as well as the continual soul-searching within the Eastern community, made the university a fine example of what a regional should be doing. And it never strayed from its original mission. In 1990, Eastern ranked twentieth in the nation, according to a survey of the American Association of Colleges of Teacher Education, in producing classroom teachers. The Model Laboratory School, with grades kindergarten through twelve, remained one of fewer than twenty such schools in the nation.[24]

Relations with the CHE improved during the Funderburk years, but not immediately. When CHE director Harry Snyder came to a campus forum in early 1985, he got an earful of complaints. One professor, alluding to the second-class status of Eastern, claimed he could not afford to get a tooth fixed. Referring to UK and UL getting a bigger share of the education pie than Eastern, Professor Carroll Hale only half-jokingly argued, "Kentucky's a pretty small pond. Any chance of sinking one of the flagships?" Relations with the CHE improved with the subsequent resignation of Snyder and the hiring of his replacement, Gary Cox.[25]

When Funderburk came to Eastern, he immediately attacked the problem of the school's being underfunded based on the CHE formula. Either new money would have to be forthcoming from the state or EKU would have to use bonds for maintenance, Funderburk said early in his term. When EKU did not get a "center of excellence" in 1987, after the General Assembly set aside funds for centers and endowed professorships, the Eastern administration renewed its efforts. The council pushed all its charges to refine their roles, including goals for hiring minority faculty and staff. The CHE also continued to set tuition rates. The funding formula and other goals became paramount, with the CHE sometimes setting nearly impossible standards. When Eastern lost more than $230,000 in new money in 1995, it was because it did not reach an impossible standard of getting a larger number of transfer students.[26]

In contrast to the Powell years, except for the Perkins Building, construction was high on the agenda again. Finally, after a struggle that spanned nine years, the Arnim D. Hummel Planetarium was dedicated on November 13, 1988. "Right now," said its director, Jack Fletcher, "this is certainly state of the art." Fletcher recalled in an interview that Funderburk told him just be-fore the new facility opened, "We don't need a planetarium here, it's a waste of time, a waste of money." The president called Fletcher into his office and told him, in effect, he would "be placed on self-sufficiency and if you can't make enough money to operate on your own we'll close the doors and lock it forever." Fortunately for both Eastern and the public at large, the planetarium paid its own way and continues its service as the third-largest college or uni-versity facility of its type in the world. Funderburk, unlike Powell, was able to tap into bonds because of lower interest rates. The 1986–87 budget included $9 million in Consolidated Educational Building revenue bonds, the first bond sale since the late Martin years, for a communications network and pressing maintenance needs. Another bond financed construction of the Donald R. Dizney Building for Allied Health and Nursing. Other bonding funds, made without pledging student fees toward payment for the first time, were used to renovate the Roark Building and construct the Funderburk Build-ing, which housed the Department of Criminal Justice Training of the Ken-tucky Justice Cabinet. A major enhancement of the John Grant Crabbe Library, with the new Thomas and Hazel Little Building connection to the completely renovated University Building, cost $11.7 million. Finally, a $4 million Gen-eral Assembly appropriation and $750,000 in private funds financed con-struction of the Harry Moberly Classroom and Wellness Building. Because this facility was designated for athletics and physical training, and not for general student use, there was some criticism of this expenditure.[27]

With the administration of Governor Paul Patton (1995–2003), higher education began to get more notice after the landmark Kentucky Education Reform Act of 1990. Primary in the governor's plans was reorganizing the CHE and wresting away from the University of Kentucky its domination of the state's community colleges. The regional universities supported Patton and pressured the legislature to go along. "I will not be deterred by any kind of pressure or threats or possible adverse consequences," the governor averred, taking on the powerful statewide UK block and its president, Eastern alum-nus Charles T. Wethington Jr. Eastern and its allies completely supported splitting the community colleges from UK and restructuring the CHE. Patton won his battle. The CHE received a new name, the Council on Postsecondary Education, and a new director. Moreover, the state's universities were now allowed for the first time to set their own tuition rates. As fallout from this episode, state representative Harry Moberly Jr., chair of the House Appropriation and Revenue Committee, began to draw fire from what critics saw as a conflict of interest because he also served as Eastern's director of student judicial affairs.[28]

Students in the Funderburk years, 1985–98, followed much the same patterns of the late Powell years. At first, an influx of nontraditional students promised not only to swell enrollments but also to radically change campus culture. Such students, who worked one or more jobs and often had families, were less apt to contribute to the frivolousness as in the old days. But, then again, many Eastern students, owing to their lack of money, had never been able to do more than work hard in the classroom while hustling to keep their heads above water financially. Single mothers increasingly found their way into the university. In contrast, when Eastern was given a rank of thirtieth among the top forty party schools in America by *Playboy* magazine in 1986, the president lamented, with typical understatement, "That's certainly not a thing I'm proud of." Deans Skip Daugherty and Jeanette Crockett blamed this reputation more on the influence of "downtown" than the campus. Nevertheless, Thursday nights at Richmond's watering holes seemed to be the highlight of many an Eastern student's week, and "Horny Corner 101" continued to be a rite of passage at Eastern.[29]

There was another side to campus life. Baptist Student Union director Rick Trexler and other campus religious leaders presented a positive religious side of campus life. "I think we need to realize that being a Christian doesn't mean you're square, or that you're totally boring," he said in a *Progress* article. Campus entertainment tended to favor the popular entertainers of the day, with fifty-five hundred people attending a Jimmy Buffett concert in 1987, while only twenty-five came to hear Harvi Griffith, a renowned harpist. Nevertheless, Eastern's music, art, drama, and literature faculties and students did their best, year in and year out, to present important intellectual stimulation on campus. Perhaps the highlight of the era was the full operatic production of *The Bartered Bride,* starring Verda Tudor, who went on to a singing career in New York. Another hometown product, Tim Brumfield, has established a career as a professional musician and organist at New York's Cathedral of Saint John the Divine.[30]

Unfortunately, the Eastern community could not escape the continued sway of violence and drug use in America. A prime example was the assault on Vice President Thomas Myers in his own office in 1994 by a mentally disturbed student. Increasing domestic violence in Brockton and even "gang fights" on campus, with some thugs using sticks and canes, were deplored in *Progress* editorials. "Marijuana has been here for a number of years," claimed director of public safety Tom Lindquist, "but alcohol is still the prevalent drug of choice on this campus." After several incidents of abusive hazing on campuses in the state, including Eastern, in 1986 the Kentucky General Assembly passed a law that prohibited endangering the health of an initiate into an organization using "the forced consumption of liquor or drugs." I found being a member of the Student Disciplinary Board in the late eighties to be an eye-opener. Nearly every Wednesday afternoon for three years, I sat in on cases involving everything from computer hacking to theft to rape. To further enhance campus security, Eastern added a $150,000 television surveillance system in 1995.[31]

After the continued liberalization of open house hours during the Powell years, the first coed dorm became a reality at Eastern in 1986, with the wings of Martin Hall being set aside for the opposite sexes. "Hopefully Martin Hall will adapt and progress easily in the future," said dorm director Nancy Ward. While not at the pace many students desired, the number of hours and coed dorms increased steadily. By 1996 Eastern added Dupree and Todd Halls to the list.[32]

The experiences of Lorraine B. Durham, who earned both B.A. and M.A. degrees in the eighties, highlighted the opportunities that Eastern offered its students. Though not in favor of coed dorms, she lived a typical campus life. Professor Harry Brown's picnics on his farm for members of Sigma Tau Delta English honorary added to the pleasures of this English major. She could go to teachers for both emotional and academic help. Money was tight for this student. "I just really thought I had won the lottery," she exclaimed when she made ten dollars a game for playing in the pep band. When resources ran short, some people in her church helped pay for her senior year at Eastern. Now into a successful teaching career, she said, "I wouldn't be here if it weren't for Eastern." Teaching "is a little frustrating, but as long as we can make a difference and influence these kids, then it's worth staying and being part of it."[33]

The story of Beverly Applegate illustrates the lives of many nontraditional students of the eighties and nineties. After her children began school, she entered Eastern. About her classes, she said, "It made me feel old," sitting in a class of students many of whom were ten years her junior, "but I can't say they didn't make me feel welcomed." Janet Snow, a mother of three, also "put college on hold to raise three kids," then earned a GED and ended up attending Eastern with a daughter. The associate degree program of Eastern offered the opportunity for Robert D. Abney, for example, to train for a second career and return to the workplace in his native state after completing a career in the air force.[34]

Other graduates of the Funderburk years excelled. G. Hunter Bates (1989) graduated first in his class at Harvard University School of Law before joining the staff of Senator Mitch McConnell. Robert R. Carr, a history major, kept a perfect 4.0 grade point average for four years. "My degree in history will help me a lot in law school. The key thing to learn is how to think and interpret information," he said upon receiving four awards on Honors Day in 1994. He went on to graduate from the UK law school. Michele Renea Bollinger, with a 1989 B.A. in business administration and a 1991 M.B.A., received the EKU National Alumni Association Young Alumnus Award in 2003 for her success as a cost analyst. "My education and social interaction at EKU heightened my reality that anything is possible through preparation, initiative and tenacity," she said.[35]

Eastern students also continued to take advantage of ROTC, a program that began in the fall of 1936. In 1986, it ranked fourth in size among fifty-two programs in its region. Two years later, homecoming offered an opportunity for three generals, Paul Collins, Merwin Jackson, and James Bickford, to be honored by their alma mater. In 1990, ROTC celebrated the fiftieth anniversary of the first graduating class, with six members of the class of 1940 returning to campus. Enrollment in the program remained vibrant and increased in the wake of the Gulf War of 1991. Two years later Michael D. Prater became the two thousandth Eastern graduate to receive a commission.[36]

Eastern athletics struggled in the Funderburk years. Money, or lack of it, continued to be the primary driving force at the school. With costs escalating for insurance, equipment, and travel, there seemed to be no answer except to cut some sports. Simply put, the revenue sports at Eastern, football and basketball, did not make enough to fund such a large program. Even though most of the student activity fee went to sports, the athletic program ran annual budget deficits as high as $1 million in the late eighties.[37]

Committees studied the problem extensively. They and Funderburk argued that budgets were stretched too far to fund properly seventeen intercollegiate sports. Title IX gender equity issues also had to be addressed. The rifle team and gymnastics, while successful, were soon eliminated. The vaunted swimming program also came under fire. When coach Dan Lichty announced he was unable to find private funds for scholarships needed to save the program, he contended that there had been "a change of philosophy," with Eastern no longer desiring "a well-rounded program." An athletic committee chaired by Robert Baugh, dean of Health, Physical Education, Recreation and Athletics (HPERA), found it was difficult to keep finances in trim even after eliminating several sports. Funderburk was "very tight," Baugh said in a 2004 interview, but "I learned to appreciate him." Regent Jim Gilbert maintained that Eastern would just have to accept the reality of funding sports: "We expect to have a first-class athletics program in keeping with our first-class university." Although touted by some of the faculty, dropping down to a lower level for football, like Morehead, for example, offered no real hope for cost containment, the regents declared in one of their reports. Responsibility fell on the Colonel Club to generate more financial support. Even after lighting the football stadium to eliminate conflicts with Keeneland and afternoon UK games, the Colonels still could not fill the stands. The *Progress*'s promotion of the president as "Fundy No. 1 Fan" did not appear to help either.[38]

The usually triumphant football Colonels still sang "Cabin on the Hill," an old country melody, after each victory. Coach Kidd continued his successful record, never having a losing season in the Funderburk years. All-American Chad Bratzke went on to a successful NFL career, as did a few other stars. While often winning the OVC championship and returning to the playoffs, Eastern could never quite get over the hump and into the I-AA championship game again. Kidd reaped several honors, such as having the stadium named for him, being named president of the American Football Coaches Association in 1998, and even serving briefly as athletic director. Later in the Funderburk years, however, he ran into stiff opposition from the president and the athletic director when he pushed for Eastern to join the football-minded Southern Conference.[39]

While Kidd continued to turn out winning teams, the men's basketball coaches, with one exception, were not so fortunate. After eight years at the helm (1981–89), Max Good resigned. Despite an overall losing record, 96–129, he had taken his team to the final four of the OVC tournament four out of his last five years. One of his players, Antonio Parris, broke the old scoring record in 1987. Mike Pollio coached for three years and had a successful record, 51–41 overall and 25–13 in the OVC. "One of the main problems with Eastern is that it's 20 miles away from Lexington," he said. "It's hard to get people excited when they hear UK, UK, UK."[40]

University Building, circa 1915.

"Looking backward," coeds in 1910.

William Jennings Bryan and Governor James McCreary on the steps of Sullivan Hall, 1911.

Longtime regent Jere A. Sullivan, author of the Sullivan Law.

Scene from *Of Mice and Men*, 1919.

The 1920 Eastern baseball team, with Earle Combs (second row, third from left).

Seniors of 1928 with Professor Charles A. Keith (first row, center).

The 1937 Eastern band, with directors James E. Van Peursem and Henri Schnabl (front row, last two on right).

High School Day in Hiram Brock Auditorium, 1937.

Stephen Foster Music Camp participants march downtown, July 4, 1938.

The 1938 advanced ROTC class.

The 1940 athletic department (from right to left, Charles T. Hughes, Tom Samuels, Thomas E. McDonough, George E. Hembree, and Rome Rankin).

Women's Army Auxiliary Corps on parade, circa 1943.

Vet's Village, late 1940s.

Jack Jackson, Eastern's first African American athlete, crosses the finish line with teammates Roger Kincer and Dennis Sprous.

Vice President Lyndon Johnson (center) leaving Blanton House for the ground-breaking at Alumni Coliseum, June 1, 1961.

Governor Edward Breathitt signing House Bill 238 designating four state colleges as universities in 1966, with a smiling President Robert R. Martin hovering over him.

Copy of Daniel Boone statue by Enid Yandell. Rubbing the statue's left toe supposedly brings good luck to a student taking a test.

Demonstrators protesting an ROTC parade during the Vietnam War era.

Coach Roy Kidd with 1979 NCAA Division I-AA championship trophy.

The 1981–82 women's basketball team, with Coach Dianne Murphy (seated on left).

President Hanly Funderburk speaking at the dedication of the Thomas and Hazel Little Building in 1994, with Mrs. Little (on left).

A night scene at the Student Services Building, dedicated in 2002.

Meanwhile, Eastern named the arena inside Alumni Coliseum for Paul McBrayer, the most successful basketball coach in its history. New basketball coach Mike Calhoun's Colonels gave Rick Pitino's UK squad all it wanted before losing in the last two minutes in an exciting game. In the midnineties Eastern may have had the only brother-and-sister duo, DeMarkus and Laphelia Doss, playing major college basketball at the same time. After five seasons, Calhoun resigned, and Scott Perry was selected as men's coach in 1997, Eastern's first black head coach in a major sport (in the seventies, Sergeant Nelson Beard, an African American, coached the rifle team). With the racial barrier overcome, the next test, according to the *Eastern Progress,* would be to "bring in the fans, with Lexington's hoop-shaped shadow always looming over McBrayer Arena." Alas, he too could not turn around the men's program.[41]

The nonrevenue sports, anything other than men's football and basketball and those for women, also changed with the times. Rick Erdmann's men's and women's track and cross-country squads always performed well, with Kenyans John Nganga and Titus Ngeno adding an international flavor to the men's team. Jackie Humphrey, the most successful track star in Eastern's history, made it to the 1988 Seoul Olympics in the 100-meter hurdles, as did Dan Durben, a 1982 graduate, in rifle competition. Owing to Title IX, women's sports received added emphasis in the Funderburk years. In the wake of a looming scandal, Eastern named Larry Joe Inman as head women's basketball coach in 1988. In 1992, Angie Cox, whom Inman called "the most competitive person I have ever coached," won many honors. The Eastern women's program continued to advance and won its first OVC championship in 1997. Geri Polvino's volleyball teams had winning seasons. Women's sports changed in other ways, as fast-pitch softball, an increasingly popular game, replaced field hockey. Associate athletic director Martha Mullins, who had helped guide women's sports to new heights, retired in 1996 after a twenty-five-year career at Eastern.[42]

Overall, Eastern athletics in the Funderburk era were successful. While athletes in the revenue sports got most of the headlines, those in the nonrevenue sports did well. Also, the number of club sports, which received no scholarships and minimal university support, grew to ten by the midnineties. Teams in rugby, soccer, and lacrosse added to the competitive opportunities for Eastern "student-athletes." With all the cost cutting of the Funderburk years, EKU athletics still posted an admirable record in the OVC, never finishing lower than second in all-sports in the late eighties.[43]

"To be a comprehensive, public, residential university of the Commonwealth of Kentucky," reads the role assigned to EKU by the state's higher education council. Eastern, in the Funderburk years, followed a careful, safe approach to higher education. Ongoing maintenance and a prudent expansion of the physical plant, improving salaries, and increasing public support and private giving all became important parts of this plan. Decreasing state support had to be offset with increases in tuition. For example, from 1994–95 to the next year, state aid dipped from 47 percent of the university's budget to just 39 percent.[44]

If there had been some controversy in Funderburk's early years at Eastern, reminiscent of his time at Auburn, by the early nineties the *Lexington Herald-Leader* reported peace on the Richmond campus. "He can squeeze a nickel until it screams," said one regent. When financial crises again hit Kentucky higher education in the early nineties, EKU appeared better off than most other schools in the state. Faculty regent Karl Kuhn claimed that Funderburk had overcome many doubts that existed at the time of his election in 1984 and deserved to be reelected. Another regent, in reviewing the president's term in 1992, noted "an almost total absence of discord." Funderburk said much of his success came from working well with faculty and students, managing the physical plant, and restructuring university programs.[45]

Beginning with the elimination of associate deans in 1984–85, many changes came in Funderburk's tenure. The merging of the Social Science Department with the History Department, foreign languages with English, natural science with geology, and other combinations corresponded to the elimination of eight department chairs and twelve administrative directors or coordinators by 1994. Nearly one dozen underproducing programs, those not graduating enough students, drew the attention of the Council on Academic Affairs and were suspended. While claiming to have released $4 million for other uses, these measures wiped out such programs as a successful, though small, oral history program. But with overall salary improvement, and some money spent for instructional equipment and maintenance, there was hardly a whimper from the stricken. When Funderburk received the "Screaming Nickel Award" at an SGA banquet, it was a sign of the Eastern community's acceptance of the administration's tough fiscal approach.[46]

While the Funderburk years witnessed the further maturation of a regional university, they were also a time of rationalization of the university community. There was more emphasis on obtaining grants and following a comprehensive facilities master plan. For the faculty, rationalization meant more stress on merit pay and tightened rules for sabbaticals, funded from within each department, as well as an end to summer sabbaticals. Through the flush times and the lean years, Funderburk improved Eastern's finances, facilities, and salaries compared with those at both Kentucky and the neighboring benchmark institutions. The Board of Regents approved the first $100 million budget in April 1990. At least one major change on campus came from a suggestion of the president's wife. While attending their first football game at Hanger Stadium, "Helen punched me in the arm and asked me, 'What is that smell?'" the president explained. The campus dairy was moved in 1995 to the Meadowbrook Farm, and the campus took on even more of a cosmopolitan appearance. While Eastern continued to pursue purchasing the Elmwood Estate, Funderburk's intemperate remarks about building a large parking lot on the property irrevocably hardened the executors against selling.[47]

Funderburk's cautious approach seemed to work most of the time. By 1991 enrollment topped sixteen thousand, but then it started to slide because "nontraditional" enrollment began to decline. Even with the three extended campuses in Corbin, Manchester, and Danville, by 1996 enrollment had fallen by more than one thousand. With a lower number of graduating high school seniors in Eastern's region, generally southeastern Kentucky counties, there seemed no way to keep ahead of the pack. Director of admissions James L. "Les" Grigsby reported that enrollment decreased by nearly 4 percent from 1991 to 1995. In contrast, private giving to the EKU Foundation from 1984 to 1997 increased six fold, to more than $4 million a year. Alumni giving, encouraged by using students in an annual phoneathon, topped the $50 million mark. Specific gifts to the foundation created endowed funds in the names of several patrons. Funderburk's emphasis on outside funding resulted in grants and contracts totals increasing from $2.4 million in 1984–85 to $23.7 million in 1996–97.[48]

There were shortcomings. While faculty and staff pay increased, salaries and hourly wages for classified employees did not seem to be a priority. This finally led to a miniprotest at a 1997 meeting of the regents and a promise that the matter would be studied. The board adopted a grievance policy for classified employees, but their salaries did not increase substantially. There was an actual decline in the number of black students beginning in the late eighties. Eastern did make some progress in the nineties in hiring black faculty and staff, but it was still woefully low in total numbers. Moreover, it took an inordinate amount of time for the state of Kentucky and Eastern to adopt a holiday for Martin Luther King Jr.'s birthday.[49]

If Funderburk could be farsighted as well as tightfisted about finances, he fell short on other matters. For example, by not responding to a *U.S. News & World Report* questionnaire, the magazine automatically ranked EKU in the bottom tier of similar schools in a national listing. *Progress* editor Tim Mollette scolded the president for not paying attention to needed change. With a low graduation rate compared with other Kentucky universities, how could the school attract talented students without a better national ranking?[50]

However, the Funderburk record must be balanced with his successes, with what he thought was most important. "He left a pot of money and [Eastern] in the best shape of any school in the state," said Al Smith in a 2002 interview. "It was clear to me now in these hard times that the faculty appreciated the fact that he got their raises up. He was exactly what Henry Stratton said he would be." Funderburk's $13 million fund balance was his hedge against future economic downturns.[51]

To Professor Nancy Forderhase, Funderburk appeared to be a "faceless bureaucrat, not an evil man, a decent man, a good budget person, but more interested in the nuts and bolts of the university." "He had a difficult time opening up to people on the campus and in the community," said Larry Bailey, alumni director from 1986 to 1999. And, while carefully shepherding Eastern's money, he did not spend when he should have, particularly to entice new students to the campus. "He came across to many people here as being a sort of cold individual," stated Branley Branson. "He wasn't a people person," said Bob Bagby. On the other hand, when it came to campus improvements, Chad Middleton found the president to be "a good listener," who considered the views of many people on maintenance and building projects.[52]

Many faculty never warmed to Funderburk and suspected that money was his only concern. As part of a Southern Association of Colleges and Schools self-study in 1995, a faculty questionnaire revealed that they believed themselves overworked and underpaid and that things were not getting any better. With declining enrollment and performance-based funding the rule, the president maintained that the key was "becoming more efficient and effective." Like many colleges and universities, Eastern increased its use of part-time instructors to save money. However, with declining enrollment, Eastern was caught in a classic catch-22, where raising admission standards, as done at Western, would have led to even further falling enrollments and declining tuition revenues.

"Welcome to Eastern High," fretted a *Progress* editorial about the university's open admissions policy. The president placed his faith in the eventual success of Kentucky Education Reform Act (KERA) in improving and increasing Eastern's student clientele.[53]

Expanded technology and computerization, enhanced scholarships for good students, the initiation of an honors program, a refurbished campus with several new buildings, and raising faculty and staff salaries to the highest among the regional universities were all positive signs of the Funderburk legacy. He had redeemed himself after the bitter experience at Auburn and had proved to be a very capable, if not inspiring, administrator.[54]

CHAPTER 9

Change, Controversy, and Continuity, 1998–Present

WITH THE RETIREMENT of President Funderburk scheduled for the end of June 1998, the regents began their search for his successor in April 1997. Just about everybody had an opinion about what type of person was needed to lead the university into the next century. Although praising Funderburk for his fiscal savvy, the *Eastern Progress* wanted a new president "who will listen to the students and faculty about problems and ideas." Board of Regents chairman James Gilbert asked for "a reformer" with "vision." This time the search committee chaired by Gilbert included a broad cross section of the Eastern community, with student regent Melody Mason, the faculty regent, and two other faculty members, as well as representatives from the dean's council, department chairs, alumni, retired Eastern community, and staff. Of course, the final decision would be made by the regents.[1]

Throughout the fall and winter of 1997–98, the selection process went on unabated. The committee set February 1 as the time for cutting the nominee list to five or fewer prime candidates. The final list included President Philip W. Conn of Dickinson State University, President Charles D. Dunn of Henderson State University, President William Fulkerson of the State Colleges of Colorado, and Lieutenant Governor Robert W. Kustra of Illinois. All made two-day obligatory appearances before campus forums. Kustra, the first to be grilled, told a packed Faculty Senate meeting, "The final call is up to you." When asked how he would get money for much-needed improvements to the university, he replied, "In suitcases." The audience "roared" in appreciation, according to the *Progress*. Government Professor Glenn Rainey found Kustra to be "a very gregarious, outgoing fellow, very charming." In contrast, an Illinois friend of *Courier-Journal* reporter Dick Wilson said of Kustra,

"Watch him closely. There is no one he likes to hear talk more than himself."
The other candidates also made impressive campus visits.[2]

As time neared for the final vote by the regents, Dunn withdrew his name
because Kentucky's nepotism laws would prevent his wife from teaching at
Eastern, and, in effect, he would be taking a salary cut. With the field suddenly narrowed to three, the regents elected Kustra, unanimously, at their
February 18 meeting. His contract, which extended through June 30, 2002,
included an evaluation every two years, a base salary of $150,000, a deferred
incentive payment plan, and the usual perks of the office, insurance, and so
forth. Everyone appeared excited about the new president, with the *Progress*
asking Kustra to be more of a spender, particularly on students, than
Funderburk. The fifty-four-year-old Kustra promised to be a good commu-
nicator, keeping an open door for the entire campus community.[3]

The school paper presented the appointment story with the headline "'Perfect' Fit?" and a picture of Kustra donning an EKU windbreaker. A twenty-
seven-year veteran of the classroom, though never an administrator, Kustra
told the campus, "I'm first and foremost a teacher." "I'm moving into a school
that's clearly not broken," he said. He had nothing but praise for the campus,
its heritage, and its "reputational currency."[4]

Coming from a political as well as an academic background, the new president of EKU decided to get out of the former when stymied by the exigencies
of Illinois politics. Losing a 1996 United States senatorial primary to a well-
heeled conservative Republican opponent, he first considered running for secretary of state, which is the real stepping-stone to the governorship of Illinois.
His appointment as chairman of the Illinois Board of Higher Education gave
him valuable experience in the field. He and his wife, Kathy, the former director of the Illinois Department of Public Aid, decided to seek a new path. He
was looking for an opportunity in higher education when a friend put him on
to the Eastern advertisement in the *Chronicle of Higher Education*. Two
"headhunting" firms approached him about this and other positions, and his
name became available to the Eastern search committee. Governor Paul Patton's
educational reform efforts also enticed Kustra to seek the Eastern post, according to two oral history interviews with Kustra early in his tenure.[5]

On October 2, 1998, the university installed Kustra as its ninth president
at an outdoor ceremony in the Ravine's Van Peursem Pavilion that included
Kentucky governor Paul Patton and Illinois governor Jim Edgar. Both praised
Kustra, Patton for his potential, and Edgar, his former boss, for the "enthusi-

asm" he would bring to the job as a "doer." The pomp and circumstance of the event, tempered somewhat by the outdoor scene, still lent itself to the age-old passing of the torch to a new generation of leadership. President Funderburk made gracious remarks about his successor and helped with the investiture of the new president.[6]

Kustra and the audience all laughed when he repeated the Kentucky statutory requirement that he had never taken part in a duel. "What's past is prologue," Kustra said in his inaugural address, borrowing from Shakespeare. He developed the theme that Eastern had come far in its history, but urged its students, faculty, alumni, and friends to accept the challenges of a new age. "We have to move from a faculty-teaching focus to a student-learning focus," he explained. That would be best accomplished by developing a "sense of community," where learning took place outside as well as inside the classroom. Stressing his own teaching experience, he promised to share governance with the Faculty Senate.[7]

The first year of Kustra's presidency was breathtaking, with several initiatives breaking the old molds of the Funderburk years. "First Weekend" events were aimed at ending the old suitcase-college syndrome, creating a necessary change in "campus culture." Kathy Kustra took a special role in this successful venture. Thrill rides and free bowling and billiards in the Powell recreation center added to the festive occasions. Enrollment management and a study of grade inflation and other areas of concern were addressed. Kustra had his own unbending agenda and a few days after arriving on the Eastern campus told athletic director Robert J. Baugh that he would be replaced.[8]

Moreover, a $155 million budget promised to push Eastern successfully toward the opening of a new century. Owing to declining student enrollment, new initiatives were aimed at aiding retention rates and improving technology, where Eastern lagged behind other state schools. Creation of three new centers, Teaching and Learning, Appalachian Studies, and Kentucky History and Politics, as well as enhancement of the athletic budget, were all far-reaching and costly.[9]

President Kustra proved to be a master publicist in some ways, bringing attention to the university from far and wide. Drawing on his experience of hosting a radio program while lieutenant governor, he soon began a weekly WEKU-FM program, *New Horizons in Education*. This show engaged guests from a broad spectrum, including Robert Kennedy Jr., in interesting conversations and gained an audience beyond the confines of the Richmond community. Comedian Michael Feldman's National Public Radio program *Whad'ya Know?* came to the campus in January 2000 and broadcast before a packed house in Hiram Brock Auditorium. That year was busy. In October, Democratic vice presidential candidate Senator Joe Lieberman tuned up at Arlington House, where security was tight, for his debate with Dick Cheney at Centre College. Lieberman also visited the Eastern campus and "pressed the flesh" with students and faculty, as any good politician would do. A few weeks later, Eastern became the only Kentucky university to host a program called "America's Promise," headed by former chairman of the joints chiefs of staff General Colin Powell. Before a near-capacity crowd in McBrayer Arena, Powell's speech highlighted the program aimed at helping the youth of America succeed. Moreover, Meridian Communications of Lexington received a contract, funded by the EKU Foundation, to develop a new campus identity and suggested a new slogan, "Get the Know-How," and other "branding" ideas.[10]

With the announced retirements of vice president of academic affairs Russell Enzie and vice president for business affairs Earl Baldwin prior to Kustra's election, there appeared to be no other major changes on the immediate horizon. Then, Baldwin was persuaded to delay his retirement. "His experience will be valuable to me as a new president at EKU," Kustra said. Initially Kustra, like his predecessor, appointed from within. James R. Clark became the new vice president for government relations and planning; Doug Whitlock, vice president for administrative affairs; and Baldwin, vice president for financial affairs and treasurer. A new dean of business, Robert Rogow, had earlier come on board in the summer of 1998. Then, a few months into the Kustra administration, changes began to be felt in the old Coates Building. First, vice president for university relations Donald Feltner, who had modernized Eastern's public relations and helped guide fund-raising, retired after serving in a variety of posts for forty-two years. Mark Wasicsko became dean of the College of Education in August 1999. "I was the first in my family to attend college," he said, and he could readily identify with Eastern being a "school of opportunity."[11]

Toward the end of the first year of his administration, Kustra began to assemble his own "team." Vern Snyder became vice president for university advancement, with responsibilities for alumni relations, development and public relations, and marketing programs. Fund-raising became his primary task as Kustra dipped heavily into the nearly $13 million reserve left by his predecessor for initiatives. The hiring of Enzie's successor took longer than expected when the first finalists did not pass muster. However, by early June 1999, Michael Marsden, a specialist in popular culture from Northern Michigan University, was appointed to essentially a new post, provost and vice president for academic affairs. Impressed with the reformist attitudes of both Kustra and Patton, Marsden said an "openness to new thrusts" encouraged his move to Eastern. "I think he brings together a set of qualities that are very special to Eastern," Kustra affirmed. "He's a teacher and a scholar." In more reshuffling of assignments, it was not long before Baldwin resigned and Whitlock assumed some responsibilities that were later taken over by newcomer James K. Johnston as vice president of financial affairs. Lee Van Orsdel replaced Marsha Myers as the new dean of libraries in August 1999.[12]

Believing he had a mandate from the regents, Kustra announced a major restructuring of the university on April 1, 1999, claiming it would save more than a half-million dollars. Although retired Vice President Joe Schwendeman had met with many faculty about the project, the campus was clearly not prepared for what was announced: the immediate reorganization of the nine colleges. First, the colleges of Arts and Humanities, Social and Behavioral Sciences, and Natural and Mathematical Sciences merged into a new College of Arts and Sciences, reminiscent of the old alignment prior to 1979. Moreover, the College of Arts and Technology and the College of Business would be merged into a College of Business and Technology, and three departments in the College of Health, Physical Education, Recreation, and Athletics would be combined with the College of Allied Health and Nursing. Only the College of Education and the College of Justice and Safety remained unchanged. In effect, the nine colleges would be reduced to five, offering administrative cost savings that could be applied to other campus needs, Kustra argued. The reorganization also included staff changes, the creation of two new associate vice presidents, and the realignment of some posts and academic departments.[13]

A firestorm developed about what many referred to as the "April Fool's Day Massacre." Many faculty and administrators of the stricken colleges rebelled, claiming that they had not been part of the discussion of such changes. After a heated meeting between University Foundation professors and Kustra, which I attended, five deans said that the president, contrary to what he had said at that meeting, had led them to believe that reorganization was only in the talking stage and not imminent. Kustra defended his position by claiming that it had to be in place before the university entered the new fiscal year and that Eastern needed to get in line with its benchmark institutions. "I hope that is behind us now," he wrote to the faculty. He could not have been more wrong. By the time the regents met for their late April meeting, the lines were being drawn. Faculty regent Merita Thompson expressed concerns about the lack of campus input. "A lot of faculty are very hopeful about the results," she said, "but are very concerned about the way they came about it." After a long, serious discussion, the regents decided to allow the changes without a formal vote. "My feeling is, we hire a president," said regent Jane Boyer. "If we don't like what he does, we fire the president. I don't think we should get involved on that level [micromanaging the university]."[14]

Though most faculty and staff tried to adjust quickly to reorganization, this issue did not go away and continued to be debated in the *Progress,* around departmental coffee machines, and off campus. Many alumni were not happy with the change. Acting dean of arts and sciences Dominick Hart had the task of molding a college quickly. "I know that this merger is not welcome news to all," he said. "However, it also does present opportunities." Besides facing declining enrollment and increasing money problems, Provost Marsden had the unenviable task of coming into the breach just after reorganization. It was his responsibility to tie the reorganization together in Phase II.[15]

Undeterred and full of optimism, Kustra opened the fall 1999 semester at Eastern with the traditional president's address to faculty and staff. "We are here to serve students," he said, touting many changes made during his first year. Following a trend, Eastern even outsourced its food services, giving a contract to Aramark, in an attempt to keep more students eating on campus by relying on new marketing techniques. The university was also already exploring outsourcing the bookstore operation, a search that would culminate in Wallace's Bookstore soon taking over this role.[16]

Efforts to contain costs and increase enrollment, as well as continued controversy, highlighted Kustra's second year. Very soon faculty, *Eastern Progress* editor Jacinta Feldman, and others began asking, "We're reorganized, but where's the money?" The $13 million Funderburk reserve seemed to melt away quickly. Kustra increased spending on athletics, which itself drew criticism from some faculty. The "Buck Study," begun in 1998 by a consultant firm to bring equity to Eastern's compensation for faculty, staff, and hourly workers, also never seemed to produce much except confusion, as well as a good bit of administrative obfuscation. An across-the-board $900 increase for all employees, suggested by the study, helped those at the lower end of the income scale while infuriating some faculty. Whatever was being saved went into new initiatives, pushing growth at the centers in Corbin, Manchester, and Danville; funding a new Chautauqua lecture series directed by Bruce Maclaren; promoting athletics; and confronting declining enrollments and retention. All these initiatives cost money and added to budgetary problems.[17]

The meeting of the 2000 legislature highlighted many of the unresolved issues in Kentucky higher education. The Council on Postsecondary Education (CPE), under the leadership of Gordon Davies, wanted to control the higher education budget while cooperating with Governor Patton and the General Assembly. The question always remained in Kentucky higher education: Who would get the bigger piece of the pie, UK, UL, or the regional universities? By linking goals and performance, Eastern, with its enrollment problems, faced stiff competition from its sister institutions. When the new funding package appeared to favor Northern Kentucky University, Kustra complained bitterly to the CPE and legislature that EKU was getting short shrift. "I was carrying five presidents' water on that one," he later said in his defense. Kustra clashed with the crusading Davies, who envisioned molding Kentucky into the model he had once developed for Virginia. The *Lexington Herald-Leader* called this "whining for dollars," and David Hawpe in the Louisville *Courier-Journal* chided the Eastern president for using "well-placed legislative help," that is, EKU employee and state representative Harry Moberly, to seek favor with the legislature and thereby bypass Governor Patton's well-considered budget. In the end, EKU got a slight increase in its state aid, as well as funding for a new wellness center.[18]

The enrollment decline that bedeviled the late Funderburk years had to be reversed if Eastern was to keep up with its sister institutions. And since enrollment was tied to state funds, it became imperative that Eastern confront this issue head-on. Decreasing numbers of freshmen, as well as retention problems, confounded the school and made it difficult to meet the CPE goals. As always, a strong economy pulled potential students into the workforce who might otherwise go to schools like Eastern, which continued to draw many first-generation students. Moreover, several of Eastern's twenty-two county service areas had declining high school populations. First Rita Davis and then Aaron Thompson led the effort to reverse these trends as associate vice president for enrollment management. The Student Success Institute was one of several programs that worked to retain students. This initiative finally began to pay off in the fall of 2002, as total enrollment again climbed toward fifteen thousand. Money was at the heart of all problems. Retrofitting sprinklers in Keene, Clay, Dupree, and Todd Halls could be done with bonds, stretching the payments out. And it cost $750,000 to get Eastern's computers ready for the dreaded millennium "Y2K" bug. Now able to set the school's tuition rates, the regents approved a 7.5 percent increase for the 2001–2 school year. Only with that increase could all employees receive a 3 percent raise, after a hiring freeze in late 2000 when expenditures exceeded revenue at Eastern and further decreased Funderburk's fund balance.[19]

If the Funderburk era had been marked by administrative stability, the Kustra years were just the opposite. Several holdovers from the Martin-Powell era began to be dismissed or to retire. Stephen Byrn replaced James L. Grigsby as director of admissions. While the departure of director of alumni affairs Larry W. Bailey was peaceful, that of vice president for student affairs Thomas Myers was not. Former SGA president and current state representative Ken Upchurch came to Myers's defense and urged alumni not to contribute to the university. "Dr. Myers hasn't asked me to do anything," Upchurch said. "I'm doing this because I feel this president has done him a great injustice. It's atrocious." "When I came here to Eastern as president," Kustra retorted, "I was told by the Board to choose my own team and that is what I have done." In the end, Kustra got his way and a new vice president for student affairs, yet he suffered another wound, administratively and publicity-wise. Kustra "ran off most directors," claimed another victim, former personnel director Dale Lawrenz, who found Kustra's years to be a "huge mistake." Other longtime administrators such as Doug Whitlock, Skip Daugherty, and Jim Clark, moved into new positions.[20]

The young presidency of Robert W. Kustra continued to be troubled. By 2000, Daisy French, a retired accounting professor; alumni Fred Rice and Gary Abney; and faculty representative Merita Thompson gave an entirely new complexion to the board from the one that had elected Kustra in early 1998. Thompson voiced strong opposition to the president's giving across-the-board raises to all staff and faculty. Changing and even minimally raising entrance standards also became another point of contention as Eastern moved slowly away from the old tradition of "open admission." Unconditional admission would now require a composite score of 18 on the American College Test, a policy the *Eastern Progress* openly opposed. However, students could still get in under provisional or special admissions but then, as always, would have to prove themselves capable of doing college work. Clearly, Kustra and Marsden wanted to take Eastern into the realm of a more selective student body like that at Western. Already up for debate was an evaluation of the president, mandated every two years in his contract. With Kustra well into his third year, there was no consensus or plan for how to do so until a consultant was hired. With a growing antagonism between Kustra and the new board members, nothing seemed to get resolved. More important, when the board elected Rice as its new chair, replacing Gilbert, a new regime was clearly in power, and Kustra sensed that his days as EKU president were numbered.[21]

Eastern was not the only school in turmoil, as this was a turbulent era for the state's universities. The UK faculty often criticized Charles Wethington, as much for his personality as anything else, until he finally retired; Murray State University president Kern Alexander resigned in early 2001 after long squabbles with his faculty and regents; and President George Reid went through the revolving door at Kentucky State University. Western, Northern, and Morehead universities appeared to be spared from conflict as their presidents, faculties, and regents seemed compatible. Rumors circulated, quite publicly, that Kustra would soon leave and that a faculty vote of confidence was in the works.[22]

Just as Kathy Kustra was settling into a special post in Frankfort, helping steer the state's Medicaid program, her husband announced his resignation on February 14, 2001, with a year remaining in his contract. "I created a few people who took me off their Christmas card list, you could say," he said at an informal campus forum. "The decision seems appropriate to me in light of the significant number of new regents who have been appointed or elected since I was hired three years ago," he told the press. "I think this essentially new Board deserves the opportunity to hire a new president." Most of the regents reacted respectfully, especially Ernest House and Gilbert, to word of the resignation. "I'm devastated," regent Barbara Ricke said. "I think he did an unbelievable job." Describing himself as more of a "changer" than a "maintainer," Kustra claimed he never intended to stay long at EKU.[23]

Having a lame-duck president with a year remaining on his contract, the regents appeared in no hurry to begin the search for Kustra's successor. Regent chair Rice stated his desire to see Eastern "prosper and continue to do a great job." "We don't want to lose any ground that we've gained under Dr. Kustra," said staff regent David Williams. Moreover, money woes continued to dog the Richmond school. The regents passed a 2001–2 budget with a 1.5 percent across-the-board increase for faculty and staff and 1.5 percent for merit, with twenty-five positions being cut and a 7.5 percent tuition hike.[24]

Eastern remained in the news, for good or ill. When the regents met in executive session on March 27 to discuss hiring A. T. Kearney as the executive search consultant, the possibility of their violating the open meeting law made the press. Meanwhile, the regents and Kustra's lawyer negotiated a buyout of his contract. In early June the participants agreed that Eastern's ninth president would leave one year early for a buyout of $171,878, 20 percent of his deferred incentive package, and up to $1,000 for moving from Blanton House. Kustra already had a new job as a senior fellow with the Council of State Government in Lexington. In the end, all seemed to agree that Kustra's heart would not be in the effort for the coming year, and it was better for Eastern to cut its losses and get on with finding a new president.[25]

The spring and summer of 2001 were traumatic for the Eastern community, with almost everyone who had not already done so choosing up sides and further assessing the presidency of Robert W. Kustra. Citing the many innovations introduced, former faculty regent Richard Freed claimed, "Eastern is a better place than it was when he began his tenure." Government professor Jane D. Rainey also supported the positive side, praising the Illinoisan for his personal touch and sensitivity to campus issues. However, there were probably even more critics. One alumnus called Kustra a "better spinmeister than university president," who "was quick to declare himself an outstanding success—even as his lawyer negotiated his exit." "His role was to promote the values and mission of the university and not himself," argued Professor Norman Spain, who supported the buyout of the beleaguered president's contract. Others claimed that Kustra pushed athletics to the detriment of academic programs. When, in a newspaper piece, some regents too highly praised the Kustra administration and denigrated that of Funderburk, former vice president John D. Rowlett publicly challenged them to a debate. To him, EKU had obviously not been, as suggested by some, a "bloated and mediocre" institution when Kustra took over in 1998.[26]

It was doubtful that Kustra ever fully understood the Eastern culture and the Kentucky political environment. *Courier-Journal* reporter Dick Wilson observed that Kustra could never overcome the image of the "brash Yankee," who ran afoul of a more laid-back southern university community. Moreover, the president's wife did not fit the traditional mold of a campus first lady and said that she never intended to do so. A few months after he left office, Kustra took a swipe at the state while praising UK for appointing native Lee Todd as president. "In a state whose culture is still suspicious of outsiders with reform agendas," Kustra charged, "the new president can trump his critics with an earnestness, sincerity and love for the state and university that few can question." It was hard to be lukewarm either way about Kustra. One recent retiree called him, "a showman . . . a Rick Pitino of college and university presidents." Some agreed with the changes he pushed, like reorganization, but argued that he often rushed into decisions without adequate preparation and counsel. Provost Marsden believed that many of the initiatives Kustra instituted began to bear fruit only as he was leaving. Some faculty thought from the beginning that he meant to stay only a short while and build a name for himself. It was amazing to many Kustra watchers that, for all his political experience and alleged acumen, he got so brutally mauled in the Kentucky atmosphere. I found Kustra, unlike his predecessor, to be very interested in preserving Eastern's history, fully encouraging, for example, the writing of this history. Provost Marsden came up with the idea, adopted by the regents, of naming me as University Historian. Moreover, Kustra gave more encouragement to the arts than any previous president.[27]

Throughout all this turmoil, life went on at Eastern Kentucky University: classes met, students studied and played, committees deliberated, and issues and problems, other than the presidency of Bob Kustra, needed to be addressed. Dean David Gale of the newly renamed College of Health Sciences headed a project to incorporate the study of genetics into health curricula nationwide. The renamed College of Justice and Safety, further enhancing its reputation as "A Program of Distinction," entered into agreements with Russian and Finnish authorities to help train police personnel. The university community continued its never-ending dialogue about general education, the grade inflation bugaboo, the university writing requirement, a new plus/minus grading system, and, perhaps most explosive of all, post-tenure review. Just as Kustra was exiting, the old campus received an infusion of new life with the arrival of 320 students under the Governor's Scholars Program, a prestigious program that EKU had to bid for and work hard to host.[28]

A university campus is a never-ending creation and re-creation. The transition to the campuswide Banner computer program did not always go well, as the pesky system took longer than expected to implement. When Wallace's Bookstores deteriorated into bankruptcy due to the financial finagling of its founder, former governor Wallace Wilkinson, Eastern switched over to Barnes

& Noble as its outsourced book supplier. The university community entered into a dialogue, often divisive, about serving alcohol at official campus functions and at Arlington.[29]

Thankfully, institutions like Eastern Kentucky University have an inertia, a longevity, that can sustain them in times of crisis. At the 2001 spring commencement, Kustra's last, nearly fifteen hundred graduates celebrated with family and friends and looked forward to joining the workforce. These students had combined scholarships, grants, and work into successful college careers, with a little bit of luck thrown in by rubbing old Daniel Boone's left toe on occasion. For some, ROTC offered an opportunity for both college funds and a career. The three Eastern centers, as well as distance learning through the Kentucky Telelinking Network, offered more options to students than ever before. Students from the typically economically depressed Appalachian region continued to find success at EKU, "the school of opportunity." For example, when she graduated from Eastern, Cherish Charles from Wolfe County proved that with good teachers you could break out of the old stereotypes. "Eastern students become well-rounded individuals with an extensive sense of self," she testified during a graduation day speech.[30]

The physical campus, the built environment, also outlives most of its students, faculty, and staff. Eleven buildings on campus received recognition in 1999 by the Blue Grass Trust for Historic Preservation. The University Building's use has spanned three centuries, from the founding of old Central University in 1874. Of course, Eastern still desired Elmwood, Miss Emma Watts's old estate, within reach just across Lancaster Avenue, but the property always evading the university's grasp. A campus does change. As Eastern entered a new millennium, the old trailer park, which had never been seen as a permanent site, was finally demolished. Two landmarks, O'Donnell and Ellendale Halls, also were taken down to make room for the new $20 million Student Services Building. To keep up with the times, Eastern also began planning and then constructing a wellness center for all students just behind the Moberly Building. And, of course, there are never enough parking spaces for faculty, staff, and students. "I think parking sucks," said one exasperated coed in the *Progress,* claiming that faculty had too many spaces.[31]

Alumni, who remain connected to a school, also give it a sense of place and meaning. Annually voting several into Eastern's Hall of Distinguished Alumni was only one way of recognizing key individuals who served their alma mater. Alumni Weekends just before spring graduation become annual pilgrimages for many. However, Larry Bailey, former alumni director, noted in an interview that this "connectedness" became ever more difficult, as more recent alumni did not have the old traditional college experience. At the same time, alumni donations became more important as state support declined and tuition increased. Alumni Jean and Darrell Baker cochaired one fundraising effort. "Eastern is special to me, and I want to do what I can to help the university serve others as it has served me," Darrel said in an interview. Chryssa Zizos donated scholarship money to the journalism program in honor of her parents and Professor Libby Fraas. The sheer grit of some alumni amazes me. Aimee Bruder, a cum laude graduate who has been wheelchair-bound from childhood with cerebral palsy, won medals in Paralympics swimming events. Showing their love for each other as well as for Eastern, in 2001 Jane and Gene Wright renewed their marriage vows on their sixtieth anniversary at Walnut Hall in the Keen Johnson Building. Perhaps alumnus and sports information director Karl Park set a record. Before retiring in 2003, he spent a half century, beginning in the first grade at Model, on the Eastern campus.[32]

There are other signs of continuity on the old Richmond campus as it approaches its one hundredth anniversary. Since 1928, three generations of the Engle family have taught at Eastern, with Allen currently teaching in the College of Business and Technology. The Stephen Collins Foster Music Camp celebrated its sixty-ninth season in 2004, having had only a short hiatus during World War II. Programs such as ROTC have thrived in Richmond; Eastern's ROTC continues to graduate officers at a higher rate than much larger universities. "I look at who I've become and marvel that a skinny, red-headed girl from the hills of eastern Kentucky could be charged with defending this land," said air force pilot Captain Danielle L. Barnes. Since the early 1920s, the *Eastern Progress* has been an award-winning campus newspaper. Auxiliary groups, such as the EKU Women, founded in 1955, continued to be a source of support for the university by funding scholarships. WEKU-FM, managed by Tim Singleton, annually won awards for its news coverage by reporters Marie Mitchell, Ron Smith, and Stu Johnson. In early 2004 assistant manager John Gregory won a coveted Peabody Award for his documentary *Sisters in Pain*. And Model Laboratory School, so often written off as unnecessary, will, like Eastern, celebrate its one hundredth anniversary in 2006. Parenthetically, the Lancaster parking lot will continue to be controversial. Should it be for commuters or residents? Though the topic is often discussed, Greek societies may enter the next century without housing in a sorority and fraternity row.[33]

As at all institutions there is a campus culture, or at least subculture, at Eastern. It has changed over time, even in the thirty years I spent on campus as a student and a faculty member. The hallways have often been abuzz when the rumor mill was churning. Who is doing what? Who is up for tenure or promotion?

There have always been humorists at Eastern, from the time of Charles Keith to the present. Carl Hurley, who taught at Eastern from 1966 to 1969 and again from 1974 to 1982, became so adept at standup comedy he left teaching to become "America's Funniest Professor." He performs all over the nation with a gentle folksy humor based on his upbringing in East Bernstadt.[34]

The student sense of humor has always followed closely the popular culture and argot of the day, "you know." The *Eastern Progress* and other campus forums often included such humor. Students made jokes about the appearance, mannerisms, and speech habits of faculty members that sometimes reached my ears. For example, sometimes students good-naturedly called me Dr. Ike because of an apparent resemblance to Dwight D. Eisenhower. Several times I was mistaken on campus for redheaded Father Ronald Kettler, who appreciated the joke, given that I am a Baptist. In the midnineties students swore that one history prof looked like the actor who played Niles on the TV show *Frasier*. The rapid speech and malapropisms of one administrator became legendary. The list could go on and on, and alumni of different eras had similar experiences.

Faculty humor ranged from the sardonic to the sarcastic to self-deprecating to jesting about the none-too-secret peccadilloes of some colleagues. Examples of the latter included the foibles of faculty who had difficulties with the Seventh Commandment and other social anomalies.

When I first came to Richmond in 1970, an old hand explained one day that it was amazing that the United States of America got along fine with one vice president while Eastern needed four. Faculty sometimes thought of councils of deans or chairs in the same light that workers in the old Soviet Union viewed their commandants. One time, as the job market worsened, this oft-repeated joke circulated: "What is the most important thing for an arts and sciences major to learn to say? . . . Do you want fries with that?"

"What is green and sleeps eight?" asked one faculty member. The answer:

"an Eastern maintenance van." During one of my terms in the Faculty Senate, one member often bored the group to tears with his unnecessary orations. Once, while the miscreant was in the middle of one of his perorations, a fellow senator leaned over and whispered, "There he goes again, feigning intelligence."

Many on campus made good-natured fun of the southern accent of Alabamian Funderburk. Though not known as a scintillating public figure, he was very personable and even rather humorous in a small group. Most Funderburk jokes told by the faculty revolved around his well-known pecuniary prowess. After the hallways of the administration building were painted a battleship-like gray, someone said it was because the paint was navy surplus and therefore cheap. When Eastern started following five-year planning cycles, one teacher uttered a warning that the USSR had done so, and look what had happened to it.

Sometimes the humor could have quite a bite. The controversial era of Bob Kustra is a case in point. One local wag said the school name had been changed from EKU to BKU, or Bob Kustra University, while a Louisvillian called the administration the "Illinois Mafia." As another example of sarcasm, when the early retirement option began, with faculty receiving full retirement pay while teaching half-time, a cynic claimed that this was particularly appropriate for one individual because he had been teaching half-time for many years anyway. When controversy began to hit Eastern with Kustra's arrival and eventual departure, many humorists on campus likened the Richmond school to Murray State University, which had been going through similar turmoil for decades.

The Board of Regents of Eastern proceeded slowly and deliberately in naming Kustra's successor after his resignation and subsequent buyout. Chairman Rice headed a broad-based thirteen-person committee that included a member of the local community. Because the process began late in the school year, the regents made a wise decision and chose an interim president, Dr. Eugene M. Hughes, who had presidential experience at Northern Arizona University and Wichita State University, to serve for at least four months. Some believed the search might stretch much longer as the university faced a possible $4 million cut in state support.[35]

However, by early August, the search committee settled on five finalists, all vice presidents or provosts at universities. The list included two women. All the candidates made visits to the campus. Joanne Glasser, with training as a lawyer and executive vice president for institutional advancement at Towson University in Maryland, came to visit in the middle of the pack. "I truly believe the fit is good," she said. "I am the right person at the right time." On August 24, 2001, the regents named Glasser as Eastern's tenth president at a salary of $175,000 on a four-year contract. When asked over a speakerphone for her response, Glasser replied, "I accept it with pleasure and enormous gratitude."[36]

"I think she will really knock some people's socks off," said one regent. "Petite president packs a punch," the campus paper intoned, referring to the fifty-year-old Glasser's small stature and boundless energy. "Now, it's time to sit back and watch as the Glasser presidency unfolds and she demonstrates how a female president is a 'perfect match' for this university," the editorial continued. The Lexington paper urged her to "get behind higher-education reform." A widowed mother of two, Glasser brought her teenaged daughter to Richmond and settled into Hampton Inn while Hughes remained on the job until November 1. However, Eastern's tenth president wasted no time settling in as heir apparent.[37]

The 2001 fall semester got under way with renewed hope for a turnaround of enrollment and revenue problems. The regents approved a 9 percent tuition increase and took advantage of lower interest rates to refinance some bonds. Interim president Hughes planned for a 3 percent budget downturn in anticipation of further state cuts. Moreover, the Funderburk fund reserve had been entirely depleted by the time Kustra left office.[38]

The old Richmond campus warmly welcomed the new president and equally celebrated Roy Kidd's three hundredth win at Eastern in early September. Vice President Ken Johnston planned for further budget cuts, while students complained about tuition hikes. The Banner computer system inexorably made its way across campus. News about Greek Row returned to the front page of the campus newspaper, and the new plus/minus grading scale became a reality. Barnes & Noble took over the campus book sales with apparent success after the Wallace's Bookstore debacle.[39]

No one could have been prepared for what happened on September 11, 2001. Newspapers called it "The Day That Changed America." Nothing since the attack on Pearl Harbor on December 7, 1941, impacted the Eastern campus with such suddenness. Classes and normal activities came to a near standstill as everyone, spellbound, shocked, and grief stricken, witnessed an unimaginable tragedy on television. The campus pulled together in many ways. Military reservists awaited a call for active duty. The Counseling Center and other services made extra efforts to calm students' fears. A week later, "A Day of Remembrance and Reflection" on campus only slightly healed the wounds. An upsurge of prayer vigils and patriotism swelled numbers at several places, including a service ending with a candlelight vigil in the Ravine. President Glasser assured students, "We do not have to feel helpless, and we do not have to feel alone." First Baptist Church minister Bill Fort offered solace by insisting, "You're never going to find a good explanation for the evil that was carried out all over our country." The regents approved a total refund for all students called into active military duty. As usual, 9/11 touched off a campus debate, with some professors seemingly taking an Arabist position, arguing that the United States gave too much support to Israel or that we should not be meddling in other nations' affairs. Retired history professor Walter M. Odum retorted in the *Progress,* "Since when is terrorism an understandable reaction by states that feel diplomatically or economically slighted?"[40]

In the face of the international crisis and domestic economic doldrums, Joanne Glasser became president, officially, on October 29, 2001. Speaking at a November 8 convocation, she stressed the need for unity, promising that "the best is yet to come." "We are on the threshold of taking this university to the next level," she maintained. "Together, we must dream big dreams. And together, we must work hard to achieve them." She challenged the university community to set higher academic goals and its professors to work harder. To the students she assured, "You are our number one priority."[41]

Glasser faced a daunting challenge. Kustra's brief sojourn at Eastern divided the community, the university, and the Board of Regents. The economic problems of the state and nation continued to affect the Richmond campus. Moreover, enrollment, maintenance, and badly needed construction projects had to be addressed.

After the almost informal Kustra inauguration in the Ravine, the ceremony for Glasser returned much of the old pomp and circumstance to the occasion in Alumni Coliseum. With the theme "Passion for Life and Learning," the ceremonies included music by university ensembles. The University Singers and poetry readings by faculty members highlighted the day. Comments from Governor Patton included his admonition that "a true revenue crisis" would force hard decisions for the new president. The oath delivered by Joseph E.

Lambert, chief justice of the Kentucky Supreme Court, with Glasser flanked by her two children, and the presentation of the presidential medallion by C. Fred Rice, chair of the regents, completed the formalities of the day.[42]

In her inaugural address, Glasser exuded energy and confidence that captivated the audience. "Passion" seemed to be the watchword as she promised "this won't be a one-woman show." "I have a passion for the life of the mind for life-long learning. My task as EKU president is to make the crucial interchange between teacher and student easier to conduct, in an atmosphere that encourages inquiry and discussion." Moreover, she stressed the continued need for shared governance with faculty and staff. "We want to be known as a UNIVERSITY OF DISTINCTION. Together we can lift Eastern to that next level of excellence." A first-ever Presidential Ball the following evening as part of First Weekend celebrated the launching of a new administration.[43]

With the bleak fiscal forecast, the tenth president of Eastern faced a difficult task in improving the university's stature. Moreover, she did not know just how bare the cupboard was, since her predecessor had run through Funderburk's nearly $13 million slush fund in less than three years. Some wondered when the new president, who was noted for her work habits, ever slept or ate. Representative Harry Moberly noted that his cohorts in Frankfort were impressed. "It was obvious that she was knowledgeable and very passionate about higher education," he said, after Glasser spoke before legislators. Not only would working with the CPE and solons in Frankfort be important for Glasser, but she also had to quickly establish good relations with faculty, staff, and salaried employees at Eastern.[44]

Glasser's first year on campus proved to be exciting. Not only did Roy Kidd win his three hundredth victory, but the Lady Colonels, as cochampions of the OVC, made it into the second round of the National Invitational Tournament. The *Eastern Progress* celebrated its eightieth anniversary and continued winning national awards. There were the usual campus debates over issues large and small. Students and faculty discussed the merits of a plus/minus grading system, student government reorganized, and the ill-fated Lancaster crosswalk lasted only a short time. Unfortunately, the early Glasser administration had to contend with continual budget cuts mandated from Frankfort, as well as having no reserve funds. Four budget cuts in two years hit the entire state hard and frayed everyone's nerves. The Faculty Senate pushed for a cost-of-living allowance for 2002–3. The regents passed a $151 million budget that achieved three goals on which President Glasser stood firm: no layoffs, maintaining health benefits, and across-the-board raises of 2.7 percent. Faculty and staff were now in a trying period when significant raises were out of the question. Moreover, annual tuition increases were now the norm.[45]

Eastern's campus, like that at any institution, has needed constant attention and long-range planning. It has not always aged gracefully. After years of neglect the overloaded electrical system failed miserably, plunging the campus into darkness on several occasions. With $12 million needed for a general overhaul, Glasser squeezed funds out of a tight budget to match a state grant for beginning the project in mid-2002 with $1.8 million. James C. Street, director of facilities services, faced other challenges on a growing campus. The Harry Moberly Building (named for the father of the state representative), which was designated for athletics and physical training, whetted average students' appetites for their own Student Fitness and Wellness Center. In October 2002, Governor Patton took part in the dedication of the new $20 million Student Services Building, a facility housing "one-stop shopping" for everything from admissions to testing. The auditorium was named for Eastern's fifth president, William F. O'Donnell, because the residence hall named for him had been torn down to make way for the structure. Unfortunately, construction of a Business and Technology Center on the site of old Vicker's Village proceeded slowly in 2004 because of a worldwide steel shortage. Capital requests for new construction on campus would be constrained by the ebb and flow of the national and state economies.[46]

As the Glasser presidency unfolded, administrative posts changed. Like any executive, she wanted her own people in the top ranks. Allen Ault became dean of the College of Justice and Safety in April 2003, replacing Gary Cordner. Provost Marsden, resigned after one year in the Glasser administration, to be temporarily replaced by education dean Mark Wasicsko. In mid-2003, the university appointed Lyle Cook, vice president for academic affairs at Black Hills State University, as the new provost and vice president for academic affairs. At the same time Eastern put a freeze on hiring, and Glasser decided not to replace retiring vice president for administrative affairs Doug Whitlock. James Conneely, vice president for student affairs; Bart Meyer, vice president for university advancement; and a number of associate vice presidents rounded out the Glasser appointments through 2004. Marc Whitt returned to his alma mater as associate vice president of public relations and marketing.[47]

If the economy was uncertain, enrollment wavering, and the international crises troubling in the first decade of the twenty-first century, one thing was certain: Eastern continued its love of sport. After twenty-two successful seasons as head baseball coach, Jim Ward retired in 2001. Two years later, longtime head trainer Bobby Barton retired after twenty-seven years, being replaced by Johnda Wireman, one of the few female head trainers in the NCAA. Hired in the Kustra years, men's head basketball coach Travis Ford continued the uphill battle to return the Colonels to the old days of glory. Meanwhile, women's coach Larry Joe Inman won his four hundredth college game in early 2003 and continued turning out winning teams each season. The position of athletics director changed hands several times before the appointment of John Shafer in early 2003. With previous experience as athletic director at Mississippi State University, he took on the task of raising the profile of Eastern athletics, as well as enhancing its revenues through fund-raising and increasing attendance. Scholar-athletes in the non-revenue-producing sports labored as hard as ever. Alan Horton won the 2002 OVC Scholar-Athlete Award for his classroom and track prowess. Senior Jonelle Csora threw a no-hitter in her last home game in 2003 and finished her career as one of the all-time OVC softball greats. In 2002, Eastern athletes won a record eighth OVC Academic Achievement Banner for their high grade point average.[48]

All eras come to an end, and that of Roy Kidd concluded in 2002. Elected to the College Football Hall of Fame after his thirty-ninth season, Kidd represented a dying breed: a perennial winner who sticks to one school. With 310 victories (ranking eighth all-time among college coaches), two national titles, and sixteen OVC championships, he left a great legacy that will be difficult to duplicate. Nevertheless, Danny Hope, a guard on Kidd's 1979 NCAA Division I-AA championship team, took on that challenge, finishing with a 7–5 record in 2003.[49]

Politics is never far from the center of education in Kentucky, whether it be a battle over appropriations in the General Assembly or campus intrigues. A good old-fashioned political donnybrook erupted in 2002 with CPE president Gordon Davies at the center. After the education reforms of the first Patton administration, including the transfer of the University of Kentucky's community colleges to the Kentucky Community and Technical College System, the governor's legacy began to unravel. Clearly there was no love lost with leaders in the General Assembly and the head of the CPE. Davies, along with *Courier-Journal* editor David Hawpe and the editors of the *Lexington Herald-Leader,* argued that the interference of the regional university supporters in the legislature, particularly Harry Moberly for Eastern and Jody Richards for Western, had set back higher education reform. The issues were deep and wide over how funds should be allocated. President Gary Ransdell of Western Kentucky University denied that "mission creep" was at the heart of the debate. In the end the CPE decided not to renew Davies's contract, and the governor concurred. Claiming that reform had worked under his direction, Davies snapped. "What the hell do I need to apologize for?" In contrast, English professor Joe Glaser of Western chided Davies for his "epic self-puffery" and for clearly siding with the "flagships," UK, UL, and Northern Kentucky University. With the combative Davies gone, the relations among all parties involved—the CPE, Kentucky's universities, the state legislature, and the governor—clearly needed mending.[50]

With the controversial presidency of Robert Kustra, local wags often compared Eastern's recent history to that of its distant cohort, Murray State University, which has a reputation for seemingly endless roiling local and state political intrigues. When Governor Patton signed into law Senate Bill 152, sponsored by Madison Countian Ed Worley, on March 10, 2003, few understood the full repercussions. The law required that regents at Kentucky's six regional universities live within the continental United States. Because Board of Regents chairman C. Fred Rice had recently changed his permanent residence to the American Virgin Islands, the law appeared to be aimed directly at him. Rice had a challenge filed in his name in Franklin Circuit Court, claiming the bill to be unconstitutional.[51]

With charges of a Worley-Moberly "power play" voiced in the campus newspaper, lawyers, legislators, Eastern's regents, editorialists, and letters to the editor spiced up the issue. The Lexington paper claimed that Worley's actions were "more suitable to a banana republic than an institution of higher learning." A temporary restraining order allowed Rice to remain on the board in early April. Meanwhile, Moberly claimed to have quickly lost interest in the Eastern presidency in 2001 and to have had no hand in the new law. Six members of the Board of Regents, the chair of the Faculty Senate, and Eastern's representative to the state university senate coalition signed a letter to the governor supporting Rice. In an abrupt about-face, Worley and Moberly relented, asking the CPE to apply the law only to future prospective regents and not those currently serving. Finally, Rice, Patton, and the CPE agreed to this compromise, and the court ruled that way. Said Rice, "I never had any doubt about it."[52]

Since 9/11, especially with the nearby Bluegrass Army Depot, Eastern responded, like many other American institutions, to the threats to homeland security. Everyone's nerves were a bit frayed at times. The forensics courses taught by Professor Tom Thurman, who as an FBI agent helped investigate the 1988 bombing of Pan American Flight 103 over Lockerbie, Scotland, took on added meaning. More and more students left school to join reserve and National Guard units on active duty in preparation for the invasion of Iraq in early 2003. Formal and informal debates stirred the campus. At a "Colonels for Peace" rally in March, minor confrontations between students reminded some old hands of the Vietnam War days. The war gave renewed seriousness to ROTC training. Cadet Ryan Knapp spent some time training with our British allies in England, while Marine Corporal Jesse Palmer, one of dozens of students activated, patrolled the streets of Nasiriya, Iraq. Lieutenant Colonel Brett Morris's Pershing Rifles Company continued to win awards.[53]

Students at Eastern in the early Glasser years faced not only the challenges of a world seemingly bent on terrorism, reprisal, and war but many homegrown problems as well. Campus security remained a concern for students and parents alike. And ever-accelerating technologies challenged students, faculty, and staff to control "high-tech" cheating using the Internet, text messaging, and cell phones. EKU made a special effort to keep students on campus over weekends. First Weekend, more than 180 clubs and organizations, athletic events, and the arts gave students more extracurricular activities than ever before. However, when asked by the *Eastern Progress* if she was taking part in Family Weekend, one coed replied, "I didn't know of any events. I never know what's going on." More efforts than ever before were aimed at welcoming new students to campus. As a sign of a maturing university, the Honors Program continued to challenge students and participated widely in regional and national conferences. The Student Success Institute, formed to improve Eastern's retention rate, seemed to be working.[54]

Most students thrived in the Eastern environment, including nontraditional student and mother of three Kristina O'Brien, who found time to serve as Student Government Association president and later won a trip to a space program conference in Germany. EKU students traveled to Antarctica, Europe, and Asia and won awards for their research efforts. Following some bad publicity, fraternities and sororities redoubled their efforts to serve the campus and community. In 2003 the EKU Interfraternity Council won an award in an eight-state region for community service and philanthropy.[55]

Unfortunately, Eastern lost little of its reputation for being a party school in the early twenty-first century. After an extensive study the regents adopted a revised alcohol policy in late 2002, allowing beer and wine at some official university functions but only under the strictest conditions and for no one under age twenty-one. "Tailgating" regulations also allowed liquor consumption, but again with restrictions. In the fall of 2003, new Alcohol Beverage Control regulations tightened control over the downtown bars by changing licensing procedures. It remained to be seen if this would hinder the serious drinking problems of some students at First Street "watering holes," particularly when hundreds of Eastern students and others flocked downtown on Thursday evenings. At the same time, religious organizations on campus appeared to be stronger than ever, and hundreds of students attended a revival in Brock Auditorium in early 2003.[56]

Into the first decade of the new century, Eastern's faculty, staff, and alumni succeeded in an ever-changing world. In the arts the enigmatic Hal Charles kept writing mysteries. Poet Dorothy Sutton received not only a Foundation Professorship but also national awards. David Elias won an outstanding teacher award for 2002 from the South Atlantic Association of Departments of English. David Greenlee, director of choral activities before his retirement, took a group of Eastern's students and alumni to perform under his direction at world-famous Carnegie Hall. In the sciences, Walter Borowski worked as a geological chemist in ocean-drilling research. Eastern's 2004 Foundation Professor honoree, Jerry Cook, a first-generation college graduate from Knott County, worked on several large grant projects. Laura Melius, director of career services, received a Star Award from the Southern Association of Colleges and Employers in 2003. Everyone continued to be amazed by the energy of African American mathematics professor Robert Blythe, who also served as pastor of the First Baptist Church on Francis Street, worked for racial justice, and was elected to the Richmond City Commission. These are only a few of the many faculty members who went that extra mile to serve students, the commonwealth, and the nation.[57]

Eastern's academic departments also expanded their efforts. Continuing to educate more public school teachers than any other institution in the state, the College of Education also hosted important national conferences. Raising the quality of education graduates continued to be a priority of Dean Mark Wasicsko. Younger scholars in the Department of History began turning out monographs regularly. The Teaching and Learning Center, the Center for

Appalachian Studies, and the Center for Kentucky History and Politics held conferences and found new ways to serve the region. Some things always remain the same. For example, the university continued to wrestle with general education requirements.[58]

Eastern alumni also felt the challenges of a new age. Their fund-raising efforts became even more crucial in the face of a national economic crisis and depleted state funding. Alumni Crystal Wilkinson, Linda Scott DeRosier, and Silas House turned out award-winning poetry and fiction. ROTC alumni served at home and abroad. Army colonel Terry Carrico became the first warden of Camp X-Ray at Guantanamo Bay, Cuba. African American Anthany Beatty worked his way up through the ranks to become Lexington police chief in 2001. "I wouldn't trade anything for what Eastern exposed me to," he said. In another milestone for EKU, as well as the state of Kentucky, alumna Elaine Farris became the first black school superintendent in the commonwealth when she took over the Shelby County position. In late 2003 Steve Pence became Eastern's first graduate to be elected lieutenant governor of the Commonwealth of Kentucky, proving again that the school's graduates could compete with the best in the state and nation.[59]

With an increasingly stingy state legislature, outside funding became more important than ever. By raising nearly $5 million in endowed gifts Eastern reached its 2000–2 biennium goal to receive matching funds for the "Bucks for Brains" program, to be used mostly for student scholarships. In early 2003, EKU's Justice and Safety Center received a grant of $15 million from the Department of Justice to improve communication between law enforcement agencies and to test new technologies. Moreover, true to Eastern's original charge, a $1.34 million National Science Foundation grant made it possible in early 2003 to improve instruction in science, technology, and mathematics in six local middle schools.[60]

In tough economic times, Eastern and its president set high goals. "Eastern Kentucky University will be the leading comprehensive university in the Commonwealth of Kentucky, earning national distinction, where students come first," announced a new vision statement, adopted in the fall of 2003. "Eastern Kentucky University is a student-centered comprehensive public university dedicated to high-quality instruction, service, and scholarship," read its mission statement, one that had not changed significantly since the granting of university status in 1966.[61]

Positive signs in the fall of 2003 included increasing enrollment for the third year in a row and the largest in a dozen years. The university reported increases in all areas, the most important of which was retention, where Eastern had lagged behind other state institutions for years. Moreover, the average ACT entrance score also increased by nearly a point from the previous year, indicating an improving freshman class. Nearing the sixteen-thousand-student mark recalled the early days of the Martin administration, when enrollments seemed to skyrocket each autumn. Flexibility in summer school terms also encouraged an increase in enrollment. Now goals set by the CPE had to be met to comply with higher education reform tied to state funding. Eastern continued to house a larger number of students than any other state institution. Innovations such as nonsmoking floors in residence halls and two totally smoke-free dormitories were adopted.[62]

Glasser took a special interest in improving opportunities for minorities. She set a goal of greatly increasing diversity on campus, including initiating the Joanne K. Glasser Diversity Scholarship, and named Sandra Moore as a special assistant to the provost. However, Eastern's low African American student enrollment persisted.[63]

As Eastern neared it centennial celebration, budget woes challenged its attempts to fulfill its mission and vision statements. Everything on campus suffered, including something dear to the heart of an academic: library journal subscriptions. The university regents sought new sources of revenue, including having students pay for higher course loads and imposing other fees as more state budget cuts in 2003 became a reality. Jamie Vinson, editor of the *Progress,* argued that the students themselves should be a bigger part of the discussion. The *Progress* criticized Glasser for retaining recently retired Coach Roy Kidd as an ombudsman and included a cartoon of the president. There appeared to be no end in sight to state shortfalls unless the entire state revenue and tax system was reevaluated and reformed. Governor Ernie Fletcher, elected in 2003, addressed the problem, with the usual legislative infighting threatening major reform.[64]

Just as the Glasser administration and the regents appeared to solve one budget crisis, another appeared. Moreover, when the regents attempted to give the president a $20,000 annual salary supplement, the whole matter got caught up in a confused state of affairs. Whether this supplement was to be funded through the university or the EKU Foundation, the press charged that the regents broke the open meetings law when they discussed the issue in an executive session. In the end Glasser resolved the controversy by refusing to accept any salary supplement. "I love what I do and do what I love," she said.[65]

There was no respite from budget problems. Low-income students particularly felt the pressure as they faced higher tuition and other costs at the same time that federal assistance was declining. In an unprecedented move, Eastern's regents approved a midyear tuition surcharge in December 2003 for spring 2004 and later substantially increased both room rates and tuition for the 2004–5 school year. Perhaps President Glasser best summed up this conundrum, balancing student costs with university revenues, when she said, "I think our goal should always be to offer great quality at an affordable cost." It now appeared that annual tuition increases, often in the double digits, would be the norm, particularly as the General Assembly wrangled on endlessly during and after its annual 2004 session. Another budget cut seemed assured. Meanwhile, almost miraculously, student enrollment continued to climb.[66]

In early 2004 President Glasser became a high-profile candidate for the presidency at Illinois State University, a Ph.D.-granting institution somewhat larger than EKU. Faculty, students, friends, and some regents reacted with alarm. The *Progress* editorialized that "losing her would have a negative impact on Eastern" because of momentum gained after the crises of the later Funderburk and Kustra administrations. A student letter to the campus paper was not as kind, accusing Glasser of "leaving a sinking ship" and "looking for greener pastures." After being chosen as one of three finalists for the post, Glasser dropped out of the search in late February. "I need to be at my home and Eastern is really my home," she told the *Progress,* to the collective relief of the entire community. With the hiring of a new president at Kentucky State University in early 2004, Glasser became the lowest-paid president of a state school. Within weeks the EKU Foundation supplemented Glasser's salary with a $40,000 stipend from its unrestricted funds.[67]

The French have a saying: "The more things change, the more they remain the same." As a hundred years of education on the Eastern campus drew to a close, there was continuity as well as division, signs of progress and stagnating inertia. Provost Cook and Vice President Johnston resigned in mid-2004. James Chapman accepted an appointment as interim provost. Eastern's reputation as a party school remained, even though it was now tougher for the under-twenty-one-year-old crowd to drink openly downtown. Students remained apathetic about campus elections, with only one in fifteen voting for student government president. With cost a growing concern, the Faculty Senate even talked about scrapping entirely the IDEA faculty evaluation format. At the same time, completion of the new Student Fitness and Wellness Center, the Corbin Center, and the dedication of the Veterans Memorial near the Meditation Chapel testified to Eastern Kentucky University's preparation for the future and remembrance of the past.[68]

In spring 2004 a positive sign of the university's commitment to excellence came in the hiring of critically acclaimed authors Silas House and Frank X Walker in the creative writing program of the Department of English and Theatre. The institution's future depended on hiring long-term, well-trained, and dedicated faculty rather than short-timers who perhaps viewed a sojourn in Richmond as a stepping-stone to larger universities. Eastern will also need a successful Capital Campaign led by alumni Dustan and Becki McCoy as it faces diminishing direct state support and the uncertain economy of the twenty-first century. If Eastern Kentucky University is to survive another one hundred years, it will need farsighted leadership, a student base that is improving in both quantity and quality, and caring faculty and administrators. When John D. Rowlett died in April 2004, the torch had already been passed to another generation. The last nurse to attend him began her studies at the Corbin satellite campus. "She got her start because dad and many of his colleagues believed the university could reach out to you and people responded to it," said Rowlett's son, also an EKU graduate. If Eastern is to fulfill its destiny as a "school of opportunity" in the twenty-first century, it must continue to reach out to the students of Kentucky and beyond.[69]

Notes

A Note on Sources

The work of any historian is only as strong as the sources used in his or her writing and published work. Eastern Kentucky University is blessed with an extensive and well-organized archive, initiated when Charles Hay came to the school in 1976. I have used these sources extensively and intensively, particularly between 1999 and 2003. Beginning with a small but important Central University collection, I have tried to utilize as much of the Eastern collections as possible in writing this book.

The papers of the presidential administrations, the minutes of the Board of Regents, and other internal records have been perused. As one gets nearer to the present, the amount of paper material quite obviously grows, as the information age added exponentially to the bulk of the record. The work of the historian is much like that of a reaper, winnowing the chaff from the grain, the inconsequential from the important.

If all history is essentially local, it is also biographical and ultimately about the human condition. Oral histories have played a prominent role in this book. William Berge, Beckie Denton, and others, including myself, have collected enough interviews over the years with alumni, staff, administrators, and others to flesh out what is missing from the written record of the Eastern experience.

Secondary sources are always important in a study such as this. Newspapers, including the *Louisville Courier-Journal,* the *Lexington Herald-Leader,* the *Richmond Register,* and the *Eastern Progress* have been particularly useful.

I have read and used histories of other institutions, some of them extensively, especially Lowell H. Harrison's history of *Western Kentucky University* (1987). Earlier histories of Eastern, *Three Decades of Progress* (1936) and *Five Decades of Progress* (1957), edited by Jonathan Truman Dorris, provided excellent sources for the first fifty years of this institution. In addition, Frederick D. Ogden's *Gladly Learn and Gladly Teach: The College of Arts and Sciences, 1965–1979, Eastern Kentucky University* (1999) and James McClanahan and Rhonda Smith's *Justice and Safety Education at Eastern Kentucky University: "A Historical Perspective"* (2001) tell the stories of two interesting facets of Eastern life. Similar studies should be made of such subjects as the College of Education, the College of Health Sciences, and Eastern athletics through the years. Owing to its extensive collections, a separate book based entirely on oral histories of Eastern is warranted.

1. Center of a Storm

1. Stuart W. Sanders, "Family Feud," *Kentucky Humanities,* no. 1 (1999): 14–17; Lowell H. Harrison and James C. Klotter, *A New History of Kentucky* (Lexington: University Press of Kentucky, 1997), chaps. 13–17; Charles B. Castner, "Louisville & Nashville Railroad," *The Kentucky Encyclopedia* (Lexington: University Press of Kentucky, 1992), 578–80.

2. Harrison and Klotter, *A New History of Kentucky,* chap. 15, 393–99; Hambleton Tapp and James C. Klotter, *Kentucky: Decades of Discord, 1865–1900* (Frankfort: Kentucky Historical Society, 1977), 198–99.

3. Jonathan Truman Dorris, "Central University, Richmond, Kentucky," *Register of the Kentucky Historical Society* 32 (April 1934): 92–95; Randall Balmer and John R. Fitzmier, *The Presbyterians* (Westport, Conn.: Greenwood Press, 1993), 73; Louis B. Weeks, "Presbyterian Church," *The Kentucky Encyclopedia,* 736–38.

4. Dorris, "Central University," 95; Walter L. Lingle and John W. Kuykendall, *Presbyterians: Their History and Beliefs* (Atlanta: John Knox Press, 1978), chap. 8.

5. Dorris, "Central University," 95; Fred A. Engle Jr., "Central University of Richmond, Kentucky," *Register of the Kentucky Historical Society* 66 (July 1968): 280–81; Weeks, "Presbyterian Church," 737.

6. Ernest Trice Thompson, *Presbyterians in the South,* Vol. 2, *1861–1890* (Richmond, Va.: John Knox Press, 1983), 359; Richard C. Brown, *The Presbyterians: Two Hundred Years in Danville, 1784–1984* (Danville, Ky.: Danville Presbyterian Church, 1983), 99–100; Dorris, "Central University," 96; Audrea McDowell, "Stuart Robinson," *The Encyclopedia of Louisville* (Lexington: University Press of Kentucky, 2000), 766–67; Kenneth Dennis, "Bennett Henderson Young," *The Encyclopedia of Louisville,* 962–63; Klotter, "Robert Jefferson Breckinridge," *The Kentucky Encyclopedia,* 120; Klotter, "William Campbell Preston Breckinridge," *The Kentucky Encyclopedia,* 121; Lewis B. Weeks, *Kentucky Presbyterians* (Atlanta: John Knox Press, 1983), 78, 83, 86, 88, 90–92, 98–105; Minutes of the Boards of Curators and Trustees of Central University, Richmond, Kentucky, Organized May 28, 1873, June 9, 1884, Central University Records, University Archives, Eastern Kentucky University (hereafter cited as Minutes of the Boards). All Central University records cited are held in the University Archives, Eastern Kentucky University.

7. Dorris, "Central University," 97; Robert L. Breck File, undated ms., Central University Records, Townsend Room; *Richmond Register,* October 26, 1991; Robert Stuart Sanders, *Presbyterianism in Versailles and Woodford County, Kentucky* (Louisville: Dunne Press, 1963), 38–39; Engle, "Central University," 280; Central University, Box 1, the Alumni Association of Central University.

8. Breck File; *Founders Day Program* (Richmond: Eastern Kentucky State College, 1964), 6; *Richmond Register,* October 26, 1991; Sanders, *Presbyterianism in Versailles,* 38–39; Dorris, "Central University," 97–99; Dwayne D. Cox and William J. Morison, *The University of Louisville* (Lexington: University Press of Kentucky, 2000), 62; *The Kentucky Register,* September 25, 1874.

9. *Richmond Register,* November 22, 1999; William E. Ellis, H. E. Everman, and Richard D. Sears, *Madison County: 200 Years in Retrospect* (Richmond: Madison County Historical Society, 1985), 243, 245; Marion B. Lucas, "Berea College in the 1870s and 1880s: Student Life at a Racially Integrated Kentucky College," *Register of the Kentucky Historical Society* 98 (Winter 2000): 1–22.

10. Minutes of the Boards, May 28, 29, December 31, 1873; "Historical Sketch," *Cream and Crimson, 1901* (Richmond, Ky.: Central University, 1901), 9–10; Hoyt D. Gardner Jr., "Dentistry," *The Encyclopedia of Louisville,* 243–44; Penelope Papangelis, "Medical Schools," *The Encyclopedia of Louisville,* 604; *Central News,* March 6, 1897; *Richmond Register,* September 26, 1987; "Sketch of Central University," *Cardinal and Blue, 1903* (Danville: Central University of Kentucky, 1903), 12–15; Jane Elizabeth Munson, "Breathitt County, Kentucky" (M.A. thesis, University of Miami [Ohio], 1970), 44.

11. *Kentucky Register,* August 7, 1874.

12. Breck File, undated ms.; *Kentucky Register,* September 25, 1874; Dorris, "Central University," 97–99; Minutes of the Boards, December 31, 1873, April 14, 30, 1874; *First Annual Catalogue of the Officers and Students of Central University, 1874–75* (Richmond: Central University, 1875), 1, 6–7, 10.

13. Dorris, "Central University," 100; Ellis, Everman, and Sears, *Madison County,* 237–38; 127 Central University Records, 84A2, Box 4; *Kentucky Register,* August 4, 1908; *Richmond Register,* December 10, 2000; *Courier-Journal,* April 18, 1885.

14. Dorris, "Central University," 101; Minutes of the Boards, March 6, 1882, February 22, 1898; Alumni Association Minutes, Box 1, February 22, 1898.

15. *Richmond Register,* April 1, 1999; *Eastern Progress,* April 1, 1999; *Courier-Journal,* April 18, 1885; Dorris, "Central University," 106–7; "Central University," *Atlantis* 8 (November 1889): 108; Engle, "Central University," 295; Minutes of the Boards, March 6, 1882, March 2, 1883; *Central News,* August 6, 1898.

16. Dorris, "Central University," 101–2; *Eleventh Catalogue of Central University, 1884–85,* 26–29; Engle, "Central University," 293–94.

17. *Kentucky Register,* June 6, 1879, May 14, 1880; Minutes of the Boards, March 9, 1880; Breck File, undated ms.

18. Weeks, *Kentucky Presbyterians,* 119; Robert Stuart Sanders, *Presbyterianism in Paris and Bourbon County, Kentucky, 1786–1961* (Louisville: Dunne Press, 1961), 106–8; Sanders, *Presbyterianism in Versailles,* 40; Minutes of the Boards, June 9, July 1, 1880; Blanton to Dr. ?, April 19, 1889, Central University Records, Townsend Room.

19. Tapp and Klotter, *Kentucky: Decades of Discord,* 199–200, 202, 204; Hopkins, *The University of Kentucky,* chap. 6; *Kentucky Register,* November 25, 1881, March 10, 1882.

20. List of Scholarships, Central University Records; Central University Records, Student's Series, List of Students Graduating from Central University, 1875–1901; *Central University, Fourteenth Annual Commencement, Wednesday, June 13th, 1898*, Program; Central University Tuition Account Books, Central University Records, Townsend Room; Dorris, "Central University," 120; Financial Series, Account Books, Tuition, 1885, Box 2; Ellis, Everman, and Sears, *Madison County*, 244; Lloyd J. Graybar, "Husband Edward Kimmel," *Encyclopedia of Kentucky*, 517.

21. *Nineteenth Annual Catalogue of the Central University of Kentucky, 1892–93*, 54; Engle, "Central University," 291; Central University Faculty Report, 1883–91, microfilm; *Central News*, October 6, 1897; Archie Woods to A. G. Woods, n.d., 1874, September 26, October 2, 1874.

22. *Founder's Day Program*, 7; Engle, "Central University," 301; *Kentucky Register*, June 30, 1880, June 16, September 1, 1882; Shannon Wilson and Daniel G. Stroup, "Day Law," *The Kentucky Encyclopedia*, 258–59; *Central News*, April 3, 1897; *Cream and Crimson, 1901*, 129; *University Hot Times*, April 1900; Dennis Cusick, "Walter Newman Haldeman," *The Encyclopedia of Louisville*, 365–66.

23. Minutes of the Boards, June 7, 1887, June 8, 1891, May 6, 1893, June 12, 1895, June 10, 1896, June 8, 1898, June 13, 1899, June 12, 1900, June 4, 1901; *Atlantis* (March? 1894): 18; Engle, "Central University," 294; *Central News*, October 6, 1897, June 23, 1900; *Cream and Crimson of '98*, vol. 4, 26.

24. Minutes of the Boards, September 5, 1892; Dorris, "Central University," 118–19; Engle, "Central University," 290; *Central News*, March 6, 1897, January 26, 1898, May 16, June 23, 1900; *Cream and Crimson, 1896*, 89–90; *Cream and Crimson, 1895*, 53.

25. *Cream and Crimson, 1896*, 101–8; *Cream and Crimson of '98*, 143, 145–48.

26. Dorris, "Central University," 105; Engle, "Central University," 288; *Cream and Crimson, 1896*, 79–80; *Atlantis* (April 1887): n.p.; *Atlantis* 8 (January 1890): 4; Third Anniversary Celebration of the Epiphyllidian and Walters Literary Societies of Central University, Wednesday, June 13, 1877; *Central News*, February 16, 1898; *Courier-Journal*, April 18, 1885.

27. Faculty Records, Central University Microfilm, 1883–1901; Dorris, "Central University," 107; Engle, "Central University," 288; Central University Records, Student's Series, Fraternity History; *Cream and Crimson, 1900*, 67–89; *Atlantis* (February 1895): 2–9; *Atlantis* (February 1896): 2–9; Helen Lefkowitz Horowitz, *Campus Life: Undergraduate Cultures from the End of the Eighteenth Century to the Present* (Chicago: University of Chicago Press, 1987), chap. 6.

28. *University Hot Times* 1, no. 23 (April 1900) (this is the only extant issue found in the University Archives at Eastern Kentucky University); *Cream and Crimson, 1896*, 8.

29. *Oxford American* (November/December 1999): 9; Tapp and Klotter, *Kentucky: Decades of Discord*, 112–13.

30. Tapp and Klotter, *Kentucky: Decades of Discord*, 112–13; "Football," *The Kentucky Encyclopedia*, 339–41.

31. Gerald Griffin, "Footbrawl in Old Kentucky," *Courier-Journal Magazine,* October 12, 1952, 33, 35; *Atlantis* (? 1894): 7; *Atlantis* (February 1896): n.p.; *Cream and Crimson, 1896,* 94; *Cream and Crimson, 1900,* 19, 120; Dorris, "Central University," 106–7.

32. *Central News,* October 6, 27, 1897, November 30, 1898, December 6, 1899; *Editor and Publisher 72* (February 11, 1939): n.p., found in Central University Records; *Kentucky Register,* May 22, 1885; *Central News,* October 31, 1900.

33. *Cream and Crimson, 1896,* 99; *Kentucky Register,* May 22, 29, 1885; *Atlantis* (February 1896): n.p.; *Central News,* April 24, May 1, 8, 15, 22, 29, October 6, 1897, March 23, 30, May 4, 1898, May 24, 1899.

34. Engle, "Central University," 288–90; *Cream and Crimson, 1896,* 79–80; *Kentucky Register,* February 24, 1882; *Central News,* February 13, 20, April 24, 1897, January 26, March 9, 30, April 13, 20, 27, 1898, March 13, 1901; *Atlantis* (December 1887): 11.

35. Horowitz, *Campus Life,* chap. 2.

36. Faculty Records, Central University Microfilm, 1883–1901; *Atlantis* (December 1887): 11; *Atlantis* (? 1894): 12; Clarence E. Woods to H. L. Donovan, June 7, 1930, Herman L. Donovan Papers.

37. Faculty Records, Central University, Microfilm, 1883–1901; The Robb Case, 84A2, Chancellor's Series, Robb Case Subseries, Box 2; Minutes of the Boards, April 11, 1899; *Atlantis* 4 (June 1886): 15; *Central News,* January 15, 1899.

38. *Lexington Herald-Leader,* November 21, 1999; Horowitz, *Campus Life,* chap. 2; Dorris, "Central University," 108; *Founders Day Program,* 7–8; *University Hot Times,* April 1900; Helen Deiss Irvin, *Hail Kentucky: A Pictorial History of the University of Kentucky* (Lexington: University Press of Kentucky, 1965), 24.

39. S. C. Bains to Blanton, January 14, 1895, Central University Records, Townsend Room; Thomas H. Little to J. S. Whittmeier, June 14, 28, 1896, Central University Records, Student's Series, Miscellaneous Records, 1892–1900.

40. Minutes of the Boards, November 6, 1884, letters appended to the minutes.

41. *Central University Third Annual Commencement, Thursday, June 14, 1877; Central University 17th Annual Commencement, Wednesday, June 10, 1891; Central University Twenty-fourth Commencement, Wednesday, June 8, 1898; Kentucky Register,* June 12, 1885, June 4, 11, 1886; *Central News,* June 23, 1900.

42. Breck File, undated ms.; Dorris, "Central University," 97–99; Minutes of the Boards, December 31, 1873, April 14, 30, 1874; *First Annual Catalogue of the Officers and Students of Central University, 1874–75,* 1, 6–7, 10; Weeks, *Kentucky Presbyterians,* 119; Alvin Fayette Lewis, *History of Higher Education in Kentucky* (Washington, D.C.: Government Printing Office, 1899), 204–10; speech by Blanton, 1899, Chancellor's Series, Box 1; Brown, *The Presbyterians: Two Hundred Years in Danville,* 100.

43. Minutes of the Boards, May 16, 1895, April 13, 1896, February 22, November 10, 1898, June 13, October 18, 1899, March 28, 1900.

44. Board of Curators Minutes, November 10, 1898; Chancellor's Report and Statement Made to the Alumni Association, June 4, 1901, Manuscript by L. H. Blanton, Chancellor's Series, Box 1; *Cream and Crimson, 1900–1901,* 148.

45. *Louisville Evening Post,* April 2, 1901; *Courier-Journal,* April 7, 11, 21, 24, May 14, 1901; Brown, *The Presbyterians: Two Hundred Years in Danville,* 100–111; Minutes of the Boards, April 5, 1901; *Central News,* April 3, May 1, 1901; *Christian Observer,* May 1, 1901; To Members of the Synod of the Presbyterian Church of Kentucky in Connection with the Southern General Assembly, April 16, 1901, Box 2.

46. *Central News,* June 12, 1901; *Courier-Journal,* June 6, 17, 19, August 24, 1901; *Louisville Commercial,* May 1, 1901; Blanton to D. M. Sweets, June 11, 13, 1901, Chancellor's Series, Box 1; Engle, "Central University," 299–300.

47. Minutes of the Boards, 202–9; *Richmond Semi-Weekly Pantagraph,* June 21, 1901; *Central News,* August 28, 1901; *Catalogue of Central University of Kentucky, 1902–1903,* 8; "Agreement for Consolidation of Centre College and Central University under Name of Central University of Kentucky," 1–20, Central University Records, Box 2; Weeks, *Kentucky Presbyterians,* 147.

48. Engle, "Central University," 300; "The Old U-ni-ver-si-tee," copy in Central University Records, Student's Series, Miscellaneous Records, 1892–1901, Box 7; Norman L. Snider, "Centre College and the Presbyterians: Corporation and Partnership," *Register of the Kentucky Historical Society* 67 (April 1969): 114–15.

49. Ellis, Everman, and Sears, *Madison County,* 272–73; Minutes of the Boards, June 17, 1875.

50. Ellis, Everman, and Sears, *Madison County,* 273–74; *Lexington Morning Herald,* September 2, 1900; *Courier-Journal,* September 2, 1900; *Richmond Climax,* September 5, 1900.

2. "The Best Is Hardly Good Enough"

1. Dorris, *Three Decades,* 9–20; "Kentucky State University," *The Kentucky Encyclopedia,* 514; J. Blaine Hudson, "Afro-American Education," *The Kentucky Encyclopedia,* 286; John R. Thelin, *A History of American Higher Education* (Baltimore, Md.: Johns Hopkins University Press, 2004), 84–86.

2. Dorris, *Three Decades,* 9–20; Hopkins, *The University of Kentucky,* 209–14; Lawrence A. Cremin, *American Education: The National Experience, 1783–1876* (New York: Harper and Row, 1980), 146–47; Jurgen Herbst, *And Sadly Teach: Teacher Education and Professionalization in American Culture* (Madison: University of Wisconsin Press, 1989), 3–11; Terry L. Birdwhistell, "Divided We Fall: State College and the Normal School Movement in Kentucky, 1880–1910," *Register of the Kentucky Historical Society* 88 (Autumn 1990): 433–35.

3. Jessie M. Pangburn, *The Evolution of the American Teachers College* (New York: Teachers College, Columbia University, 1932), 32; Jurgen Herbst, "Beyond the Debate over Revisionism: Three Educational Pasts Writ Large," *History of Education Quarterly* 20 (Summer 1980): 226–27; Junius Lathrop Meriam, *Normal School Education and Efficiency in Teaching* (New York: Teachers College, Columbia University, 1906), 112–13, 116–18; Herbst, *And Sadly Teach,* 109–39.

4. Dorris, *Three Decades,* 19, 25–27; Richard Hofstadter and C. Dewitt Hardy,

The Development and Scope of Higher Education in the United States (New York: Columbia University Press, 1952), 96; W. N. Beckner, "Normal Schools in Kentucky," *Southern School Journal* 16 (November 1905), 5; *Southern School Journal* 17 (February 1906): 25–28; *Southern School Journal* 17 (March 1906): 25.

5. Dorris, *Three Decades,* 29–33; Lowell H. Harrison, *Western Kentucky University* (Lexington: University Press of Kentucky, 1987), 15–18; Hopkins, *The University of Kentucky,* 211–16; *Courier-Journal,* June 30, 1906; *Richmond Climax,* April 25, 1906, June 23, 1909; *Lexington Leader,* May 20, 1915; Birdwhistell, "Divided We Fall," 431, 437.

6. *Richmond Daily Register,* January 16, 1926; *Richmond Climax,* February 7, 1906; Barksdale Hamlett, *History of Education in Kentucky* (Frankfort: Kentucky Department of Education, 1914), 282–87; Pangburn, *The Evolution of the American Teachers College,* 93.

7. *Richmond Daily Register,* January 16, 1926; Dorris, *Three Decades,* 32–35; *Richmond Climax,* February 7, 1906; *House Journal, 1906,* 92, 516, 585, 1173, 1183.

8. Hamlett, *History of Education in Kentucky,* 282–85; *Senate Journal, 1906,* 996, 1121; Dorris, *Three Decades,* 34–38; *Kentucky Register,* January 26, May 1, 4, 1906; *Southern School Journal* 17 (May 1906): 25–26; *Richmond Climax,* April 26, May 2, 9, 1906; *Courier-Journal,* May 8, 1906; *Acts of the General Assembly of the Commonwealth of Kentucky, 1906,* 102, 393–404. Twelve acres of the original thirty-five were reserved in the event that donors to Walters wanted their money returned.

9. *Lexington Herald,* June 3, 1906; *Courier-Journal,* June 3, 1906; Harrison, *Western Kentucky University,* 16–18; *Kentucky Register,* May 4, 1906; Jonathan T. Dorris, ed., *Five Decades of Progress, Eastern Kentucky State College, 1906–1957* (Richmond: Eastern Kentucky State College, 1957), 27.

10. Dorris, *Three Decades,* 43–45; *Kentucky Register,* December 4, 1908.

11. Birdwhistell, "Divided We Fall," 448, 451; Ruric Nevel Roark to Henry Hardin Cherry, July 31, August 20, 1907, Box 1, General Letters, Henry Hardin Cherry Papers, Western Kentucky University (hereafter cited as Cherry Papers).

12. *Lexington Herald,* June 3, 1906; Dorris, *Three Decades,* 45–50; Board of Regents Minutes, July 25, August 14, November 8, 1906 (hereafter cited as Regents Minutes); Executive Committee Minutes, August 31, 1906; Joint Boards of Regents Minutes of Eastern Kentucky State Normal School and Western Kentucky State Normal School, June 2, 19, July 25, November 8, 1906 (hereafter cited as Joint Boards Minutes).

13. *Eastern Kentucky Review* 1 (October 1906): 7, 10–13, 15, 23; *Eastern Kentucky Review* 3 (July 1909): 5–6, 67–93; *Eastern Kentucky Review* 6 (January 1912): 9–10.

14. Dorris, *Three Decades,* 71–72; *Eastern Kentucky State Normal Student,* 8 (March 1915), end page; *Richmond Daily Register,* February 2, 1922; *Yearbook of Eastern Kentucky State Normal School, Richmond, Kentucky* 5 (July 1911): 33–36; *Yearbook of Eastern Kentucky State Normal School, Richmond, Kentucky* 9 (1915): 84; Dorris, *Five Decades,* 50.

15. Thomas D. Clark and Terry L. Birdwhistell, "Sullivan Law," *The Kentucky Encyclopedia,* 860; *Eastern Progress,* October 5, 1931; Hamlett, *History of Education in*

Kentucky, 200–211; Dorris, *Three Decades,* 45–47; Regents Minutes, June 3, September 1, 1908; Joint Boards Minutes, August 25, 1908; *Kentucky Register,* December 4, 1908; Birdwhistell, "Divided We Fall," 454–56. A copy of the song lyrics is in the Cherry Papers. There is also an "Eastern Hymn" with words by Wren Jones Grinstead and music by John G. Koch. *E.K.S.N. Student, 1915,* 96.

16. Dorris, *Three Decades,* 61–62, 109–10, 114–15, 118; Regents Minutes, September 13, 1907, September 1, 1908.

17. Janet Gaynor Hibbard, "Eastern Kentucky University, 1906–1960: Administrative Problems" (Ed.D. diss., Indiana University, 1973), 30–43; Roark to Cherry, April 23, May 18, 1908, April 23, 1909, Cherry Papers.

18. Clark and Birdwhistell, "Sullivan Law," 860; *Eastern Progress,* October 5, 1931; Sullivan to Cherry, May 18, June 3, 1911, Cherry Papers.

19. *Eastern Kentucky Review* 1 (April 1907): n.p.; *Eastern Kentucky Review* 1 (October 1907): n.p.; *E.K.S.N. Student* 2 (August 1909): cover page.

20. Regents Minutes, February 18, 19, March 12, April 16, 1909; *Courier-Journal,* April 15, 1909; *Lexington Herald,* April 15, 1909; *Eastern Kentucky Review* 3 (January 1909): 26, 39; *Eastern Kentucky Review* 3 (April 1909): 3, 25; *Eastern Kentucky Review* 3 (July 1909): 3; *Eastern Kentucky Review* 4 (January 1910): 2; "Ruric Nevel Roark," *Dictionary of American Biography,* 643–44; Mary Roark to Cherry, April 23, 1909, Cherry Papers; S. B. Chandler to H. L. Donovan, October 5, 1934, Herman L. Donovan Papers, Eastern Kentucky University Archives.

21. Regents Minutes, March 12, April 16, June 12, 17, October 1, 1909; *Richmond Climax,* June 23, 1909, April 13, 1910; *Richmond Daily Register,* February 2, 1922; *Eastern Kentucky Review* 4 (January 1910): 4, 8, 12, 14, 24; *E.K.S.N. Student* 3 (April 1910): 4–5; Bob Kustra, "Mary Roark Remembered for Contributions to Eastern," *Eastern Today,* 12(Fall 1998), 2.

22. *E.K.S.N. Student* 3 (April 1910): 3; *Richmond Climax,* March 9, April 13, 1910; Regents Minutes, March 18, 1910; *Southern School Journal,* 18 (December 1907), 42.

23. R. F. Ramsey, excerpt from letter, 1913; Dorris, *Five Decades,* 123–26.

24. Regents Minutes, vol. 2A covers the Crabbe years; *E.K.S.N. Student,* 4 (September–October 1910), 7.

25. *E.K.S.N. Student* 4 (September–October 1910): 7–9; *E.K.S.N. Student* 4 (November 1910): 7–10; *E.K.S.N. Student* 4 (December 1910): 2–3; *E.K.S.N. Student* 4 (January 1911): 8–10; *E.K.S.N. Student* 4 (May 1911): 13; *E.K.S.N. Student* 5 (November 1911): 17; *Yearbook of E.K.S.N.S., 1911,* 44; *Richmond Climax,* March 6, May 3, 1911.

26. *E.K.S.N. Student* 4 (January 1911): 8; *E.K.S.N. Student* 4 (February 1911): 11; *E.K.S.N. Student* 5 (December 1911): 9; *E.K.S.N. Student* 5 (June 1912): 18–19.

27. *E.K.S.N. Student* 6 (November 1912): 10; *E.K.S.N. Student* 6 (December 1912): 14–15; *E.K.S.N. Student* 7 (September–October 1913): 7–8; *E.K.S.N. Student* 8 (October 1914): 11; *E.K.S.N. Student* 8 (November 1914): 19; *E.K.S.N. Student* 8 (May

1915): 16; Dorris, *Five Decades,* 151; Dorris, *Three Decades,* 184; *Richmond Climax,* May 22, 1912.

28. *E.K.S.N. Student* 6 (September 1912): 3–4; *E.K.S.N. Student* 8 (May 1915): 16; *E.K.S.N. Student* 8 (June 1915): 5–6; Dorris, *Three Decades,* 279, 286; Regents Minutes, July 14, 1911, May 8, December 5, 1914; Fannie Noe Hendren interview, July 13, 1986.

29. *E.K.S.N. Student* 7 (September–October 1913): 8; *E.K.S.N. Student* 8 (November 1914): 19; *Eastern Kentucky Review* 1 (July 1907): 27; *Eastern Kentucky Review* 4 (October 1909): 5, 24; *Eastern Kentucky Review* 4 (July 1910): 7; Dorris, *Three Decades,* 215–16, 224–25, 265, 269; *Bluemont, 1910,* 34; Hendren interview; Virginia H. Waters interview, July 25, 1986.

30. Regents Minutes, April 22, 1915, June 16, 1916; *Eastern Kentucky Review* 10 (1916): n.p.; *Eastern Progress,* May 6, 1938.

31. *Eastern Kentucky Review* 9 (1915): 2–3; Dorris, *Five Decades,* 242–47. Unfortunately for the researcher, there are large gaps in the extant copies of the *Eastern Kentucky Review, E.K.S.N. Student,* and the *Talisman.*

32. *E.K.S.N. Student* 4 (February 1911): 5–6; *E.K.S.N. Student* 4 (April 1911): 5–8; *E.K.S.N. Student* 5 (December 1911): 15; *E.K.S.N. Student* 6 (December 1912): 4; *E.K.S.N. Student* 8 (June 1915): 10. For a general history of Progressivism, see Dewey W. Grantham, *Southern Progressivism: The Reconciliation of Progress and Tradition* (Knoxville: University of Tennessee Press, 1983).

33. *Eastern Kentucky Review* 11 (1917): n.p.; *Eastern Kentucky Review* 12 (1918): 37; Regents Minutes, June 11, 17, 1909, March 18, 1910; *Bluemont, 1910,* 106. For a review of the racial climate in Kentucky in this period, see George C. Wright, *Life behind a Veil: Blacks in Louisville, Kentucky, 1865–1930* (Baton Rouge: Louisiana State University Press, 1985); Betty Tevis Balke, "The Dean in Profile," *Eastern Alumnus* 4 (Spring 1965): 3.

34. Herbst, "Beyond the Debate over Revisionism," 137; *Eastern Kentucky Review,* I (January 1907), 22–23; Herbst, *And Sadly Teach,* 109–39.

35. *E.K.S.N. Student* 5 (June 1912): 8; Hibbard, "Eastern Kentucky University," 44–45; Balke, "The Dean in Profile," 3.

36. Birdwhistell, "James Kennedy Patterson," *The Kentucky Encyclopedia,* 713; Harrison, "Henry Hardin Cherry," *The Kentucky Encyclopedia,* 181–82; Harrison, *Western Kentucky University,* 55–58; Carl P. Chelf, "A Selective View of the Politics of Higher Education in Kentucky and the Role of H. H. Cherry" (Ph.D. diss., University of Nebraska, 1968), 235–50; *Eastern Kentucky Review* 6 (January 1912): 20; Charles Gano Talbert, *The University of Kentucky: The Maturing Years* (Lexington: University of Kentucky Press, 1965), 7–9.

37. Crabbe to Cherry, May 5, 1910, March 12, 25, December 3, 1914, July 31, 1915, February 12, July 26, 1916; Cherry to Crabbe, January 22, 1913, March 17, 18, October 14, 1914, August 2, October 7, 1915, July 20, August 24, 1916; E. C. McDougle to Crabbe, July 31, 1915, Cherry Papers.

38. Regents Minutes, October 21, 1910, July 19, 1912, March 11, September 26, 1913; Crabbe to Cherry, September 30, 1913, Cherry Papers; *Bluemont, 1910; Eastern Kentucky Review* 7 (April 1913): 4–7; Hibbard, "Eastern Kentucky University," 52–56.

39. Hibbard, "Eastern Kentucky University," 59–64; *Eastern Kentucky Review* 6 (January 1912): 69; *Eastern Kentucky Review* 8 (Summer School 1913): 1–54.

40. Waters interview; *Talisman, 1916,* 24.

41. Ethel Merritt Lisle, July 17, 1986; *Talisman, 1916,* 16; Balke, "The Dean in Profile," 4.

42. *School Bell Echo,* Winter Issue, 2001, 7–8; Hendren interview.

43. *Eastern Kentucky Review* 11 (1917): n.p.; *Eastern Kentucky Review* 15 (1921): 4–5; Dorris, *Three Decades,* 123–26; Regents Minutes, February 18, November 19, 1909, March 13, July 19, September 20, 1912, April 11, 1913, May 8, 1914; *Richmond Climax,* June 23, 1909.

44. Dorris, *Three Decades,* 63–64, 146; Crabbe to Cherry, June 24, 1916; Cherry to P. W. Grinstead, October 23, 1912, Cherry Papers; Regents Minutes, June 16, 1916.

45. *E.K.S.N. Student* 7 (February 1914): 15–16; Hibbard, "Eastern Kentucky University," 45; Dorris, *Three Decades,* 146, 266; Dorris, *Five Decades,* 261; Waters interview.

3. From Normal School to Teachers College

1. Regents Minutes, June 16, August 28, September 5, 1916; *Eastern Progress,* March 23, 1928; Cherry to Coates, September 7, 1916; Coates to Cherry, September 8, 21, 1916 (unless otherwise noted, the Coates correspondence is located in the Thomas Jackson Coates Papers, Eastern Kentucky University Archives); Flossie Dotson to Coates, December 6, 1922, Cherry Papers.

2. Regents Minutes, September 6, October 26, 1916.

3. Regents Minutes, April 14, September 22, 1917, March 22, June 1, July 27, November 20, 1918; *Eastern Kentucky Review* 12 (Review of the Second Term, 1917–18): 3; Executive Committee Minutes, September 14, 19, 1918; Dorris, *Five Decades,* 194–95; Mabel G. Pullen interview, October 4, 1986.

4. *Eastern Kentucky Review* 14 (Summer School 1919): 42; *Eastern Kentucky Review* 12 (Review of the Third Term, 1917–18): 3; *Eastern Kentucky Review* 13 (September–October, 1918): 23–24, 32; Executive Committee Minutes, September 14, 1918; Regents Minutes, November 20, 1918; Cherry to Coates, January 18, 1918; Dorris, *Five Decades,* 195.

5. *Eastern Kentucky Review* 13 (September–October 1918): 29–32; Regents Minutes, November 20, 1918.

6. Regents Minutes, November 20, 1918; *Eastern Kentucky Review* 13 (September–October 1918): 1, 23, 24; *Eastern Kentucky Review* 13 (Summer School 1919): 47–48.

7. Regents Minutes, November 20, 1918; Executive Committee Minutes, January 9, February 17, 1919; Dorris, *Five Decades,* 194; Harrison and Klotter, *A New History of Kentucky,* 290; Pullen interview; Nancy D. Baird, "Epidemics," *The Encyclopedia of Louisville,* 273.

8. *Kentucky Register,* April 20, 1917; Regents Minutes, April 14, June 15, July 14, September 22, November 5, December 8, 1917, March 11, 22, June 1, September 21, 1918; Dorris, *Five Decades,* 21; *Courier-Journal,* April 27, 1919.

9. Dorris, *Three Decades,* 125; *Eastern Kentucky Review* 13 (January–February–March 1920): 4; Regents Minutes, May 8, 15, July 10, September 13, 1920, May 8, 1923, January 14, 1928; *Courier-Journal,* October 12, 1919, July 14, 1925; Dorris, *Five Decades,* 18–21.

10. Executive Committee Minutes, August ?, 1920; Regents Minutes, September 13, November 20, 1920, November 19, 1921.

11. *Courier-Journal,* April 28, October 12, December 27, 1919; Hibbard, "Eastern Kentucky University," 74; Harrison, *Western Kentucky University,* 56–58; Regents Minutes, January 24, 1920.

12. Coates to Cherry and enclosure, December 1, 1919, Cherry Papers; Dorris, *Three Decades,* 147, 194; Regents Minutes, June 1, 1918; *Richmond Daily Register,* June 27, 1921; Confidential Report and Recommendations of the President to the Board of Regents, April 23, 1921, Robert R. Martin Papers, Eastern Kentucky University Archives.

13. Dorris, *Three Decades,* 67–68; Joint Boards Minutes, November 19, 1921; *Acts of the Kentucky General Assembly,* Approved March 20, 1922, chap. 25, p. 97; Harrison, *Western Kentucky University,* 59–62; Rudolph, *The American College and University,* 463; Pangburn, *The Evolution of the American Teachers College,* 93; John R. Duncan, "Morehead State University," *The Kentucky Encyclopedia,* 649–50; Ernie R. Bailey, "Murray State University," *The Kentucky Encyclopedia,* 664–65; Chelf, "A Selective View of the Politics of Higher Education in Kentucky and the Role of H. H. Cherry," 235–50.

14. *Eastern Kentucky Review* 13 (Summer 1919): 16–20; *Eastern Kentucky Review* 14 (January–February–March 1920): 22–23; *Eastern Kentucky Review* 15 (1921): 11–13; *Eastern Kentucky Review* 16 (1921): 20–21; Harrison, *Western Kentucky University,* 59; enclosure from Joyce Hardin about her aunt, Leoti Hardin, to the author.

15. Karen O. Skaff, "Herman Lee Donovan," *The Kentucky Encyclopedia,* 269; Donovan to Cherry, May 23, August 13, 1921, July 7, 1924, Cherry Papers; Regents Minutes, April 14, 23, 1921, July 19, October 4, 1924; Dorris, *Three Decades,* 66–67; *Eastern Kentucky Review* 17 (August 1923, "Bulletin"): 3–4.

16. "Minutes of an Emergency Meeting of President H. H. Cherry of the Western Normal School and T. J. Coates of the Eastern Normal School, April 24, 1924," Cherry Papers; *Richmond Daily Register,* April 14, 1925; Chelf, "A Selective View of the Politics of Education in Kentucky and the Role of H. H. Cherry," 235–50.

17. Dorris, *Five Decades,* 51; "Faculty Rules, March 21, 1926"; *Eastern Progress,* May 6, 1938, May 25, 1962; *Richmond Register,* August 27, 2000; Regents Minutes,

January 16, 1926, January 14, 1928; *Eastern Kentucky Review* 13 (January–February 1919): 34; Willie B. Norton interview, September 17, 1987; Betty Tevis Balke, "The Dean in Profile," *Eastern Alumnus* 4 (Spring 1965): 2–3; William J. Moore interviewed by Charles Hay, March 27, 1978; Ethel B. Pearson interview, November 12, 1987; Allie Ruth Spurlin interview, July 10, 1987; Rova and Judson Harmon interview, September 7, 1987; Coates to G. S. Napier, January 6, 1928, Donovan Papers.

18. *Richmond Register,* August 27, 2000; Dorris, *Three Decades,* 150; *Eastern Kentucky Review* 13 (January–February 1919): 35; *Eastern Kentucky Review* 13 (Summer School 1919): 41–42; Regents Minutes, November 20, 1920; *Talisman* 9 (February 1919): n.p.; Katie Carpenter interview, November 24, 1986; Balke, "The Dean in Profile," 4.

19. *Eastern Kentucky Review* 15 (Senior Issue 1921): 4, 16, 20–21, 33, 35; Mattie T. Roberts interview, October 30, 1986.

20. *Richmond Daily Register,* April 14, 1925; Susan H. Fields interview, August 4, 1986; Ruth Allen interview, July 29, 1986; Norton interview; Colonel Hammond interview, November 12, 1987; Talton K. Stone interview, October 20, 1986; Allie Ruth Spurlin interview, July 10, 1987.

21. Norton interview; Lucille Strother Hogge interview, July 28, 1986; *Eastern Progress,* February 1922.

22. *Richmond Daily Register,* April 14, 1930; *Eastern Kentucky Review* 13 (Summer School 1919): 33–34, 37–38; "The Training School," *Eastern Kentucky Review* 20 (August 1926), special issue; *Eastern Kentucky Review* 24 (July 1930): 5–6, 17–18; *Courier-Journal,* July 3, 1929; *Richmond Register,* August 18, 1990; Dorris, *Five Decades,* 94, 278–79; Regents Minutes, January 8, November 19, 1921, October 13, 1923, April 11, 1925, April 30, 1927; Carpenter interview.

23. Dorris, *Five Decades,* 79–84; Regents Minutes, June 7, 1907, December 8, 1916, April 14, 1917, May 15, 1920; Dorris, *Three Decades,* 91–107.

24. Regents Minutes, August 9, 1919, April 14, 1923, October 9, 1926; *Eastern Kentucky Review* 14 (September–October 1919): 5; Executive Committee Minutes, October 19, 1919, January 6, 1920, October 13, 1925; Harmon and Harmon interview; Dorris, *Three Decades,* 227–31; Coates to Sullivan, March 12, 1927; Extra Curricular Organizations, Second Semester, 1926–27, Donovan Papers.

25. Harrison, *Western Kentucky University,* 68–69; Regents Minutes, November 5, 1917, July 27, 1918, May 30, October 14, November 11, December 20, 1922, September 1, 1923, April 12, May 30, July 19, 1924, December 18, 1926; Executive Committee Minutes, February 17, October 9, 1919, November 2, 1920, May 5, July 6, 1921, December 4, 1922; *Courier-Journal,* December 27, 1919; Hibbard, "Eastern Kentucky University," 72–75; Joint Boards Minutes, November 19, 1921; *Eastern Kentucky Review* 17 (August 1923): 3–4; S. R. Green to Coates, December 17, 1926.

26. Regents Minutes, January 8, 1921, January 13, February 15, June 29, 1923, April 17, 1926; Executive Committee Minutes, July 31, November 29, 1922, January 9, 1924, September 1, 1926; "Stateland Purchase," December 9, 1922, Coates Papers.

27. Dorris, *Three Decades,* 175–86; *Richmond Daily Register,* November 17, 1916;

Talisman 9 (October 1915): n.p.; *Talisman* 9 (December 1915): n.p.; *Talisman* 10 (November 1916): n.p.; Regents Minutes, May 15, July 10, 1920.

28. Regents Minutes, September 13, November 20, 1920, May 26, 1921, August 14, 1926; Executive Committee Minutes, July 31, 1922.

29. *Eastern Kentucky Review* 16 (1921): 21; Regents Minutes, January 13, 1923, January 15, November 12, 1927, January 14, 1928; Cherry to Coates, October 10, 1921, November 14, 1922, February 26, 1923; Coates to Cherry, November 9, 1921, November 13, 1922; Harrison, *Western Kentucky University,* 58, 84–87; *Eastern Progress,* December 19, 1922.

30. Dorris, *Five Decades,* 151–53; *Eastern Kentucky Review* 13 (January–February 1919): 33–34; *Richmond Daily Register,* November 7, 1999; *Talisman* 9 (May 1916): n.p.; *Eastern Progress,* November 7, December 19, 1922, May 11, 1925; *Milestone, 1922,* 108; *Milestone, 1923,* 67; C. R. Rouse interview, September 19, 1987; Beckham Combs interview, October 11, 1986; Talton K. Stone interview, October 20, 1986.

31. *Lexington Herald-Leader,* July 15, 1999; *Eastern Progress,* December 2, 1999; *Richmond Daily Register,* November 7, 1999; Colonel Hammonds interview, November 12, 1987; Stone interview; William Marshall, "Earle Bryan Combs," *The Kentucky Encyclopedia,* 218–19.

32. Dorris, *Five Decades,* 142–43; Dorris, *Three Decades,* 133–35, 274; *Eastern Kentucky Review* 11 (1917): n.p.; *Eastern Kentucky Review* 16 (1921): 35; Regents Minutes, October 9, 1926; Norton interview; Rouse interview; *Eastern Progress,* May 12, 1923.

33. Dorris, *Five Decades,* 325–28, 264–65; Regents Minutes, July 14, 1917, August 20, October 9, 1926; Executive Committee Minutes, August 28, 1920; Coates to A. J. Crabbe, November 10, 1925.

34. Dorris, *Five Decades,* 109–10; *Richmond Register,* May 12, 19, 1990; Regents Minutes, February 10, April 14, 1917, July 14, September 1, 1923; Executive Committee Minutes, February 17, August 9, 1919.

35. *Eastern Kentucky Review* 12 (1917): 25; *Eastern Kentucky Review* 13 (January–February 1919): 7, 16–17; Dorris, *Three Decades,* 158–61; *Talisman* (Senior Number 1916): 11; Patrick Henry Callahan to Coates, June 17, 1927. See William E. Ellis, *Patrick Henry Callahan: Progressive Catholic Layman in the American South* (Lewiston, N.Y.: Edwin Mellen Press, 1989).

36. Beckham Combs interview; *Courier-Journal,* March 18, 1928; Regents Minutes, March 19, 1928; Mary F. Richards interview, July 22, 1986.

37. Dorris, *Three Decades,* 65–66, 221–24; Regents Minutes, March 19, 1928; *Eastern Progress,* March 23, 1928; Jere A. Sullivan to Homer E. Cooper, March 22, 1928, Sullivan Correspondence, Eastern Kentucky University Archives.

38. Dorris, *Three Decades,* 59–60, 65–66; *Eastern Progress,* March 23, 1928; Regents Minutes, August 14, 1926, January 15, 1927, March 26, 1928.

39. Regents Minutes, May 15, 26, 1920, April 11, 1925, April 17, 1926, April 30, 1927; Hibbard, "Eastern Kentucky University," 75–80; *Eastern Kentucky Review* 14 (September–November 1919): 14–15.

40. Hibbard, "Eastern Kentucky University," 80–82; Dorris, *Five Decades,* 50, 133; Regents Minutes, April 6, 1921, January 14, 1928; Executive Committee Minutes, September 14, 1918, February 17, 1919; Dorris, *Three Decades,* 56, 73–75; Ruth L. Allen interview, July 29, 1986; Coates to Anna A. Schnieb, October 7, 1927; Balke, "The Dean in Profile," 2–3; Homer E. Cooper to Coates, February 18, 1927; Cooper to the Members of the Board of Regents, May 21, 1928, Donovan Papers.

41. Emma Y. Case interview, August 18, 1986; Ruth Lane interview, July 29, 1986; Dorris, *Three Decades,* 275; Norton interview; Dovie M. Combs interview, September 29, 1988; Myrtle Lee Baker Watts interview, December 5, 1986; Amelia Vanover interview, July 24, 1986; Pearson interview; Fields interview; Beckham Combs interview; Cecil A. Washburn interview, July 7, 1987; Valley G. McGee interviewed by Janet White, November 5, 1987; Coates to Homer E. Cooper, March 21, 1927, Coates Papers.

42. Richard A. Edwards, "Looking Backward," ms., 1972, 174–75; Moore interview.

43. William E. Ellis, "Frank LeRond McVey: His Defense of Academic Freedom," *Register of the Kentucky Historical Society* 67 (January 1967): 37–54.

4. The Donovan Years

1. Regents Minutes, March 19, 1928.

2. Regents Minutes, March 26, 1928; *Eastern Progress,* April 6, 1928.

3. *Courier-Journal,* March 27, 28, 1928; Lee Kirkpatrick to Donovan, June 21, 1928 (unless otherwise noted, all Herman L. Donovan correspondence and papers are located in the Eastern Kentucky University Archives).

4. Frederick Rudolph, *The American College and University: A History* (New York: Knopf, 1962), 463; Herbst, "Beyond the Debate over Revisionism," 137.

5. *Richmond Daily Register,* April 6, 1928; Herman L. Donovan, "I Remember Eastern," unpublished manuscript in the Donovan Papers, University of Kentucky and Eastern Kentucky University, 1; Donovan 1928–29 Contract; Donovan to William A. McCall, December 29, 1928.

6. Regents Minutes, May 5, 1928; Dorris, *Three Decades,* 67–69.

7. "The Inauguration of Herman Lee Donovan as President of the College," *Eastern Kentucky Review* 22 (February 1929): 4–32; *Courier-Journal,* October 26, 1928.

8. Hibbard, "Eastern Kentucky University," 105–6; Donovan, "I Remember Eastern," 50–51.

9. There is a large file of Cammack correspondence in the Donovan Papers; Keen Johnson to Donovan, November 25, 1940; Donovan to H. D. Fitzpatrick, February 9, 1939; Jere Sullivan to Donovan, May 1930; *Richmond Daily Register,* September 13, 1931; Regents Minutes, April 26, 1930; Flem D. Sampson, Executive Order, March 8, 1930; Sullivan to Flem D. Sampson, May 14, 1928.

10. Donovan to Cooper, April 15, June 5, 1929, June 10, July 4, 1930; Buchanan

to Cooper, June 10, 1930; Buchanan to Donovan, June 10, 1930; Cooper to Donovan, June 10, 1930; Case to Donovan, February 1, 1931.

11. Donovan to Cooper, September 15, 1930, March 14, 1931; notes on Cooper by Donovan, n.d.; Donovan to P. N. Elbin, October 19, 1933; Regents Minutes, March 14, 1931; *Courier-Journal,* April 12, 1931.

12. Donovan, "I Remember Eastern," 22–24; Dorris, *Three Decades,* 51, 56–57; Emma Case to Donovan, May 17, 1932, March 6, 1933; *Richmond Register,* March 12, 1988; Donovan to Marie L. Roberts, April 23, 1932, May 3, 1934; Donovan to Annie C. Roberts, April 2, 1937; Regents Minutes, April 17, 1934; Donovan to Rainey T. Wells, October 3, 1929; Martha K. Barksdale interview, November 17, 1987.

13. Donovan to Charles H. Thompson, November 7, 1938; Dorris, *Five Decades,* 261; *Catalog, 1935–36; Eastern Kentucky Review* 27 (July 1935): 3.

14. Donovan, "I Remember Eastern," 4–6; Donovan to Jere Sullivan, March 23, 1929; Donovan to Van Peursem, March 22, 1929; Donovan's Notes to Teachers, Box 112.

15. James C. Burnett interview, October 9, 1977; Norman A. Deeb interview, October 1, 1987; "Schniebology 314" item; Donovan to Schnieb, April 18, 1933.

16. "Distribution of Grades, 1928–29," Box 108; petition in Box 86; Deeb interview; Burnett interview; Meredith J. Cox to Donovan, April 29, 1931; Millie H. Prater interview, January 11, 2001; Casey and Thelma Morton interview, October 1, 1977; Thomas C. and Hazel C. Little interview, August 5, 1986.

17. Donovan to D. T. Ferrell, April 15, 1929; Donovan, "I Remember Eastern," 28–30; Hibbard, "Eastern Kentucky University," 104; "Annual Report, Instructional Activities for School Year, 1933–34"; "Rating Scale of Teaching," form, July 1, 1929; Regents Minutes, July 11, 1931.

18. Donovan, "I Remember Eastern," 70–71; Donovan Papers, Box 72; Hibbard, "Eastern Kentucky University," 86–88; Donovan to W. D. Hooper, October 17, 1928; Donovan to A. W. Birdwell, November 16, 1934; Donovan to H. H. Cherry, December 11, 1930; Donovan to Talton K. Stone, November 15, 1934; Donovan to Guy E. Snavely, December 15, 1933; *Eastern Progress,* April 6, 1938; Regents Minutes, October 20, 1928, January 21, 1933, May 2, 1938.

19. Dorris, *Three Decades,* 75–76; *Richmond Register,* August 12, 2001; Regents Minutes, February 1, 1930; Little interview.

20. "Education as an Instrument of Social Progress," speech; "Secondary Education in the New Deal," speech; "Teacher Training for the New Age," speech; Clarence E. Woods to Donovan, June 7, 1930; Donovan to Woods, June 9, 1930; Donovan to Patrick H. Callahan, January 22, 1932; Callahan to Donovan, January 3, 1933; "Educating the Teacher for the Progressive Public School," speech; Donovan to Alben Barkley, November 26, 1930, December 30, 1932.

21. Burnett interview; "Is It Public Indifference or Lack of Information?" speech; Donovan to Donald McWain, August 2, 1932; Donovan to County Superintendents, form letter and questionnaire, July 13, 1931; Donovan to Vance Armentrout, July 22,

1932; Donovan to Malcolm Bayley, July 13, 1931; *Courier-Journal,* May 11, September 6, 1931, July 10, 1933; *Monticello Outlook,* May 7, 1931, *Hazard Herald,* April 30, 1931; *Owensville News,* April 23, 1931; Donovan, "I Remember Eastern," 38–44; Regents Minutes, September 18, 1931.

22. Lydia M. Garrett interview, August 2, 1986; Richard I. Greenwell interview, June 7, 1981; "Summary of Enrollment, Kentucky Collection," October 16, 1930; Little interview; Ted C. Gilbert interview, October 15, 1986; Prater interview; Burnett interview; Hiram Brock Jr. interview, May 29, 1987.

23. Donovan, "I Remember Eastern," 1–71; Linda L. Eads, "The Donovan Years," Eastern Kentucky University student paper, 1977, 9–10; *Catalog, 1928–29; Eastern Kentucky Review* 22 (August 1928): 31.

24. *Eastern Progress,* September 4, 1935; Dorris, *Five Decades,* 134, 258; Emma Y. Case interview, August 18, 1986; Robert L. Smith to Donovan, January 6, 1929; Norman L. Lee Jr. to Donovan, ca. 1934; Burnett interview.

25. *Eastern Progress,* November 8, 1940; Donovan to Mrs. Eugene R. Kelley, January 24, 1941; Donovan to Charles A. Keith, May 15, 1930.

26. Donovan, "I Remember Eastern," 7–10; Donovan to R. O. Moberly, June 19, 1928; Donovan to Marie L. Roberts, October 30, November 12, 1928; "Report of a Conference Which Took Place in the Office of President H. L. Donovan on May 20, 1929"; J. Ed McConnell interview, August 4, 1986; Case interview; Greenwell interview; "Committee on Student Welfare, Discipline, and Grievances, December 12, 1928"; Donovan to Faculty, September 15, 1928, April 23, 1930; order dated April 25, 1931, Box 11; Regents Minutes, April 14, June 17, 1937; Donovan to Case, December 5, 1932; *Courier-Journal,* October 19, 1935.

27. Donovan to A. L. Young, July 27, 1933; Donovan, "I Remember Eastern," 11–14; Ingrid B. Fagan, "Chapel Service at Eastern Kentucky State Teachers College during the Donovan Years," Eastern Kentucky University student paper, 1988, 1–5.

28. *Richmond Daily Register,* January 18, 28, March 25, 1935; Donovan, "I Remember Eastern," 12–15; *Eastern Progress,* March 14, 1941; *Catalog, 1935–36; Eastern Kentucky Review* 28 (July 1935): 31; Mary F. Richards interview, July 22, 1986; Jean Stocker True interview, November 12, 1986; Gilbert interview.

29. *Eastern Progress,* March 10, 1939; Donovan to Frank H. Shaffer, September 28, 1934; Donovan to L. A. Pechstein, May 9, 1939; Harry Elmer Barnes to Donovan, July 31, 1940; A. B. Chandler to Donovan, June 29, 1939; Donovan to McVey, July 12, 1939.

30. *Eastern Progress,* April 7, October 31, 1939, January 17, 1941; Assembly Programs, September 25 to October 11, 1940.

31. Student Representation on Committees, October 10, 1941; *Eastern Progress,* January 13, 1939, November 22, 1941; Eads, "The Donovan Years," 14–16; Results of Elections, Box 112; Dorris, *Three Decades,* 141; Hibbard, "Eastern Kentucky University," 111, 151; Donovan to Warner W. Willey, November 28, 1938.

32. Approved Activities to be Carried Out by the Open Forum, ca. late 1930s; *Eastern Progress,* November 22, 1941; Mildred Redding and Fred Dial to Coates, January 13, 1928; Student Aid Society, May 22, 1934; Student Loan Committee, July 7, 1932;

Meredith J. Cox to Donovan, February 29, 1931; Anna Schnieb, Notes on Our Student Loan Fund and on Student Assistance, December 21, 1928; Donovan to Achsa Kinnett, January 23, 1931.

33. "A Family Chat," November 29, 1937, January 5, 1940; D. L. Hignite to Donovan, February 7, 1937.

34. *Richmond Daily Register,* February 11, 1935; *Eastern Progress,* September 30, October 14, 1938; Dorris, *Five Decades,* 131–32; *Catalog, 1935–36; Eastern Kentucky Review* 28 (July 1935): 42; Regents Minutes, October 18, 1930; Burnett interview; Marion S. Roberts interview, October 9, 1987; "The Mystic Six" to Dear Sirs, n.d.; "Rules for Freshmen," W. F. O'Donnell Papers.

35. Martin to Donovan, July 8, 1932, May 26, 1934, March 11, 1938; Donovan to D. L. McConnell, January 2, 1940; Burnett interview; Donovan to Martin, March 21, 1939; *Courier-Journal,* May 19, 1934.

36. Dorris, *Three Decades,* 181–83; Donovan, "I Remember Eastern," 23–24, 64; Dorris, *Five Decades,* 152–53, 296–98; Alfred S. Portwood interview, February 26, 1987.

37. Charles Hay III, "Virtual Historical Tour of Eastern Kentucky University"; Bobby Pollard, "History of the Weaver Health Building: From Inception to Dedication," Eastern Kentucky University student paper, 1992, passim; Donovan, "I Remember Eastern," 59–61; Dorris, *Five Decades,* 297–98; Regents Minutes, June 28, October 18, 1930; Burnett interview; Dorris, *Three Decades,* 181.

38. Hibbard, "Eastern Kentucky University," 112; *Milestone, 1930,* 114; *Lexington Herald-Leader,* February 17, 2000; Donovan to Maurice F. Seay, November 4, 1932; Burnett interview; Dorris, *Three Decades,* 186–87; *Richmond Register,* November 14, 1999; Charles T. Hughes interview, February 23, 1978; H. D. Tartar interview, August 2, 1990; *Eastern Progress,* July 27, August 10, December 7, 1928.

39. Regents Minutes, October 26, 1929; Donovan to Cherry, November 7, 1932; Donovan to Robert T. Hinton, December 7, 1929; Donovan to Robert K. Salyer, September 27, 1929; Meeting of the Committee on Athletics, November 11, 1932; *Milestone, 1933,* n.p.; Burnett interview; Portwood interview; McConnell interview.

40. Regents Minutes, October 18, December 13, 1930, January 31, March 14, 1931, February 6, April 27, 1932; Donovan to Rainey T. Wells, October 3, 1929; Donovan to Achsa Kinnett, January 24, 1931; Donovan to Charles B. Meyers, January 1, 1935; *Courier-Journal,* September 17, 1932; Katherine Morgan to Donovan, August 26, 1930; Clarissa Hicks interview, August 14, 1987; Smith and Nancy Park interview, November 15, 1983; Robert R. Martin interviews, November 4 and December 13, 1976.

41. Regents Minutes, April 27, June 27, July 19, 1932, April 29, 1933, April 17, 1934; *Richmond Register,* July 30, 2000; Donovan, "I Remember Eastern," 61–62; Donovan to Ray A. Smith, December 26, 1933; *Courier-Journal,* April 10, 29, 1932; Donovan to C. F. Weaver, May 10, 1932; *Alumni Number of Eastern Kentucky Review* 27 (December 1933): 5–7; McConnell interview; Donovan to W. C. Jones, April 18, 1932.

42. Donovan to J. C. W. Beckham, April 4, 1933; Donovan to Vance Armentrout, December 26, 1933; Donovan to R. L. Bedwell, April 28, 1932; Regents Minutes, April 27, October 22, 1932; *Richmond Register,* July 3, 2000; Donovan to R. S. Newcomb, March 18, 1933; Donovan to R. A. Palmore, March 8, 1933; Ethel Squires to Donovan, June 16, 1932; Donovan to Squires, June 21, 1932; Donovan to Charles J. Turck, July 28, 1932.

43. David O. Levine, *The American College and the Culture of Aspiration, 1925– 1940* (Ithaca, N.Y.: Cornell University Press, 1986), 185–95; Burnett interview; Morton interview; Hughes interview; Gilbert interview; Dorris, *Five Decades,* 69; McConnell interview; Emma Y. Case to Donovan, July 18, 1934; Prater interview; Malcolm W. Willey, *Depression, Recovery, and Higher Education: A Report of Committee 4 of the American Association of University Professors* (New York: McGraw-Hill, 1937), 281– 84; "Ability of Students to Pay Tuition Fees and Population of Home Counties," Office of the Director of Research, April 6, 1933; George L. Stith interview, October 5, 1990; Morton interview.

44. Donovan to Opal Pierson, May 20, 1940; Donovan to Cherry, January 8, 1930; Donovan to C. F. Weaver, January 15, 1930; Donovan to Uel W. Lamkin, August 10, 1932; Donovan to A. L. Crabb, February 9, 1932.

45. Donovan to Lamkin; Donovan to W. P. Morgan, December 28, 1931; Donovan to Cherry, December 28, 1931; Donovan to John K. Norton, April 4, 1932; Gary S. Cox, "Council on Higher Education," *The Kentucky Encyclopedia,* 494–95; Harrison and Klotter, *A New History of Kentucky,* 362; Donovan to Keen Johnson, June 30, 1934; Donovan to Allie Young and John Y. Brown, January 15, 1932; Donovan to Cammack, March 24, 1934; Regents Minutes, April 17, 1934.

46. Donovan to "Dear Student," January 30, 1932; Regents Minutes, April 17, 1934; Donovan to Sewell, October 12, 1933; Sewell to Laffoon, December 17, 1934; Donovan to Laffoon, February 16, 1935; Donovan to Vance Armentrout, February 19, 1935; Donovan to Laffoon, February 11, 1935; Donovan, "I Remember Eastern," 58–59.

47. Donovan to Vance Armentrout, February 19, 1935; Donovan to Honorable Member of the Budget Commission, January 11, 1932; Donovan to "My Dear Friend," December 29, 1933; *Danville Advocate Messenger,* March 25, 1933, February 12, 1934.

48. "Are There Too Many Teachers in Kentucky?" speech; "Are Teachers Colleges a Menace? A Reply," April 1932, speech; Donovan to H. D. Fitzpatrick, June 21, 1937.

49. *Richmond Daily Register,* n.d., Donovan Papers; Donovan to John Carr, March 7, 1934; Donovan to Griffenhagen and Associates, February 10, 1934; Donovan to James H. Richmond, September 27, 1933; Harrison, *Western Kentucky University,* 74, 75, 90–91; Donovan to Cammack, February 13, 1934.

50. Levine, *The American College and the Culture of Aspiration,* 195–201; Dorris, *Five Decades,* 145; Dorris, *Three Decades,* 69; Regents Minutes, December 2, 1933, January 20, 1934; Donovan to Barkley, December 2, 1936; Donovan to Virgil Chapman, August 3, 1937; Brock interview; Emilie Wiggins interview, January 5, 1987; Gilbert interview.

51. Donovan to John Howard Stamper, February 11, 1934; Donovan to Frank D. Peterson, September 5, 1935; Peterson to Donovan, October 18, 1935; Donovan to Warren Peyton, May 1, 1934; Donovan to Aubrey Williams, April 17, 1939; Donovan to Cammack, April 6, 1934; Regents Minutes, October 16–17, 1936; Boxes 88 and 89 contain NYA and FERA payrolls, information, and correspondence; Wiggins interview.

52. Regents Minutes, April 17, August 27, October 9, 1935, May 2, 1936; *Eastern Progress,* November 1, 1935; Donovan to Chester Spears, June 25, 1935; Donovan to Gayle Starnes, August 26, 1935; Glyndon E. Green, "More Than a Stadium," Eastern Kentucky University student paper, 1982, 1–9; Dorris, *Five Decades,* 278; Donovan to H. W. Schmidt, March 1, 1929; *Courier-Journal,* July 3, 1929; Rural School Construction, Box 111; Little interview; Burnett interview; Donovan to James H. Richmond, December 27, 1934.

53. Donovan to A. C. Glass, October 14, 1936; *Courier-Journal,* October 20, 1936; Thomas E. McDonough, "More Than a Stadium," *Athletic Journal* (September 1938): 26–28; Regents Minutes, January 30, December 5, 1936, April 14, 1937; Donovan to Sue Scrivner, July 3, 1935; Regents Minutes, Executive Committee, April 10, August 19, 1937.

54. *Richmond Register,* March 28, 1999; Donovan to George H. Goodman, April 30, 1935, July 1, 1939; Regents Minutes, June 23, August 27, 1935; George Goodman to Donovan, June 29, 1939.

55. *Richmond Daily Register,* November 3, 1935; *Richmond Register,* November 5, 2000; Regents Minutes, July 18, September 12, 1934, August 27, 1935, January 18, 1936; *Eastern Progress,* January 24, 1936; Donovan to George H. Sager Jr., January 28, 1936; program for "Alumni Day Dedication of Addition to College Library, Three Decades of Progress," May 16, 1936; Dorris, *Five Decades,* 21.

56. Library Report for 1927–28; Annual Report from the Library to the President, 1933–34; Robert M. Lester to Donovan, December 15, 1938; Mary Estelle Reid to Donovan, January 15, 1929; *Eastern Progress,* January 13, March 10, 1939; Regents Minutes, December 17, 1938, Dorris, *Five Decades,* 96–104; Sallie Marcum interview, January 13, 1987; E. Francis Mason interview, July 14, 1987.

57. Donovan to Dr. A. T. McCormack, July 1, 1937; *EKSTC General Information, School Year, 1939–40,* 16; Donovan to Barkley, December 2, 1936, August 3, September 8, 1937; Barkley to Donovan, telegram, August 15, 1935, June 22, 1938.

58. *Richmond Register,* April 1, May 9, 1999; *Richmond Daily Register,* October 15, 1938, March 20, 1940; Regents Minutes, June 1, 5, August 2, 10, 26, September 20, December 17, 1938, March 20, 1940; *Eastern Progress,* October 28, 1938.

59. After being nominated for governor by the Democratic Party in 1939, Johnson became governor after Chandler resigned in early October. Johnson then appointed Chandler as United States senator to replace the recently deceased M. M. Logan. A few weeks later Johnson easily won the governorship in his own right. Lowell H. Harrison, "Keen Johnson," *The Kentucky Encyclopedia,* 474; Regents Minutes, September 20, October 18, 1938, February 10, March 21, 1940; *Eastern Progress,* Octo-

ber 28, 1938; Ruth Flint Graybar, "The PWA and the Student Union Building, 1938–40," Eastern Kentucky University student paper, 1982, 1–14.

60. *Richmond Daily Register,* March 20, 1940; *Eastern Progress,* February 1, 2001; "Founders Day Dedication Ceremonies," March 21, 1940; Regents Minutes, March 21, 1940; Dorris, *Five Decades,* 29; Donovan to Johnson, March 8, 1940.

61. Regents Minutes, January 19, April 17, 1935; Dorris, *Five Decades,* 153; *Milestone, 1936,* n.p.; Greenwell interview; Donovan to A. L. Lassiter, January 23, 1935; *Richmond Daily Register,* January 18, February 19, March 6, 1935; Hibbard, "Eastern Kentucky University," 112; *Eastern Progress,* January 19, 1935; "Prologue to the New School Year at Eastern," WHAS, October 2, 1935, speech; Hughes interview; Portwood interview; Tartar interview; Bernard E. Wilson interview, February 4, 1988; Fred Darling interviews, August 29, September 3, 1986; Donovan to Rankin, January 23, 1935, O'Donnell Papers.

62. Greenwell interview; *Lexington Herald-Leader,* June 4, 1990; *Courier-Journal,* October 17, 1936; Donovan to R. H. Herndon, December 22, 1936; Athletic Workships, 1937–38; Tartar interview; Gilbert interview; Darling interviews.

63. Donovan to Cammack, November 2, 1936; Donovan to McDonough, May 8, 1938; *Eastern Progress,* September 30, October 28, 1938; Regents Minutes, May 2, 1936; Greenwell interview; Donovan to James H. Richmond, November 2, 1935.

64. *Richmond Register,* November 19, 2000; *Eastern Progress,* September 27, October 11, 25, November 8, December 13, 1940; Kenneth W. Perry interview, November 7, 1987; Dorris, *Five Decades,* 153–54; Darling interviews; press release, January 18, 1937; Dorris, *Three Decades,* 183–89; Donovan to Paul L. Garrett, August 1, 1939.

65. Deeb interview; Perry interview; Burnett interview; Darling interviews.

66. Darling interviews; Gilbert interviews; Prater interview; Perry interview; *Lexington Herald-Leader,* December 2, 2001; Mary Lois Robinson ms. See Mary Ellen Klatte, *Kentucky Woman: The Life of Viebie Catron Cantrell* (Ashland, Ky.: Jesse Stuart Foundation, 2000).

67. *Eastern Progress,* September 29, 1939, February 9, March 12, 29, 1940; Donovan to Arch A. Mercey, December 12, 1938; Donovan to M. J. Cox, July 30, 1931.

68. Dorris, *Three Decades,* 136–42, 158–61; R. R. Richards to Donovan, January 31, 1939; Dorris, *Five Decades,* 235; Campus-Church Relations Committee, October 7, 1936; F. D. Perkins to Donovan, October 21, 1938; Donovan to Perkins, October 24, 1938.

69. Dorris, *Five Decades,* 251–55; Case to Donovan, June 28, 1928; three folders of Kirkpatrick-Donovan correspondence; Box 107: Press Releases; Donovan to Beckley, December 11, 1936; Beckley to Donovan, January 14, 1937; Boxes 103–106: Publications and Publicity by County; Fred E. Russell to Donovan, January 25, 1937; "Introducing Professionally Trained Teachers," *Eastern Kentucky Review* 31 (April 1939): n.p.

70. Donovan to "Dear High School Senior," form letter, May 4, 1931; Donovan to Floyd Gaines, February 21, 1936; Donovan to W. C. Goble, August 9, 1933; Donovan to James C. Burnett, September 17, 1930; Donovan to Russell E. Helmlick,

June 14, 1938; Donovan to Marie Hamin, May 18, 1931; Donovan to Charles B. Meyers, January 1, 1935; Donovan, "I Remember Eastern," 61; Donovan to Opal Pierson, May 20, 1940.

71. Dorris, *Five Decades,* 228–29; Donovan, "Youth Is Meeting the Challenge," radio address, March 12, 1935; "Prologue to the New School Year at Eastern," speech, October 2, 1935; R. R. Richards to Robert Whitfield, March 6, 1936; "Eastern's 1935 Radio Programs," *Eastern Kentucky Review* 28 (September 1935): n.p.; "Eastern's Radio Programs, January 6–May 12, 1937," Box 108; Regents Minutes, July 7, 1934; *Eastern Progress,* November 29, 1935.

72. Donovan to Alfred B. Steigner, June 3, 1936; Dorris, *Three Decades; Eastern Kentucky Review* 19 (May 1936); Regents Minutes, May 2, 1936; Donovan to Paul L. Garrett, February 23, 1939.

73. Donovan to James H. Richmond, January 10, 1938; "Preliminary Statement of Conference between Governor Chandler and the Presidents of the State-Supported Colleges," Council on Public Higher Education, March 24, 1936; Donovan to Chandler, December 14, 1936, January 14, 1938; "Summary of Facts Regarding the Eastern Kentucky State Teachers College," Box 91, n.d.

74. An era ended with Cherry's death on August 1, 1937. Even though they often clashed, to the end Donovan thought of Cherry as his mentor. Donovan defended the Western president against charges of drunk driving in 1931, for example. Donovan to Cherry, February 26, 1931.

Regents Minutes, April 17, 1935, October 21, 1939, July 23, November 16, 1940; Harrison, *Western Kentucky University,* 90–93; Dorris, *Five Decades,* 28, 81; Donovan to Fitzpatrick, June 21, 1937; Donovan to McVey, June 16, 1934; Donovan to Cherry, May 3, 1931, February 10, 1936; Donovan to William H. Vaughn, August 3, 1940; Harrison, "Henry Hardin Cherry," *The Kentucky Encyclopedia,* 180–81; Council on Public Higher Education Minutes, March 24, 1936; Donovan to Johnson, June 30, 1934, June 22, 1937.

75. Dorris, *Five Decades,* 168–77; Donovan to Virgil Chapman, September 22, 1939; Donovan to Commanding General, Fifth Army Corps, August 5, 1935; telegram to Donovan from Fort Knox, January 22, 1936; A. J. May to Donovan, May 7, 1936; Major Charles W. Gallaher to Donovan, June 15, 1937, March 2, 1939; Major General David Stone to Donovan, March 1, 1940; Donovan to Stone, March 23, 1940; Keen Johnson to Donovan, March 27, 1940; Donovan to Johnson, September 24, 1940; Albert L. McCarthy interview, June 19, 1987; Brock interview; Regents Minutes, October 16–17, 1936, November 16, 1940, January 25, 1941; *Eastern Progress,* January 15, March 12, May 7, 1937.

76. *Eastern Progress,* December 14, 1939, January 19, 1940, January 31, March 28, 1941.

77. Donovan to William A. McCall, December 29, 1928; Donovan to M. S. Robertson, September 4, 1928; Donovan to C. A. Phillips, March 22, 1932; *Courier-Journal,* February 14, 1935; Regents Minutes, October 18, 1938.

78. Donovan to C. C. Sherrod, December 7, 1939; Donovan to Johnson, September 10, 1937; Regents Minutes, October 16, 1937, March 4, May 13, 1939, April 27, 1940; *Richmond Daily Register,* March 20, 1940.

79. Charles Gano Talbert, *The University of Kentucky: The Maturing Years* (Lexington: University of Kentucky Press, 1965), 130–34; Regents Minutes, April 4, 1941; *Eastern Progress,* April 11, 1941; *Courier-Journal,* April 5, 6, 7, 1941; Donovan to John W. Brooker, April 5, 1941; Donovan to Johnson, March 7, 1941.

80. Mary F. Richards interview; Barksdale interview; Chelf, "A Selective View of the Politics of Higher Education in Kentucky and the Role of H. H. Cherry," 246.

81. *Richmond Daily Register,* July 1, 1941.

5. Trials of War and Peace

1. Dorris, *Five Decades,* 198; *Richmond Register,* February 27, 2000; *Eastern Progress,* May 23, 1941; Regents Minutes, July 19, November 1, 1941.

2. Deeb interviews; Perry interview; Darling interviews; *Eastern Progress,* September 26, October 10, 1940

3. *Eastern Progress,* November 22, 1941; *Milestone, 1942,* 62, 72; Dorris, *Five Decades,* 153–54; Perry interview.

4. *Eastern Progress,* October 31, November 7, 1941.

5. *Eastern Progress,* December 19, 1941; *Richmond Register,* December 8, 9, 1941; Perry interview.

6. *Eastern Progress,* February 6, 1942; Assembly Programs; *Courier-Journal,* June 7, 1942.

7. *Eastern Progress,* February 26, 1942; Regents Minutes, February 14, April 8, August 8, 1942; Ellis, Everman, and Sears, *Madison County,* 331–32.

8. Regents Minutes, October 31, 1942; *Eastern Progress,* December 19, 1941, February 6, March 11, October 31, 1942; *Catalog, 1943,* 30; *Milestone, 1942,* 20–32, *Milestone, 1943,* 5, 10–11.

9. *Milestone, 1943,* 73, *Milestone, 1946,* 118; O'Donnell to Lt. Charles R. Perry, March 25, 1943 (unless otherwise noted, all correspondence noted is in the William F. O'Donnell Papers, Eastern Kentucky University Archives); Thomas E. McDonough to *Courier-Journal,* February 11, 1942.

10. *Richmond Register,* January 9, February 19, 23, March 27, April 28, 1943; W. C. Jones to O'Donnell, November 11, 1942; Virginia W. Walle interview, April 15, 1988; *Courier-Journal,* February 27, 1943.

11. O'Donnell to Lt. Charles R. Perry, July 2, 1942, February 14, 1943; O'Donnell to Lt. W. F. O'Donnell Jr., August 26, 1943; Regents Minutes, April 28, 1943; Dorris, *Five Decades,* 202–4; *Eastern Progress,* October 16, 1942, April 16, 1943; *Courier-Journal,* November 2, 1943.

12. *Eastern Progress,* December 6, 1941, October 16, 31, 1942, January 15, October 27, 1943, April 14, 1944, February 9, 1945; O'Donnell to Howard W. Odum,

February 8, 1945; Beatrice G. Dougherty interviewed by Janet White, October 29, 1987.

13. *Courier-Journal,* April 20, July 2, 1943; *Richmond Register,* February 8, 26, March 1, 19, August 19, 1943; *Cincinnati Enquirer,* February 16, 1943.

14. *Kentucky Post,* June 2, 1943; *Courier-Journal,* April 20, May 16, July 2, 1943; Joe Reister to O'Donnell, April 23, 1943.

15. Dorris, *Five Decades,* 101; Br. Gen. W. L. Weible to O'Donnell, December 24, 1943; March 4, 1943, Training Unit Contract, War Department; O'Donnell to Br. Gen. Joe N. Dalton, August 9, 1943; O'Donnell to Thomas Collier, August 10, 1943; Regents Minutes, August 19, November 15, 1943.

16. O'Donnell to Lt. W. F. O'Donnell, Jr., September 18, 1943.

17. Daily Bulletin No. 180, Headquarters, 3589th Service Unit, WAC Branch No. 6, n.p.; Daily Bulletin No. 188, n.p.; Daily Bulletin No. 191, n.p.; *Richmond Register,* September 25, 1943.

18. Press release, February 18, 1944, by Henry L. Stimson, Secretary of War, copy; Lt. Col. E. S. Farnish to O'Donnell, March 23, 1944; *Eastern Progress and Engineer,* March 3, 17, 1944; *Courier-Journal,* February 19, 1944; Regents Minutes, March 6, 1944; O'Donnell to Senator A. B. Chandler, December 6, 1943; O'Donnell to Lt. Col. J. E. Haywood, December 4, 1943.

19. *Life at Eastern, May 1944,* passim; Harvey H. LaFuze interview, February 18, 1988; O'Donnell to H. D. Fitzpatrick, December 3, 1943; Laura A. Holt interview, August 9, 1988.

20. Donovan to O'Donnell, January 25, 1944; Regents Minutes, March 6, May 8, July 14, December 11, 1944; O'Donnell to Warfield Miller, June 4, October 6, 1943.

21. Regents Minutes, December 11, 1944; *Courier-Journal,* June 1, 1944; *Eastern Progress,* December 1, 13, 1944; Dorris, *Five Decades,* 300–301.

22. *Eastern Progress,* May 12, June 13, October 6, 1944; Dorris, *Five Decades,* 254–55; Mary F. Richards interview, July 22, 1986; Jack Lockhart to Editor, *Eastern Progress and Engineer,* January 31, 1944.

23. Questionnaire, "Former Students in the Service," 1944–45, ASTP File, Alumni Affairs.

24. Beatrice G. Dougherty, "Through a Veil of Darkness," *Eastern: The EKU Alumnus* 14 (Winter 1945): 9–18; Dougherty interview.

25. *Eastern Progress,* October 6, November 8, 1944, January 12, 23, March 15, 30, May 15, 1945; Regents Minutes, September 15, December 11, 1944, May 10, 1945; Hughes interview; Barksdale interview; Dorris, *Five Decades,* 155; O'Donnell to Donovan, July 26, 1944; *Milestone, 1946.*

26. *Eastern Progress,* May 18, June 22, 1945, October 22, 1946; Regents Minutes, May 10, August 14, 1945; Dorris, *Five Decades,* 203–16.

27. Hughes interview; Regents Minutes, May 10, September 17, November 19, 1945; *Courier-Journal,* September 18, 1945; Hibbard, "Eastern Kentucky University," 126–28; O'Donnell to Keen Johnson, September 14, 1945.

28. Hibbard, "Eastern Kentucky University," 135–38; *Eastern Progress,* October 5, 19, 1946; Regents Minutes, November 19, 1945; Horowitz, *Campus Life,* 185–87; Louis Menard, "Undisciplined," *Wilson Quarterly* 25 (Autumn 2001): 55–56; Alva M. Thompson to O'Donnell, February 13, 1946; Willmer Halcomb interview, November 30, 1990; Thelin, *A History of American Higher Education,* 262–63.

29. Veterans Petition to O'Donnell, October 16, 1946; *Eastern Progress,* October 19, 1946, March 14, October 24, 1947; Deeb interviews; Ethan Colton to O'Donnell, November 14, 1946.

30. O'Donnell to Senator Virgil Chapman, May 6, June 4, 1946; O'Donnell to Senator Alben Barkley, May 6, 1946; *Eastern Progress,* November 17, December 6, 1945, March 6, 27, 1946, October 23, 1953; O'Donnell to Max Reed, December 19, 1945; O'Donnell to S. F. Choden, July 22, 1946; Veterans Club to O'Donnell, November 14, 1945; O'Donnell to Jesse C. Moberly, January 1, 1946; O'Donnell to Education Editor, *New York Times,* March 15, 1945; Veterans Club, meeting, October 8, 1953; O'Donnell to Judge Kenneth E. Parke, October 15, 1953; Holt interview; Carl and Mary Snyder Ward interview, December 31, 1991.

31. Carl Keen interview, August 1, 1990; Anita Allen interview, June 24, 1987; Grant Foster and Florence E. Asher interview, June 23, 1987; Edsel Mountz interview, May 9, 1990; Halcomb interview; Holt interview.

32. *Eastern Progress,* June 22, 1945, February 1, March 6, May 10, November 2, 27, 1946; *Richmond Register,* September 17, 1946; *Milestone, 1946,* 26, 28, 97, 118; Darling interviews; *Milestone, 1947,* 168.

33. Deeb interviews; Darling interviews; *Eastern Progress,* April 25, 1947; O'Donnell to J. C. Codell, April 11, 1947; *Lexington Herald-Leader,* June 18, 1981; *Milestone, 1947,* 148; Dorris, *Five Decades,* 157–58, 298–99.

34. Regents Minutes, January 22, May 20, 1947, February 16, 1948, July 18, 1950; Dorris, *Five Decades,* 157–59, 298–99; *Eastern Progress,* February 15, 1949, March 19, 1951; *Milestone, 1948,* 148; *Milestone, 1950,* 133; O'Donnell to C. D. Harmon, February 5, 1949; Paul D. Hicks interview, April 16, 1988.

35. *Eastern Progress,* May 10, 1946, April 25, October 10, 1947, November 19, December 10, 1948; Regents Minutes, May 20, October 20, 1947; *Milestone, 1948,* 128–29, 135; *Milestone, 1949,* 123; *Milestone, 1950,* 122; Glenn E. Presnell interviewed by William Berge, September 12, 13, 1978.

36. O'Donnell to Paul Garrett, April 5, 1944; *Eastern Progress,* February 27, 1948; Garrett to O'Donnell, September 23, 1949.

37. Regents Minutes, May 20, October 20, 1947, February 16, June 19, December 13, 1948, April 14, 1949; *Eastern Progress,* February 7, 1948.

38. Regents Minutes, July 27, 1948, August 15, September 30, 1949, February 20, 1950; *Eastern Progress,* January 16, 1948; *Courier-Journal,* February 21, September 20, 1949.

39. *Courier-Journal,* January 1, November 26, 1944, May 5, November 26, 1946, March 28, April 9, May 21, 1947; Robert G. Wood, "The Election of William F.

O'Donnell," Eastern Kentucky University student paper, 1982, 1–5; Hibbard, "Eastern Kentucky University," 140–41; Regents Minutes, July 18, 1950.

40. Regents Minutes, February 20, 1950.

41. *Eastern Progress,* January 18, 1946, June 3, 1948; Dorris, *Five Decades,* 178–90, 208–9; *Courier-Journal,* February 27, 1955; O'Donnell to Gen. George C. Marshall, April 4, 1945; Regents Minutes, February 12, November 10, 1951, May 4, 1959.

42. *Eastern Progress,* January 31, 1947, October 9, 23, 1953, April 2, 1954, January 21, 1955, October 24, 1958, November 6, 1959; Regents Minutes, November 3, 1956; O'Donnell to H. Clay Chambers, November 6, 1956; *Milestone, 1959,* n.p.

43. *Eastern Progress,* October 5, 1945, October 9, 1953, March 5, April 2, September 22, 1954, February 18, 1955, November 7, 1958, November 19, 1959; Regents Minutes, March 22, November 13, 1954.

44. *Eastern Progress,* January 18, 1946, February 18, 1955; Dorris, *Five Decades,* 131–33, 135; O'Donnell to Ralph Woods, January 31, 1949, February 1, 1955; *Courier-Journal,* May 22, 1957; Regents Minutes, June 2, 1954; Carl and Mary Cole interview, April 3, 2002.

45. *Eastern Progress,* February 18, 1955, October 25, 1957; Regents Minutes, July 10, 1957; Dorris, *Five Decades,* 127–45; Jewish Chautauqua Society File; Adron Doran to O'Donnell, January 17, 1957.

46. Regents Minutes, May 20, 1947, January 15, 1949, February 20, 1950, November 21, 1955, November 2, 1957, May 4, July 23, October 18, 1959, January 11, 1960; O'Donnell to J. M. Godard, January 15, 1951; Godard to O'Donnell, January 17, 1951.

47. *Catalog, 1951–52,* 54; *Catalog 1955–1956,* 55; *Catalog, 1957–58,* 54; *Catalog, 1958–59,* 57; *Catalog, 1959–60,* 59; O'Donnell to Helen Murray, September 6, 1956; Tom Rece to O'Donnell, May 24, 1958; O'Donnell to Rece, May 28, 1958; Scholarship File, Donald R. Swindler, February 3, 1959; Regents Minutes, May 13, July 10, 1957, May 4, 1959; Emma Case to O'Donnell, February 3, 1959; 50 Dollar Scholarship File; Fellowship File.

48. *Richmond Register,* April 7, 1958; Student File; O'Donnell to Case, November 15, 1945; *Courier-Journal,* August 19, November 2, 1956.

49. *Eastern Progress,* January 20, 1951, February 19, March 19, 1954, October 25, 1957, April 4, 1958; *Courier-Journal,* December 25, 27, 1950; O'Donnell to Sheriff Russell Turpin, April 7, 1954.

50. Regents Minutes, September 17, 1945, May 20, 1947, August 15, 1949, February 20, March 27, 1950, May 4, November 7, 1953, March 22, 1954, July 23, 1958; citation from Charles Hay's notes in Eastern Kentucky University Special Collections and Archives.

51. Regents Minutes, March 21, July 20, 1956, March 1, November 2, 1957, January 18, July 23, September 17, 1958.

52. Dorris, *Five Decades,* 21; *Eastern Progress,* September 23, 1955, October 10, 1958; *Courier-Journal,* March 10, 1956, June 1, 1957.

53. *Courier-Journal,* February 27, 1955, February 11, 1956, July 25, 1958; Regents Minutes, February 20, 1950, May 29, November 10, 1951, March 22, June 2, 18, July 8, 1954, March 4, May 9, November 21, December 6, 1955, March 21, May 13, July 20, 1956, July 10, November 2, 1957, January 18, April 28, June 4, 23, September 17, October 18, 1958, May 4, 1959, January 11, February 26, March 17, 1960; *Eastern Progress,* May 23, 1959; "The Students of Keith Hall" to O'Donnell, December 18, 1958; Cole interview.

54. *Milestone, 1950,* 133; Cole interview.

55. *Milestone, 1952,* 112–13; *Milestone, 1953,* n.p.; *Milestone, 1958,* n.p.; *Eastern Progress,* March 1, 1952.

56. *Milestone, 1955,* 78–79; *Milestone, 1956,* 146, 149; *Eastern Progress,* January 21, March 4, 1955.

57. Athletic Scholarships, 1958–60 File; Regents Minutes, February 12, 1951, March 27, 1952, August 1, 1955, February 21, 1958; Cole interview.

58. Dorris, *Five Decades,* 156; *Eastern Progress,* February 14, 1947; March 19, 1954, April 1, 1955; Lynn Harvell, "Gertrude Hood: Four Decades of Contribution, 1928–1972," Eastern Kentucky University student paper, 1985, 4–12; Lynn Harvell, "The Women's Athletic Association at Eastern Kentucky State College: Early Beginnings (1946–1955)," Eastern Kentucky University student paper, 1985, 1–22.

59. *Courier-Journal,* November 5, 1954; Dorris, *Five Decades,* 160–61.

60. *Milestone, 1955,* 69; *Milestone, 1956,* 139; *Milestone, 1960,* 98; *Eastern Progress,* December 10, 1954, January 21, 1955; Tangerine Bowl File, Contract between Eastern and Elks Lodge, November 29, 1954; *Richmond Register,* January 5, 1955.

61. Garrett to O'Donnell, March 9, 1954; O'Donnell to Garrett, April 2, 1954; *Courier-Journal,* February 17, 23, 24, 1960; *Eastern Progress,* February 26, 1960; Cole interview; Gary P. West, "The Play," *Kentucky Monthly* 5 (November 2002): 22–23, 49.

62. *Eastern Progress,* February 12, 1951, July 20, 1956; Regents Minutes, June 19, 1948, September 27, 1951, November 21, 1955.

63. Regents Minutes, September 27, 1951, May 4, November 7, 1953, July 8, 1954, July 20, 1956, May 13, 1957, April 28, June 4, 1958; Barksdale interview.

64. Regents Minutes, July 20, 1956, November 19, 1959, April 13, 1960; Dorris, *Five Decades,* 99; *Eastern Progress,* October 5, 1956, *Courier-Journal,* October 1, 1954, September 22, 1955, September 25, 1956, October 26, 1958; Grace and Dean Gatwood interview, January 15, 1987.

65. Regents Minutes, March 1, 1957; Dorris, *Five Decades,* 96–104; *Eastern Progress,* October 25, 1957; *Courier-Journal,* May 22, 1956; O'Donnell to Chandler, December 17, 1957.

66. *Catalog, 1946–47,* passim; Dorris, *Five Decades,* 309–10.

67. Dorris, *Five Decades,* 130, 307–10; *Eastern Progress,* February 28, 1947, June 3, 1948, May 21, 1954, January 27, September 22, 1955, January 13, 1956, October 11, December 13, 1957; John Hardin Best, "The Revolution of Markets and Management: Toward a History of American Higher Education since 1945," *History of Education Quarterly* 28 (Summer 1988): 183–86.

68. Regents Minutes, October 20, 1947, May 12, July 18, 1950; Barksdale interview. See cartoon in *Eastern Progress,* May 8, 1942; *EKU Alumnus* 16 (Summer 1977): 11–12.

69. Regents Minutes, June 2, 1954, August 1, 1955, March 21, 1956; *Milestone, 1960,* 223; *Milestone, 1959,* 203; *Milestone, 1961,* 80.

70. *Eastern Progress,* May 8, 1942, November 7, 1958, November 20, 1959.

71. O'Donnell to Hitomi Tsuji, September 17, 1952; O'Donnell to Alsoto Wafik Taha, January 19, 1954.

72. William E. Sexton interview, September 3, 1987; Regents Minutes, July 23, October 18, September 17, 1958, June 3, 1959.

73. *Courier-Journal,* October 3, 1959, May 22, 1960; Barksdale interview; Sexton interview; *Eastern Progress,* May 31, 1960; Hibbard, "Eastern Kentucky University," 148–49, 151.

74. Cole interview; *Richmond Register,* December 10, 2000.

6. Robert R. Martin

1. Donna M. Masters, "Robert Richard Martin," *Kentucky Encyclopedia,* 612–13.

2. Ibid.

3. Albert B. Chandler interview, December 6, 1976; James L. Sublett interview, August 9, 1977; *Maysville Daily Independent,* April 2, 1958; Robert R. Martin interview, November 29, 1976; J. C. Powell interview, April 14, 1978; Ellis Hartford interview, December 14, 1976.

4. William G. Adams conversation, March 3, 2002; Regents Minutes, May 13, 1957; Adron Doran interview, February 23, 1977; Martin interview, November 29, 1976; *Courier-Journal,* November 9, 1957, April 1, 1958, October 3, 10, 1959; Jo M. Ferguson interview, March 9, 1977.

5. Robert F. Matthews interview, November 30, 1976; Edward F. Prichard Jr. interview, January 25, 1977; Bert T. Combs interview, December 12, 1976; Sublett interview; Ferguson interview; Edward T. Breathitt Jr. interview, March 15, 1977.

6. Bert T. Combs interview; Breathitt interview; Doran interview; Lyman Ginger interview, November 15, 1977; Matthews interview; Chandler interview; Ferguson interview; *Courier-Journal,* July 20, September 5, 6, 9, 14, 1958; *Lexington Herald,* April 14, 1960; Earl C. Clements interview, January 5, 1977.

7. *Courier-Journal,* December 10, 1959; Bert T. Combs interview; Breathitt interview; Wendell P. Butler interview, February 3, 1977; Sublett interview; Ralph Whalin interview, May 14, 1978.

8. Regents Minutes, April 13, 1960; *Courier-Journal* April 14, 1960; Combs to Flem D. Sampson, April 4, 1960 (unless otherwise noted, all manuscripts in this chapter are from the Robert R. Martin Papers, Eastern Kentucky University Archives); Doran interview.

9. Regents Minutes, April 13, 1960; *Courier-Journal,* April 14, 1960; *Eastern Progress,* April 19, 1960.

10. Regents Minutes, April 13, 1960; Martin interview, November 29, 1976; *Eastern Progress,* April 19, 1960; Doran interview; Butler interview.

11. Martin interview, November 29, 1976; Butler interview; Powell interview; Combs interview; Breathitt interview; Robert B. Hensley interview, March 25, 1977.

12. *Lexington Herald,* April 14, 1960; *Richmond Daily Register,* April 13, 1960; Sublett interview; Chelf, "A Selective View of the Politics of Higher Education in Kentucky and the Role of H. H. Cherry," 246–47.

13. J. C. Powell interviews, April 14, 1978, May 1, 3, 1985; Martin interview, November 29, 1976; *Courier-Journal,* June 14, 1960; Martin to O'Donnell, May 27, 1960.

14. *Sunday Herald-Leader,* June 11, 1960; Schedule and Speech Files; Albert P. Smith Jr. interview, September 19, 2002; Sublett interview; Thomas D. Clark interview, October 29, 2002.

15. Sublett interview; Cornelius Grafton interview, March 9, 1977; Otis A. Singletary Jr. interview, May 3, 1978; Thomas D. Myers interview, April 21, 1978; John P. DeMarcus interview, April 25, 1978; John D. Rowlett interview, May 2, 1978; Martin to C. F. Schafer, September 30, 1963; Martin to Arnold Hanger, June 13, 1973; Martin to James O. Filburn, May 6, 1974; William E. Sexton interview, September 3, 1987; Shirley M. Castle interview, November 4, 1977; Lawrence O. Martin interview, April 16, 1987; Speech File, August 2, 1973; Martin to James Anderson, December 7, 1978.

16. *Courier-Journal,* June 2, 1960; Powell interviews, April 14, 1978, May 1, 3, 1985; Regents Minutes, July 8, September 3, 1960.

17. *Eastern Progress,* September 29, October 20, 27, November 3, 1960.

18. *Eastern Progress,* November 17, 1960; *Courier-Journal,* November 18, 1960; Martin, "A Vision of Greatness," November 17, 1960, Speech File; Allan Ostar interview, March 15, 1977.

19. "A Vision of Greatness" speech; Dean and Grace Gatwood interview, January 15, 1987.

20. Regents Minutes, March 4, April 19, 1961; *Eastern Progress,* December 1, 1960, February 17, March 3, 10, November 3, 17, 1961.

21. Clements interview; Regents Minutes, April 19, 1961; *Richmond Daily Register,* June 1, 1961; *Eastern Progress,* June 1, 1961, February 14, 2002; *Milestone, 1961,* 61; Martin to Johnson, March 28, 1961.

22. Martin interview, December 13, 1976; Johnson to Martin, May 2, 1961; Martin to J. L. Pruett, June 27, 1975.

23. Martin to Pruett, June 27, 1975; Martin interview, December 13, 1976; Thomas Stovall interview, March 15, 1977; Jo M. Ferguson to Martin, January 19, 1971; copy, "Last Will and Testament of Emma Parkes Watts, June 10, 1970"; Watts Codicil, August 13, 1970; Clay Shackelford to Watts, April 24, 1963; contract for 4.5 acres of Watts Estate, June 14, 1971.

24. Regents Minutes, August 3, 1961; *Courier-Journal,* August 3, 1961; Martin to Romulo, August 4, 1961; *Milestone, 1969,* 35; *Eastern Progress,* May 1, November 20,

1964, March 25, 1966, May 9, 1968; Martin to Parker, July 21, 1967; Parker to Martin, June 17, 1968; Martin to J. S. Cooper, March 22, May 18, 1962.

25. Martin interview, December 13, 1976; Sexton interview; "In Pursuit of a Vision," *Fifteen Year Report,* Eastern Kentucky University, 1959–60/1974–75, passim.; Grafton interview; Prichard interview; Butler interview; Ludwig Caminita Jr. to Carl D. Perkins, October 22, 1965, copy; *Lexington Herald,* July 17, 1970.

26. *Courier-Journal,* November 17, 1960; *Eastern Progress,* March 17, 1961, December 7, 14, 1962; *Richmond Register,* August 16, 1960.

27. *Eastern Progress,* December 15, 1960, September 21, November 30, 1962, January 10, 1964; Daniel P. Webster to the author, June 18, 2002; Regents Minutes, January 9, 1963; Roger Green Jr. telephone conversation, November 7, 2002; Jim Barrett, e-mail to author, March 23, 2003; Sue Campbell Barrett, e-mail to author, March 24, 2003.

28. Webster letter; *Eastern Progress,* February 2, 1960, March 9, 1962, September 21, November 27, 1963, September 18, 1964; Regents Minutes, November 3, 1962.

29. Webster letter; *Eastern Progress,* February 2, 1960, November 17, December 8, 1961, March 9, April 27, 1962, February 8, March 29, June 28, November 15, 1963, February 14, September 18, 1964; Donald Henrickson conversation, April 28, 2003.

30. Castle interview; Lawrence O. Martin interview; Emma Y. Case interview, August 18, 1986; William J. Moore interview, October 23, 1977.

31. Powell interview, May 1, 1985; *Eastern Progress,* December 15, 1960; Larry W. Bailey interview, May 22, 2002; R. R. Richards interview, March 23, 1978; Branley Branson interview, April 18, 2000.

32. Robert L. Oppelt to President Robert Krustra, e-mail message, January 2, 2000, copy to author; *Eastern Progress,* September 19, 1968; Regents Minutes, September 12, 1968, May 30, 1969.

33. *Eastern Kentucky University Magazine* 1 (Spring 2000): 10; Bailey interview; Nancy and R. E. Forderhase interview, February 4, 2000.

34. *Eastern Progress,* October 5, 1962; Martin to James S. Pope Jr., March 23, 1961.

35. Martin to Dorcas Ruthenburg, March 29, 1962; *Eastern Kentucky University Magazine* 2 (Summer 2001): 6; *Eastern Progress,* September 6, October 20, 1961, May 1, 29, September 25, October 23, 1964, April 2, 1965; *Milestone, 1963,* 236; *Milestone, 1965,* 224–32.

36. *Eastern Progress,* May 17, 1963; *Richmond Register,* December 18, 2000; *Milestone, 1963,* 236.

37. Charley E. Gillispie interview, May 9, 1987; *Eastern Kentucky University Magazine* 1 (Spring 2000): 9.

38. *Eastern Kentucky University Magazine* 1 (Spring 2000): 25; John W. Smith interview, March 27, 2002; Bailey interview.

39. James S. and Anna W. Way interview, April 29, 2000; *Eastern Progress,* February 23, 1989; Regents Minutes, June 17, 1965, December 19, 1966.

40. *Lexington Herald-Leader,* August 24, 1986, January 2, 1999; "Paul S. McBrayer,"

The Kentucky Encyclopedia, 590; *Richmond Register,* January 2, 1999; Regents Minutes, March 21, 1962, August 6, 1964; *Eastern Progress,* December 8, 1961, February 2, March 9, 1962, March 19, 1965, May 27, 1966.

41. *Eastern Progress,* January 18, February 22, 1963; Martin to Hughes, September 20, 1967; Martin to Doran, March 23, 1961.

42. *Eastern Progress,* November 30, 1962, November 22, 1963, September 17, October 15, 1965, September 21, November 3, 1966, November 30, December 14, 1967; *Richmond Register,* July 26, 1999; Regents Minutes, December 4, 1964; *Lexington Herald-Leader,* August 29, 2001; *Milestone, 1965,* 218–23; *Milestone, 1966,* 316–23; *Milestone, 1967,* 340–47; *Milestone, 1968,* 335–43, *Milestone, 1969,* 298–307.

43. *Eastern Progress,* February 18, March 12, 1965, May 11, 18, 1967; *Milestone, 1965,* 224–32; *Milestone, 1966,* 325–31.

44. "State University System," *The Kentucky Encyclopedia,* 850–51; *Lexington Herald,* November 3, 1961; *Lexington Leader,* November 3, 1961; *Richmond Daily Register,* November 13, 1961; Doran to Martin, October 19, 1963.

45. Ginger interview; *Paducah Sun-Democrat,* June 9, 1963; *Courier-Journal,* October 25, 1963, December 10, 1965; H. D. Fitzpatrick Jr. to Martin, December 19, 1960; *Kentucky Kernel,* November 13, 1963; Ralph H. Woods to Martin, June 7, 1963, March 3, 1964; Martin to Oswald, January 4, 1964.

46. Best, "The Revolution of Markets and Management," 185; Martin interview, December 3, 1976.

47. Martin and John D. Rowlett interview, April 20, 1990; Regents Minutes, October 23, 1964, October 30, 1965; Martin interview, December 3, 1976; *Eastern Progress,* April 4, 2002; *Courier-Journal,* May 26, 1965; John D. Rowlett interview, May 2, 1978.

48. Rowlett interview; Martin and Rowlett interview, May 8, 1990; James McClanahan and Rhonda Smith, *Justice and Safety Education at Eastern Kentucky University: A Historical Perspective,* 2001, 4–7; *Eastern Progress,* February 25, 1966; Regents Minutes, October 4, 1972; Robert E. Bagby interview, May 22, 2000; J. C. Powell interview, May 3, 1985.

49. Harrison, *Western Kentucky University,* 175–81; *Eastern Progress,* September 17, October 8, 1965; Frederic D. Ogden, *Gladly Learn and Gladly Teach: The College of Arts and Sciences, 1965–1979, Eastern Kentucky University* (Richmond: Eastern Kentucky University, 1999), 8–17, 56–57; Frederic D. Ogden interview, January 27, 1987.

50. Breathitt interview; Regents Minutes, January 21, March 7, June 17, 1966; Harrison, *Western Kentucky University,* 161–62; *Courier-Journal,* June 9, 1963; *Richmond Daily Register,* February 26, 1966.

51. *Eastern Progress,* January 21, February 11, 18, 25, March 4, 18, 25, 1966; *Courier-Journal,* February 26, March 19, 1966; Breathitt interview; *Milestone, 1966,* 416; Regents Minutes, March 7, 1966; Richard Wilson interview, April 18, 1977; M. M. Chambers, *Higher Education in the Fifty States* (Danville, Ill.: Interstate Printers and Publishers, 1970), 158.

52. Doran interview; Frank L. Dickey interview, January 5, 1977; Louie B. Nunn interview, February 16, 1977; A. D. Albright interview, June 7, 1977; John P. DeMarcus interview, April 25, 1978; Lowell H. Harrison, "Louie B. Nunn," *Kentucky Encyclopedia,* 686; Will Frank Steely, "Northern Kentucky University," *Kentucky Encyclopedia,* 684–85; Singletary interview; Richard Wilson interview, March 9, 2000; Martin interview, December 3, 1976; *Kentucky Post,* October 10, 1968; Dwayne D. Cox and William J. Morison, *The University of Louisville* (Lexington: University Press of Kentucky, 2000), 144–45.

53. Ferguson interview; Grafton interview; Nunn interview; Martin to Nunn, February 27, 1968; Regents Minutes, January 10, 1968.

54. Martin to Thomas H. McGregor, April 16, 1963; Martin to Hanger, January 27, 1967; Regents Minutes, September 3, 1960, October 30, 1965, March 21, May 30, December 19, 1966, October 21, 1967, August 1, 1968, January 15, 1969; *Eastern Progress,* September 14, 1966.

55. *Eastern Progress,* February 18, 1966, September 14, 1967, May 4, 1970, May 2, November 7, 1974, May 4, 1977; *Richmond Register,* May 13, 1974; *Milestone, 1969,* 35; Martin to Seth Tuska, January 7, 1974; Regents Minutes, August 2, 1973; *Courier-Journal,* January 13, 1974; Martin to Russell McClure, June 7, 1976, Powell Papers.

56. Harrison, *Western Kentucky University,* 162–63, 195; *Eastern Progress,* May 21, 1965, February 25, April 8, October 20, December 1, 1966, February 16, 1967, October 25, 1973; Regents Minutes, May 30, 1966, October 19, 1971.

57. Regents Minutes, January 21, 1970; *Eastern Progress,* March 5, 1965, August 30, 1973, January 8, December 11, 1975; *Milestone, 1970,* 193–95, 199, 264–65, 278.

58. David Brooks, "The Organization Kid," *Atlantic Monthly,* April 2001, 46; *Eastern Progress,* February 18, 1966; Martin, faculty speech, September 13, 1969; Prichard interview.

59. Martin to Major General Frederick M. Warren, May 11, 1962; Martin to Major General Andrew R. Lolli, July 24, 1962.

60. *Eastern Progress,* May 21, November 5, 12, 19, December 3, 17, 1965, March 25, April 1, 8, 22, 1966; Regents Minutes, September 12, 1968, July 11, 1969, August 6, 1970; *Eastern Kentucky University Magazine* 2 (Summer 2002): 16; Mike Embry, e-mail to author, September 15, 2003.

61. *Eastern Progress,* October 20, 1966, March 16, 23, 30, November 9, 1967; *Milestone, 1967,* 246; W. Stephen Wilborn interview, April 25, 1978; Stovall interview; Regents Minutes, April 22, 1968.

62. Regents Minutes, March 20, April 22, May 8, 30, November 21, 1968; Wilborn interview; *Eastern Progress,* October 26, November 9, 16, December 7, 1967, January 11, February 8, 29, March 7, 1968; Wilborn to Martin, May 6, 1968.

63. *Eastern Progress,* September 19, October 3, November 7, 14, 21, December 5, 12, 1968.

64. Regents Minutes, January 15, March 19, April 16, June 5, 1969, April 2, 1971; Myers interview; telephone conversation with David Wainscott, December 1, 2002; *Courier-Journal,* June 6, 1969; *Eastern Progress,* October 25, 1973, September 19, 1974.

65. Regents Minutes, March 19, June 5, 1969; *Courier-Journal,* March 20, 26, 27, 28, April 1, 1969; Richard Wilson interviews; *Eastern Progress,* February 13, 20, 27, March 6, 13, 20, 27, April 3, 1969; Attorney General John B. Breckinridge to W. Stephen Wilborn, March 4, 1969; Wilborn interview.

66. *Eastern Progress,* April 3, 10, 24, May 15, 22, 29, June 26, 1969; Regents Minutes, March 19, June 5, 1969.

67. *Eastern Progress,* October 9, 16, 30, 1969; *Milestone, 1970,* 48–49.

68. Regents Minutes, July 11, 29, 1969, June 5, September 11, 1970; *Courier-Journal,* June 6, 1970; *Eastern Progress,* May 7, 14, 1970; Marvin Dodson and Richard VanHoose interview, December 17, 1976; Nunn interview; *Lexington Herald,* August 19, 1970.

69. Regents Minutes, December 19, 1966, June 5, July 29, 1969, August 3, 1972, May 12, 1973; *Eastern Progress,* January 12, 1967, June 25, 1970; *Milestone, 1970,* 123; Powell interview, May 1, 1985.

70. Regents Minutes, June 17, 1965, June 5, 1970, October 4, 1972, January 5, August 2, 1973; Martin to Marion Brown, February 13, 1968; *Courier-Journal,* April 15, 1966.

71. Wilson interviews; Mary Joe Jones to Martin, September 16, 1968; Martin to Jones, September 18, 1968.

72. Regents Minutes, November 22, 1967, June 5, August 6, 1970, February 6, October 19, 28, 1971, March 21, 29, August 2, 1973, October 4, 1975.

73. *Eastern Progress,* May 28, 1970, April 27, 1972.

74. Singletary interview; *Courier-Journal,* May 9, 13, 20, 1972; *Lexington Leader,* May 9, 1972; Martin to Singletary, May 18, 1972; "Statement by Robert R. Martin," n.d.; Combs to Martin, June 1, 1973; Martin to Combs, June 6, 1973; Stratton to Martin, May 17, 1972; Regents Minutes, March 20, April 25, May 19, August 3, 1972, March 29, October 6, December 6, 1973; Flonnie C. Walton to Martin, May 27, 1972; *Eastern Progress,* March 29, June 21, October 25, 1973, September 5, December 6, 1974; John B. Breckinridge to Martin, August 17, 1970; Carl and Mary Cole interview, April 3, 2002.

75. Clark interview; Smith interview; O. Leonard Press interview, March 11, 1977; Regents Minutes, April 2, 1971; *Courier-Journal,* November 10, 1971; Ostar interview; *Lexington Herald,* November 18, 1970; Earl C. Clements to Martin, November 25, 1970; Martin to Clements, December 3, 1970.

76. "Alum to Dear Sir," January 31, 1962; Dr. Stephen C. Schindler to Martin, April 7, May 11, 1972; Martin to Gertrude Adams, December 6, 1960; Martin to C. F. Schafer, September 30, 1963.

77. Regents Minutes, August 2, October 6, 1973, October 5, 1974, January 4,

1975; Wilson interviews; *Eastern Progress,* July 27, September 14, October 5, 1972, March 1, 7, 23, April 26, 1973, January 24, March 21, 1974, February 21, 2002.

78. Regents Minutes, August 2, 1973, April 27, August 1, 1974, January 4, March 25, August 7, 1975, April 3, 1976; Ogden, *Gladly Learn and Gladly Teach,* 49–56; *Eastern Progress,* October 25, 1973, April 4, August 29, September 26, October 3, 10, 24, 1974, January 16, 1975.

79. *Eastern Progress,* July 26, August 23, 1973, October 4, 1975, January 8, 1976; Regents Minutes, January 2, 1976.

80. *Eastern Progress,* March 21, 28, April 11, 1974, January 29, 1976.

81. *Eastern Progress,* September 26, November 7, 1974, January 9, April 17, May 1, August 28, 1975; *Eastern Kentucky University Magazine* 2 (Summer 2002): 17; *Milestone, 1970,* 303; *Courier-Journal,* October 12, 1972.

82. *Courier-Journal,* April 1, 4, 1969, August 4, 1971; Nunn interview; Wilson interviews; Martin to Wallace G. Wilkinson, July 5, 1967; Martin to Thomas Stovall, February 29, 1968; Doran interview; Doran to John W. Keith Jr., September 15, 1971.

83. Singletary interview; Martin and Rowlett interview, May 8, 1990; Regents Minutes, January 23, October 4, 1972, March 25, 1975; Donald R. Feltner, "The Story of the Birth and Maturation of a University," *Eastern Kentucky University Alumnus* 15 (Summer 1976): 31; Prichard interview; *Eastern Progress,* October 19, 1972; *Lexington Herald,* September 22, 1969; Rowlett to Martin, September 22, 1969; Bagby interview; Martin to Nunn, April 4, 1971; McClanahan and Smith, *Justice and Safety Education at Eastern Kentucky University,* 1–32; Bob Schulman, "One Man's Opinion," WHAS-TV, October 16, 1972.

84. Larry VanDyne, "The Spotlight Turns to Voc-Tech," *Chronicle of Higher Education,"* April 7, 1975, 9.

85. *Milestone, 1969,* 318; *Milestone, 1970,* 207; Regents Minutes, May 12, August 2, October 18, 1973, April 1, 1974, March 25, October 2, 1975; *Eastern Progress,* April 4, August 29, 1974; *Eastern Kentucky University Alumnus* 14 (Winter 1975): 37.

86. *Eastern Progress,* March 29, April 5, 1973, February 12, March 18, 1976.

87. *Milestone, 1973,* 243; *Eastern Progress,* November 29, 1973; *Eastern Kentucky University Alumnus* 14 (Winter 1975): 40–41.

88. Regents Minutes, April 3, 1976; *Courier-Journal,* April 4, 1976; *Eastern Progress,* October 23, 1975, April 8, 1976; "Statement," Robert R. Martin, April 3, 1976; *Milestone, 1976,* 25.

89. Myers interview; *Eastern Progress,* September 4, October 2, 1975, March 4, 18, July 1, 1976; Martin interview, December 13, 1976.

90. *Eastern Progress,* April 29, 1976, November 11, 1999; Martin interview, December 13, 1976; Clark interview; *Lexington Herald-Leader,* December 2, 1997; *Courier-Journal,* December 19, 1976; Regents Minutes, September 30, 1976; Richard Wilson interviews.

91. Ostar interview.

7. J. C. Powell

1. W. Stephen Wilborn interview, April 25, 1978; Richard Wilson interview, March 9, 2000; Robert R. Martin to Dean William G. Monahan, April 29, 1976; *Eastern Progress,* April 22, 1976; *Richmond Daily Register,* April 5, 1976; Emma Y. Case interview, August 18, 1986.

2. *Eastern Progress,* April 4, July 1, 29, 1976; Morris Taylor interview, August 23, 1976; Regents Minutes, June 5, 1976; *Lexington Leader,* August 10, 1976; Faculty Senate Minutes, May 5, 1976; Composite of All Committees, Presidential Search File; William E. Ellis to Robert B. Begley, May 5, 1976 (unless otherwise noted, all correspondence and archival material in this chapter are in the J. C. Powell Papers, Eastern Kentucky University Archives).

3. Robert Bagby interview, May 22, 2000; *Eastern Progress,* July 29, 1976; *Richmond Daily Register,* June 26, August 5, 10, 1976; Regents Minutes, June 5, August 14, 1976; *Courier-Journal,* August 5, 10, 15, 1976; Resolution, Presidential Search Committee; Faculty/Staff Advisory Committee, Final Report and Minority Report, August 10, 1976; Report of the Student Advisory Committee, August 6, 1976.

4. Report of the Presidential Search Committee to the Board of Regents, August 14, 1976; Taylor interview; *Lexington Herald,* August 13, 17, 1976; *Richmond Daily Register,* August 14, 1976; *Sunday Herald-Leader,* August 15, 1976; *Lexington Leader,* August 16, 1976; *Eastern Progress,* August 26, 1976; Beverly Yeiser interview, April 5, 1978.

5. Richard Wilson interview, April 18, 1977; Richard Wilson interview, March 9, 2000; J. C. Powell interview, April 14, 1978; Wilborn interview.

6. Regents Minutes, June 5, August 14, November 20, 1976; *Courier-Journal,* October 1, 1976; Eastern Kentucky University Institutional Plan, 1976–80; *Eastern Progress,* August 25, 1977; Regents Minutes, October 1, 1977; Faculty Senate Minutes, September 10, 1979.

7. *Courier-Journal,* December 19, 1976; "The Robert R. Martin Tribute Dinner, September 16, 1976"; *Lexington Herald,* October 1, 1976; Regents Minutes, September 30, 1976; *Eastern Progress,* September 16, October 28, 1976, November 10, 1977; *Milestone, 1978,* 158.

8. Recording, "Opening Session, Rowlett and Powell, August 20, 1976"; *Courier-Journal,* March 24, 1977; Eastern Kentucky University, *Report to Education* 7 (April 1977): 1, 8; James and Anna Way interview, April 27, 2000; *Eastern Progress,* April 21, 1977.

9. Eastern Kentucky University, *Report to Education* 7 (April 1977): 1, 8; *Eastern Progress,* March 24, 1977; J. C. Powell to Governor Julian Carroll, February 3, 1977; *Milestone, 1977,* 168B–171.

10. Frederick D. Ogden interview, January 27, 1987; Branley Branson interview, April 18, 2000.

11. Regents Minutes, January 7, 1978, January 9, 1982; *Eastern Alumni* 17 (Sum-

mer 1977): 39–40; *Eastern Alumni* 18 (Summer 1979): 23; Ogden, *Gladly Learn and Gladly Teach,* 72; Ogden interview; *Eastern Progress,* December 2, 1976, July 12, 1979; *Milestone, 1978,* 97.

12. Powell to Harry Snyder, July 27, 1981; John Y. Brown Jr. to Cabinet Secretaries, etc., February 4, 1980; *Eastern Progress,* April 21, May 5, September 15, 29, 1977, March 19, 1981, January 21, 1982; Regents Minutes, August 6, 1981, October 6, 1984; Faculty Senate Minutes, February 2, 1981; Harrison, *Western Kentucky University,* 255–57.

13. Governor's Press Conference, January 28, 1982, copy; *Eastern Alumnus* 20 (Summer 1981): n.p.; A. D. Albright interview, June 7, 1977; *Eastern Progress,* October 20, 1977, August 28, 1980, March 5, 19, 1981, February 4, 1982; Dwayne D. Cox and William J. Morison, *The University of Louisville* (Lexington: University Press of Kentucky, 2000), 180–81.

14. *Eastern Alumnus* 23 (Winter 1984): n.p.; *Eastern Progress,* March 1, 1984; Powell to Board of Regents, April 16, 1983; Powell to Secretary Larry M. Hayes, February 23, 1984; Nancy Forderhase to Powell, October 19, 1979; Regents Minutes, April 17, 1982, January 7, 1984.

15. Chad Middleton interview, April 10, 2000; Regents Minutes, April 12, 1978, April 25, 1981; *Eastern Progress,* December 2, 1976, January 19, February 3, 1977, August 22, 1979, September 11, 1980, September 3, 1981, November 10, 1983.

16. *Eastern Progress,* October 28, 1976; Powell to Miss Truly Fair, April 25, 1980; Regents Minutes, January 7, 1978, January 5, 1980; *Eastern Alumnus* 19 (Summer 1981): 1; Faculty Senate Minutes, September 19, 1977, September 10, 1979.

17. *Eastern Progress,* July 28, October 27, 1977, February 14, 1980, January 15, 1981, August 26, 1982; Regents Minutes, August 4, 1977, August 5, 1982, April 16, 1983; Jack Fletcher to William E. Sexton, October 15, 1979; Regents Minutes, April 12, 1978, October 28, 1982; contract with Spitz Space Systems, July 8, 1976, Box 130, Powell Papers.

18. *Eastern Progress,* September 2, 1976, May 5, August 25, 1977, August 28, 1980, August 24, 1978; Regents Minutes, October 20, 1979, August 7, October 4, 1980; *Milestone, 1981,* 39.

19. Ernest E. Weyhrauch interview, February 4, 2000; Box 129, Powell Papers; Powell to Dorothy Dorris Wilcox, May 14, 1981; *Eastern Progress,* March 24, 1977, April 20, 1978, August 28, 1980, September 10, October 1, 1981; Regents Minutes, April 12, 1978, April 21, 1979.

20. Robert Hemenway to Larry Martin, August 7, 1984; Lawrence O. Martin interview, April 16, 1987.

21. Powell to William Berge, August 5, October 27, 1977; Regents Minutes, April 16, 1977; *Eastern Progress,* October 28, 1976, October 22, 1981, September 30, 1982, April 7, 1983; *Eastern Alumnus* 21 (Summer 1982): 16.

22. Regents Minutes, January 7, 1978, April 4, August 6, 1981, August 2, November 26, 1984; *Eastern Progress,* November 9, 1978, January 22, April 19, 1981,

September 20, 1984; Rodney T. and Viola Gross interview, June 11, 1987; *Eastern Alumnus* 19 (Summer 1980): 30.

23. *Eastern Alumnus* 17 (Winter 1978): 35; *Eastern Alumnus* 18 (Winter 1979): 24; *Eastern Alumnus* 19 (Summer 1980): 25; Ursel D. Boyd interview, June 16, 2000; Milos Sebor de Wsseborzicz interview, July 23, 1986; *Eastern Progress,* March 24, November 10, 1983, November 1, 1984; Regents Minutes, April 26, 1980; *Eastern Alumnus* 24 (Winter 1984): 10–12.

24. *Eastern Progress,* August 25, 1977, August 22, 1979, October 7, 1982; Regents Minutes, April 21, 1979, April 26, 1980.

25. *Eastern Progress,* October 7, 1976, April 14, 1977, October 6, 1983; *Milestone, 1984,* 17, 38–39; Horowitz, *Campus Life,* 245–77.

26. *Eastern Progress,* November 18, 1976, April 14, July 28, 1977, April 27, 1978, May 1, 1980; Regents Minutes, June 18, 1977; Lisa A. Irwin interview, September 29, 2002.

27. *Eastern Progress,* September 10, 1981, January 13, 1983.

28. *Eastern Progress,* August 25, September 29, 1977, January 12, October 5, 1978; *Eastern Alumnus* 17 (Winter 1978): 25–27; *Eastern Alumnus* 21 (Summer 1982): 1.

29. *Eastern Progress,* April 21, 1977; Nancy Elliott Simpson conversation, June 12, 2003.

30. *Eastern Progress,* October 5, 19, 1978, September 11, 1980, January 21, 1981; Regents Minutes, June 18, 1977; *Milestone, 1977,* 30; *Milestone, 1981,* 70–73.

31. Irwin interview.

32. Timothy V. Tingle, e-mail to the author, March 11, 2003.

33. Cynthia Bohn interview, June 30, 2000; Carl K. Greene interview, June 8, 2000; *EKU Magazine* 1 (Spring 2000): 14–15, 27, 29.

34. "A Concerned Parent" to Robert R. Martin, November 10, 1980; *Eastern Progress,* October 13, 1983; Regents Minutes, April 21, 1979; Margaret Echsher to Powell, November 20, 1982; *Milestone, 1977,* 94–95.

35. Regents Minutes, October 20, 1979, August 7, 1980, June 11, 1982; *Eastern Progress,* February 11, 1982; Dixie Bale Mylum interview, April 21, 1986.

36. *Eastern Progress,* April 14, May 5, October 27, 1977, February 3, 1983; Regents Minutes, August 3, 1978; *Eastern Alumnus* 18 (Winter 1979): 24; *Eastern Alumnus* 20 (Summer 1981): 19.

37. Regents Minutes, April 26, 1980, January 9, 1982, October 6, 1984; *Eastern Progress,* December 2, 1982, March 10, 1983; *Milestone, 1982,* 23.

38. Powell Papers, Box 27; Regents Minutes, October 1, 1977, October 9, 1982; *Eastern Alumnus* 20 (Summer 1981): 9; *Eastern Alumnus* 23 (Winter 1984): 12; *Eastern Progress,* February 4, July 22, 1982; *Milestone, 1985,* 129.

39. Peggy Stanaland interview, June 28, 2000; *Eastern Progress,* August 26, 1976, November 19, 1981; Regents Minutes, July 16, 1983; *Milestone, 1976,* 90.

40. *Eastern Alumnus* 19 (Winter 1979): 4–11; *Eastern Progress,* January 19, 1978, October 25, 1979, January 10, 1980, January 6, 1981.

41. *Eastern Progress,* February 3, 1977, October 29, 1981, January 14, 21, July 1,

1982, January 13, 1983, October 13, 1994; *Eastern Alumnus* 22 (Winter 1983): 12–14; *Milestone, 1977,* 150.

42. *Eastern Progress,* September 30, October 21, 1982; Regents Minutes, August 3, 1978, September 10, 1983.

43. *Milestone, 1977,* 145; *Milestone, 1978,* 186–95; *Milestone, 1979,* 188–89; *Milestone, 1981,* 96; *Eastern Progress,* March 2, 1978, February 22, March 8, 1979, August 27, 1981.

44. *Eastern Progress,* January 26, 1978, November 18, 1982, January 13, 1983; *Milestone, 1983,* 100.

45. *Milestone, 1977,* 110–11; *Milestone, 1978,* 168–69; *Eastern Progress,* August 22, 1979, February 7, 28, April 24, 1980, October 29, 1981, November 4, 1982; *Eastern Alumnus* 20 (Winter 1981): 25; *Milestone, 1981,* 132.

46. *Milestone, 1982,* 21.

47. Regents Minutes, April 16, 1977, June 11, 1982, January 15, April 16, 1983, October 6, 1984; *Eastern Progress,* March 3, 1977, April 12, 1979, September 30, 1982; *Eastern Alumnus* 19 (Summer 1980): 22; *Eastern Alumnus* 20 (Winter 1981): 21; Planning Evaluation Committee, April 15, 1984.

48. *Eastern Progress,* November 4, 1976, November 10, December 8, 1977, August 25, 1983; Regents Minutes, July 16, 1983, January 7, 1984; *Milestone, 1977,* 174.

49. *Eastern Progress,* April 7, 1977, March 22, 1979; Regents Minutes, June 18, 1977; Faculty Senate Minutes, December 12, 1966, March 3, 1976, May 2, 10, 1977, March 5, 1979, February 2, 1981, January 17, 1983; Harrison, *Western Kentucky University,* 257.

50. *Eastern Progress,* April 7, 1977, February 3, April 20, 1978, November 4, 1982, April 7, October 13, November 10, December 1, 8, 1983, February 9, 1984; Regents Minutes, August 3, 1978; Faculty Senate Minutes, May 2, 1977, May 5, 1980, January 17, 1983, February 6, 1984.

51. Regents Minutes, October 1, 1977, September 10, 1981, October 4, 1980, February 6, August 2, 1984; *Eastern Progress,* September 10, 1981.

52. *Eastern Progress,* September 23, 1976, August 25, October 27, 1977, February 3, 1978, September 10, 1981, September 9, 1982, July 7, 1983; Regents Minutes, October 20, 1979, July 16, 1983.

53. Regents Minutes, April 25, 1984; *Eastern Progress,* April 26, 1984; *Milestone, 1986,* 126–28.

54. *Eastern Progress,* December 2, 1982.

55. William E. Sexton interview, September 3, 1987; Larry W. Bailey interview, May 22, 2000; *Eastern Alumnus* 23 (Summer 1984): 2–8; *Eastern Progress,* December 6, 1984; *Milestone, 1984,* 125.

56. *Eastern Progress,* February 24, 1983, August 30, September 13, October 4, November 1, 1984; *Milestone, 1976,* 34–35; *Milestone, 1981,* 44; *Milestone, 1983,* 18–19; *Milestone, 1985,* 70.

57. *Milestone, 1984,* 58–59; *Milestone, 1985,* 23, 28–29; *Eastern Progress,* October 15, 1981.

8. "To Make a Good University a Better One"

1. Regents Minutes, draft copy, Bonnie Gray, April 13, 1984; Regents Minutes, April, 25, 1984; Powell Papers, Box 167; Dept. Chairs to Hallie Shouse, Vice-Chairman of the Regents, May 9, 1984 (unless otherwise noted, all collections are in the Eastern Kentucky University Archives).

2. *Eastern Progress,* November 1, 8, 1984; Hanly Funderburk interview, June 9, 1987.

3. Funderburk interview; *Eastern Progress,* November 8, 15, 1984; Dwayne Cox, Auburn University archivist, to William E. Ellis, October, 25, 1988; *USA Today,* February 18, 1983; *Birmingham News,* November 10, 1982, February 27, 1983; *Montgomery Advertiser,* November 2, 3, 1982; *Time,* February 21, 1983, 66; *Auburn Plainsman,* November 2, December 4, 7, 1982, February 16, March 3, 1983; *Auburn Bulletin,* January 26, 1983.

4. Funderburk interview; Regents Minutes, November 26, 1984; *Courier-Journal,* November 27, 1984; *Richmond Register,* November 27, 1984.

5. *Courier-Journal,* November 27, 1984; *Eastern Progress,* November 29, 1984; *Richmond Register,* November 27, 1984; Smith interview, September 19, 2002; Mary Ellen Klatte interview, April 25, 2000.

6. *Eastern Progress,* November 29, 1984.

7. Funderburk interview; *Milestone, 1985,* 68–69; *Eastern Progress,* November 29, 1984.

8. Regents Minutes, August 8, 1985; *Eastern Progress,* December 6, 1984, January 10, 17, 1985.

9. Inauguration of H. Hanly Funderburk Jr., May 11, 1985, Schedule of Events; *Richmond Register,* May 13, 1985.

10. *Eastern Progress,* April 7, 1988, August 22, 1991, February 1, 1996, October 24, 2002; *Milestone, 1988,* 46–47.

11. Funderburk to Board of Regents, April 22, 1989; Regents Minutes, March 7, 1985, July 16, 1994, July 31, 1997; Funderburk to Martha Grise, September 8, 1986; William E. Ellis to Funderburk, December 16, 1986; Funderburk to Ellis, December 19, 1986; Charles L. Nelson to William Ellis, n.d.; *Lexington Herald-Leader,* January 20, February 15, April 27, 1988; *Eastern Progress,* March 28, 1985, October 1, 1987.

12. Regents Minutes, February 16, November 9, 1985, April 26, 1986, April 4, 1987, January 16, 1988.

13. *Eastern Progress,* February 4, 18, 25, April 28, 1988, January 18, 1990, September 5, October 24, 1991; Smith interview; *Milestone, 1988,* 76–77.

14. *Eastern Progress,* September 5, 1991, January 16, February 6, 13, April 23, August 20, 1992, February 3, 1994, September 11, 1997; Regents Minutes, July 24, 1992; Harrison and Klotter, *A New History of Kentucky,* 422–25.

15. Ellis to Funderburk, August 25, 1987; Regents Minutes, April 6, 1987, Octo-

ber 10, 1987, August 3, 1989; *Eastern Progress,* April 10, 1987; Faculty Senate Minutes, March 2, April 6, 1987; *EKU Faculty/Staff Handbook, 1998–2000,* 85.

16. Regents Minutes, October 10, 1987, April 22, August 3, 1989.

17. Ellis to Funderburk, August 25, September 20, 1985, August 1, 1986, August 25, 1987; Regents Minutes, October 21, 1989, April 28, 1990.

18. Lawrence A. Cremin, *Popular Education and Its Discontents* (New York: Harper and Row, 1990), 51–78; *Eastern Progress,* March 24, April 14, 1988, April 2, 1992; *Milestone, 1987,* 57.

19. Nancy and R. E. Forderhase interview, February 4, 2000; *Eastern Progress,* August 27, 1987, September 22, 1994, February 21, 2002; *Richmond Register,* January 18, 1990, September 1, 1999; *Milestone, 1997,* 129; *Milestone, 1999,* 107; *Eastern Today* 12 (Fall 1998): 4.

20. *Eastern Progress,* February 3, 1989, April 19, 1990, November 3, 1994, October 3, 1996; Harold R. Blythe Jr. and Charles A. Sweet Jr., vitae; Forderhase interviews; *EKUpdate* 3 (January 28, 2002): 3; *EKU Magazine* 1 (Spring 2000): 5.

21. William H. Martin to Ellis, September 2, 2002; Elizabeth R. Wachtel to Ellis, October 25, 2002; *Eastern Progress,* September 24, 1987; Regents Minutes, October 8, 1994.

22. Regents Minutes, April 26, 1986, January 22, 1994, January 18, November 1, 1997; Regents Minutes, May 22, 1993, April 16, 1994; *Eastern Progress,* February 20, 1986, July 10, 1990, August 20, September 3, 1992, December 7, 1995; *Milestone, 1990,* 103.

23. *Eastern Progress,* November 5, 1987, April 7, 1988, April 20, 1989, September 11, 1997; enclosures from Bonnie Gray; Regents Minutes, April 4, 1987, April 27, 1996; *Milestone, 1998,* 133.

24. Regents Minutes, April 20, 1991, January 9, April 25, 1998; McClanahan and Smith, *Justice and Safety Education at Eastern Kentucky University,* 17, 19, 22, 25, 33, 43; *Richmond Register,* January 18, 1990; *Eastern Progress,* April 23, 1998.

25. *Eastern Progress,* April 4, 1985; Richard Wilson interview, March 9, 2000.

26. *Eastern Progress,* April 30, 1987, October 26, 1989, March 4, November 11, 1993, October 20, November 10, 1994, May 4, September 28, 1995, March 7, 1996; Regents Minutes, August 8, 1985; *Eastern Today* 11 (Spring 1998): 3–5; *Eastern Today* 11 (Winter 1998): 7.

27. *Eastern Progress,* October 10, 1985, November 10, 1988, December 2, 1993, April 4, 1996; Jack K. Fletcher interview, December 9, 2003; Regents Minutes, April 26, October 5, November 5, 1986, April 22, October 21, 1989, January 20, 1990, April 20, October 16, 1991, December 2, 1993, October 26, 1996, November 1, June 14, 1997, January 9, 1998; *Milestone, 1989,* 46–47.

28. Harrison and Klotter, *A New History of Kentucky,* 420, 424; *Eastern Progress,* February 1, March 7, 1996, January 30, March 13, April 3, October 23, 1997; Richard Wilson interview; *Richmond Register,* April 20, 1999; *Lexington Herald-Leader,* December 10, 1996.

29. Horowitz, *Campus Life,* 263–94; *Eastern Progress,* December 4, 1986, January 25, 1990; Lorraine B. Durham interview, March 13, 2001; *Milestone, 1988,* 12–13, 30–31.

30. *Eastern Progress,* February 27, March 6, 1986, March 5, April 9, 1987, January 25, 1990.

31. *Eastern Progress,* October 17, 1985, March 27, April 10, 21, 1986, April 30, 1987, November 20, 1989, July 10, 1990, October 24, 1991, March 4, 1993, January 13, March 10, July 12, September 15, November 3, 1994, April 27, December 7, 1995, March 7, 1996; Regents Minutes, August 7, 1986; *Milestone, 1987,* 46–47.

32. Regents Minutes, November 9, 1985; *Eastern Progress,* March 28, 1996.

33. Durham interview.

34. *Eastern Progress,* February 1, 1996; Robert D. Abney conversation; *Milestone, 1998,* 121.

35. *Eastern Progress,* April 28, 1994; EKU National Alumni Association, Award Banquet Program, April 26, 2003, 6.

36. *Eastern Progress,* October 9, 1986, March 12, November 17, 1988, November 1, 1990, August 22, 1991; *Milestone, 1998,* 114–15; *Milestone, 1993,* 44.

37. *Eastern Progress,* December 7, 1989.

38. *Eastern Progress,* April 10, September 25, October 23, 1986, April 9, September 24, 1987, February 3, 1994; Regents Minutes, April 13, 1985, April 26, 1986, April 4, 1987, June 11, 1990, February 4, 1993, October 23, 1997; *Milestone, 1988,* 222–23; Robert J. Baugh interview, January 15, 2004.

39. *Eastern Progress,* November 29, 1984; September 25, October 26, 1986, September 24, 1987, September 13, 1990, January 31, 1991, January 13, February 3, 1994, July 13, 1995, October 23, 1997; January 15, 1998; Michael Embry, "Roy Kidd," *Kentucky Monthly* 5 (September 2002): 19.

40. *Eastern Progress,* November 29, 1984, July 13, 1995, October 23, 1986, February 26, 1987, January 15, 1998; Regents Minutes, January 20, 1990, January 26, 1991, July 13, 1995; *Milestone, 1990,* 124–29.

41. *Richmond Register,* January 11, 1989, December 19, 1999; *Eastern Progress,* March 16, 1989, February 23, 1995, February 27, March 13, April 17, 1997; *Milestone, 1988,* 217, *Milestone, 1993,* 172–73; *Milestone, 1997,* 148–49, 151; *Milestone, 1998,* 144–45; *Milestone, 1999,* 134–35.

42. *Eastern Progress,* February 25, April 14, 28, September 29, October 6, 1988, March 26, 1992, March 28, 1996, March 6, 1997, March 12, 1998; *Richmond Register,* April 22, 1993, January 8, 2002; *Milestone, 1988,* 146–47, 208–9, 224–31, 243; *Milestone, 1994,* 178–81.

43. Regents Minutes, June 11, 1990; *Eastern Progress,* October 12, 1995.

44. Regents Minutes, January 26, 1991; *Direction, Eastern Kentucky University Strategic Plan, 1991–1995,* 1–9; *Eastern Kentucky University, 1985–1990: An Assessment,* 1–27; *Eastern Progress,* May 4, August 24, 1995.

45. *Lexington Herald-Leader,* February 11, 1992, February 20, 1995; Regents Minutes, February 1, 1992.

46. Regents Minutes, April 20, 1991, February 1, 1992, May 22, 1993, January 22, 1994, April 16, 1994; *Eastern Progress,* September 16, 1993.

47. Regents Minutes, April 26, August 7, October 5, 1986, January 17, October 10, 1987, January 16, November 5, 1988, April 28, 1990, January 26, April 20, 1991, July 10, 1993, May 22, October 30, 1993, October 28, 1995, April 27, 1996; *Eastern Progress,* April 23, 1988, August 19, 1993, April 23, 1998.

48. *Eastern Progress,* November 14, 1997, April 23, 1998, March 7, 2002; Regents Minutes, October 26, 1996, January 9, April 25, 1998; *Milestone, 1987,* 137.

49. Regents Minutes, November 1, 1997; *Eastern Progress,* January 14, 1987, January 18, 1990, March 4, 1993, November 14, 1996, October 16, November 6, 1997, January 15, 1998.

50. Michael Marsden interview, February 4, 2003; *Eastern Progress,* August 28, September 4, 1997.

51. Smith interview.

52. Forderhase interviews, Larry W. Bailey interview, May 22, 2000; Branley Branson, April 18, 2000; Robert Bagby interview, May 22, 2000; Richard Wilson interview, March 9, 2000; Middleton interview; *Eastern Progress,* April 23, 1998.

53. *Eastern Progress,* January 19, 26, February 2, March 2, April 6, 1995, August 29, 1996.

54. *Milestone, 1998,* 107, 110–11; *Eastern Progress,* April 23, 1998; *Making a Good University Better, A Report on the Presidency of Hanly Funderburk, January 1, 1985–June 30, 1998,* 1–14; *Lexington Herald-Leader,* May 10, 1998.

9. Change, Controversy, and Continuity

1. Regents Minutes, April 28, July 1, 1997; *Eastern Progress,* April 17, 24, May 1, September 4, October 9, 1997.

2. Regents Minutes, November 1, 1997; *Eastern Progress,* January 22, February 5, 1998; Richard Wilson interview, March 9, 2000.

3. Regents Minutes, February 18, March 27, 1998; *Eastern Progress,* February 26, April 30, July 9, 1998.

4. *Eastern Progress,* February 26, July 9, 1998; *Milestone, 1998,* 110–11; *Eastern Today* 11 (Spring 1998): 1; *Eastern Today* 11 (Summer 1998): 1–2.

5. Robert W. Kustra interviews, October 19, December 9, 1998.

6. *Richmond Register,* October 1, 1998; *Eastern Progress,* October 8, 1998; *Milestone, 1999,* 94–98; program: "The Installation of Robert Walker Kustra as the Ninth President of Eastern Kentucky University."

7. *Eastern Progress,* October 8, 1998; *Milestone, 1999,* 94.

8. *Lexington Herald-Leader,* March 7, 1999; Kathleen Kustra interview, October 26, 2000; Robert J. Baugh interview.

9. *Milestone, 1999,* 30, 41, 99–101; *Lexington Herald-Leader,* October 25, 1999; *Richmond Register,* August 17, 1999; Regents Minutes, October 10, 1998; *EKUpdate* 2 (August 21, 2000): 1; Robert J. Baugh interview.

10. *Eastern Progress,* November 5, 1998, October 5, November 9, 16, 2000; Richard Wilson interview, March 9, 2000; *EKU Magazine* 1 (Spring 2000): 20; *Richmond Register,* October 4, 2000; *EKUpdate* 2 (October 16, 2000): 1; *EKUpdate* 2 (November 27, 2000): 1; *EKUpdate* 2 (December 11, 2000): 3; *Lexington Herald-Leader,* February 20, 1999, November 10, 11, 2000; *Eastern Kentucky University Magazine* 1 (Spring 2000): 3; Regents Minutes, October 21, 2000, January 27, 2001.

11. Regents Minutes, July 30, 1998, January 16, 1999; *Eastern Progress,* July 9, 1998, August 28, 1999; *Richmond Register,* December 27, 1998.

12. *Richmond Register,* June 5, 10, 1999; *Eastern Progress,* January 14, February 11, April 1, August 26, December 9, 1999, December 7, 2000; Bob Kustra to University Community, June 9, 1999; Michael T. Marsden interview, February 4, 2003; *EKUpdate* 2 (November 13, 2000): 2; *Richmond Register,* August 9, 1999; *Lexington Herald-Leader,* March 17, 2002.

13. Bob Kustra to University Faculty and Staff, April 1, 1999; Kustra to Faculty, May 5, 1999; *Lexington Herald-Leader,* April 3, 1999; *Richmond Register,* April 3, 1999; *Eastern Progress,* April 29, 1999; Regents Minutes, April 24, 1999; Branley Branson interview, April 18, 2000; Carolyn J. Baugh interview, January 15, 2004.

14. Kustra to Faculty, May 6, 1999; Deans Robert J. Baugh, Donald L. Batch, Vance Wisenbaker, Jack L. Culross, and Virginia Falkenberg to Eastern Kentucky University Foundation Professors, ca. early May 1999; *Eastern Progress,* April 29, 1999; Robert J. Baugh interview.

15. *Regents Minutes,* July 29, 1999; *Richmond Register,* April 7, 19, 1999; *Eastern Progress,* April 15, 22, 1999; Marsden interview; Dominick Hart to All the Faculty of College of Natural and Mathematical Sciences, Colleges of Social and Behavioral Sciences, and College of Arts and Humanities, April 29, 1999.

16. Regents Minutes, April 24, July 29, October 9, 1999, April 28, 2000; *Richmond Register,* March 24, April 26, August 17, 26, October 25, 1999, April 29, 2000; Kustra to Faculty and Staff, May 14, 1999.

17. *Eastern Progress,* April 6, May 4, August 24, 2000, February 8, March 22, 2001; Regents Minutes, October 9, 1999, May 19, October 21, 2000, March 1, 2001; *EKUpdate* 2 (October 16, 2000): 1; *EKUpdate* 2 (December 11, 2000): 2; *EKUpdate* 2 (March 19, 2001): 2.

18. Robert W. Kustra interview, May 2, 2001; *Lexington Herald-Leader,* March 15, April 15, August 8, September 2, 1999, February 23, March 3, 11, 15, 2000; *Courier-Journal,* February 23, June 18, 2000; *Eastern Progress,* December 9, 1999, April 20, 2000; Regents Minutes, January 16, February 5, 2000; Smith interview.

19. Regents Minutes, October 9, 1999, February 5, April 28, 2000, January 27, 2001; *Eastern Today* 12 (Fall 1998): 4; *EKUpdate* 2 (September 18, 2000): 3; *Eastern Progress,* January 14, August 26, October 14, 1999, April 6, November 9, 2000, February 8, April 26, 2001, October 24, 2002; *Richmond Register,* August 8, September 27, 2000, February 9, April 22, 2001.

20. *Eastern Kentucky University Magazine* 1 (Spring 2000): 22; Kustra interview, May 2, 2001; Larry W. Bailey interview, May 22, 2000; *Eastern Progress,* March 2, 9,

2000, March 7, 2002; *EKUpdate* 2 (August 21, 2000): 3; Richard Wilson interview, March 9, 2000; Dale Lawrenz interview, February 23, 2004; Regents Minutes, February 5, August 3, 2000.

21. *Eastern Today* 11 (Summer 1998): 7; *Eastern Progress,* September 16, 1999, March 2, 9, August 31, October 12, November 16, 2000; Kustra interview, May 2, 2001; *Lexington Herald-Leader,* May 5, 2000; Mardsen interview; Employment Agreement, Regents Minutes, April 25, 1998; Regents Minutes, May 19, 2000, January 27, 2001; *Eastern Kentucky University Undergraduate Catalogue, 2003–4.*

22. *Lexington Herald-Leader,* March 8, April 24, 26, June 20, 1999, February 14, 2001; *Richmond Register,* July 3, 2000, February 14, 2001; Wilson interview.

23. Kathleen Kustra interview; Robert Kustra interview, May 2, 2001; Marsden interview; *EKUpdate* (February 3, 2001): 2; *Eastern Progress,* February 22, 2001; *Lexington Herald-Leader,* February 15, 16, 2001; *Richmond Register,* February 15, 16, 22, 2001.

24. *Lexington Herald-Leader,* March 2, 2001; *Eastern Progress,* February 22, 2001; *Richmond Register,* February 22, March 2, 2001; Regents Minutes, March 1, 27, 2001.

25. Regents Meeting, March 27, April 12, June 5, 2001; Agreement and Release, June 5, 2002, Regents Minutes; *Richmond Register,* March 28, April 13, June 6, July 1, 2001; Kustra interview, May 2, 2001; Marsden interview; *Eastern Progress,* April 19, 2001.

26. *Richmond Register,* July 1, 7, 2001; *Lexington Herald-Leader,* March 5, July 17, August 29, September 7, 2001; *Eastern Progress,* August 30, 2001; Carolyn L. Baugh interview; Robert J. Baugh interview.

27. Wilson interviews; Kathleen Kustra interview; Robert Bagby interview, May 22, 2000; *Lexington Herald-Leader,* March 25, 2002; Marsden interview; Mary Ellen Klatte interview, April 25, 2000; Nancy and R. E. Forderhase interview, February 4, 2000; Smith interview; *Eastern Kentucky University Magazine* 2 (Spring 2000): 22; *Eastern Progress,* September 30, 1999; Regents Minutes, February 5, 2000.

28. *EKUpdate* 2 (December 11, 2000): 1; Marsden interview; *Lexington Herald-Leader,* March 20, 23, 1999, August 30, 2000; McClanahan and Smith, *Justice and Safety Education at Eastern Kentucky University,* 22, 33; *Eastern Progress,* March 4, 11, April 15, 1999; *Richmond Register,* March 24, 1999, June 24, 2001; Regents Minutes, July 30, 1998.

29. *Eastern Progress,* March 9, 2000, February 8, 2001; *Lexington Herald-Leader,* March 28, April 20, 2001; *Richmond Register,* April 20, 2001; Regents Minutes, January 27, 2001; *EKUpdate* 2 (April 30, 2001): 2; *EKUpdate* 3 (February 11, 2002): 4.

30. *Richmond Register,* March 28, 1999, March 8, 2000, May 7, July 21, 2001; *Lexington Herald-Leader,* February 11, 2000; *Eastern Progress,* April 26, 2001; *All Around Kentucky,* September 2000, 15.

31. "Recognition Ceremony for Historic Buildings, Eastern Kentucky University, April 1, 1999"; *Eastern Progress,* April 1, 1999, April 6, 2000, April 10, 2003; *Richmond Register,* January 18, April 2, 1999, June 21, 2000; *Lexington Herald-Leader,* March 31, December 11, 1999.

32. *Richmond Register,* April 19, 1999, May 27, 2002; *Eastern Progress,* February 8,

March 1, April 12, 2001, September 25, 2003; *EKU Magazine* 2 (Winter 2001): 27, 31; *EKU Magazine* 3 (Winter 2002): 17; *Lexington Herald-Leader,* April 24, 1999; Bailey interview; *Eastern Today* 12 (Fall 1998): 6; *EKUpdate* 2 (April 30, 2001): 3; *EKUpdate* 3 (September 4, 2001): 4; *EKUpdate* 4 (October 21, 2002): 3.

33. *Richmond Register,* October 11, 1998, March 23, 1999, August 6, 2001, March 27, 2003; *Lexington Herald-Leader,* October 29, 2001; *Eastern Progress,* January 14, 1999, February 21, October 31, 2002, April 10, August 21, 2003; *EKU Magazine* 3 (Summer 2002): 11.

34. *Eastern Progress,* October 8, 1987.

35. Regents Minutes, April 12, June 29, 2001; Eugene M. Hughes interview, October 22, 2001; *Richmond Register,* June 30, 2001; *Eastern Progress,* October 25, 2001; *EKUpdate* 2 (July 9, 2001): 1; *EKUpdate* 3 (August 6, 2001): 1.

36. Regents Minutes, August 24, 2001; *EKUpdate* 2 (April 2001): 1; *EKUpdate* 3 (August 6, 2001): 1; *Lexington Herald-Leader,* August 14, 25, 2001; *Richmond Register,* August 22, 25, 2001; *EKUpdate* 3 (August 20, 2001): 1; *Eastern Progress,* August 23, 30, 2001; Joanne Glasser interview, January 7, 2002.

37. *Richmond Register,* August 25, 2001; *Eastern Progress,* August 30, 2001; Glasser interview, January 7, 2002; *Lexington Herald-Leader,* August 28, 2001; *EKUpdate* 3 (September 4, 2001): 1.

38. Regents Minutes, August 2, 2001; *Eastern Progress,* August 23, 2001; Hughes interview; *Richmond Register,* August 30, 2001; *Lexington Herald-Leader,* March 17, 2003.

39. *Eastern Progress,* April 26, August 23, 2001; *Lexington Herald-Leader,* September 9, 2001; Hughes interview.

40. *Louisville Courier-Journal,* September 11, 2001; *Lexington Herald-Leader,* September 16, 2001; *Eastern Progress,* September 13, 20, 2001; *EKUpdate* 3 (October 1, 2001): 1, 3; Regents Minutes, October 20, 2001; Hughes interview; *EKU Magazine* 3 (Winter 2002): 18–19.

41. *Eastern Progress,* October 25, November 15, 2001; *EKUpdate* 3 (November 12, 2001): 1, 3.

42. "The Inauguration of Joanne Kramer Glasser, Esquire, as the Tenth President of Eastern Kentucky University," program; *EKUpdate* 3 (February 25, 2001): 1; *EKU Magazine* 3 (Winter 2002): 3–8.

43. "Remarks, Joanne Kramer Glasser, Esq., Presidential Inauguration"; *Richmond Register,* March 3, 9, 10, 2002; *Lexington Herald-Leader,* March 5, 9, 2002; *EKUpdate* 3 (March 25, 2002): 1, 4; *Eastern Progress,* March 7, 14, 2002; Joanne Glasser interview, January 7, 2002.

44. *Lexington Herald-Leader,* March 5, 2002, March 17, 2003; *EKU Magazine* 3 (Winter 2002): 6; *EKUpdate* 3 (October 15, 2001): 1.

45. *Eastern Progress,* March 3, May 2, April 11, October 10, 2002; *Richmond Register,* December 18, 2001, November 23, 2003; Regents Minutes, June 17, 2002; *Courier-Journal,* June 18, 2002; *Lexington Herald-Leader,* March 17, 2003; Joanne Glasser interview, January 10, 2003.

46. Regents Minutes, April 26, November 8, 2002; Joanne Glasser interview, May 9, 2002; *Eastern Progress,* August 26, 1999, February 14, August 29, September 5, 2002, January 16, 2003, February 5, September 23, 2004; *Richmond Register,* August 15, 1999, November 9, 2000, November 1, 2002; *EKUpdate* 3 (October 29, 2001): 1; *EKUpdate* 3 (February 11, 2002): 1; *EKUpdate* 4 (August 12, 2002): 1; *EKUpdate* 4 (November 18, 2002): 1, 4; *EKUpdate* 4 (April 7, 2003): 1; Glasser to Dear Colleague, September 19, 2002; *EKU Magazine* 4 (Summer 2003): 20.

47. Marsden interview; *Richmond Register,* April 26, June 20, September 14, 2003; Joanne Glasser interviews, May 9, 2002, December 2, 2003; *Eastern Progress,* January 16, 30, March 13, April 3, May 1, August 21, September 5, 11, 23, October 30, 2003; *EKUpdate* 4 (January 21, 2003): 1; Regents Minutes, April 25, 2003; *EKU Magazine* 4 (Summer 2003): 7–9.

48. *EKU Magazine* 1 (Spring 2000): 21; *Eastern Progress,* March 9, 2000, April 26, August 23, 2001, October 31, 2002, January 8, February 13, 27, April 10, November 13, 2003; *EKUpdate* 4 (September 23, 2002): 4; *EKUpdate* 4 (February 3, 2003): 3; *EKUpdate* 4 (March 3, 2003): 1; *Richmond Register,* May 5, 27, 2003; *Courier-Journal,* May 25, 2003; *Lexington Herald-Leader,* July 5, 2003.

49. *Courier-Journal,* August 29, October 1, 2002; *Lexington Herald-Leader,* October 1, November 22, 2002, April 25, August 10, 2003; Michael Embry, "Coaching Legend," *Kentucky Monthly* 5 (September 2002): 13–15, 19; *Richmond Register,* October 1, 2002; *EKUpdate* 4 (January 21, 2003): 3; *Eastern Progress,* January 23, 2002.

50. *Lexington Herald-Leader,* September 28, 2001, April 4, May 17, 26, June 3, 2002, April 3, May 13, August 7, 2003; *Courier-Journal,* May 5, 9, 10, 12, June 5, 2002; *Richmond Register,* May 13, 20, 2002; Al Smith interview, September 19, 2002.

51. *Lexington Herald-Leader,* March 17, 26, 2003; *Eastern Progress,* May 1, 2003.

52. *Eastern Progress,* March 13, April 10, May 1, 2003; *Lexington Herald-Leader,* March 11, 15, 16, 17, 18, April 22, 2003; *Richmond Register,* March 7, April 25, 2003; *Courier-Journal,* April 26, 2003.

53. *Eastern Progress,* September 12, 2002, January 23, March 6, 13, April 10, May 1, September 25, 2003; *Lexington Herald-Leader,* March 15, 2003; *Richmond Register,* April 9, 2004.

54. *Courier-Journal,* May 26, 2002; *Lexington Herald-Leader,* April 3, 2002, August 13, 2003; *EKUpdate* 3 (November 26, 2001): 3; *EKUpdate* 3 (January 14, 2002): 3; *EKUpdate* 4 (December 3, 2002): 3; *Eastern Progress,* October 2, 2002, February 20, 2003.

55. *Eastern Progress,* April 24, 2002, September 18, 2003, January 15, 2004; *Lexington Herald-Leader,* November 21, 2001, April 10, 2002, March 19, 2003; *EKUpdate* 3 (February 25, 2002), 1–4; *EKUpdate* 4 (April 22, 2002): 3; *Richmond Register,* April 6, 2004.

56. *Eastern Progress,* February 7, 2002, February 8, August 21, 2003; Glasser interview, January 10, 2003; Regents Minutes, November 8, 2002; *EKUpdate* 4 (November 18, 2002): 1.

57. Regents Minutes, April 16, 2002; *EKU Magazine* 3 (Summer 2002): 10; *EKU*

Magazine 3 (Winter 2002): 14; *EKUpdate* 3 (February 25, 2002): 3; *EKUpdate* 4 (January 21, 2003): 1; *Eastern Progress,* January 16, September 11, 2003; *Richmond Register,* August 8, 2003; *EKU Magazine* 4 (Summer 2003): 22.

58. *EKUpdate* 3 (May 6, 2002): 2; *EKU History Department Newsletter,* Winter 2002–3, 1; *Richmond Register,* April 10, November 1, 2002, November 21, 2003; *Eastern Progress,* March 29, 2001; *EKUpdate* 3 (April 22, 2002): 1.

59. *EKUpdate* 4 (November 4, 2002): 1; *EKUpdate* 4 (April 21, 2003): 1; *Lexington Herald-Leader,* March 11, June 29, 2002, March 6, August 3, 2003; *EKU Magazine* 3 (Winter 2002): 23; *EKU Magazine* 5 (Fall 2004), 11; *Richmond Register,* March 11, 2002.

60. Regents Minutes, November 8, 2002; *EKUpdate* 4 (November 18, 2002): 1; *EKUpdate* 4 (January 21, 2003): 1; *Richmond Register,* February 7, 2003; *Eastern Progress,* February 20, October 2, 2003; *EKU Magazine* 4 (Summer 2003): 23.

61. "Remarks: Joanne K. Glasser, Fall Convocation, Wednesday, August 13, 2003," author's copy; *Richmond Register,* August 14, 2003.

62. *Richmond Register,* March 25, 2001, August 16, 2002, February 7, May 5, October 7, 2003; *Lexington Herald-Leader,* February 4, August 18, October 4, 2003; *Eastern Progress,* September 27, 2001, February 13, April 10, October 9, 2003; *EKUpdate* 3 (January 28, 2002): 1.

63. Glasser interview, December 2, 2003; *EKUpdate* 3 (April 8, 2002): 1; *EKUpdate* 4 (February 3, 2003): 4; *Richmond Register,* June 28, 2003; *Lexington Herald-Leader,* March 5, 2003.

64. *Eastern Progress,* March 7, April 10, 2002, April 10, January 23, October 2, 2003; *Richmond Register,* February 9, 2003; *Lexington Herald-Leader,* January 28, 2003; *EKUpdate* 4 (May 5, 2003): 1.

65. *EKUpdate* 4 (May 5, 2003): 1; *Richmond Register,* February 9, 21, June 22, April 26, August 11, September 7, December 5, 2003, February 22, 2004; *Eastern Progress,* February 13, 20, 27, April 24, September 11, 2003, February 12, 24, 2004; Regents Minutes, November 8, 2002, April 25, December 4, 2003; Joanne Glasser to "Dear EKU Colleague," September 19, 2003; *Lexington Herald-Leader,* September 11, 2002, December 5, 2003; Glasser interview, December 2, 2003.

66. *Lexington Herald-Leader,* September 11, 2002, December 5, 2003, March 4, April 23, 2004; Jennifer Washburn, "The Tuition Crunch," *Atlantic Monthly,* January–February 2004, 140; *Eastern Progress,* January 13, March 17, April 8, 2004; *Richmond Register,* December 5, 2003, April 23, 2004; Joannne Glasser interview, May 3, 2004.

67. *Eastern Progress,* February 5, 12, 26, April 8, 2004; *Richmond Register,* February 22, July 7, 2004; *Lexington Herald-Leader,* January 31, July 10, 2004.

68. *Eastern Progress,* March 4, 25, April 8, 2004; *Richmond Register,* April 23, 24, June 9, August 11, 2004; *EKU Magazine* 5 (Summer 2004), 5; *EKU Magazine* 5 (Fall 2004), 13.

69. *Lexington Herald-Leader,* April 6, 10, 2004; *EKU Magazine* 5 (Fall 2004), 17.

Index

Index

Parris, Antonio, 186
party school, 163, 183, 215, 218
Passion for Life and Learning, 209
Patrick, Dale, 144
Patridge, Lelia E., 33, 48
Patterson, James K., 13, 22–24, 26, 35
Patton, Paul, 179, 182, 194, 199, 209, 213
Paxton, E.J., 134
Payne, Bruce R., 61
Peale, Norman Vincent, 126
Pearl Buchanan Theatre, 81, 171
Pearl Harbor, 7, 92, 208
Pence, Steve, 216
Periclesian Literary Society, 46
Perkins, Carl D., 126
Perkins Building, 159
Permanent Court of International Justice, 65
Perry, Kenneth W., 84, 92
Perry, Scott, 187
Perry, Shirley K., 84
Pershing Rifles, 103, 164, 214
Pfaadt, Buddy, 133
Philaletheans, The, 10, 13
phonathon, 189
Photo Club, 96
physical education, 51, 84
physical plant, growth of, 60, 126
physician, campus, 52
Pi Omega Pi, 71, 104
Pickels, Thomas H., 24
Pille, Roy, 83
Piotrowska, Helena, 32
planning, long range, 170
Planning Council, 156
plus/minus grading system, 203, 208
politics, 18, 90, 102, 212
Pollio, Mike, 186
Pollitt, Mabel, 74
Polvina, Geri, 187
Portwood, Al, 73, 82
Posey, Robert W., 135, 181
post-tenure review, 203
Powell, Colin, 196
Powell, Julius C., 153–57, 165, 168–70; appointment as president, 153–54; as executive assistant, 121, 128, 128, 140, 143; financial expertise of, 157, 159; retirement of, 170, 173; review of tenure of, 170–71
Powell Building, 144

pranks, 14, 37, 47, 104, 163
Prater, Michael D., 185
Prater, Millie, 75
Pratt, J.W., 3, 4, 6
preparatory schools, 3
Presbyterian Church, 1–2
Presidential Ball, 210
presidential search committee, 119, 150, 154, 173, 193, 207
Presnell, Glenn, 101, 110, 132
Press, O. Leonard, 146
Prichard, Ed, 118, 149, 155
Program Evaluation Committee, 167
Program of Distinction, 180, 203
Progressive Era, 33
prohibition, 65, 66
promotion and tenure, 177
Public Works Administration, 78, 79
publications, 10, 32, 96. *See also Eastern Kentucky Review; Eastern Progress; Milestone, The; Student*
publicity, 49, 86, 125

quarter system, 92–93, 101

radio, 87
Rainey, Glenn, 193
Rainey, Jane D., 202
Rankin, Rome, 82–83, 92, 95–97, 100
Ransdell, Gary, 213
rape, 169
Rat Court, 99
Rauch, Joseph, 69
Ravine, 79, 104
Rawlins, Claude, 92
Rebilas, Tom, 162
recruitment, 86
Reeves, Clyde, 118
Regents Awards, 126
registration, 147, 161, 170
Reid, George, 201
Reid, Mary Estelle, 54
religion, 1, 54, 85, 104, 138, 163, 183, 215
Religious Emphasis Week, 104
retention, 199, 217
retirement, 177
retirement system, 56, 63, 89, 112, 168
Rex, campus mascot, 89
Rhoads, McHenry, 45
Rice, C. Fred, 200–201, 207, 210, 213

278